Insurance Operations
Volume 2

Insurance Operations
Volume 2

Bernard L. Webb, CPCU, FCAS, MAAA
Consultant

Connor M. Harrison, CPCU, AU
Director of Underwriting Education
American Institute

James J. Markham, J.D., CPCU, AIC, AIAF
Senior Vice President and General Counsel
American Institute

Second Edition • 1997

American Institute for Chartered Property Casualty Underwriters
720 Providence Road, Malvern, Pennsylvania 19355-0770

Second Edition • July 1997

Library of Congress Catalog Number 97-73245
International Standard Book Number 0-89463-077-6

 *Printed in the United States of America on recycled paper.*

Contents

8 Reinsurance 1

Functions of Reinsurance 2

Policyholders and Reinsurance 8

Types of Reinsurance 10

Financial Reinsurance 30

Reinsurance Through Pools 32

The Reinsurance Market 33

Summary 36

Glossary of Reinsurance Terms 37

9 The Reinsurance Transaction 45

Reinsurance Planning for a Primary Insurer 46

Reinsurance Negotiations 60

Reinsurance Administration 66

Loss Experience in Reinsurance 71

Reinsurance Pricing 71

Regulation of Reinsurance 77

Reinsurance and the Capacity Problem 82

Summary 83

Glossary of Reinsurance Terms 84

10 Ratemaking Principles 87

Actuarial Services 88

Principles of Ratemaking 89

Rate Regulation 109

Summary 111

Glossary 112

11 The Ratemaking Process 117

Development of Ratemaking Data 117

Comparison of Ratemaking Methods 139

Other Lines of Insurance 140

Rate Filings 143

Summary 144

Glossary 146

12 Insurer Financial Management 147

Loss Reserve Analysis and Verification 148

Planning 168

Analysis of Reinsurance Requirements 172

Evaluation of Insurers 174

Best's Ratings 175

Risk-Based Capital 186
IRIS 192
Summary 195
Glossary 196

13 Claims Adjusting 199
The Claims Environment 199
The Claims Adjusting Process 216
Summary 250

14 Property Claims Adjusting 253
General Issues in Property Claims Adjusting 254
Challenges Facing Specific Types of Property Claims 289
Summary 313

15 Liability Claims Adjusting 317
General Issues in Liability Claims 318
Challenges Facing Specific Types of Liability Claims 348
Summary 369

Index 371

Chapter 8

Reinsurance

An insurer, like any other business firm, obtains insurance for those loss exposures that are too great for the insurer to retain. This is true of all of the insurer's loss exposures, whether they are the exposures inherent in its own business operations, such as fire damage to the home office building, or loss exposures of others assumed under insurance contracts. This chapter discusses only the transfer of loss exposures assumed under insurance contracts. The practice is known as reinsurance. (In life insurance, this practice is referred to as reassurance.)

Reinsurance can be defined as a contractual agreement under which one insurer, known as the primary insurer, transfers to another insurer, known as the **reinsurer**, some or all of the loss exposures accepted by the primary insurer under insurance contracts it has issued or will issue in the future. The primary insurer may also be referred to as the ceding insurer, ceding company, cedent, or reinsured. This text will consistently use the term **primary insurer** to denote an insurer that provides insurance to the general public rather than to other insurers.

In almost all reinsurance agreements, the reinsurer does not assume all of the exposure of the primary insurer. The reinsurance agreement usually requires the primary insurer to keep a portion of the exposure. This is known as the insurer's **retention** and can be expressed as a dollar amount, a percentage of the original amount of insurance, or a combination of the two. The reinsurance agreement usually contains an upper limit above which loss exposures are the responsibility of the primary insurer.

Reinsurers, like primary insurers, share loss exposures with other reinsurers. Those transactions are very similar to the reinsurance agreements between the primary insurer and the initial reinsurer. In this way, loss exposures are shared globally in the reinsurance community. These transactions are known as **retrocessions**, whereby loss exposures are transferred from the **retrocedent** to the **retrocessionaire**.

Functions of Reinsurance

At first, it might seem odd that an insurer would go to the trouble and expense of selling a policy and then pay a reinsurer to relieve it of some or all of the loss exposures assumed. There are several practical business constraints that are specific to the nature of the insurance business and the regulatory environment in which it operates. Reinsurance functions to alleviate these constraints.

Reinsurance can provide the following to primary insurers:

- Stabilization of loss experience
- Large-line capacity
- Financing (surplus relief)
- Catastrophe protection
- Underwriting assistance
- Withdrawal from a territory or class of business

Stabilization of Loss Experience

An insurer, like any other business firm, must have a reasonably steady flow of profits in order to attract and retain capital and increase its capital and surplus to support growth. Insurance losses sometimes fluctuate widely because of demographic, economic, social, and natural forces, as well as simple chance. Smoothing the peaks and valleys of the loss experience curve is a major function of reinsurance. Stabilization of loss experience is closely related to the function of catastrophe protection, discussed later.

For example, a primary insurer might purchase reinsurance to limit the amount of any one loss it would pay. The primary insurer obtains stability in its underwriting results through the reinsurance transaction. How reinsurance provides stability is illustrated in Exhibit 8-1.

Exhibit 8-1
Stabilization of Loss Experience

Hypothetical Loss Experience of an Insurer for a Line of Business

Time Period (Year)	Losses (000)	Amount Reinsured (000)	Stabilized Loss Level (000)
1	$10,000	$ —	$10,000
2	22,500	2,500	20,000
3	13,000	—	13,000
4	8,000	—	8,000
5	41,000	21,000	20,000
6	37,000	17,000	20,000
7	16,500	—	16,500
8	9,250	—	9,250
9	6,000	—	6,000
10	10,750	—	10,750
Total	$174,000		

Average Annual Losses $17,400

The total losses are $174,000,000, or an average of $17,400,000 each time period. If a reinsurance agreement were in place to cap losses to $20,000,000, the primary insurer's experience would be limited to the amounts shown in the stabilized loss level column. The solid line that fluctuates dramatically shown in the graph below represents actual losses; the horizontal line represents average losses.

Graph of Hypothetical Loss Data

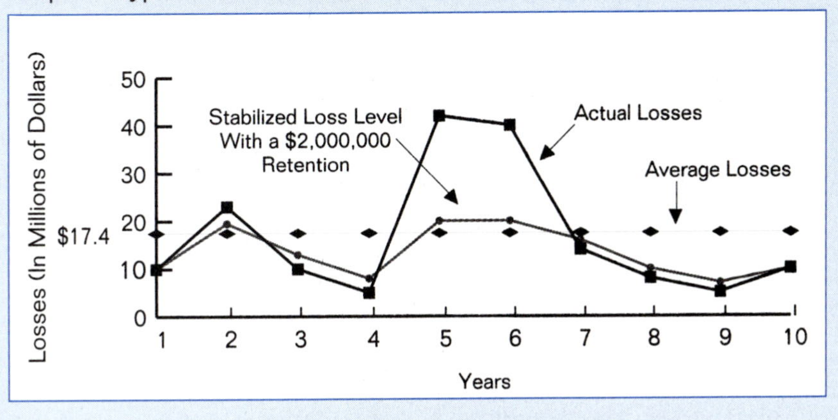

Large-Line Capacity

Large-line capacity refers to an insurer's ability to provide a high limit of insurance on a single loss exposure. For example, an insurer might be called on to write $150 million of coverage on a commercial office building or $160 million of physical damage (hull) coverage on a new jumbo jet. The liability coverage on a large passenger airplane could exceed $100 million.

Few primary insurers could write such a large amount of insurance on a single loss exposure without reinsurance. State insurance regulations prohibit an insurer from writing an amount of insurance in excess of 10 percent of its policyholders' surplus on any one loss exposure. An insurer can write a large line by keeping its retention within a reasonable relationship to its capital and surplus and reinsuring the balance of the risk.

An insurer might want to write a higher limit than it can retain for its own accounts for many valid reasons. For example, a primary insurer might consider accepting an application for hull coverage on a new jumbo jet valued at $160 million if it can minimize its retention to an acceptable level. Reinsurers, operating through pools or individually, take shares of the exposure. In turn, many reinsurers retrocede part of their exposure to other reinsurers. On large exposures like the jumbo jet, the participation of many reinsurers is common.

Financing (Surplus Relief)

There is a limit to the amount of premiums an insurer can write. The limit for a given insurer is a function of policyholders' surplus. As a practical matter, an insurer is likely to be considered overextended if its net written premiums, after deducting premiums on reinsurance ceded, exceed its policyholders' surplus by a ratio of more than three to one. That is, a ratio below 3-to-1 is favorable.

A growing insurer might have difficulty maintaining an acceptable ratio because the premium-to-surplus ratio of a rapidly growing insurer is like a candle burning at both ends. As the premium volume grows, it causes the surplus to shrink. The shrinkage results from the prepaid expense portion of the unearned premium reserve, such as agents' commission and policy issuance, being charged against surplus.

In U.S. statutory insurance accounting, income and expense are mismatched. The insurer must establish an initial unearned premium reserve equal to the total premium for the policy and then recognize the income over the life of the policy. The insurer pays most of its expenses at the inception of the policy and is required to charge these expenses against income immediately rather than amortize them throughout the policy period. Since it has not yet earned any income, the insurer must take money from surplus to pay these initial expenses. This is referred to as the *surplus drain* caused by growth in written premium. This problem is illustrated in Exhibit 8-2.

Exhibit 8-2
Financing

Assume that Casualty Insurance Company opened for business on December 31, 19X1. On that date, it had $2 million of paid-in capital and surplus but no premiums. On January 1, 19X2, it wrote and collected $5 million of premiums on one-year policies. Its initial expenses for the policies were $1.5 million for producer commissions, premium taxes, underwriting expenses, policy writing, billing and collection, and so forth. Casualty also had to establish an unearned premium reserve, a liability, equal to the total amount of premium, $5 million. Consequently, the money for the expenses must be taken from surplus, leaving surplus to policyholders of only $500,000. Below is Casualty's balance sheet as it appeared on December 31, 19X1, before writing the premiums, and on January 1, 19X2, after writing the premiums and paying the initial expense resulting from them.

As can be seen in the balance sheet below, the shrinkage of the policyholders' surplus caused the ratio that originally was 2.5-to-1 ($5 million of premiums to $2 million of net worth) to become a ratio of 10-to-1 ($5 million of premiums to $500,000 of net worth). This is an extreme example, of course, but it does illustrate the problems that can be encountered by a rapidly growing insurer.

Balance Sheets for Casualty Insurance Company
December 31, 19X1 and January 1, 19X2

	12/31/X1	1/1/X2
Assets		
Cash	$ 500,000	$4,000,000*
Investments	1,500,000	1,500,000
Total Assets	$2,000,000	$5,500,000
Liabilities		
Unearned Premium Reserve	$ 0	$5,000,000
Total Liabilities	$ 0	$5,000,000
Policyholders' Surplus		
Capital	$ 500,000	$ 500,000
Surplus	1,500,000	0
Total Policyholders' Surplus	$2,000,000	$ 500,000
Total Liabilities and Policyholders' Surplus	$2,000,000	$5,500,000
Ratio of Written Premium to Surplus	2.5	10

* The cash for 1/1/X2 was calculated by adding the premiums collected ($5,000,000) to the cash for 12/31/X1 ($500,000) and subtracting the expenses paid ($1,500,000).

Continued on next page.

Reinsurance, in various forms, can provide some relief to the premium-to-surplus ratio problem. First, the ratio is calculated on the basis of net premiums, after deducting premiums for reinsurance. Second, the unearned premium reserve is also calculated on the basis of net premiums. With some forms of reinsurance, the reinsurer pays a **ceding commission** to the primary insurer to cover its expenses in selling and issuing the policies, plus an override for profit. Thus, although the primary insurer takes credit for the full reinsurance premium in calculating its unearned premium reserve, it actually pays out only the net amount after deducting the ceding commission. The relief to surplus is therefore a direct result of the ceding commission received by the ceding primary insurer.

Balance Sheet for Casualty Insurance Company, January 1, 19X2, Net After Ceding 50 Percent of Premiums and Receiving 30 Percent Ceding Commission

Assets	
Cash	$2,250,000
Investments	1,500,000
Total Assets	$3,750,000
Liabilities*	
Unearned Premium Reserve	$2,500,000
Total Liabilities	$2,500,000
Policyholders' Surplus	
Capital	$ 500,000
Surplus	750,000
Policyholders' Surplus	$1,250,000
Total Liabilities and Policyholders' Surplus	$3,750,000
Ratio of Written Premiums to Surplus	

*50% of written premiums

Above is the balance sheet for Casualty Insurance Company on January 1, 19X2, as it would have appeared if Casualty had ceded half of its premiums to a reinsurer and received a 30 percent ceding commission on the *reinsurance premium.*

Casualty's premium-to-surplus ratio has fallen from 10-to-1 to 2-to-1, solely through the use of reinsurance. First, the net written premiums dropped from $5 million to $2.5 million because of the reinsurance cession. Second, the policyholders' surplus increased from $500,000 to $1.25 million because of the recapture of $750,000 of prepaid expenses. This arises from the 30 percent ceding commission paid by the reinsurer for the $2.5 million of written premium ceded.

Exhibit 8-2 illustrates the financing function of reinsurance—the reduction of surplus drain for a growing insurer that results from having to recognize all expenses when they are incurred. This function is usually called **surplus relief**. It is so important to poorly financed insurers that a special kind of reinsurance, sometimes called **surplus-aid reinsurance**, was offered in the past to insurers with inadequate surplus. A surplus-aid reinsurance agreement appeared on superficial examination to be a typical reinsurance contract, but it often contained an agreement requiring the primary insurer to reimburse the reinsurer for any claims paid under the reinsurance contract. The primary insurer would take credit for the reinsurance in setting its unearned premium reserve, even though no transfer of risk was involved. A similar device involved purchasing a normal treaty near the end of the year and cancelling it early in the following year so that it would be in force on December 31 for Annual Statement purposes. Fortunately, these devices for circumventing solvency regulation have largely disappeared. Changes in accounting rules have eliminated the benefit that insurers sought in these arrangements.

A different form of reinsurance that provides surplus relief has recently received considerable attention, although it has been used on a limited scale for many years. There are several forms of such reinsurance, but they are known collectively as **financial reinsurance**. The name results from the primary purpose of such contracts: to improve the financial status, or at least the apparent financial status, of the primary insurer. Financial reinsurance involves very little transfer of risk; in some cases, no risk at all is transferred. Financial reinsurance is discussed in more detail later in this chapter.

Catastrophe Protection

Property-liability insurers are subject to major catastrophe losses from earthquakes, hurricanes, tornadoes, industrial explosions, plane crashes, and similar disasters. These events can result in large property-liability claims to a single insurer. Total industry losses have reached more than $16 billion for one hurricane and $13 billion for one earthquake, and winter storm losses in excess of $100 million are not uncommon.

Special forms of reinsurance, to be discussed in a later section of this chapter, have been developed to protect against the adverse effects of catastrophes. This purpose of reinsurance is closely related to the purpose of stabilizing loss experience, since catastrophes are major causes of the instability of losses.

Underwriting Assistance

Reinsurers deal with a wide variety of insurers in many different circumstances. Consequently, they accumulate a great deal of information regarding the experience of various insurers with particular coverages and the methods of rating, underwriting, and handling various coverages. This experience can be helpful to primary insurers, particularly small insurers or larger insurers planning to enter a new line. For example, one medium-sized insurance company reinsured 95 percent of its umbrella liability coverage over a period of years and relied heavily on the expertise of the reinsurer in rating and underwriting the policies. Without this technical assistance, many small and medium-sized insurers could not write some coverages with which they have limited expertise.

This service of reinsurers is very important in both the life and the property-liability fields. Of course, reinsurers must be careful when offering advisory service so that they do not reveal or use proprietary information obtained through confidential relationships with other primary insurers.

Withdrawal From a Territory or Class of Business

Occasionally, an insurer or a reinsurer decides to withdraw from a territory or a class of business, or perhaps to go out of business entirely. There are at least two ways to achieve either end. The insurer could merely cancel or nonrenew the unwanted policies and refund the unearned premiums to its policyholders. That process is unwieldy, expensive, and likely to create ill will among policyholders, producers, and insurance regulators. An alternative method is to reinsure the unwanted business with another insurer or a reinsurer. This method avoids the ill will resulting from terminating the insurance, and the cost of reinsurance might be less than the cost of processing and paying return premiums on cancelled policies.

The process of reinsuring all losses for an entire class, territory, or book of business is known as **portfolio reinsurance**. This reinsurance process is an exception to the general rule that reinsurers usually do not assume all of the exposures of the primary insurer. In the absence of fraud, the portfolio reinsurer does not normally have any recourse against the primary insurer if the loss experience on the business does not turn out as expected.

Policyholders and Reinsurance

Reinsurance involves a contractual relationship between a primary insurer and a reinsurer. The persons or firms insured by the primary insurer are not parties to the reinsurance contract and usually have no rights under that contract. For example, assume that the Manufacturing Company buys insurance on its factory for $1 million from the Insurance Company. Insurance Company, in turn, reinsures 90 percent of the exposure with Reinsurance

Company. Fire destroys the factory. Since writing the policy, Insurance Company has become insolvent and is now unable to pay its claims. Because there is no contractual relationship between the insured and the reinsurer, Manufacturing Company cannot collect directly from Reinsurance Company. Reinsurance Company pays its share of the loss to the receiver of Insurance Company, and this money is distributed proportionately to all creditors of Insurance Company. Manufacturing Company must settle for only its proportionate share as one creditor of Insurance Company.

There are some exceptions to the general rule that the policyholder has no direct right of action against a reinsurer. Occasionally, a reinsurer authorizes a primary insurer to attach to its policies an endorsement, executed by the reinsurer, called a cut-through endorsement. The **cut-through endorsement** generally provides that in the event of the insolvency of the primary insurer, the obligation under the policy becomes a direct obligation of the reinsurer. The cut-through endorsement is sometimes attached to fire insurance or homeowners contracts because a mortgagee has refused to accept the primary insurer's policies without it. Less frequently, it is attached at the request of the risk manager of a commercial policyholder or an industrial firm, and sometimes it is needed because the primary insurer is not rated by Best's.

There are some other minor exceptions to the rule that the primary insurer's policyholder does not have a right of direct action against the reinsurer. For example, Section 315(1)(a) of the New York Insurance Law does not permit a primary insurer to take credit for surety and fidelity reinsurance unless the reinsurance agreement permits direct suit by the obligee against the reinsurer. New York courts have held that this section of the law creates a direct right of action by the obligee.[1] On the other hand, a case decided in Puerto Rico casts some doubt on the value of a cut-through endorsement, at least in that Commonwealth. The Supreme Court of Puerto Rico has held that cut-through endorsements are contrary to public policy and that the reinsurance proceeds should be paid to the liquidator of the insolvent primary insurer despite the existence of the cut-through endorsement.[2] This ruling is contrary to several other decisions that have upheld and enforced such contracts.[3]

The fact that the policyholders of the primary insurer do not have the right of direct action against the reinsurer does not mean that they receive no benefit from the reinsurance. Policyholders might, in fact, receive several benefits. The availability of reinsurance might enable them to obtain all of their insurance from one insurer instead of buying it in bits and pieces from several insurers. This avoids the potential problems of coverage gaps and loss collections when dealing with several insurers. Also, the availability of reinsurance helps to maintain the solvency of primary insurers, with obvious advantages to policyholders. The Best's rating of primary insurers is affected by the strength of their reinsurance. Finally, reinsurance allows small insurers to compete effectively against larger ones, thus increasing the options available to insurance buyers. Of course, reinsurers might, in some cases, lessen price and coverage competition, since their rating and underwriting practices influence the rates and policy forms used by their primary insurers.

Types of Reinsurance

Several different kinds of reinsurance have developed to serve the various functions listed in the first section of this chapter. No single kind of reinsurance serves all of the purposes effectively.

The section that follows discusses several forms of reinsurance as though they are standardized contracts. Although that method of presentation is necessary for clarity, each reinsurance contract is tailored to the specific needs of the primary insurer and the reinsurer. Consequently, a given reinsurance contract might include combinations of the reinsurance forms discussed here, or it might bear only a superficial resemblance to any of these forms.

Reinsurance contracts can be categorized in several ways. The first major categorization is between facultative and treaty reinsurance. In **facultative reinsurance,** the primary insurer negotiates a separate reinsurance agreement for each risk it wishes to reinsure. The primary insurer is not under any obligation to purchase reinsurance on a policy it does not wish to reinsure, and the reinsurer is not obligated to reinsure policies submitted to it.

In **treaty reinsurance,** the primary insurer agrees in advance to reinsure certain lines of business in accordance with the terms and conditions of the treaty, and the reinsurer agrees to accept the business that falls within the treaty. Although the primary insurer might have some discretion in reinsuring individual policies, all of the policies that come within the terms of the treaty are expected to be placed with the reinsurer.

Despite this seemingly clear-cut distinction between facultative and treaty reinsurance, some reinsurance contracts are a hybrid and are called facultative treaties.

One authoritative source defines a **facultative treaty** in the following manner:

> A reinsurance contract under which the ceding company has the option to cede and the reinsurer has the option to accept or decline classified risks of a specific business line. The contract merely reflects how individual facultative reinsurances shall be handled.[4]

On rare occasions, a facultative treaty might be called a **facultative obligatory treaty,** automatic facultative treaty, or another treaty with mixed nomenclature.

Such a treaty might provide that the primary insurer has the option to submit risks within a specified class that the reinsurer is obligated to accept. Because of the obvious opportunities for adverse selection, reinsurers are careful in selecting the primary insurers for which they write facultative obligatory treaties.

Information regarding the relative importance of facultative and treaty reinsurance within the portfolios of reinsurers is limited. Some reinsurers specialize in facultative agreements, and others prefer treaty business.

Another system for categorizing reinsurance depends on the manner in which the obligations under contracts are divided between the primary insurer and the reinsurer. These two approaches to dividing losses are called pro rata reinsurance and excess of loss reinsurance.

Under **pro rata reinsurance** (or proportional reinsurance), the amount of insurance, the premium, and the losses are divided between the primary insurer and the reinsurer in the same agreed proportions. That is, if the reinsurer gets 35 percent of the coverage under a given policy, it also gets 35 percent of the premium and pays 35 percent of each loss under the policy, regardless of the size of the loss. Under pro rata reinsurance treaties, the reinsurer usually pays a ceding commission to the primary insurer to cover its expenses and possibly an allowance for profit.

Under **excess of loss reinsurance** (or nonproportional reinsurance), no amount of insurance is ceded. Excess of loss reinsurance does not become involved until the primary insurer has sustained a *loss* that exceeds its retention under the contract and is covered by the excess of loss agreement. Both facultative reinsurance and treaty reinsurance can be written as pro rata or excess or a combination of the two. Exhibit 8-3 shows the various ways of categorizing reinsurance. Note the inclusion of financial reinsurance, which is a nontraditional and specialized type of reinsurance. Financial reinsurance and the other forms of reinsurance shown in Exhibit 8-3 will be discussed in detail in the paragraphs that follow.

Treaty Reinsurance

Most insurers depend heavily on treaty reinsurance because it provides several advantages over facultative reinsurance. The reinsurer is obligated to accept all business that falls within the terms of the treaty. Consequently, the primary insurer can underwrite, accept, and reinsure such business without prior consultation with the reinsurer on each pending application. Also, since prior negotiation is not required, the handling expense for each policy reinsured is less under a treaty than under facultative reinsurance. Whether an insurer chooses to use a pro rata or an excess of loss treaty is determined by the kind of exposures to be reinsured, the financial needs of the primary insurer, and other factors.

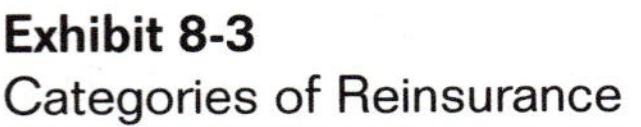

Exhibit 8-3
Categories of Reinsurance

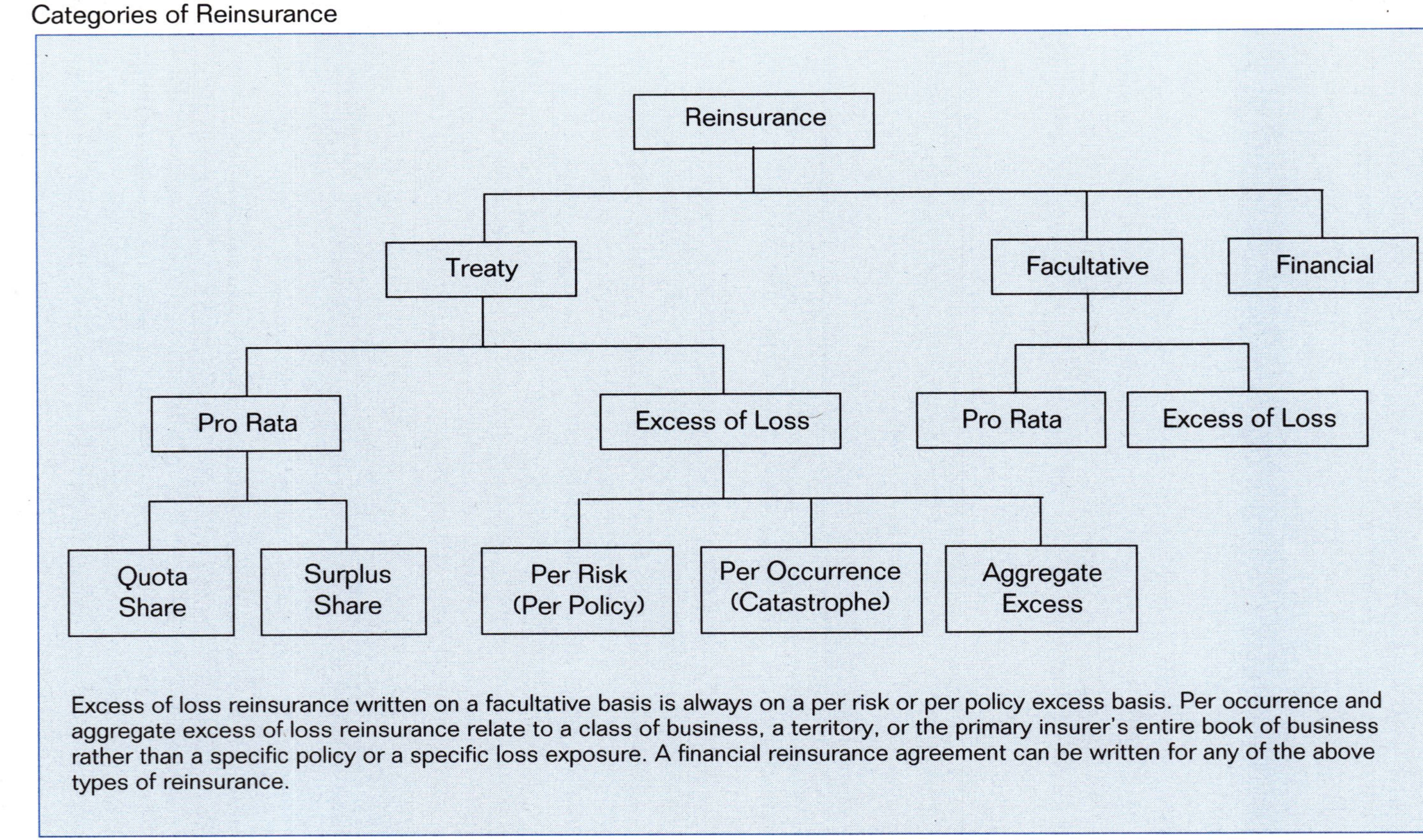

Excess of loss reinsurance written on a facultative basis is always on a per risk or per policy excess basis. Per occurrence and aggregate excess of loss reinsurance relate to a class of business, a territory, or the primary insurer's entire book of business rather than a specific policy or a specific loss exposure. A financial reinsurance agreement can be written for any of the above types of reinsurance.

Adapted from Michael W. Elliott, Bernard L. Webb, Howard N. Anderson, and Peter R. Kensicki, *Principles of Reinsurance*, vol. 1 (Malvern, PA: Insurance Institute of America, 1995), pp. 5, 148.

Pro Rata or Proportional Treaties

Pro rata reinsurance is the choice for a thinly financed insurer, whether writing property or liability insurance, since it is more effective than excess of loss coverage in providing surplus relief. Its greater effectiveness in that respect stems largely from the practice of paying ceding commissions under pro rata treaties, a practice not common under excess of loss treaties. Also, the premium for a pro rata treaty is likely to be a larger percentage of the original premium than is the case with an excess of loss treaty.

The two kinds of treaties in the pro rata category are quota share and surplus share (sometimes simply called surplus). The principal difference between them is the way in which the primary insurer's retention is stated. (The term "surplus" should not be confused with the policyholders' surplus of either the primary insurer or the reinsurer.)

Quota Share

Under a **quota share treaty**, the primary insurer cedes a fixed, predetermined percentage of every risk it insures within the class or classes subject to the treaty. Even the smallest risks are reinsured.

The primary insurer's retention is stated as a percentage of the amount of insurance so that the dollar amount of its retention varies with the amount of insurance. The reinsurer assumes the amount of insurance less the primary insurer's retention, up to the reinsurance limit, which is expressed as a maximum dollar amount per one risk. The reinsurer receives the same percentage of the premium (less the ceding commission) as it does of the amount of insurance and pays the same percentage of each loss. An example of a quota share treaty is shown in Exhibit 8-4.

Quota share treaties can be used with either property or liability coverages, but property quota share treaties are much more common. They have the advantage of being simple to rate and simple to administer, since the reinsurer receives the agreed percentage of all covered premiums. The principal disadvantage is that a quota share treaty results in ceding a large share of presumably profitable business. Because of this disadvantage, quota share reinsurance has been declining in popularity. However, it is still widely used, especially by small insurers and insurers that need surplus relief. Quota share is the most effective treaty for that purpose.

Quota share treaties are not effective in stabilizing underwriting results, since they do not affect the primary insurer's loss ratio. Of course, a favorable ceding commission might affect the primary insurer's combined ratio, since reinsurance commissions received are credited against direct commissions paid in the

Exhibit 8-4
Quota Share Treaty Example

Assume that Insurance Company has purchased from Reinsurance Company a quota share treaty with a $250,000 limit and a retention of 25 percent and a cession of 75 percent. Insurance Company has written three policies. Policy A insures Building A for $10,000 for a premium of $100, with one loss of $8,000. Policy B insures Building B for $100,000 for a premium of $1,000, with one loss of $10,000. Policy C insures Building C for $150,000 for a premium of $1,500, with one loss of $60,000. The table and graph below show how the insurance, premiums, and losses under these policies would be split between the primary insurer and the reinsurer. In each case, the primary insurer retains 25 percent of the insurance and the premium and pays 25 percent of the losses. However, the dollar amount of its retention increases as the amount of insurance increases.

Division of Insurance, Premium, and Losses Under Quota Share Treaty

	Insurance Company (25%)	Reinsurance Company (75%)	Total
Policy A			
Insurance	$ 2,500	$ 7,500	$ 10,000
Premium	25	75	100
Loss	2,000	6,000	8,000
Policy B			
Insurance	$25,000	$ 75,000	$100,000
Premium	250	750	1,000
Loss	2,500	7,500	10,000
Policy C			
Insurance	$37,500	$112,500	$150,000
Premium	375	1,125	1,500
Loss	15,000	45,000	60,000

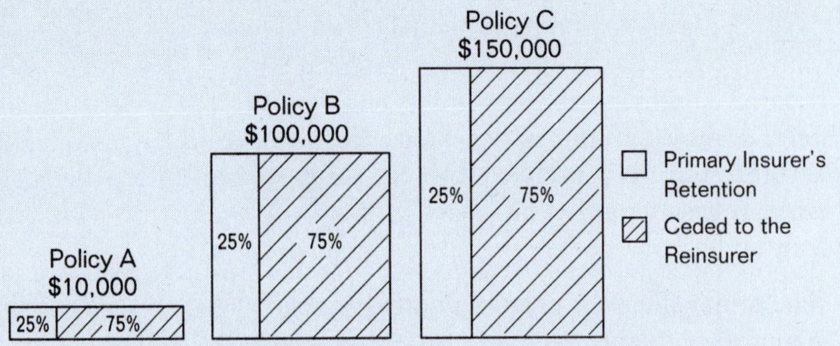

primary insurer's Annual Statement. Over many years, one insurer showed a negative expense ratio on its Annual Statement because the ceding commissions on its reinsurance treaties were greater than all of its expenses paid. A reinsurer must anticipate an extremely low loss ratio in order to pay such a high ceding commission.

A quota share treaty can be reasonably effective in improving the primary insurer's large-line capacity, depending on the percentage retention required. However, it is not as effective in that regard as surplus share and per risk excess treaties.

Surplus Share

Surplus share treaties, like quota share treaties, are pro rata or proportional reinsurance. That is, the primary insurer and the reinsurers share the amount of insurance, the premium, and the losses in the same percentage. The difference between them is in the way the retention is stated. The retention under a quota share treaty is stated as a *percentage* of the amount insured, and the retention under a surplus share treaty is usually stated as a minimum *dollar amount*. However, the primary insurer might elect to retain more than the minimum retention stated in the treaty if it wishes to do so. If the amount of insurance under a given policy is less than the retention amount, no insurance under the policy is ceded. If the amount of insurance under a policy exceeds the retention amount, the amount of insurance above the retention is ceded to the reinsurer, subject to the reinsurance limit and other limitations of the treaty. The reinsurer receives premiums and is responsible for all losses, regardless of size, in the same proportion that the amount ceded bears to the amount retained. Even though an individual loss might be less than the retention of the ceding company, it will be shared between the ceding company and the surplus share reinsurer if the amount of insurance exceeds the retention amount. The major distinction between quota share and surplus share is that although the same *percentage* of reinsurance applies to all eligible policies under quota share, the percentage *varies* from policy to policy in a surplus share treaty, depending on the amount of the insurance ceded. This is illustrated in Exhibit 8-5.

Surplus share reinsurance has been a common form of reinsurance for property insurers, though it has recently been losing ground to excess of loss reinsurance. It has seldom been used for liability insurance. If pro rata reinsurance is written for liability lines, it is done on a quota share basis.

The principal advantage to the primary insurer of surplus share treaties over quota share treaties is that surplus share treaties, because of their fixed dollar retentions, avoid ceding reinsurance on loss exposures so small that the

Exhibit 8-5
Surplus Share Treaty Example

Assume that Insurance Company has purchased from Reinsurance Company a surplus treaty with a retention of $25,000 and a limit of $250,000. This would be referred to as a "ten-line surplus treaty," since the primary insurer will cede coverage up to ten times the retention amount. The table and graph below show how this treaty would apply to the same three policies used previously to illustrate the application of a quota share treaty. For Policy A, no amount of insurance is ceded because the amount of insurance is less than the $25,000 retention. For Policy B, the proportion in which premiums and losses are shared is determined by the retention divided by the insurance amount. The same applies to Policy C. Under a quota share treaty (Exhibit 8-4), the percentage retention remains constant, and the dollar amount of retention increases as the amount of insurance increases. Under a surplus share treaty for insurance amounts above the retention, the dollar amount of retention remains constant while the percentage retention decreases as the amount of insurance increases.

Division of Insurance, Premium, and Losses Under Surplus Share Treaty With $25,000 Retention and $250,000 Limit

	Insurance Company (%)	Reinsurance Company (% Ceded)	Total
Policy A			
Insurance	$10,000 (100%)	$ 0 (0%)	$ 10,000
Premium	100	0	100
Loss	8,000	0	8,000
Policy B			
Insurance	$25,000 (25%)	$ 75,000 (75%)	$100,000
Premium	250	750	1,000
Loss	2,500	7,500	10,000
Policy C			
Insurance	$25,000 (16.67%)	$125,000 (83.33%)	$150,000
Premium	250	1,250	1,500
Loss	10,000	50,000	60,000

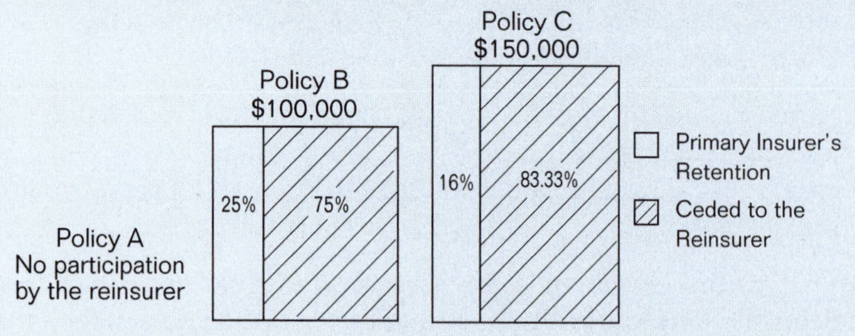

primary insurer can afford to retain them. A surplus share treaty also provides a more logical approach to purchasing proportional reinsurance, because no reinsurance is purchased unless the risk is beyond the capacity of the primary insurer to absorb.

The principal disadvantage of surplus share treaties in comparison with quota share is the increased administrative expense. Since not all risks are reinsured, the primary insurer must maintain a record of those which are reinsured and furnish a report of them to the reinsurer each month or at some other regular interval. The listing of reinsured exposures, which usually includes premium and loss information, is known as a **bordereau** (for which the plural is "bordereaux"). Although reporting on a bordereau basis to reinsurers is not common practice today, the primary insurer must make records available to the reinsurer for audit purposes.

Surplus share treaties compared to quota share are of lesser importance in providing surplus relief, since no reinsurance is ceded on risks with limits of insurance less than the minimum net retention.

A surplus share treaty is superior to a quota share treaty in providing large-line capacity. Under a quota share treaty, the primary insurer's total *dollar exposure to loss* increases in direct proportion to that of its reinsurers, resulting in a limited line capacity. However, under a surplus arrangement, the primary insurer may cede several multiples of its net retention up to the limit of its treaty, providing significant risk capacity.

Since amounts of insurance ceded to a surplus treaty vary by risk, the financial results realized by the reinsurers can vary significantly from those of the primary insurer. In retrospect, the primary insurer may find that it has ceded very profitable business to the reinsurer. The loss of profit is part of the price the primary insurer pays in meeting a business objective through reinsurance.

Like the quota share treaty, the surplus share is not designed to protect the primary insurer from catastrophe loss occurrences. This function of reinsurance is satisfied by excess of loss treaties, described later. Until recently, *pro rata treaties generally did not have a per occurrence limit.* For example, some regional insurers wrote primarily large property exposures within a one- or two-state territory and used surplus share treaties as their major form of reinsurance. Severe earthquakes or hurricanes might damage or destroy many of the ceded exposures, resulting in very large losses to reinsurers. Recent catastrophes such as Hurricane Andrew in 1992 and the Northridge (California) earthquake in 1994 have resulted in occurrence limits on most proportional treaties.

Excess of Loss or Nonproportional Treaties

Excess of loss treaties, sometimes referred to as nonproportional treaties, differ from pro rata, or proportional, treaties in that the primary insurer and the reinsurer do not share the amount of insurance, premium, and losses in the same proportion. In fact, *no insurance amount is ceded under excess of loss treaties, only losses and premiums*. The reinsurance premium is usually stated as a percentage of the primary insurer's premium income for the covered lines of business, but the percentage is subject to negotiation and varies by line and by insurer. Generally, ceding commissions are not paid under excess of loss treaties.

The excess reinsurer is only responsible for losses that exceed the retention and fall within the coverage provided by the reinsurance contract. Although coverage provided by the pro rata treaty is always concurrent (identical) with the coverage provided by the primary insurer's policy, the coverage provided by the excess reinsurance contract is not necessarily the same as that of the primary insurer.

There are three general classes of excess of loss treaties: per risk or per policy excess, per occurrence excess (also known as per loss excess), and aggregate excess. They differ substantially in operation and are discussed separately below.

Per Risk or Per Policy Excess

Distinguishing between a per risk and a per policy excess of loss reinsurance treaty is important. A **per risk excess treaty** applies to property insurance with the retention and limit applying separately to each risk insured by the primary insurer. A **per policy excess treaty** applies to liability insurance with the retention and limit applying separately to each policy issued by the primary insurer. The retention under a per risk or per policy excess of loss treaty is stated as a dollar amount of loss (not an amount of insurance), and the reinsurer is liable for all or a part of loss to any one exposure in excess of the retention and up to the agreed reinsurance limit. In some cases, the reinsurer might agree to pay only a stated percentage, such as 90 percent or 95 percent, of the loss in excess of the retention.

The retention amount is usually set at a level to exclude a large majority, by number, of expected claims. This is consistent with the theory that excess of loss treaties are intended to protect the primary insurer against unusually large losses. However, the retention is sometimes set low enough so that reinsurance claims occur frequently. Treaties with such low retentions are frequently referred to as **working covers** (or working level excess treaties). Working covers permit the primary insurer to spread losses over a number of years so that profitable years can offset unprofitable ones. A small or inexperienced insurer might choose a working cover to minimize its exposure to loss until it gains confidence in the lines of business written.

The retention under a per risk or per policy excess of loss treaty *applies separately to each subject of insurance.* For example, if Insurance Company insured Company A at 1110 Main Street and Company B next door at 1112 Main Street, and they both burned, the retention under a per risk excess treaty would apply separately to each. If Insurance Company issued automobile liability policies to each of the above companies, and an auto accident occurred involving both policies, the retention under a per policy excess treaty would apply separately to each policy. As the next two sections explain, the retention applies differently for the other forms of excess treaty.

Unlike pro rata treaties, excess reinsurers do not participate in all losses, but only in those that exceed the primary insurer's retention, and then only in the part in excess of the retention. This difference is emphasized here because it is a frequent source of confusion. Exhibit 8-6 shows how a primary insurer and a reinsurer would split losses under a per risk excess of loss treaty.

From the viewpoint of the primary insurer, the principal advantage of a per risk or per policy excess of loss treaty in comparison with pro rata treaties is that less premium is submitted to the reinsurer. This permits the primary insurer to earn income on the investment of these funds. Administration costs are also lower, since fewer reinsurance claims are processed. Also, keeping track of the loss exposures reinsured, as is required under a surplus share treaty, might not be necessary. The excess of loss treaty is concerned only with losses.

Because the reinsurance premium is lower than for pro rata treaties and because commissions are normally not paid to the primary insurer, excess of loss treaties are not effective in providing surplus relief.

Per risk or per policy excess treaties are very effective in providing large-line capacity, since they absorb the large losses that make large lines hazardous to the primary insurer. They are much more effective in this regard than quota share treaties and more effective than surplus share treaties, particularly if the reinsurance premium cost is considered.

Per risk or per policy excess treaties are very effective in stabilizing the loss experience of the primary insurer because they lessen the effect of large losses, which contribute disproportionately to fluctuations of loss experience. The loss experience of the reinsurer is not the same as that of the primary insurer in any given year. However, over the long run, each primary insurer should expect to pay its own losses plus the reinsurer's operating expenses and profit. That is, the primary insurer gives up a part of its profits in the good years in

Exhibit 8-6
Per Risk Excess of Loss Treaty Example

Assume Insurance Company has purchased from Reinsurance Company a per risk excess of loss treaty with a $25,000 retention. The table and graph below show how losses will be split. Policy A and Policy B have losses below the retention amount, so the reinsurer is not involved. Policy A (see Exhibit 8-5) only has a $10,000 limit, so even a total loss will not come under this treaty. No mention is made here of policy limits or premium amounts because they are not relevant to the division of losses under an excess treaty.

Division of Losses Under Per Risk Excess Treaty With $25,000 Retention

	Loss Amount	**Insurance Company**	**Reinsurance Company**
Policy A Loss	$ 8,000	$ 8,000	$ 0
Policy B Loss	$10,000	$10,000	$ 0
Policy C Loss	$60,000	$25,000	$35,000

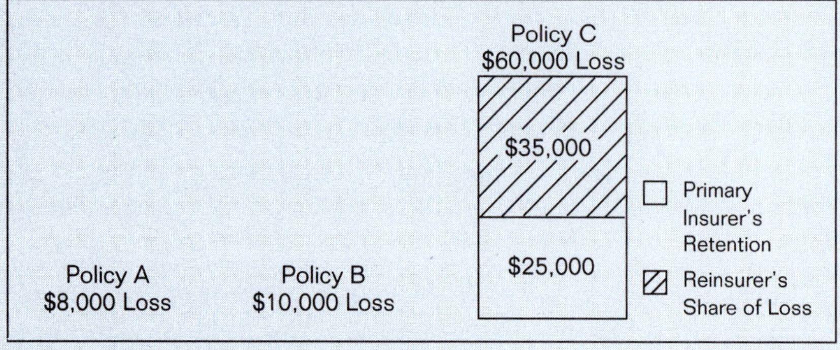

order to transfer its losses to the reinsurer in the bad years, thus stabilizing its loss experience over time.

Per risk excess treaties are helpful in catastrophes, since they pay the amount in excess of the primary insurer's retention on each individual claim. However, they are far less effective in this regard than per occurrence excess treaties, since a catastrophic loss from a hurricane, a tornado, or an earthquake can affect a large percentage of the insurers' policies written in a geographic area.

Per Occurrence Excess

Per occurrence excess of loss reinsurance provides indemnity against loss sustained in excess of the net retention of the primary insurer, subject to a reinsurance limit, regardless of the number of risks (number of separate policies or specifically scheduled items) involved in respect to one accident, occurrence, or event. Per occurrence excess of loss reinsurance applies to either property or liability coverages and is called **catastrophe excess** when applied to property coverages and **clash cover** when applied to liability coverages.

A liability per occurrence excess treaty is extremely important to primary insurers with very high limit requirements. Even insurers writing modest amounts of workers compensation, for example, might feel that $5 million, $10 million, or more of per occurrence reinsurance protection is advisable.

The distinguishing feature of liability per occurrence excess is that auto liability, general liability, workers compensation, umbrella, and perhaps other coverages can be combined to form a single excess claim, and there might also be multiple claimants. When the per occurrence retention is set higher than the limit of any single liability policy, the coverage is sometimes known as a clash cover because it would take more than a single policy to involve the reinsurance coverage.

Another feature materially different from the property classes is the length of time required for the full development and settlement of all losses. The time between date of loss and notice to excess reinsurers might be several years. Final settlement of known losses may require many more years. In some cases, questions might be raised as to the time of the occurrence, such as carcinogenic exposures that might not manifest themselves for decades. Inflation and the late development of claims make this a difficult class to underwrite.

Property insurers are especially prone to large accumulations of losses arising from a single catastrophe, such as a hurricane or an earthquake that damages many insured properties. Most of the individual claims are relatively small, but the accumulated amount can be staggering. Catastrophe treaties are designed to cope with this problem.

Like the per risk and per policy excess treaties, the retention under a per occurrence excess treaty is stated as a dollar amount. The difference is that all of the net losses (that is, gross loss less deduction for all other per risk reinsurance) arising from a single occurrence are totaled to determine when the retention has been satisfied. The reinsurance limit also applies to the aggregate amount of losses from one occurrence. Consequently, the definition of occurrence becomes important. One catastrophe treaty defines an occurrence as follows:

C. The term "Loss Occurrence" will mean the sum of all individual losses directly occasioned by any one disaster, accident, or loss or series of disasters, accidents, or losses arising out of one event which occurs within the area of one state of the United States or province of Canada and states or provinces contiguous thereto and to one another. However, the duration and extent of any one "Loss Occurrence" will be limited to all individual losses sustained by the Company occurring during any period of 168 consecutive hours arising out of and directly occasioned by the same event except that the term "Loss Occurrence" will be further defined as follows:

(1) As regards windstorm, hail, tornado, hurricane, cyclone, including ensuing collapse and water damage, all individual losses sustained by the Company occurring during any period of 72 consecutive hours arising out of and directly occasioned by the same event. However, the event need not be limited to one state or province or states or provinces contiguous thereto.

(2) As regards riot, riot attending a strike, civil commotion, vandalism and malicious mischief, all individual losses sustained by the Company occurring during any period of 72 consecutive hours within the area of one municipality or county and the municipalities or counties contiguous thereto arising out of and directly occasioned by the same event. The maximum duration of 72 consecutive hours may be extended in respect of individual losses which occur beyond such 72 consecutive hours during the continued occupation of an assured's premises by strikers, provided such occupation commenced during the aforesaid period.

(3) As regards earthquake (the epicenter of which need not necessarily be within the territorial confines referred to in the opening paragraph of this Article) and fire following directly occasioned by the earthquake, only those individual fire losses which commence during the period of 168 consecutive hours may be included in the Company's "Loss Occurrence."

(4) As regards "Freeze," only individual losses directly occasioned by collapse, breakage of glass and water damage (caused by bursting of frozen pipes and tanks) may be included in the Company's "Loss Occurrence."

For all "Loss Occurrences," other than (2) above, the Company may choose the date and time when any such period of consecutive hours commences, provided that it is not earlier than the date and time of the occurrence of the first recorded individual loss sustained by the Company arising out of the disaster, accident, or loss and provided that only one such period of 168 consecutive hours will apply with respect to one event, except for any "Loss Occurrences" referred to in (1) above where

> only one such period of 72 consecutive hours will apply with respect to one event.
>
> However, as respects those "Loss Occurrences" referred to in (2) above, if the disaster, accident, or loss occasioned by the event is of greater duration than 72 consecutive hours, then the Company may divide that disaster, accident, or loss into two or more "Loss Occurrences," provided no two periods overlap and no individual loss is included in more than one such period and provided that no period commences earlier than the date and time of the occurrence of the first recorded individual loss sustained by the Company arising out of that disaster, accident, or loss.
>
> No individual losses occasioned by an event that would be covered by 72 hours clauses may be included in any "Loss Occurrence" claimed under the 168 hours provision.

The word "company" in the foregoing quotation refers to the primary insurer. The treaty quoted above does not cover flood damage, but another treaty uses a similar definition applicable to flood. It uses a period of hours similar to the above and specifies that the flood damage must occur in "the same river basin (river basin being defined as the basin of a river including the basin of all of the tributaries of said river, which flows directly into an ocean, bay or gulf, or one of the Great Lakes of the United States)."[5]

This definition of occurrence is important because it controls the application of the retention and the reinsurance limit. The retention would apply separately, but only once, to each occurrence, as would the reinsurance limit. For example, if a hurricane travels up the East Coast and causes wind damage over three days, all of the damage would be from a single occurrence. Consequently, the primary insurer would be required to absorb only one retention, and the reinsurer's liability could not exceed the amount stated in the treaty.

If the same hurricane brought heavy rains causing flooding in one river that drained into the Atlantic Ocean and another that drained into the Gulf of Mexico (not an uncommon circumstance), the floods in the two rivers would be two separate occurrences by the above definition. Consequently, the retention and the treaty limit would apply separately to each river, even though both floods originated from the same storm system.

The definitions quoted are merely illustrative. Different reinsurers, or even the same reinsurers in different treaties, might use different definitions.

Per occurrence excess treaties are very effective in smoothing the fluctuations in loss experience to the extent that such fluctuations result from an accumulation of losses from a single occurrence. Such treaties do not contribute to the primary insurer's premium capacity (except to the extent that they stabilize loss experience), since they are not designed to cover individual losses, nor do they contribute to large-line capacity unless written to cover for a single large loss as well as an accumulation of losses.

Per occurrence excess treaties do not provide significant surplus relief. Since the reinsurance premium is a relatively small percentage of the direct premiums and the reinsurer usually does not pay a ceding commission, the benefit to surplus from this transaction is incidental.

Per occurrence excess treaties usually provide that the reinsurers will pay up to a stated percentage, that is, 90 or 95 percent, of the loss in excess of the retention. Therefore, not only does the primary insurer pay the losses up to the retention, but it also participates in the loss above the retention. This encourages the primary insurer to settle losses economically, since it will be participating in the loss even though the retention is exhausted.

Per occurrence treaties also differ from per risk and per policy excess of loss contracts in that they are usually written for a specific period of time (twelve months) and are usually noncancelable by either party.

Aggregate Excess

Aggregate excess treaties, sometimes called excess of loss ratio or stop loss treaties, are less common than the other forms of excess of loss treaties. However, they have been used with some frequency in connection with crop hail insurance and for small insurers in other lines.

Under an **aggregate excess treaty**, the reinsurer begins to pay when all the primary insurer's claims for some stated period of time, usually one year, exceed the retention stated in the treaty. The retention can be stated in dollars, as a loss ratio percentage, or as a combination of the two. The size of the retention is subject to negotiation between the primary insurer and the reinsurer, but it usually would not be set so low that the primary insurer would be guaranteed a profit. Also, the reinsurer normally does not pay all losses in excess of the primary insurer's retention, but only a percentage of the excess, usually 90 or 95 percent. This last feature is intended to discourage the primary insurer from relaxing its underwriting or loss adjustment standards after its retention has been reached.

Since the aggregate excess treaty limits the primary insurer's losses (or loss ratio), it would appear that no other reinsurance would be needed. However, when aggregate excess treaties are used, other treaties are commonly used to support the reinsurance program. In some cases, the reinsurer might insist on other treaties as a condition of providing the aggregate excess cover. In those cases, the other treaties would be written for the benefit of both the primary insurer and the aggregate excess reinsurer. That is, the primary insurer's retention and the aggregate excess reinsurer's liability would both relate to the net loss after the proceeds of all other reinsurance had been deducted.

The aggregate excess treaty is the most effective of all forms of reinsurance in stabilizing the loss experience of the primary insurer, particularly if the cost of reinsurance is ignored. It is also effective in providing large-line capacity and coping with catastrophes, since the cap it puts on losses would apply equally to large individual claims and an accumulation of claims from a catastrophe.

However, an aggregate excess treaty usually does not involve ceding commission. Therefore, it does not provide significant surplus relief or premium capacity. Logically, it should increase premium capacity because the primary insurer would need less surplus to absorb the remaining fluctuation in loss experience. However, current regulatory techniques are not sophisticated enough to adjust premium-to-surplus ratio requirements to reflect the greater loss stability provided by aggregate excess covers.

A summary of the functions or purposes of reinsurance and how well each type of reinsurance serves those purposes is shown in Exhibit 8-7.

Facultative Reinsurance

Making specific statements about facultative reinsurance is difficult because each item of coverage is negotiated separately and can be of almost any form and at almost any rate that is agreeable to both parties. In the past, facultative reinsurance on property was almost always written on a pro rata basis. Now, facultative excess is commonly used.

Regardless of the form, excess or pro rata, the approach to underwriting facultative reinsurance is substantially different from that for treaties. In underwriting a treaty, the principal emphasis is on the management of the primary insurer, the classes reinsured, the geographical spread, and the primary insurer's historical loss experience for the lines of insurance covered by the treaty. The reinsurer does not underwrite individual loss exposures under the treaty.

Under facultative reinsurance, the reinsurer underwrites each loss exposure individually as it is submitted for consideration. The primary insurer is required to furnish detailed information on each exposure (essentially the same information that a prudent primary insurer would require when underwriting an account).

The facultative reinsurer is not bound by the rates quoted or charged by the primary insurer. It may, if it chooses and if the primary insurer is willing, charge a higher rate for the reinsurance than was charged on the direct policy. For this

Exhibit 8-7
Function of Specific Types of Treaty Reinsurance

Type of Reinsurance	Financing (Surplus Relief)	Large-Line Capacity	Catastrophe Protection	Stabilization of Loss Experience	Main Purpose
Quota share	Yes	Yes	Yes, but not purchased for this purpose	No	To provide surplus relief
Surplus share	Yes	Yes	No	No	Primarily to provide large-line capacity while providing some surplus relief
Per risk or per policy excess	No	Yes	Possibly to some extent but not purchased for this purpose	Yes	To provide large-line capacity while stabilizing loss experience
Per occurrence excess	No	No	Yes, sole purpose	Yes	To protect against an accumulation of losses from one event (property or liability coverages)
Aggregate excess	No	Yes	Yes	Yes	To stabilize loss experience

reason, primary insurers that expect to depend heavily on facultative reinsurance frequently obtain a reinsurance commitment before they quote a premium to their prospective policyholders. Of course, this precaution is taken only partly because of rates and partly to be sure that reinsurance will be available. When an exposure is accepted, the reinsurer formalizes the agreement with a **certificate of reinsurance**.

In view of the uncertainty and handling burden of facultative reinsurance, why would a primary insurer use it? Why not rely solely on treaties? There are several reasons.

First, treaties have exclusions. Property treaties, for example, usually exclude reinsurance coverage for a list of so-called "target risks," such as large art museums, major bridges, tunnels, nuclear generating facilities, and other properties of high value. These properties are excluded primarily because their large values require them to buy insurance from a number of primary insurers. If they were not excluded in treaties, a reinsurer might find, after a loss, that its accumulated loss through several different primary insurers exceeded the amount it deemed prudent to accept. It would not know of such an exposure before a loss because the reinsurer does not underwrite each individual exposure under a treaty. Treaties might also exclude certain hazardous operations, either for property or liability lines. If an exposure is excluded under the primary insurer's treaties, it must turn to facultative reinsurers for protection.

Second, a primary insurer might use facultative coverage to protect its treaties, to protect a favorable commission allowance under its treaties, or to protect a profit-sharing agreement. A favorable reinsurance treaty is a valuable relationship for a primary insurer, facilitating its operations and contributing to its profits. However, the continuation of the treaty on favorable terms, or perhaps on any terms, depends on the quality of business placed with it. The ceding commission or rates under treaties are determined by loss experience under the treaty. Some treaties include retrospective rating plans or profit-sharing commission plans that tie the rates or commission directly to losses incurred under that treaty. The rates or commissions under other treaties are negotiated on the basis of past loss experience. If an insurer must write coverage on a loss exposure that might have an adverse effect on its treaty relationships, it can reinsure it facultatively instead. Since each facultative submission is an independent transaction and is underwritten separately, a loss under one facultative agreement has little or no effect on the terms or rates under subsequent transactions.

Another reason for using facultative reinsurance is to cover a loss exposure that exceeds the limits under the applicable treaties. The limit under a reinsurance treaty is one of the major determinants of reinsurance costs. Consequently, a primary insurer should set the limit at an amount that is adequate for the vast majority, say 98 percent, of the loss exposures it insures and rely on facultative coverage for the excess over treaty limits for the unusually large exposures.

There is one exception to the statement that each facultative submission is separately and independently underwritten. Reinsurers sometimes enter into what is called a facultative obligatory treaty. Under such a treaty, the primary insurer is not required to place any exposures, but the reinsurer is obligated to accept any business the primary insurer elects to place as long as it is within the class of business covered by the treaty. Under a facultative obligatory treaty, the reinsurer underwrites the management of the primary insurer at least as carefully as under the more common treaties, and possibly more carefully.

Facultative obligatory treaties are not common because of the opportunity for adverse selection against the reinsurer. Facultative treaties that are nonobligatory to the reinsurer are slightly more common. Such treaties merely set forth the conditions under which business will be placed and accepted if the primary insurer elects to place it and the reinsurer elects to accept it.

Pro Rata Facultative Reinsurance

As previously mentioned, facultative reinsurance for property exposures has traditionally been written on a pro rata basis, though excess of loss reinsurance has become more prominent in recent years. **Pro rata facultative reinsurance** functions similarly to a surplus share treaty except, of course, that each facultative agreement relates to a single subject of insurance. Exhibit 8-8 shows the operation of a pro rata facultative reinsurance transaction.

Excess Facultative Reinsurance

Excess of loss facultative reinsurance operates just like a per risk or per policy excess treaty. That is, the primary insurer pays all losses equal to or less than its agreed retention. The reinsurer is involved only if the loss exceeds the primary insurer's retention, and then it pays only the amount in excess of the retention, up to the reinsurance limit.

Excess of loss reinsurance has been the traditional form of facultative reinsurance for liability and workers compensation coverages. As previously mentioned, it has been used with increasing frequency for property insurance.

For liability insurance, the per policy excess reinsurance premium is usually based on the increased limits factors used by the primary insurer. However, the reinsurance premium might be higher or lower than the primary insurer's increased limits premium, depending on the facultative reinsurer's judgment as to the adequacy of that premium for the particular exposure.

Exhibit 8-8
Pro Rata Facultative Reinsurance Example

As an illustration, assume that Insurance Company has received an application from one of its producers to write $1 million of property insurance on the Foundry Corporation. Insurance Company has established its net retention limit on foundries at $100,000. In addition, it has automatic surplus share treaties that will cover five lines, or, in this case, $500,000. The surplus reinsurers pay Insurance Company a 35 percent ceding commission under the treaties.

Insurance, Premium, and Loss Division Through Surplus Share and Pro Rata Facultative Reinsurance

	Insurance	Premium	Loss	Ceding Commission to Insurance Company
Insurance Company	$ 100,000	$ 3,000	$ 2,000	$ 0
Surplus Share Reinsurers	500,000	15,000	10,000	5,250
Facultative Reinsurer	400,000	12,000	8,000	3,600
Totals	$1,000,000	$30,000	$20,000	$8,850

Insurance Company then approaches the facultative department of Facultative Reinsurer with a request for $400,000 of pro rata facultative reinsurance. After Facultative Reinsurer reviews all of the information furnished by Insurance Company, it agrees to provide the $400,000 of coverage, for which it will receive 40 percent of the direct premium and will pay Insurance Company a 30 percent ceding commission. The direct premium charged to Foundry Corporation by Insurance Company is $30,000.

Having obtained the necessary reinsurance, Insurance Company issued the policy to Foundry Corporation. A $20,000 loss occurred shortly thereafter. The insurance, premium, and loss would be divided as shown below.

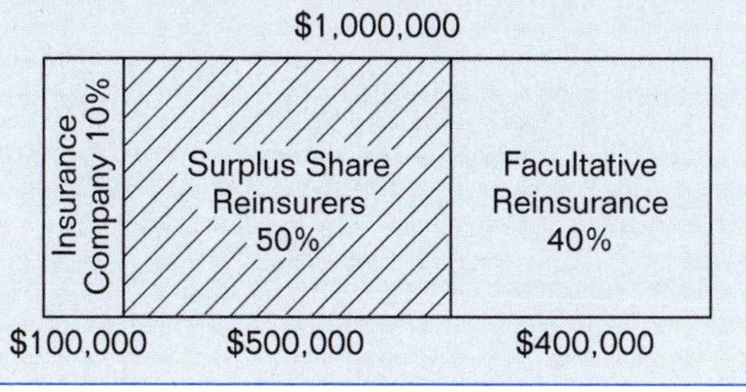

Specifying a method for rating excess of loss facultative coverage for property insurance is difficult. The rate would largely depend on the judgment of the facultative underwriter, reinforced to the extent possible by statistics from the reinsurer's experience with similar exposures, guides such as Lloyd's first loss scale, and what the competition is charging. Lloyd's first loss scale is used by property facultative underwriters in much the same way increased limit factor tables are used in liability lines.

Functions of Facultative Reinsurance

The principal functions of facultative reinsurance, whether pro rata or excess of loss, are to provide large-line capacity, to cover those exposures specifically excluded from treaties, and to protect treaties from unusual or hazardous exposures. Facultative reinsurance can also be used to secure a second opinion from the facultative reinsurer as to acceptability, price, policy terms, and conditions. Since facultative coverage must be negotiated separately on each subject of insurance, it is not likely to provide significant surplus relief unless a very large number of facultative covers are purchased. The same characteristic prevents facultative reinsurance from effectively coping with catastrophes. It does help smooth the fluctuations in loss experience, however, by providing a means of limiting the effect of a single large loss.

Financial Reinsurance

All reinsurance contracts are financial contracts. The characteristics that distinguish the traditional reinsurance contracts, discussed up to this point, from the so-called financial or finite reinsurance contracts, discussed here, are the kinds and amounts of risks transferred. Traditional reinsurance contracts are designed primarily to transfer underwriting risk—the risk that losses and expenses will exceed premium.

Financial reinsurance contracts usually transfer very little underwriting risk; some of them transfer no underwriting risk at all. They can also transfer some investment risk, some timing risk, or both. **Investment risk** is the chance that a reinsurer's investment portfolio will yield a lower return than expected. **Timing risk** is the risk that losses will be paid more quickly than expected, thus producing less investment income than expected.

A primary insurer's major motivation for purchasing financial reinsurance is to enhance its surplus position. However, because of accounting restrictions imposed in 1992, U.S. insurers are restricted from benefiting from some forms of financial reinsurance. According to these accounting guidelines, the following must be present in order for a transaction to be considered "reinsurance":

1. The reinsurer must assume significant insurance risk under the reinsured portions of the underlying insurance contracts.
2. It must be reasonably possible for the reinsurer to realize significant loss from the transaction.

Although the term "insurance risk" is defined in the guidelines, the terms "reasonably possible" and "significant loss" are not. Thus, determining whether a financial reinsurance agreement meets these accounting requirements is complex.

Financial reinsurance agreements can be transacted using most types of reinsurance. Under a financial reinsurance treaty, the reinsurer's aggregate liability under the contract is limited. That limit can be set equal to the reinsurance premium plus anticipated investment income, shielding the reinsurer from the underwriting risks.

The principal categories of financial reinsurance are as follows:

- Time and distance contracts
- Loss portfolio transfers

Many variations are possible within each of these categories.

Time and Distance Contracts

Under a **time and distance contract,** the primary insurer pays an agreed premium to the reinsurer at the inception of the contract. In return, the reinsurer promises to pay to the primary insurer one or more future payments, with the date and amount of each payment specified in the contract. The payments to the primary insurer are not contingent on its underwriting experience. The premium paid by the primary insurer is determined by discounting the future payments to reflect the investment income that the reinsurer expects to earn on the premium it receives. A loading for the reinsurer's expenses and profit is added, either directly or by crediting interest at a lower rate than the reinsurer expects to earn. The only risk assumed by the reinsurer is the risk that it will not earn as much investment income as it anticipated in calculating the premium.

Time and distance contracts are no longer used much in the United States, since regulatory authorities and auditors have judged them not to be reinsurance transactions. Instead, they are treated for accounting purposes in the same way as bank deposits. The major purchasers for such contracts are syndicates at Lloyd's of London.

Loss Portfolio Transfers

Traditional reinsurance contracts cover losses incurred by the primary insurer during the term of the reinsurance contract. By contrast, loss portfolio transfers cover losses incurred by the primary insurer before the inception of the loss portfolio transfer contract. Under a **loss portfolio transfer contract**, the primary insurer cedes to the reinsurer its liability for a block of losses (or portfolio) defined in the contract. Subject to the limits stated in the contract, the reinsurer then reimburses the primary insurer for any amounts paid to settle the covered losses.

Until recently, the advantage of loss portfolio transfers to U.S. primary insurers was an immediate increase in policyholders' surplus. The premium the primary insurer must pay is usually substantially less than the aggregate amount of loss reserves transferred because they are discounted in calculating the premium. Consequently, a primary insurer might transfer $100 million of loss reserves for a premium of $75 million. The difference of $25 million would be added to its policyholders' surplus. U.S. accounting standard changes have taken away this advantage for U.S.-domiciled insurers.

Reinsurance Through Pools

Although there are some fine distinctions among pools, syndicates, and reinsurance associations, the three will be discussed together here, and no distinction will be made between them. A **reinsurance pool** (or syndicate or association) is an organization of insurers banded together to underwrite reinsurance jointly. Some pools write reinsurance only for member companies of the pool. Others write coverage only for nonmember insurers, and still others may write coverage for both members and nonmembers. Some reinsurance pools restrict their operations to relatively narrow classes of business, such as fire and allied lines coverages on sprinklered properties. Others write a wide variety of coverages.

The initiative for the organization of a reinsurance pool can come from any of several sources. Several pools were organized because groups of relatively small insurers wanted to increase their capacity to write high-value properties. None of the insurers operating alone had sufficient skill and capacity, but the group could provide the needed capacity and hire technicians by combining financial resources through a reinsurance pool. Often, such pooling results in a lowering of total expenses. Examples of such pools are the Industrial Risk Insurers (IRI) and the United States Aircraft Insurance Group (USAIG). Governmental pressure or suggestion has been the initiating force in the formation of some pools. Among these are the nuclear energy pools and the reinsurance plans and joint underwriting associations that function in some states to provide automobile, fire, and workers compensation insurance for those who cannot obtain coverage in the voluntary market.

A reinsurance broker, also known as a reinsurance intermediary, might organize a pool as a means of providing reinsurance to clients of the brokerage firm. Such pools are likely to be fluid, with old member firms departing and new member firms entering on a fairly frequent basis. Needless to say, the broker would need to have some inducement to offer in order to entice an insurer to participate. The inducement might be an established book of desirable business, some special expertise on the part of the broker, or some similar benefit to the insurer. Although many broker-initiated pools have operated successfully over many years, a few have failed, with severe results for the participating companies. With increasing exposure for legal liability resulting from such pool operations, broker-oriented pools are not as evident today as in past years.

Pooling, by itself, does not necessarily improve the underwriting results of the pooled business. Poor business placed in the pool simply develops poor pool results.

The operating methods of reinsurance pools vary as widely as their purpose of organization, or perhaps more so. Automobile residual market mechanisms, discussed in Chapters 1 and 6, exemplify how the property-liability industry has combined resources to address a market need. Similarly, insurance-industry-backed nuclear energy pools were created to protect the public from the peacetime use of nuclear energy.

The Reinsurance Market

The boundaries of the reinsurance market are difficult to define. It is a surprisingly international market, and a single large loss might be shared by reinsurers throughout the world. In 1995, U.S. insurers bought almost half of their reinsurance, measured by premiums, from nonadmitted alien reinsurers. These alien reinsurers are located in many countries of the world, including Russia and China. However, Britain, Bermuda, and Switzerland overwhelmingly account for the largest shares. The share of U.S. reinsurance premiums going to nonadmitted alien insurers does not fully indicate the international nature of the reinsurance business. Of the twenty largest U.S.-based reinsurers in 1995, four were owned by foreign reinsurers. Of course, some of the nonadmitted, alien reinsurers to which U.S. companies ceded premiums were owned by U.S. insurers, especially those reinsurers domiciled in the United Kingdom and Bermuda.

Insurers based in the United States sell much reinsurance abroad, but not nearly as much as they buy abroad. The United States is a net importer of reinsurance.

Exhibit 8-9 shows a list of the largest reinsurers in the world in 1995, along with their estimated 1995 written premiums. All of the reinsurers listed in Exhibit 8-9 are active in the U.S. market, either directly or through subsidiaries. Lloyd's of London is not included in Exhibit 8-9, but probably would rank near the middle if included.

Note the geographic diversity in top reinsurers, with eight headquartered in the United States, three each in Germany and Japan, two each in Switzerland and France, and one each in England, Italy, and Bermuda. Numerous smaller reinsurers are located in many other countries.

In addition to the geographic spread of the largest reinsurers, one other fact stands out in Exhibit 8-9. Many reinsurers are substantially smaller financially than the primary insurers to which they provide reinsurance protection. However, any one professional reinsurer does not write or retain for its own account all of the exposures assumed under a treaty with a major primary insurer. A major treaty is usually shared by several reinsurers on a percentage basis, or if one reinsurer initially writes the entire treaty, it might cede much of it to other reinsurers under retrocession agreements.

Multiplicity of Reinsurers

In addition to its geographic spread, the boundaries of the reinsurance market are difficult to define for another reason. Any insurer can provide reinsurance unless it is subject to statutory or charter prohibitions. Few such prohibitions exist, and many primary insurers also provide some reinsurance. Even relatively small insurers can engage in the reinsurance business by participating in various reinsurance pools and syndicates, their participation sometimes being a very small fraction of a percentage point of the pool business. Such small companies are not major factors in the reinsurance market, either individually or collectively.

As a practical matter, the reinsurance market for U.S. insurers is composed of (1) U.S. insurers or licensed alien insurers that specialize in reinsurance, frequently referred to as professional reinsurers; (2) U.S. insurers or licensed alien insurers whose primary business is direct insurance with the public but that have professional reinsurance departments; and (3) nonlicensed (nonadmitted) alien reinsurers. U.S. reinsurance is almost evenly split between professional reinsurers and nonlicensed alien reinsurers. The former group of reinsurers accounts for 46.7 percent of the market, and the latter has 45.6 percent. The remaining share belongs to direct insurers with reinsurance departments.[6]

Exhibit 8-9
World's Twenty Largest Reinsurers: 1995*

Company	Country of Domicile	Net Reinsurance Premiums 1995 (millions of $)
Munich Re	Germany	$11,076
Swiss Re	Switzerland	8,891
Employers Re	United States	6,967
General Re/Cologne Re Group	United States	6,102
Assicurazioni Generali S.p.A.	Italy	3,816
Hannover Re Group	Germany	3,542
Lincoln National Re	United States	2,888
Gerling Global Re Group	Germany	2,461
SCOR Group	France	2,098
Tokio Marine & Fire Ins. Group	Japan	1,134
Mercantile & General Re	England	1,752
American Re	United States	1,626
AXA Re	France	1,437
Toa Fire & Marine	Japan	1,105
Transatlantic Re	United States	1,009
Everest Re	United States	945
Winterthur	Switzerland	923
Yasuda Fire and Marine Ins. Co.	Japan	806
Berkshire Hathaway	United States	777
Centre Re	Bermuda	716

Adapted from "Business Insurance Directory of Worldwide Reinsurance," *Business Insurance*, September 2, 1996, pp. 3, 29-53.

*Since this survey was conducted by *Business Insurance* in September 1996, Munich Re has acquired American Re, and Swiss Re has acquired Mercantile and General. Additionally, SCOR U.S. bought Allstate Corporation's U.S. reinsurance operation, and General Re bought National Re. These consolidations are evidence of the dynamics in the global reinsurance marketplace.

Reciprocity

Another complicating factor in the measurement of the reinsurance market is the practice of reciprocal reinsurance among primary insurers. In **reciprocal reinsurance**, two (or possibly more) primary insurers enter into an agreement under which each cedes to the other an agreed percentage of its business. For example, a U.S. automobile insurer and a Canadian automobile insurer entered into an agreement whereby the U.S. insurer ceded approximately 80 percent of its business to the Canadian insurer in exchange for 30 percent of the Canadian insurer's direct premiums. Because of the sizes of the two insurers, the dollar amounts of ceded premiums were approximately equal. The transaction provided both insurers with some protection against fluctuations in loss experience both by sharing losses and by providing each insurer with a better spread of exposures geographically and in numbers.

In this case, both insurers were writing substantially the same class of business—private passenger automobile insurance predominantly for blue-collar workers. Similarity of business is a prime consideration in any reciprocal reinsurance arrangement. If the exchanged business is not substantially similar, one insurer is likely to profit at the expense of the other.

The two insurers in this case also possess another characteristic that is highly desirable for successful reciprocal reinsurance. They do not compete in the same market area. Since each partner in a reciprocal arrangement must furnish the other partner with a great deal of proprietary information, such arrangements are generally not satisfactory in a competitive situation. This fact, perhaps more than any other, contributed to the decline of reciprocity as a major force in the reinsurance market.

In years past, when professional reinsurance was less available and few insurers operated nationally, reciprocity was an important reinsurance technique. Today, its use is relatively limited except for the special case of reciprocal reinsurance arrangements among several insurers under common ownership or common management or both. In that special case, reciprocity is still common.

Summary

Reinsurance describes the contractual relationship between insurers when risk is transferred from one to another. Individual business enterprises purchase insurance to reduce the chance of financial loss. Likewise, insurers purchase reinsurance primarily to ensure financial stability. Specifically, these functions include stabilization of loss experience, large-line capacity, financing, and catastrophe protection. Additional functions include underwriting assistance and assistance provided to an insurer withdrawing from a territory or class of business.

The reinsurance relationship exists exclusively between the primary insurer and the reinsurer. The individual policyholder is *not* a party to the reinsurance contract unless an endorsement is attached to the primary insurer's policy. This endorsement permits the policyholder to cut through the primary insurer and present a claim directly to the reinsurer.

Several forms of reinsurance have been developed to serve the functions of reinsurance. A reinsurance agreement could contain several of the forms described in this chapter. The reinsurance program of a primary insurer might contain many agreements with many reinsurers, each comprising several forms of reinsurance. For instructional purposes, this text described each reinsurance form separately even though most insurer reinsurance programs would use several forms in combination.

Reinsurance is arranged in two general ways. Treaties are ongoing relationships between parties. The usual treaty arrangement obligates both parties to a specified transfer and acceptance of risk. Facultative reinsurance is usually a one-time negotiated arrangement between parties. Facultative arrangements often serve as a stop-gap for treaty exclusions or when the treaty limits are lower than needed.

Financial reinsurance is a relatively new type of reinsurance arrangement in which the underwriting risk traditionally present is absent. Financial reinsurance contracts transfer the risk that the reinsurer's portfolio will yield a lower return than expected and that losses will be paid more quickly than expected.

In some instances, insurers have banded together into reinsurance pools. The composition, operation, and purpose of pools vary. Some pools were formed to meet the needs of small insurers, and others were formed to combine the technical resources needed to offer certain forms of insurance. The state and federal governments have been the initiating force of some pool organizations.

The market for reinsurance is international. Like primary insurers, reinsurers share risks with other reinsurers through retrocession. In this process, the effect of a reinsured loss is diluted. In addition, primary insurers might join together to meet the reinsurance needs of one another through reciprocal reinsurance arrangements.

Glossary of Reinsurance Terms[7]

Acquisition Costs—All expenses directly related to acquiring insurance or reinsurance accounts, i.e., commissions paid to agents, brokerage fees paid to brokers, and expenses associated with marketing, underwriting, contract insurance, and premium collection.

Admitted (Authorized) Reinsurance—Reinsurance for which credit is given in the ceding company's Annual Statement because the reinsurer is licensed or otherwise authorized to transact business in the jurisdiction in question.

Aggregate Excess of Loss Reinsurance—A form of excess of loss reinsurance which indemnifies the ceding company against the amount by which all of the ceding company's losses incurred during a specific period (usually 12 months) exceed either (1) a predetermined dollar amount or (2) a percentage of the company's subject premiums (loss ratio) for the specific period. This type of contract is also commonly referred to as "stop loss" reinsurance or "excess of loss ratio" reinsurance.

Alien—An insurer domiciled outside the United States.

Annual Statement (Also Statutory Annual Statement and Convention Blank)—The annual report format prescribed by the NAIC and the states.

Assume—To accept all or part of a ceding company's insurance or reinsurance on a risk or exposure.

Assumption—A procedure under which one insurance company takes over or assumes the direct policy liabilities of another insurer.

Automatic Facultative Binder (AFB) or Automatic Facultative Treaty—See Facultative Treaty.

Bordereau—A report provided periodically by the reinsured detailing the reinsurance premiums and/or reinsurance losses with respect to specific risks ceded under the reinsurance agreement.

Bulk Reinsurance—A transaction sometimes defined by statute as any quota share, surplus aid, or portfolio reinsurance agreement through which, by itself or in combination with other similar agreements, an insurer assumes all or a substantial portion of the liability of the reinsured company.

Capacity—The largest amount of insurance or reinsurance available from a company or the market in general. Also used to refer to the maximum amount of business (premium volume) which a company or the total market could write based on financial strength.

Catastrophe Reinsurance—A form of excess of loss reinsurance which, subject to a specific limit, indemnifies the ceding company in excess of a specified retention with respect to an accumulation of losses resulting from a catastrophic event or series of events arising from one occurrence. Catastrophe contracts can also be written on an aggregate basis under which protection is afforded for losses over a certain amount for each loss in excess of a second amount in the aggregate for all losses in all catastrophes occurring during a period of time (usually one year).

Cede—To transfer to a reinsurer all or part of the insurance or reinsurance risk written by a ceding company.

Ceding Commission—In calculating a reinsurance premium, an amount allowed by the reinsurer for part or all of a ceding company's acquisition and other overhead costs, including premium taxes. It may also include a profit factor. See Overriding Commission.

Ceding Company (Also Cedent, Reinsured, Reassured)—The insurer which cedes all or part of the insurance or reinsurance risk it has written to another insurer/reinsurer.

Cession—The amount of insurance risk transferred to the reinsurer by the ceding company.

Clash Cover (or Contingency Cover)—An excess of loss reinsurance agreement with a retention level equal to or higher than the maximum limits written for any one reinsured policy or contract. Usually applicable to casualty lines of business, the clash cover is intended to protect the ceding company against accumulations of loss arising from multiple insureds and/or multiple lines of business for one insured involved in one loss occurrence.

Cut-Through Endorsement—An endorsement added to an insurance policy to provide that, in the event of the insolvency of the insurance company, the amount of any loss which would have been recovered from the reinsurer by the insurance company will be paid instead directly to the policyholder by the reinsurer. Also referred to as an Assumption of Liability Endorsement (ALE). See Guarantee Endorsement.

Excess of Loss Ratio Reinsurance—See Aggregate Excess of Loss Reinsurance.

Excess of Loss Reinsurance—A form of reinsurance which, subject to a specified limit, indemnifies the ceding company against the amount of loss in excess of a specified retention. It includes various types of reinsurance, such as catastrophe reinsurance, per risk reinsurance, per occurrence reinsurance, and aggregate excess reinsurance. See also Non-Proportional Reinsurance.

Excess Per Risk Reinsurance—A form of excess of loss reinsurance which, subject to a specified limit, indemnifies the ceding company against the amount of loss in excess of a specified retention for each risk involved in each occurrence.

Facultative Certificate of Reinsurance—A contract formalizing a reinsurance cession on a specific risk.

Facultative Obligatory Treaty (Also Semi-Obligatory Treaty)—A reinsurance contract under which the ceding company may cede exposures or risks of a defined class that the reinsurer must accept if ceded.

Facultative Reinsurance—Reinsurance of individual risks by offer and acceptance wherein the reinsurer retains the "faculty" to accept or reject each risk offered by the ceding company.

Facultative Treaty—A reinsurance contract under which the ceding company has the option to cede and the reinsurer has the option to accept or decline classified risks of a specific business line. The contract merely reflects how individual facultative reinsurance shall be handled.

Finite Reinsurance (Nontraditional Reinsurance, Limited Risk Reinsurance, and Financial Reinsurance)—A term used to describe a broad spectrum of treaty reinsurance arrangements which provide reinsurance coverage at lower margins than traditional reinsurance, in return for a lower probability of loss to the reinsurer. This reinsurance is often multi-year and financially oriented, and can provide a means of financial management beyond that usually provided by traditional reinsurance.

Foreign—A U.S. domiciled insurer which is domiciled in a state other than the jurisdiction in question.

Guarantee Endorsement—An endorsement added to an insurance policy covering the policyholder's mortgaged property to provide that, in the event of the insolvency of the insurance company, the reinsurer shall pay directly to the mortgagee and/or the policyholder the amount of loss which would have been recovered from the reinsurer by the insurance company. The endorsement may provide that the reinsurer will pay the full loss amount in accordance with the insurance protection afforded by the insurance company. The guarantee endorsement is also known as the mortgagee endorsement, and is similar in concept to the cut-through endorsement.

Net Loss—The amount of loss sustained by an insurer after deducting all applicable reinsurance, salvage, and subrogation recoveries.

Net Retained Liability—The amount of insurance which a ceding company keeps for its own account and does not reinsure in any way (except in some instances for catastrophe reinsurance).

Nonadmitted Reinsurance—Reinsurance for which no credit is given in the ceding company's statutory statement because the reinsurer is not licensed or authorized in the jurisdiction in question.

Nonproportional Reinsurance—See Excess of Loss Reinsurance.

Obligatory Treaty—A reinsurance contract under which business must be ceded in accordance with contract terms and must be accepted by the reinsurer.

Overriding Commission—An allowance paid to the ceding company over and above the acquisition cost to allow for overhead expenses and often including a margin for profit.

Participating Reinsurance—See Pro Rata Reinsurance.

Pool (Also Association, Syndicate)—An organization of insurers or reinsurers through which pool members underwrite particular types of risks with premiums, losses, and expenses shared in agreed amounts.

Portfolio—The liability of an insurer for the unexpired portion of the in-force policies or outstanding losses or both for a described segment of the insurer's business.

Portfolio Reinsurance—The transfer of portfolio via a cession of reinsurance. See also Assumption.

Primary—In reinsurance this term is applied to the nouns: insurer, insured, policy, and insurance, and means respectively: (1) the insurance company which originates the business, i.e., the ceding company; (2) the policyholder insured by the primary insurer; (3) the initial policy issued by the primary insurer to the primary insured; (4) the insurance covered under the primary policy issued by the primary insurer to the primary insured (sometimes called "underlying insurance").

Proportional Reinsurance—See Pro Rata Reinsurance.

Pro Rata Reinsurance (Also Quota Share, Proportional, and Participating Reinsurance)—A generic term describing all forms of quota share and surplus reinsurance in which the reinsurer shares a pro rata portion of the losses and premiums of the ceding company.

Quota Share Reinsurance—A form of pro rata insurance indemnifying the ceding company for a fixed percent of loss on each risk covered in the contract in consideration of the same percentage of the premium paid to the ceding company.

Reassured—See Ceding Company.

Reciprocity—A mutual exchange of reinsurance between two or more companies.

Reinstatement—A provision in an excess of loss reinsurance contract, particularly catastrophe and clash covers, that provides for reinstatement of a limit which is reduced by the occurrence of a loss or losses. The number of times that the limit can be reinstated varies, as does the cost of the reinstatement.

Reinsurance—The transaction whereby the assuming insurer, for a consideration, agrees to indemnify the ceding company against all, or a part, of the loss which the latter may sustain under the policy or policies which it has issued.

Reinsurance Premium—The consideration paid by a ceding company to a reinsurer for the coverage provided by the reinsurer.

Reinsured—See Ceding Company.

Reinsurer—The insurer which assumes all or a part of the insurance or reinsurance risk written by another insurer.

Retention—The amount of risk the ceding company keeps for its own account or the account of others.

Retrocession—A reinsurance transaction whereby a reinsurer (the retrocedent) cedes all or part of the reinsurance risk it has assumed to another reinsurer (the retrocessionaire).

Stop Loss Reinsurance—See Aggregate Excess of Loss Reinsurance.

Surplus Reinsurance—A form of pro rata reinsurance under which the ceding company cedes that portion of its liability on a given risk which is greater than its net line. As consideration, the reinsurer receives that portion of the total premium which the surplus bears to the total liability.

Target Risk—(1) Certain high-valued bridges, tunnels, and fine arts collections which are excluded from reinsurance contracts and release the reinsurer of any potential high accumulation of liability on any one risk from various sources; (2) a large hazardous risk for which insurance is difficult to place; or (3) a large attractive risk which is considered a target for competing insurance companies and producers.

Treaty—A reinsurance contract under which the reinsured company agrees to cede and the reinsurer agrees to assume risks of a particular class or classes of business.

Underlying—The amount of insurance or reinsurance on a risk (or occurrence) which applies to a loss before the next higher excess layer of insurance or reinsurance attaches.

Working Cover—A contract covering an amount of excess reinsurance in which loss frequency is anticipated.

Chapter Notes

1. Jonathan F. Bank, "The Contract v. The Contact," *Reinsurance*, August 1983, p. 161.
2. Jonathan F. Bank, "Cut-Through Endorsements: Puerto Rico Ruling Tarnishes Their Attractiveness," *Business Insurance*, October 10, 1983, p. 51.
3. For a brief review of such cases, see the references cited in the two preceding footnotes.
4. *Glossary of Reinsurance Terms* (Washington, DC: Reinsurance Association of America, 1992), p. 7.
5. *Reinsurance and Reassurance*, vol. 5 (New York, NY: Munich Reinsurance Company, 1965), p. 107.
6. Craig Elkind and Thomas Walsh, "U.S. Re Market Shaken But Not Stirred, Standard & Poor's Says," *National Underwriter* (Property & Casualty/Risk & Benefits Management Edition), July 17, 1995, p. 56.
7. The definitions in this glossary were adapted with permission from *Glossary of Reinsurance Terms*.

Chapter 9

The Reinsurance Transaction

A well-planned and well-executed reinsurance program is a valuable asset to a primary insurer. It can help to stabilize loss experience, provide capacity, and provide surplus for growth. In periods of severe catastrophe, a good reinsurance program can mean the difference between survival and failure.

An optimal reinsurance program requires careful planning by the primary insurer, possibly with assistance from reinsurers, reinsurance brokers, and consultants. The persons planning and executing the plan must understand several aspects of reinsurance. Among them are the following:

1. How the characteristics of the primary insurer affect its reinsurance needs
2. The information needed to design a reinsurance program and negotiate the required reinsurance contracts
3. The administrative procedures involved in various forms of reinsurance
4. The methods used by reinsurers in pricing their services
5. The effects of regulation on reinsurance at both the primary insurer level and the reinsurer level

This chapter provides an introduction to those subjects.

Reinsurance Planning for a Primary Insurer

There are many kinds of reinsurance, and, with rare exceptions, any primary insurer can find a combination of reinsurance contracts that meets its needs. The development of such a reinsurance program requires careful analysis of the primary insurer's needs as well as a thorough understanding of the reinsurance market.

The principal purposes of reinsurance are to provide large-line capacity, stabilize the primary insurer's loss ratio, and provide surplus relief. The first step in planning a reinsurance program for a primary insurer is to determine how much large-line capacity, how much stability, and how much surplus relief are needed.

At a minimum, the loss ratio must be sufficiently stable so as not to pose a threat to the insurer's continued solvency. It is also desirable for the insurer to be able to pursue its future growth plans. Beyond those considerations, managements of different insurers may differ as to the degree of stability they demand and the amount they are willing to pay to obtain it. The reinsurance program for a given primary insurer must reflect the attitude of its management toward risk.

Mutual insurers, for example, may be willing to accept greater loss ratio volatility than stock insurers. Mutuals are controlled by their policyholders, who are likely to be less concerned with short-term profits than are the stockholders of stock companies.

Management must be concerned with the stability of operating profit, which consists of the sum of underwriting profit and investment profit. Reinsurance deals only with the underwriting profit, yet management must also consider the stability of investment profit when designing the reinsurance program. Stable investment profit permits greater variation in underwriting profit. Several large insurers have suffered severe financial strains when their underwriting experience and their investment experience turned unfavorable at the same time.

Although the stability of investment profit must be considered in designing a primary insurer's reinsurance program, the goals of the program will ordinarily be stated in terms of net loss ratios, that is, the primary insurer's loss ratio after adjustment for reinsurance premiums ceded and losses recovered under the reinsurance program.

Other goals in addition to loss ratio stability may be specified for the reinsurance program. For example, the goals of an insurer's reinsurance program might include the following:

1. Avoid any increase in net loss ratio in excess of five percentage points as a result of chance variations in frequency or severity of losses, including catastrophes
2. Provide single risk capacity of at least $20 million for commercial property insurance and $10 million for commercial liability insurance under automatic treaties
3. Increase surplus by $10 million

The goals might be much more elaborate, listing many lines of insurance and classes of risks within each line.

Achievement of the specified goals might not always be possible or practical because of market conditions and cost considerations. Also, one must recognize that reinsurance planning is largely judgmental. Although some actuarial tools may be used in the process, it is still far short of an exact science. Despite those limitations, setting goals or objectives provides valuable guidance in reinsurance planning and reinsurance negotiations.

Factors Determining Reinsurance Needs

The reinsurance needs of a primary insurer depend on several factors. Among the most important are the following:

1. Kinds of insurance written
2. Exposures subject to catastrophic loss
3. Volume of insurance written
4. Available financial resources
5. Stability and liquidity of investment portfolio
6. Growth plans

All of those factors must be considered in designing a comprehensive reinsurance plan.

Kinds of Insurance Written

The characteristics of the various lines of insurance that help determine reinsurance needs include stability of loss frequency and stability of loss severity.

Catastrophe exposure, discussed below, is an element in both loss frequency and loss severity.

There is no common form of reinsurance that deals directly with loss frequency variations, but several forms of reinsurance can be used to reduce their financial effect. Perhaps the most effective form of reinsurance for handling loss frequency variations (especially if reinsurance costs are ignored) is an aggregate excess treaty. It puts a cap on the primary insurer's loss ratio (subject to percentage participations and treaty limits), whether such variations occur from catastrophes, other frequency variations, or variations in loss severity.

Reinsurance products are much more effective in reducing the effects of fluctuations in loss severity than they are for fluctuations in loss frequency. For large individual losses, both surplus share and per risk excess treaties are especially effective. The choice between them should be based on a consideration of cost and the need for surplus relief. Facultative cessions are also very useful tools for controlling large losses from unusually hazardous or unusually large exposures. The delays and heavy administrative burden associated with facultative cessions limit their use to relatively unusual situations.

Exposures Subject to Catastrophic Loss

Several lines of insurance are especially susceptible to catastrophes, such as windstorm, earthquake, hail, and winter storms. Other lines have less serious catastrophe exposures.

Catastrophe exposures vary widely from one geographic area to another. For example, hurricane losses are more common along the Gulf Coast and the south Atlantic coast than elsewhere in the United States, although they do sometimes cause damage for some distance inland or along the north or middle Atlantic coast. Tornadoes, on the other hand, are more common in the middle of the country. Hail losses are more severe at higher altitudes. Earthquake losses tend to be concentrated around certain well-known geologic faults.

In designing a catastrophe reinsurance program, a primary insurer must carefully analyze the geographic distribution of its insured properties. Such an analysis should consider the number of properties that could be damaged in a single occurrence and the maximum aggregate amount of damage from such an occurrence. Extensive data are available to assist in such an analysis. Data concerning the occurrence and intensity of hurricanes, tornadoes, and earthquakes are available from various governmental agencies. Insurance loss data are available from industry organizations.

It is essential to consider such data in establishing retentions and coverage limits under catastrophe excess treaties. Several South Carolina insurers were forced into insolvency by losses from Hurricane Hugo. More thorough analyses of their hurricane loss exposures might have enabled them to obtain additional reinsurance to ensure their survival.

The analysis of hurricane loss exposures is fairly typical of the techniques that can be used to analyze potential catastrophe losses. The first step in the analysis is to plot on a map the distribution of the properties insured in areas subject to hurricane damage, showing both the number and value of properties insured. Those properties should be shown for the smallest practical geographic units, at least by county and preferably by postal ZIP Code area.

The second step is to superimpose on the plot of insured properties a plot of historic hurricane tracks, showing both the path and the intensity of past storms. Insurance industry loss data for such storms should also be analyzed. Such loss data should be adjusted to reflect inflation and increased population density since the past storms occurred.

Through such careful analysis, an insurer can derive a reasonable estimate of the largest amount of aggregate losses it is likely to sustain in a single storm. Similar techniques can be used for earthquakes, floods, or other natural disasters. Although such analyses are time-consuming and expensive, they are necessary to provide reasonable assurance that adequate catastrophe reinsurance limits are obtained. Some reinsurers and reinsurance brokers have computer models to assist in the process. Because they have already collected the necessary historical data, the primary insurer need only provide its own data concerning the distribution of insured properties.

Volume of Insurance Written

The volume of insurance written is another major determinant of the reinsurance needs of a primary insurer. According to the law of large numbers, an insurer with a large volume of insurance should have a more stable loss ratio than one with a small volume, all else being equal. The increased stability resulting from large volume reduces the need for reinsurance. Of course, the volume needed to provide stability differs from one line of insurance to another. A line of insurance that has frequent, small losses can achieve stability with a smaller volume than one that has infrequent, large losses.

For example, an insurer that specializes in physical damage coverage for private passenger automobiles could achieve reasonable stability with a relatively small premium volume. Some catastrophe reinsurance might be needed unless the insurance is widely distributed across the country.

On the other hand, it is doubtful that any attainable premium volume would provide acceptable stability without reinsurance for an insurer that specializes in property insurance on large industrial facilities. Such an insurer would be likely to need a relatively complex reinsurance program, involving both treaty agreements and facultative cessions, regardless of its premium volume.

Available Financial Resources

The financial resources available to the primary insurer affect its reinsurance needs in two ways: through its need for stability and its need for surplus relief. An insurer with a weak surplus position needs a highly stable net loss ratio in order to avoid serious financial difficulties and possible insolvency. The weak surplus position may also require the use of pro rata reinsurance to provide surplus relief.

An insurer with a very strong surplus position can afford to risk a more volatile net loss ratio because it has the financial strength to absorb some unanticipated losses. However, the absolute size of the insurer's surplus is not the only concern. The quality of the surplus, as indicated by the invested assets that stand behind it, must also be considered.

Stability and Liquidity of Investment Portfolio

The stability and liquidity of a primary insurer's investment portfolio are important considerations in designing its reinsurance program. If an insurer plans to rely on its surplus to absorb abnormal losses, that surplus must be invested in assets that are (1) readily marketable and (2) not subject to wide fluctuations in market price. Otherwise, the surplus might not be sufficient to pay losses in a timely manner.

An insurer that holds large amounts of common stock in its investment portfolio would need to be more heavily reinsured than an insurer that holds short-term bonds, all other things being equal, since the common stock might be marketable only at a substantial loss in an unfavorable market. A large portfolio of long-term bonds might also sustain substantial market losses. An insurer that invests a large part of its funds in wholly owned subsidiaries needs to have a substantial reinsurance program because the stock of the subsidiaries might not be marketable when unusual losses occur.

Growth Plans

An insurer's growth plans also affect its reinsurance requirements. In general, an insurer that plans to grow rapidly needs to be reinsured more heavily than one that plans to grow more slowly. That greater need for reinsurance for a rapidly growing company stems from two sources.

First, new business constitutes a larger part of the premium volume of a rapidly growing insurer. The loss ratio on new business is likely to be higher and less predictable than the loss ratio on business that has been seasoned through renewal underwriting.

Also, a rapidly growing insurer is more likely to need surplus relief than an insurer that is growing more slowly. An insurer might earn a reputation for being an unreliable market if it has to discontinue writing new business because it has already written too much.

A primary insurer might reduce its long-term profits by entering into the reinsurance agreement because it has potentially ceded away profitable business. Sacrificing these profits is a short-term strategy that enables the primary insurer to continue to grow and, it is hoped, earn greater profits in the future.

Examples

Some examples can help to clarify the reinsurance planning process. These examples are hypothetical but are intended to be reasonably realistic.

Example 1—Large Personal Lines Insurer

The first example is a very large insurer. It specializes in personal lines insurance, primarily private passenger auto and homeowners insurance. Its annual direct premium volume is $20 billion. Its business is spread across the country, with the proportion of its business in any one state being approximately the same as that state's proportion of the nation's population. Its policyholders' surplus is $12 billion. Its investment portfolio consists mostly of federal government bonds and high-grade industrial and utility bonds. The insurer normally holds about $500 million in treasury bills, high-grade commercial paper, and other short-term assets. Common stocks account for only about 5 percent of its invested assets and less than 10 percent of policyholders' surplus. The insurer has shown an operating profit every year for the past decade. An analysis of the geographic spread of its homeowners and auto physical damage exposures indicates that losses in excess of $500 million in any one catastrophe are very unlikely.

After reviewing all of the available data, the insurer has decided that it does not need any reinsurance. Its large premium volume, wide spread of small individual risks, strong surplus position, and stable, liquid investment portfolio would enable it to cope with any loss ratio variation it might reasonably expect to occur, including catastrophes.

Example 2—Small Multi-Line Mutual Insurer

The second example is near the other end of the spectrum of U.S. property-liability insurers. It is a small mutual insurer whose business is confined to a single state. Its annual direct premium volume is $20 million, and its policyholders' surplus is $5 million. It writes homeowners coverage and property insurance for small commercial risks. It is headquartered in a city on the south Atlantic coast, and about half of its business is in or near the coastal region. Virtually all of its policies provide windstorm coverage; many also provide earthquake coverage. Minor quakes occur in or near its headquarter's city several times each year. The most recent damaging quakes occurred in the last century.

An analysis of the geographic distribution of its business indicates that a major hurricane could cause losses of as much as $10 million to the properties currently insured. An earthquake could cause losses of as much as $5 million. Its investment portfolio consists primarily of U.S. government bonds, with some bonds issued by its home state and local governments within that state. The insurer has experienced moderate growth in the past and expects to continue to grow at about 5 percent each year. Although it has shown an operating profit in most years of the last decade and for the decade as a whole, its loss ratio fluctuated substantially from year to year even though no major catastrophes occurred during that period.

With a premium-to-surplus ratio of 4-to-1, this insurer needs surplus relief if it is to continue to grow. Consequently, a quota share treaty is needed. Management has decided to cede 25 percent of its business under a quota share treaty, and the reinsurer has agreed to pay a 25 percent ceding commission. That transaction would reduce its net written premiums to $15 million, and the ceding commission would increase its policyholders' surplus to $6.25 million, giving it a premium-to-surplus ratio of less than 3-to-1. That ratio is acceptable to the regulatory authorities in the insurer's home state.

Management has decided that an aggregate excess treaty offers the best solution to stabilizing the insurer's net loss ratio. A reinsurer has offered to provide such a treaty with a retention of an 80 percent loss ratio. The reinsurer would pay 95 percent of losses in excess of the retention along with its proportional share of loss adjustment expenses. However, the reinsurer is willing to provide that aggregate excess treaty only if the primary insurer purchases a per occurrence excess treaty with a limit of at least $8 million and a retention of $500,000 or less. The per occurrence excess treaty would apply only to the primary insurer's net losses after deducting amounts recoverable under the quota share treaty. The aggregate excess treaty would apply only to the primary insurer's net losses after deducting recoveries under both the quota share treaty and the per occurrence excess treaty. The per occurrence excess treaty would apply only to property losses. The other two treaties would cover liability losses under the homeowners policies also.

Example 3—Large Multi-Line Stock Insurer

The final example, typical of U.S. property-liability insurers, is a stock insurer with annual direct written premiums of $1 billion and policyholders' surplus of $500 million. It has averaged 10 percent annual growth over the past decade and expects to continue to grow at about the same rate.

Its combined ratio has exceeded 100 percent each year for the last decade, averaging 102 percent for the period. It has reported an operating profit each year for the last decade, but the profit has been small in some years. A high-grade portfolio of bonds and other fixed-income securities accounts for about 95 percent of its invested assets. The balance consists of carefully selected preferred and common stocks.

The insurer writes commercial automobile insurance, general liability, commercial multi-peril, and commercial fire and allied lines insurance. It writes small to medium-sized commercial and industrial risks. A survey of its outstanding policies showed that about 95 percent of its liability policies had occurrence limits of $10 million or less, and about 95 percent of its property policies provided coverage of $15 million or less. Management has decided to set its treaty limits to cover those amounts and to depend on facultative reinsurance for the policies with greater limits.

The insurer does not need surplus relief, so no pro rata reinsurance will be purchased. Per risk or per policy excess treaties will be purchased for both liability and property insurance. Management has decided that the insurer can afford to assume individual losses up to 0.5 percent of direct written premium, or 1.0 percent of policyholders' surplus. Consequently, the retention under both the liability and property treaties will be set at $5 million per loss. Treaty limits will be $5 million for liability and $10 million for property losses. Thus, the primary insurer's retention and the treaty limits will fully cover about 95 percent of all policies issued.

The properties insured by the primary insurer are spread widely across the country, but several areas have high concentrations of values subject to catastrophe losses. The worst of those is a metropolitan area on the Gulf Coast, where management estimates that a direct hit by a major hurricane could cause losses of up to $50 million. A catastrophe treaty with a limit of $50 million and a retention of $5 million will be purchased to cover that exposure.

Setting Retentions

Although actuaries have experimented with mathematical methods for establishing reinsurance retentions, such methods have not been generally accepted. The setting of retentions is still more a matter of judgment than an exact science. However, some general considerations can be mentioned.

The method of setting retentions varies with the kind of treaty as well as other factors. The reasons for buying a pro rata treaty differ from the reasons for buying an excess treaty, so the factors considered in setting the retention also differ.

The principal reason for choosing a pro rata treaty in preference to an excess treaty is to provide surplus relief. Consequently, the amount of surplus relief needed must be an important factor in the selection of the retention. The amount of surplus relief received will be a function of the percentage of premiums ceded and the percentage ceding commission received. Exhibit 8-2 (in Chapter 8) illustrates the effect of pro rata reinsurance on policyholders' surplus and indicates the general method of making such calculations.

The principal purposes of excess of loss treaties are to stabilize loss experience and to provide large-line capacity. Providing large-line capacity is a function of the treaty limit, rather than the retention. Therefore, the principal consideration in setting the retention of an excess of loss treaty is the size of loss that the primary insurer can absorb without undue effect on the policyholders' surplus or the loss ratio for the line or lines covered by the treaty. That amount is, in turn, a function of the premium volume and the policyholders' surplus of the primary insurer.

Most states have a statutory provision that puts an upper limit on an insurer's retention under its reinsurance treaties. That provision usually states that an insurer cannot retain net for its own account an amount on any one loss exposure in excess of 10 percent of the insurer's policyholders' surplus. Thus, if an insurer has policyholders' surplus of $10 million, its legal maximum net retention for any one loss exposure would be $1 million. Very few insurers retain their legal maximum.

One of the principal purposes of excess reinsurance is to stabilize loss experience. It seems logical, therefore, that the primary insurer should retain that part of its aggregate losses that is reasonably stable and predictable and should cede that part that is not reasonably stable and predictable. However, that simple statement raises two complex questions. First, what is meant by "reasonably stable and predictable"? Second, given criteria for "reasonably stable and predictable," how does one determine what portion of aggregate losses meets those criteria?

Managers of insurers differ in their criteria for what is reasonably stable and predictable. However, some general rules can be given. Losses can be said to be reasonably stable and predictable if the maximum probable variation is not likely to affect the insurer's loss ratio or surplus to an extent unacceptable to management.

For example, the management of one insurer might conclude that it could accept a maximum variation of 3 percentage points in the loss ratio and 9 percent in policyholders' surplus due to chance variation in losses during the year. Another insurer with less surplus or less venturesome management might decide that it could risk only 2 percentage points of the loss ratio and 4 percent of surplus to policyholders. All other things being equal, the second insurer would probably elect a lower retention. Of course, the selection of a retention requires a balancing of the desirability of stability against the undesirability of high reinsurance costs. Lowering the retention increases stability, but it also increases reinsurance costs.

Based on the foregoing considerations, two methods have been used to select the retention level under an excess treaty. Both assume that the primary insurer should retain losses within the size category in which sufficient frequency exists for reasonable predictability. Consequently, both methods require an analysis of a loss-size distribution such as that shown in Exhibit 9-1, but the method of analysis differs somewhat. The losses in Exhibit 9-1 have been adjusted for inflation from the date of occurrence to the midpoint of the period for which the treaty will be in effect.

The simpler of the two methods is to examine a table such as the one shown in Exhibit 9-1 for the point at which there seems to be a sudden change in the frequency trend. For example, in Exhibit 9-1 the frequency of each size bracket is approximately one-half of the next lower bracket for losses up to $20,000. However, the frequency for the $20,001 to $25,000 bracket is only one-third of the next lower bracket. Consequently, a retention of $20,000 might be selected. A retention of $20,000 would include 97 percent of the number of claims and 94 percent of the dollar amount of losses (all of the losses up to $20,000 plus the first $20,000 of each loss in excess of $20,000).

Exhibit 9-1
Distribution of Losses by Size for Past Ten Years, Adjusted for Inflation

	Losses		Percentage of	
Loss Size	Number	Total Amount	Number	Amount
$ 1– 5,000	11,381	$ 23,774,909	48%	14.4%
5,001–10,000	6,639	48,033,165	28	29.2
10,001–15,000	3,557	43,804,455	15	26.6
15,001–20,000	1,423	24,664,859	6	15.0
20,001–25,000	474	10,564,986	2	6.4
Over 25,000	237	13,845,777	1	8.4
	23,711	$164,688,151	100%	100.0%

Alternatively, management might prefer a retention of $15,000, at which a smaller break in the trend occurs. That retention would include 91 percent of the losses by number and 89.6 percent by amount.

The second method of setting the retention under an excess treaty involves a determination of the largest loss for which underwriting results are acceptably stable. The first step is to restructure the loss distribution from Exhibit 9-1 into a new distribution as shown in Exhibit 9-2. This table shows the losses by size for each of the past ten years, but instead of showing the number or dollar amount of losses, it shows them as loss ratios. That is, the dollar amount of losses in each bracket has been divided by the earned premium for the year. The premiums and losses should be adjusted to reflect rate changes and inflation, respectively, before the loss ratios are calculated.

The retention is set at the upper limit of the highest loss size class for which the variation in loss ratio is acceptable to management. In Exhibit 9-2, the statistics would probably indicate a retention of either $15,000 or $20,000, depending on the amount of variation management is willing to accept. In the $15,001 to $20,000 bracket, the difference between the worst year and the best year is 7.9 percentage points (13.4 – 5.5) of loss ratio, or about 84 percent of the mean loss ratio for that bracket for the ten-year period. In the $20,001 to $25,000 bracket, the difference between the best year and the worst year is 8.7 percentage points (9.7 – 1.0) of loss ratio, or approximately 229 percent of the mean loss ratio for that bracket for the ten-year period.

In these hypothetical illustrations, both methods resulted in the same retention, depending on the choice between the two possible retentions in the second method. They would not necessarily be in such close agreement in actual practice.

The first step in setting the retention for a catastrophe treaty is for management to decide how much policyholders' surplus and how many points of loss ratio can be risked on one year's catastrophes. These must, of course, be translated into dollars.

The second step is to estimate the maximum number of catastrophes that might reasonably be expected to occur in one year. That number would depend on the line or lines of insurance concerned, the territory in which the primary insurer operates, and the concentration of insured properties within the territory. For jurisdictions that have windstorm pools, the effects of such pools must be considered when setting windstorm retentions. The retention per catastrophe would be found by dividing the number of dollars from the first step by the number of catastrophes from the second step.

Retention setting is easier under an aggregate excess treaty than under any other kind of reinsurance. The primary insurer should select for its retention the lowest loss ratio (1) for which the reinsurance premium is affordable and (2) that is acceptable to the reinsurer. Those two considerations almost inevita-

Exhibit 9-2
Loss Ratios by Loss Size for Past Ten Years, Adjusted for Rate Changes and Inflation

	Loss Ratios by Year					
Loss Size	**1**	**2**	**3**	**4**	**5**	**6**
$ 1– 5,000	8.6%	8.4%	8.8%	8.7%	8.9%	9.0%
5,001–10,000	16.9	17.4	17.4	17.6	17.0	18.1
10,001–15,000	15.0	16.1	16.3	16.9	17.3	14.8
15,001–20,000	8.4	9.7	9.3	5.8	10.8	13.4
20,001–25,000	1.3	3.5	4.6	5.4	2.1	2.9
Over 25,000	6.3	4.9	9.8	7.3	8.1	1.0
Totals	56.5%	60.0%	66.2%	61.7%	64.2%	59.2%

Loss Size	**7**	**8**	**9**	**10**	**Mean**
$ 1– 5,000	8.8%	8.5%	8.5%	8.8%	8.7%
5,001–10,000	18.3	17.1	17.3	17.9	17.5
10,001–15,000	16.0	16.3	15.2	16.1	16.0
15,001–20,000	12.1	6.0	5.5	9.0	9.0
20,001–25,000	1.1	1.0	9.7	6.4	3.8
Over 25,000	4.1	5.7	2.1	0.7	5.0
Totals	60.4%	54.6%	58.3%	58.9%	60.0%

bly result in a retention loss ratio somewhat higher than the primary insurer's break-even loss ratio.

Most of this discussion of retention setting has ignored the cost of reinsurance and the role of the reinsurer in setting retentions. However, those factors cannot be overlooked in actual practice. Most insurers purchasing excess treaties accept retentions higher than they would prefer, either to reduce reinsurance costs or because the reinsurer insists on it.

Under surplus share treaties, the position of the reinsurer may be reversed. That is, the reinsurer may sometimes insist on a lower retention than the primary insurer would prefer. Under a surplus share treaty, no reinsurance is ceded on properties for which the amount of insurance is less than the retention. Consequently, a very high retention would mean that the reinsurer would be excluded from participating in a large part of the primary insurer's business. If the business below the retention is the most desirable part of the primary insurer's portfolio, the reinsurer may insist on a lower retention to enable it to participate in that business.

If the primary insurer carries several treaties that may cover the same loss, the retention under each of them should be set with due consideration for the relationships between them. For example, an insurer's reinsurance program might have a quota share treaty, a per risk excess treaty, and a catastrophe treaty. The retention under the catastrophe treaty should be higher if that treaty is written for the benefit of both the primary insurer and quota share reinsurers than if written only for benefit of the primary insurer.

To illustrate the difference, assume that the retention under the quota share treaty is 25 percent and the retention under the catastrophe treaty is $1 million. Assume further that a catastrophe causes losses totaling $3 million under coverages reinsured under the catastrophe treaty. If the catastrophe treaty is written for the benefit of the primary insurer only, it will not pay any of the loss. The primary insurer's portion of the losses would be 25 percent, or $750,000, which is less than the catastrophe retention.

If the catastrophe treaty is written for the benefit of the primary insurer and quota share reinsurers, the catastrophe reinsurer would pay $2 million, assuming that the treaty limit is at least that high. The quota share reinsurer would then pay 75 percent of the remaining $1 million, leaving the primary insurer with a net retention of only $250,000.

A similar analysis could be made for the per risk excess treaty and the quota share treaty or, for that matter, for all three of them. This is another reason why an insurer's reinsurance program should be a carefully integrated program and not merely a collection of treaties.

Setting Reinsurance Limits

Setting reinsurance limits is only slightly less subjective than setting retentions. Pro rata and per risk or per policy excess treaties, in whatever combination carried, should have sufficiently high limits to cover, in combination with the primary insurer's retention, a substantial majority of the loss exposures insured by the primary insurer. Exactly how large a majority will be covered will depend on cost considerations, since reinsurance costs can be expected to increase as the limit increases and the retention remains constant. This increased cost for a higher limit must be weighed against the premium, administrative expense, and inconvenience of facultative reinsurance for those exposures not fully covered by treaties.

Limit setting for a catastrophe treaty is even more subjective. The goal is to select a limit just adequate to cover the largest catastrophe that might reasonably be expected. The difficulty is in determining the potential amount of loss in the largest catastrophe likely to occur. The primary insurer's past experience is not a satisfactory guide. Catastrophe losses are notoriously variable, and the largest catastrophe the insurer sustained in the past might not be the largest that is likely to occur in the future. In addition, circumstances change. For example, the insurer might now be writing more business in a catastrophe-prone area than it wrote in the past.

Perhaps the best way to set the limit for a catastrophe treaty is through a careful analysis of the concentration of loss exposures as previously explained.

The limit for an aggregate excess treaty should be set at an amount adequate to cover the highest loss ratio the primary insurer might reasonably expect to sustain, provided the reinsurance premium for such a limit is acceptable to its management. Unfortunately, there is no reliable method of estimating accurately the highest loss ratio an insurer might expect to sustain. However, some general guidelines can be followed. The variation in loss ratios is, in part, a function of the lines of insurance written. A property insurer can expect a greater variation in loss ratios than a liability insurer because of the catastrophe exposure in property insurance. The existence of a catastrophe treaty (in addition to the stop loss treaty) would lessen the variation from catastrophe.

The size of the insurer is another important determinant of loss ratio variability. All other things being equal, a smaller insurer (measured by premium volume) can expect more variation in loss ratio than a larger one. It would, therefore, need a higher treaty limit relative to its premium volume.

Perhaps the most important factor is the geographic distribution of the insurer's business. An insurer writing property classes in one territory is much more vulnerable to loss ratio fluctuation than an insurer having a nationwide spread in its exposures. Again, this is primarily due to catastrophe possibilities.

In setting the limit for any kind of reinsurance, the interaction between all applicable treaties must be considered. For example, the limit for an aggregate excess treaty can be lower if adequate catastrophe reinsurance is carried. Also, the limit of a catastrophe treaty can be lower if it applies only to the retention of the primary insurer after recoveries from pro rata reinsurance, rather than to the direct losses.

Cost of Reinsurance

The cost of reinsurance might not be easy to determine in advance. The cost is not simply the premium paid to the reinsurer. Several other major factors must be considered. One of those factors is the losses recovered or to be recovered under the reinsurance agreement. The losses are an especially important factor under a pro rata treaty or a working cover for which substantial loss recoveries are anticipated.

A primary insurer is expected to pay its own losses and the reinsurer's expenses and profit under any treaty if the treaty is continued over a sufficiently long period of time. Consequently, the amount included in the premium for the reinsurer's expenses and profit becomes an important factor in assessing the cost of reinsurance.

Reinsurance transfers some loss reserves and unearned premium reserves from the primary insurer to the reinsurer. Since the assets offsetting these reserves are invested, this transfer results in some loss of investment income to the primary insurer. The loss of investment income is likely to be greater under a pro rata treaty than under an excess treaty because the reinsurance premium for a pro rata treaty is usually greater. However, some investment income is lost in either case, and the lost income is an additional cost of the reinsurance transfer.

The cost to the primary insurer of administering the reinsurance program must also be considered. Facultative reinsurance is especially expensive to administer because each reinsurance transaction must be negotiated individually. Pro rata treaties, especially surplus share, are generally more expensive to administer than excess treaties because of the more detailed record keeping and the greater frequency of reinsurance claims. In any case, the cost of administering the program must be considered in evaluating reinsurance costs.

Finally, one additional factor must be considered in a reciprocal reinsurance arrangement. The business assumed might not be as profitable (or more unprofitable) than the business ceded. This profit or loss on the assumed insurance under a reciprocal arrangement must be included in the estimated cost of the reinsurance program.

Reinsurance Negotiations

Reinsurance negotiations may be conducted in several ways, depending on the nature of the primary insurer and the reinsurer, the kind of reinsurance concerned, and other factors. This section discusses in general terms some of the major factors involved in the negotiation of reinsurance agreements.

Information Needed

The primary insurer's first step in reinsurance negotiations is the compilation of necessary information. Depending on the kind of reinsurance involved, the required information might be voluminous, and compilation might require a substantial effort. However, the task should not be taken lightly. Favorable reinsurance terms and rates might depend on the thoroughness of the data provided by the primary insurer.

The information required in reinsurance negotiations varies with the kind of reinsurance arrangement under negotiation. In treaty negotiations, the reinsurer is interested primarily in information concerning the management and underwriting operations of the primary insurer. Little attention is given to individual loss exposures insured, but the reinsurer is concerned with product mix and geographic spread. In negotiations for facultative cessions, the reinsurer is interested primarily in the details of the individual loss exposure and only secondarily in the general operations of the primary insurer. Of course, if the subject of negotiation is an obligatory facultative treaty, the information needed would be essentially the same as any other treaty. However, the reinsurer might underwrite the primary insurer even more carefully because of the greater opportunity for adverse selection under an obligatory facultative treaty.

The reinsurer's principal considerations in underwriting a treaty are the primary insurer's management characteristics, underwriting policies, underwriting results, and financial condition. The integrity of the primary insurer's management is a primary consideration. There are numerous opportunities for fraud in the administration of a reinsurance treaty, and numerous cases of fraud have occurred.

The reinsurer is interested in more than just honesty. It is also interested in the demonstrated capability and stability of management and the experience and capabilities of the underwriting staff. Reinsurance treaties are intended to be long-term arrangements. Consequently, the reinsurer is concerned with the possibility of a change in management personnel or a change in management objectives or both.

A reinsurer is also concerned with the financial strength of the primary insurer. The insolvency of a primary insurer normally does not increase the liability of the reinsurer, but it does complicate the administration of a treaty, and it could involve the loss of part of the reinsurer's premiums. The reinsurer's role might get especially complicated if many cut-through endorsements are outstanding because the reinsurer might be required to adjust losses under such endorsements directly with the original insured. Depending on state law, the reinsurer may be required to pay some losses twice: to the beneficiary under the cut-through endorsement and to the receiver of the insolvent primary insurer. If local courts permit, the reinsurer will offset net premiums due against claims payable. Otherwise, the reinsurer is just another general creditor of the insolvent primary insurer. Also, as noted above, reinsurance treaties are usually considered to be long-term relationships, and the insolvency of the primary insurer is hardly consistent with that concept.

The reinsurer would be especially interested in the solvency of the primary insurer if the treaty provides for payment of premiums as earned rather than as written or if the treaty permits the primary insurer to hold funds of the reinsurer so that the primary insurer can take credit for the reinsurance in calculating its unearned premium or loss reserves. The latter provision is fairly common if the reinsurer is unlicensed in the primary insurer's state of domicile.

Perhaps the most important considerations in reinsurance negotiations are the underwriting policies and underwriting results of the primary insurer. Factors to consider in assessing an underwriting policy are shown in Exhibit 9-3.

Exhibit 9-3
Factors To Consider in Assessing the Underwriting Policy of a Primary Insurer

1. What classes of business is the primary insurer writing?
2. Is it writing primarily personal lines, small mercantile, industrial, or others?
3. What is its geographic area of operation?
4. Are the primary insurer's underwriting guidelines (e.g., acceptable, prohibitive, and submit for approval lists) satisfactory?
5. Are its gross line limits and net line limits in keeping with the financial strength of the primary insurer?
6. Are the primary insurer's loss control and loss adjustment practices adequate for the classes of business written?
7. Have the primary insurer's underwriting results been satisfactory in the lines covered by the proposed reinsurance treaty?
8. Does the primary insurer anticipate any substantial changes in its management, marketing, or underwriting practices?
9. Are the primary insurer's rates adequate for the risks covered under the treaty?

The existence of and the terms of other reinsurance would also be important considerations. In property insurance, for example, pro rata reinsurers would be interested in the terms of any catastrophe treaty and other excess reinsurance. Is it written only for the interest of the primary insurer, or does it protect the interest of pro rata reinsurers as well?

The reinsurer would also be interested in the primary insurer's loss experience over the most recent several years. Loss ratio is especially important in connection with a pro rata treaty because it is used for underwriting selection, rating, and setting commission terms. The reinsurer is interested not only in the level of the loss ratio but also in its stability or volatility over time.

For a per risk or per policy excess treaty, the reinsurer requires data concerning distribution of losses by size. A distribution of amounts of insurance by size may also be required.

The discussion up to this point has concentrated on the information the reinsurer is likely to require from the primary insurer. However, in most cases reinsurance negotiations are two-sided; that is, the primary insurer is also interested in obtaining information about the reinsurer. The information needed by the primary insurer, while less detailed, is approximately the same as that needed by any consumer in purchasing insurance. Is the reinsurer financially sound and well managed? Are its claims practices satisfactory? Can it offer the services needed by the primary insurer? Are its rates competitive? Is it licensed in the primary insurer's state of domicile, or can it make other arrangements so that the primary insurer can take credit for the reinsurance in calculating its unearned premium and loss reserves?

Use of Reinsurance Brokers

The first step in the negotiation of any contract is for the parties to get together. The primary insurer and reinsurer may get together directly or work through an intermediary called a reinsurance broker.

The function of a **reinsurance broker** is essentially the same as that of any other broker: to bring together two potential contracting parties and to assist them in reaching agreement on the terms of the contract. The reinsurance broker, in this case, is compensated for those efforts through a commission paid by the reinsurer. The percentage commission may be small in comparison with the commission rates paid to primary insurance brokers, frequently as low as 1 percent of the reinsurance premium. However, the premiums are often large, so the dollar amount of commission may also be large.

When reinsurance is handled by a reinsurance broker, premium payments usually pass through the reinsurance broker en route from the primary insurer to the reinsurer. Also, loss payments and premium refunds pass through the reinsurance broker en route from the reinsurer to the primary insurer. The reinsurance broker may be able to earn substantial amounts of investment income on these funds in its custody, adding significantly to its income.

Should a primary insurer use a reinsurance broker in the negotiation of its reinsurance program even though many large reinsurers are willing to deal directly? The question has been asked on many occasions, but still no single answer applies to all cases. The answer depends on an insurer's own needs and circumstances.

If the primary insurer is well staffed with people who are thoroughly familiar with reinsurance markets, capable of designing its reinsurance program, and negotiating its reinsurance contracts, it might not need a reinsurance broker. Consequently, it might be able to negotiate a slightly lower reinsurance cost because of the absence of a brokerage commission.

However, many insurers, especially the small- and medium-sized ones, do not have the personnel needed to manage their reinsurance affairs effectively. They must rely on some outside person for advice. That person could be a consultant or an employee of a reinsurer, but frequently it is a reinsurance broker.

A broker handles the reinsurance needs of several primary insurers. That exposure to a variety of problems enables brokerage personnel to develop expertise in handling reinsurance problems. This expertise, when coupled with a knowledge of available reinsurance markets and access to such markets, can make a reinsurance broker a very valuable ally for the negotiation of a reinsurance program.

Reinsurance brokers have one other advantage. Some reinsurers might not be staffed to deal directly with potential buyers of reinsurance. This is particularly likely with respect to small professional reinsurers and primary insurers with limited reinsurance operations. Also, some very large reinsurers deal only through reinsurance brokers. A reinsurance broker might be the only practical means of access to such reinsurers, either through a pool managed by the brokerage firm or through individual negotiation.

Precise figures are not available to show the proportion of U.S. reinsurance handled by reinsurance brokers. One estimate places the market share of all reinsurance brokers combined at approximately 75 percent of U.S. reinsurance premiums.[1] Most of the reinsurance premiums controlled by reinsurance brokers are for treaty reinsurance. Many reinsurance brokers prefer not to handle facultative reinsurance agreements because of the extensive amount of effort and paperwork involved in handling individual placements.

Historically, reinsurance brokers were small, independent business firms, controlled by one or a few individuals. Most recently, the trend has been to larger reinsurance brokers controlled by even larger retail brokerage firms, such as J & H Marsh & McLennan and Aon Risk Services, or insurance companies. Of the ten largest U.S. reinsurance brokers, five are controlled by large retail brokerage firms, and two are controlled by insurance company groups.[2]

Whether the reinsurance broker is acting as a representative of the primary insurer or the reinsurer is not always clear. The question is more than academic because it could determine, among other things, whether a reinsurance contract is void because of misrepresentation or concealment.

For example, the primary insurer might make full disclosure to the reinsurance broker, but the reinsurance broker might fail to transmit some material fact to the reinsurer. In that situation, if the reinsurance broker is the agent of the primary insurer, the treaty might be voidable at the option of the reinsurer for concealment. If the reinsurance broker is the agent of the reinsurer, the treaty would not be voidable because the reinsurer would be charged with the knowledge of the reinsurance broker. Consequently, there would not be any concealment.

In most cases, the courts have held that reinsurance brokers are agents for the primary insurer. However, the reinsurance broker may become the agent of the reinsurer either by specific contractual agreement to that effect or by actions of the reinsurer that lead the primary insurer to believe that the reinsurance broker is the agent of the reinsurer.[3]

Reinsurance Commissions

Two kinds of commissions may be involved in reinsurance transactions: (1) ceding commissions paid by the reinsurer to the primary insurer and (2) brokerage commissions paid by the reinsurer to the reinsurance broker. Ceding commissions are intended to reimburse the primary insurer for the expenses it incurred in selling and servicing the business ceded to the reinsurer. Such commissions are common under pro rata treaties but not under excess treaties. The ceding commission is subject to negotiation between the parties and usually depends on (1) the actual expenses of the primary insurer (including acquisition costs along with administrative, information system, and accounting costs), (2) the reinsurer's estimate of the premium volume and loss experience expected under the treaty, and (3) the competitive state of the reinsurance market at the time the treaty is being negotiated. Treaties frequently provide for a retrospective adjustment of the ceding commission if the actual loss ratio under the treaty varies substantially from the expected loss ratio.

Brokerage commissions vary, but a typical commission scale might be 1 percent to 2 percent on pro rata treaties and 5 percent to 10 percent on excess treaties. The higher commission percentage on excess treaties reflects the fact that they produce lower premiums while requiring substantially the same amount of effort on the part of the reinsurance broker. Thus, a higher percentage commission is needed in order to provide the same dollar remuneration. Some reinsurance brokers negotiate a fee for their services to the primary insurer instead of a commission.

Reinsurance Administration

The administration of a reinsurance program is a joint effort by the primary insurer and the reinsurer. Each of the parties has specified duties, obligations, and rights under the reinsurance contract.

Role of the Primary Insurer

After the reinsurance agreement has been negotiated and has become effective, the heaviest burden of administration falls on the primary insurer; the reinsurer depends on the primary insurer's capabilities, good faith, and good luck. The primary insurer is obligated to conduct its underwriting and loss adjustment operations in the manner contemplated by both parties when the reinsurance was negotiated or to notify the reinsurer of any substantial changes.

Within the contemplated policies, the primary insurer is free to exercise its best judgment in underwriting individual risks or adjusting individual claims, and the reinsurer is bound by the primary insurer's actions in such matters. In the words common to reinsurance, the reinsurer "follows the fortunes" of the primary insurer.

The treaty may require the primary insurer to notify the reinsurer promptly upon receiving notice of a large loss, and the reinsurer may reserve the right to participate in the investigation or defense of such claims. Such right is exercised only in unusual circumstances, but these are becoming more frequent.

The primary insurer should design its information system to capture and process the data required to fulfill its administrative duties. If the reinsurance program is a simple one, including only quota share and excess treaties covering all policies issued by the primary insurer with the same retentions and limits, the data requirements can be rather simple. In such a case, the primary insurer would need to collect only direct premium data in order to calculate the reinsurance premiums payable to the reinsurers. Data for individual losses would be needed to apply treaty limits and excess retentions. Such data are needed for other accounting purposes in any case, so there would be little additional burden for reinsurance administration.

If a catastrophe excess treaty is carried, the primary insurer must code losses so that those arising from catastrophes can be identified. Similarly, if casualty "clash" coverage is carried, occurrences must be identified so that all casualty losses arising from a single occurrence can readily be identified.

A surplus share treaty might have slightly more complex data requirements. Sufficient data must be provided to enable the primary insurer to determine the portion, if any, of each of its policies ceded to each surplus share reinsurer. Such information is essential for the calculation of both reinsurance premiums payable and reinsurance losses recoverable.

Extensive use of facultative reinsurance might also require a more elaborate approach to fulfilling data needs. Each facultative reinsurance cession is negotiated separately, so the retention, limits, rate, and even the reinsurer may be different for each policy. Even the nature of the coverage (excess or pro rata) may differ. The information system should be adequate to capture those differences.

Some underwriting practices of the primary insurer might also require expansion of the data collection system. If the primary insurer writes risks that are excluded from one or more of its treaties, the policies covering such risks should be coded to avoid paying reinsurance premiums for them and submitting reinsurance claims for them.

If the primary insurer elects not to cede an otherwise eligible risk under a treaty (to protect its treaty or for other reasons), special coding is necessary to avoid errors in calculating reinsurance premiums or losses. Special coding is also needed if the primary insurer elects a retention or reinsurance limit different from the standard retentions and limits provided by its treaties.

A properly designed data collection and information system greatly simplifies the reinsurance administrative process. It also simplifies the process of compiling information for the negotiation of renewal or replacement treaties.

The primary insurer is required to report premiums and losses, and perhaps other data, to the reinsurer by bordereaux or by such other means as the treaty might specify. The reinsurance agreement might also require the primary insurer to make its books and records available to the reinsurer at reasonable times and places so that the reinsurer can verify the reported data.

Exhibit 9-4 shows a segment of a bordereau used by one primary insurer in reporting required information to its reinsurer. Exhibit 9-5 shows one form of current account statement used by one primary insurer to report reinsurance premiums and losses to a reinsurer that does not require a detailed bordereau.

Historically, bordereaux were required by virtually all reinsurers. That requirement is much less common at the present time. Many reinsurers are willing to accept a current account statement such as that in Exhibit 9-5. They rely on their contractual right to audit the primary insurer's books to guard against incorrect information.

Traditionally, reinsurance treaties were considered "gentlemen's agreements" and contracts of utmost good faith. Disputes were to be settled by negotiation

Exhibit 9-4
Illustrative Bordereau—July 19X1

Insured	Policy	Effective Date	Expiration Date	Premium Ceded	Ceding Comm.	Net Ceded Premium	Losses Paid	Loss Expense	Losses Out-standing	Balance Due to Reins.
Boat Manufacturer	CPP99406	07/03/X1	07/03/X2	$17,953	$ 4,488	$13,465	$ 825	$ 75	0	$12,565
Book Store	CPP88431	09/07/X0	09/07/X1	0	0	0	7,593	487	0	–8,080
Restaurant	CPP89976	11/13/X0	11/13/X1	0	0	0	12,576	793	$8,541	–13,369
Delivery Service	CPP97865	07/01/X1	07/01/X2	24,581	7,374	17,207	0	0	0	17,207
Totals				$42,534	$11,862	$30,672	$20,994	$1,355	$8,541	$ 8,323

Summary

Gross Premiums Ceded	$42,534
Less Ceding Commissions	–11,862
Net Premiums Ceded	30,672
Less Loss and Loss Adjustment Expenses Paid	–22,349
Balance Due to Reinsurer	$ 8,323

Exhibit 9-5
Illustrative Reinsurance Current Account

Annual Statement Line	Premiums Ceded	Ceding Comm.	Net Premiums Ceded	Losses Paid	Loss Expenses Paid	Losses Out-standing
01-Fire	$ 40,560	$10,140	$ 30,420	$ 20,321	$ 2,503	$ 45,654
02-Extended Coverage	13,471	3,347	10,124	4,783	3,977	26,894
05-C.M.P.	180,478	45,140	135,338	97,728	10,539	140,000
09-Inland Marine	53,547	13,436	40,111	21,649	2,374	27,652
Totals	$288,056	$72,063	$215,993	$144,481	$19,393	$240,200

Summary

Gross Premiums Ceded	$288,056
Less Ceding Commission	−72,063
Net Premiums Ceded	215,993
Less Loss and Loss Adjustment Expenses Paid	−163,874
Amount Due to Reinsurer	$ 52,119

and arbitration, rather than by legal action. Those concepts have been somewhat weakened by the competitive pressures and practices of recent years.

Role of the Reinsurer

Under a smoothly functioning treaty relationship, the reinsurer's duties, other than collecting premiums and paying claims, are minimal. Many reinsurers prefer to write excess treaties with very high retentions so that claims are rarely presented.

Yet, the reinsurer performs additional duties. Although it ordinarily does not become involved in the underwriting of individual insureds or the adjustment of individual losses, the reinsurer may audit the underwriting and claims practices of the primary insurer to be sure they are being conducted as anticipated. Large, individual losses may be examined partly as a verification that proper adjustment and reserving practices were followed and partly to extract whatever underwriting implications they provide. The reinsurer may also be consulted by the primary insurer on individual underwriting or claims problems.

A substantial amount of litigation has involved the obligation of the reinsurer to share in punitive damage judgments or judgments for bad faith against the primary insurer arising out of the primary insurer's handling of claims covered under the reinsurance contract. In most cases, the courts have held that the reinsurer is not liable for such judgments because they did not arise from the reinsured policy but from errors or unfair practices of the primary insurer. Bad faith judgments have been held to be covered in a few cases because of the wording of the specific reinsurance contract.[4] Coverage for those "extra-contractual obligations" is frequently provided under liability excess treaties.

Claim Settlement

The adjustment of claims under the primary insurer's contracts with its policyholders is usually left to the primary insurer's judgment. Reinsurance contracts usually permit the reinsurer to participate in the adjustment of direct claims that might result in reinsurance claims, but that right is exercised infrequently.

The procedure for the adjustment of claims between the primary insurer and the reinsurer may vary from one agreement to another and by type of treaty. Under a pro rata treaty, the primary insurer may be required to file a monthly bordereau showing premiums due to the reinsurer and claims due from the reinsurer. If the premiums exceed the losses, the primary insurer remits the difference. If the losses exceed the premiums, the reinsurer remits the difference. Exceptionally large individual losses may be paid individually before the end of the reporting period as a convenience to the primary insurer.

Losses under a working cover or per occurrence excess treaty may be handled by bordereau in the same manner outlined above for pro rata treaties, since a substantial number of losses is expected under a working cover treaty. For excess treaties with higher retentions, losses are reported individually as they occur. The contract usually requires the primary insurer to report all losses that are expected to exceed a specified amount, with that amount being somewhat less than the retention.

Per occurrence excess treaties are not involved until the accumulated losses exceed the retention. At that point, the primary insurer would begin presenting claims to the reinsurer as soon as it has paid them. The reinsurer is usually obligated to make payment to the primary insurer as soon as reasonable proof of loss has been received. Proof of loss is often simply a statement of total claims paid and, as additional information, current reserve estimates.

Aggregate excess treaties usually provide for an initial payment a short time, perhaps sixty days, after the end of the year. If the primary insurer's loss ratio has not been finalized at that time, a subsequent adjustment may be made. Although there is usually no contractual requirement for it, most reinsurers would begin to make initial payments before the end of the year if it becomes clear that the primary insurer's loss ratio will exceed the retention.

Loss Experience in Reinsurance

Under excess treaties and facultative reinsurance, there is no inherent relationship between the loss experience of primary insurers and reinsurers. In times of rapid inflation (assuming a fixed retention), excess reinsurers are likely to have worse underwriting experience than the primary insurers. The poorer experience results from two factors. First, the excess reinsurer covers the top of the large losses, where inflation comes into play, while the primary insurer's payment is limited by the agreed retention. Second, inflation pushes more of the smaller losses over the retention amount, resulting in payment by the reinsurer. Of course, fluctuations in the number and size of catastrophes also affect the loss experience of reinsurers. In addition, competitive pressures may differ between the primary insurance market and the reinsurance market.

Consequently, the loss experience of reinsurers as a whole may be better or worse than the experience of primary insurers in any given year. Exhibit 9-6 shows the combined ratios (loss ratio plus expense ratio) for reinsurers.

Combined ratios of individual reinsurers varied rather widely from the averages shown. The averages seem to follow the primary insurer experience reasonably closely. Historically, the combined ratios for reinsurers have been a few percentage points higher than those for primary insurers, but the magnitude of the difference has declined in recent years.

Reinsurance Pricing

As one might expect, pricing methods for reinsurance vary with the kind of reinsurance. Pricing methods also vary from one reinsurer to another, so it is not practical to discuss here all of the methods in use. Consequently, the discussion in this chapter stresses general principles rather than detailed calculations.

Pro Rata Treaties

For quota share and surplus share treaties, the reinsurance rate is customarily the same as the rate used by the primary insurer for the original policy. In other words, the pro rata reinsurer usually charges a pro rata part of the original premium, based on its pro rata share of the amount of insurance. However, the ceding commission paid to the primary insurer will vary according to the

Exhibit 9-6
Combined Ratios Compared

Year	Combined Ratio All Lines of Property and Liability Insurance*	Combined Ratio U.S. Professional Reinsurers
1975	106.6	109.9
1976	101.3	101.2
1977	96.0	99.7
1978	95.9	99.5
1979	99.1	103.0
1980	101.4	104.7
1981	104.1	105.6
1982	107.7	109.5
1983	109.9	118.0
1984	116.1	130.9
1985	114.6	124.1
1986	106.7	109.3
1987	103.3	105.9
1988	104.0	104.2
1989	107.9	108.8
1990	108.3	106.4
1991	107.6	108.5
1992	114.6	114.7
1993	105.7	105.4
1994	107.1	106.2
1995	105.0	108.9

*Combined ratio before dividends to policyholders

Data obtained from *Best's Aggregates and Averages—Property-Casualty*, 1996 Edition, p. 166; the *National Underwriter*, July 1, 1991, Section II, p. 86; and *National Underwriter*, July 15, 1996, Section II, p. 59.

reinsurer's estimate of the loss ratio to be incurred on the premium ceded under the treaty. The ceding commission, in effect, "prices" the pro rata treaty because the net amount paid by the primary insurer is the premium less the ceding commission.

For example, if the pro rata reinsurer expects to incur a loss ratio of 60 percent under the treaty and is willing to accept 15 percent of the premium for expenses, profit, and contingencies, it would pay a ceding commission of 25 percent of reinsurance premiums. On the other hand, if it expected a loss ratio of only 50 percent with the same allowance for expenses, profit, and contingencies, it would allow a ceding commission of 35 percent.

Retrospective (or profit-sharing or sliding scale) commission arrangements are quite common. Under such arrangements, the ceding commission varies with the actual loss ratio incurred under the treaty. For example, in the first illustration given in the foregoing paragraph, the treaty might provide for a provisional commission of 35 percent, to be adjusted after the end of the year according to the commission rates and loss ratios shown in Exhibit 9-7. Thus, if the actual loss ratio for the year is 50 percent, instead of the expected 60 percent, the primary insurer would receive an additional 5 percent ceding commission. In effect, the unexpected profit is shared approximately equally between the primary insurer and the reinsurer under the retrospective ceding commission scale in Exhibit 9-7.

The reinsurer's estimate of the loss ratio to be incurred is usually based primarily on the primary insurer's past experience. However, that experience may be adjusted for industry trends, changes in the primary insurer's underwriting practices, and other factors the reinsurer considers relevant.

Exhibit 9-7
Retrospective Ceding Commission Scale

Actual Loss Ratio	Commission Rate
60% or more	35%
59% but less than 60%	35.5
58% but less than 59%	36
57% but less than 58%	36.5
56% but less than 57%	37
55% but less than 56%	37.5
54% but less than 55%	38
53% but less than 54%	38.5
52% but less than 53%	39
51% but less than 52%	39.5
50% but less than 51%	40
less than 50%	41

Per Risk or Per Policy Excess Treaties

The ratemaking procedure for per risk or per policy excess treaties is somewhat more complicated than that for pro rata treaties. A traditional excess rating methodology prevalent among reinsurers is the **burning-cost method**. To compute a **burning-cost rate**, the underwriter divides the sum of known losses in the excess layer occurring over some time period, usually five years, by the premium for these policies during the same time period. To get a rate, this ratio is then multiplied by a selected loss development factor, perhaps multiplied by some selected trend factor, loaded by a factor to recognize exposure when there have been no losses, and divided by an expected loss ratio. The problem with this approach is that it does not consider underlying exposure changes, rate changes, the emergence of incurred but not reported claims, adverse claim development, or claim growth caused by inflation. Burning-cost rating is not very accurate and, in fact, can be highly misleading, even for the working cover excess of loss property treaties for which it was designed.

Catastrophe Treaties

In theory, the method of making rates for catastrophe treaties is the same as that for per risk or per policy excess treaties, except the loss distribution would show aggregate amounts per occurrence rather than for individual losses. In practice, reliable catastrophe data are not available on a company-by-company basis because of the large element of chance variation in catastrophic occurrences. Consequently, judgment plays a much larger role in the rating of catastrophe treaties than it does in per risk or per policy excess treaties. Of course, national, regional, and state catastrophe data are available and are used to the extent they are applicable. However, an individual insurer's catastrophe experience can be expected to differ from industry experience because of its geographic spread of business and the differing nature of insured exposures.

Aggregate Excess Treaties

Theoretically, the premium for an aggregate excess treaty can be calculated from a probability distribution of loss ratios. In practice, that method is seldom, if ever, used because the nature of the probability distribution is not known. In any case, the mathematical manipulations involved in such a calculation are beyond the scope of this text.

In practice, the premium for an aggregate excess treaty is likely to be based very largely on the judgment of the reinsurance underwriter. Of course, the underwriter will reinforce judgment with an analysis of the primary insurer's loss ratios over the last several years, probably five or more. The class of business and territory of operation of the primary insurer will be important factors, as will the magnitude of the retention and the treaty limit. Beyond those general statements, it is difficult to describe ratemaking for stop loss treaties in terms that are not both highly mathematical and highly theoretical.

Effect of Competition

Reinsurance is a very competitive business, both domestically and internationally. This competitiveness results, in part, from the relative ease of entry into the market. For example, a new reinsurer in the broker market does not need to invest large sums in building a marketing force.

In the United States, with one or two exceptions, an insurer's charter to write primary business also includes reinsurance for the same lines. Thus, little or no additional funding is required to capitalize a reinsurer.

Finally, a new reinsurer using reinsurance brokers needs only a minimal staff. Services to the policyholder are furnished by the primary insurer, and the reinsurer need not become involved in them except in very unusual circumstances. Even the reinsurer's claims department can be minimal, since the loss adjustment is handled by the primary insurer in the majority of cases.

Insurers move in and out of the reinsurance business as market conditions change. Those changes in the market tend to unsettle reinsurance rates and cause fluctuations in the availability of reinsurance coverage.

When reinsurance is profitable, new reinsurers may be formed, and primary insurers enter the market to sell reinsurance. Those new reinsurers must offer some inducement to prospective customers—usually price—either in the form of lower rates or higher ceding commissions. Of course, the established reinsurers must meet the prices of their new competitors, and the result is lower profits, or possibly underwriting losses, and the resulting withdrawal of marginal reinsurers.

Effect of Inflation

For pro rata reinsurance, inflation affects the loss experience of both primary insurers and reinsurers about equally. That effect is discussed in the chapters on ratemaking for direct insurance.

Excess of loss reinsurers are affected by inflation to a substantially greater degree than pro rata reinsurers. The effects are felt at both ends of the treaty: the retention and the reinsurance limit. The excess reinsurer covers the top part of the claims in excess of the retention, and, as those claims increase from inflation, the increase is at the top. If a fixed retention rather than a variable one is used, the inflationary increase in losses above the retention does not affect the primary insurer's net loss.

If a fixed retention is used, the excess reinsurer also suffers at the lower end of the loss distribution. The inflationary increase in the smaller losses pushes more and more of them over the primary insurer's retention, so the reinsurer must pay part of them. The effect of inflation is illustrated in Exhibit 9-8.

Exhibit 9-8
Effect of Inflation on Reinsurance Losses

Assume that a primary insurer, reinsured under an excess reinsurance treaty with a $100,000 retention, sustains two losses: one for $95,000 and one for $225,000. These losses would be divided as shown below.

		Amount Paid by	
	Amount	**Primary Insurer**	**Reinsurer**
Loss 1	$ 95,000	$ 95,000	$ 0
Loss 2	225,000	100,000	125,000
	$320,000	$195,000	$125,000

Now assume that two losses causing the same amount of actual physical damage as those above occurred two years later. Although the actual physical damage was the same, higher prices caused the cost of repairs to increase to $115,000 and $270,000, respectively. These two losses will be divided as shown below.

		Amount Paid by	
	Amount	**Primary Insurer**	**Reinsurer**
Loss 1	$115,000	$100,000	$ 15,000
Loss 2	270,000	100,000	170,000
	$385,000	$200,000	$185,000

The total loss has increased by $65,000, and the reinsurer's share has increased by $60,000, but the primary insurer's share has increased by only $5,000. This simplified example overstates the relative effect of inflation somewhat, but it does illustrate the nature of the problem.

Reinsurers have attempted to combat problems caused by inflation by adopting treaties with variable retentions, sometimes called indexed retentions. Under such treaties, the amount of retention increases automatically with an increase in some price index, such as a construction cost index or a consumer price index. In the illustration used above, prices seem to have increased approximately 20 percent, so the retention would have increased from $100,000 to $120,000. The resulting division of losses would be as shown below. Thus, the inflationary increase has been spread more evenly between the primary insurer and the reinsurers.

		Amount Paid by	
	Amount	**Primary Insurer**	**Reinsurer**
Loss 1	$115,000	$115,000	$ 0
Loss 2	270,000	120,000	150,000
	$385,000	$235,000	$150,000

Regulation of Reinsurance

Traditionally, reinsurance has been subject to very limited regulation. The principal purpose of insurance regulation is to protect insurance consumers from unfair practices of some insurers and from the insolvency of insurers. That protection was deemed necessary because of the unequal knowledge and bargaining power of insurers and insurance consumers. Because the reinsurance business is conducted between two insurers, the knowledge and bargaining power of the parties were deemed to be relatively equal, so the protective shield of regulation was not considered necessary. There was also a fear that rigid regulation of U.S. reinsurers would limit their ability to compete with alien reinsurers, both here and abroad.

Another factor that reduced the need to regulate reinsurance was the nature of the market and the participants in the market. Only a few reinsurers were in business, and they were well-financed firms with a long history of ethical and sound business dealings. The market situation has changed drastically in recent years. Many new firms, both reinsurers and reinsurance brokers, have entered the market. It is quite evident that some of them were lacking in ethical standards, financial strength, or both. The world of reinsurance has been shaken by several scandals in the United States, the United Kingdom, Panama, Bermuda, and other places. Those scandals have brought about increased pressure for more detailed regulation of reinsurance. The New York regulation dealing with reinsurance brokers, mentioned elsewhere in this chapter, arose from one of the scandals—the insolvency of a reinsurance broker with large losses to both reinsurers and primary insurers.

The United Kingdom also tightened its regulation of reinsurance following several scandals there. A regulation adopted by the U.K. Department of Trade requires primary insurers to furnish a report to the department each year showing the following:

(1) the names and addresses of all reinsurers to which business has been ceded during the year;

(2) any connection (other than the reported reinsurance) between the primary insurer and any of its reinsurers;

(3) the amount of premium payable to each reinsurer; and

(4) any indebtedness of a reinsurer to the primary insurer at the end of the year.[5]

With the exception of the New York Regulation 98, the regulation of reinsurance in the United States has changed little. Many changes have been proposed, and some of the proposals are discussed later in this chapter. First, a brief review of the current regulatory pattern is in order.

Present Reinsurer Regulation

Reinsurers domiciled in the United States and alien reinsurers licensed in the United States are subject to the same solvency regulations as primary insurers. They are required to file annual, and sometimes quarterly, financial statements with state regulatory authorities and adhere to state regulations regarding reserves, investments, and minimum capital and surplus requirements. They must also undergo periodic examination by the appropriate state authorities. However, those regulations cannot be applied to unlicensed alien reinsurers because they are not within the jurisdiction of state (or federal) regulatory bodies. There has been much concern in recent years about the possible insolvencies of some unlicensed alien reinsurers, but U.S. regulatory agencies can do little to prevent such failures. Primary insurers and reinsurance brokers must rely on their own efforts to detect impending insolvencies of alien reinsurers. The solvency tests for reinsurers are the same as those applied to primary insurers.

Reinsurance rates are not regulated directly in this country. The regulation of primary insurer rates could indirectly affect reinsurance rates, however. The establishment of the primary insurer's rates might place an effective ceiling on the amount it can pay for reinsurance.

Reinsurance contracts are regulated to only a slightly greater degree. Such contract regulation is aimed at the primary insurer rather than the reinsurer because many reinsurers are not within the jurisdiction of regulatory agencies.

Primary insurers are usually eager to be able to take credit against their unearned premium and loss reserves for premiums ceded to and losses recoverable from reinsurers. The availability of those credits reduces the drain on the primary insurer's surplus from writing new business. Regulators motivate primary insurers to require some desirable provisions in their reinsurance contracts by withholding permission to take credit for the reinsurance unless it contains the specified clauses. Note that those provisions are not mandatory. A primary insurer that is willing to forgo the reserve credits can enter into a reinsurance contract that does not include them.

The first clause to be required was an insolvency clause. Before the insolvency clause was required, reinsurers sometimes escaped the payment of losses if the primary insurer became insolvent. The required **insolvency clause** provides that the insolvency of the primary insurer does not affect the liability of the reinsurer for losses under the reinsurance contract. The reinsurer makes payment to the receiver or liquidator of the insolvent primary insurer for the benefit of its creditors.

More recently, some states have required an **intermediary clause** in reinsurance contracts. This clause provides that the reinsurance broker is the agent of the reinsurer for the collection of reinsurance premiums and the payment of reinsurance claims. Thus, the reinsurer assumes the risk of the reinsurance broker's being unable or unwilling to pay over to it all of the premiums collected under its reinsurance contracts. It also assumes the risk that the reinsurance broker will not transmit to the primary insurer all claim payments made by the reinsurer. This clause is very beneficial to primary insurers because the courts have held in most cases that the reinsurance broker is the agent of the primary insurer. Consequently, in the absence of this clause, the risk of insolvency of the reinsurance broker would fall most often upon the primary insurer and not upon the reinsurer.

Insurance regulatory authorities can influence the activities of primary insurers and reinsurers. The value of most proportional reinsurance transactions lies in the transfer of the unearned premium reserve to the reinsurer. If state insurance regulators do not approve of a reinsurer, they can deny the primary insurer any benefit of a reinsurance contract with the unacceptable reinsurer. Some states permit the primary insurer to take the reserve credits only if the reinsurer is licensed in the state. Others permit the credit if the reinsurer is licensed in any state of the United States. Finally, some states permit the reserve credits even if the reinsurer is not licensed anywhere in the United States, provided the primary insurer obtains the permission of the state insurance department before entering into the contract. Credit may also be permitted if reinsurance loss reserves are funded by a letter of credit or a trust fund.

Regulation of Reinsurance Brokers

Unlike primary insurance brokers, reinsurance brokers are neither required to be licensed in most states nor required by law in most states to demonstrate any special skill in their chosen field. The principal purpose in licensing primary insurance brokers, at least in theory, is to protect the public against being victimized by dishonest or incompetent brokers. Because reinsurance brokers deal only with insurers, that protection has not been deemed necessary in their case. Some discussion of licensing reinsurance brokers has occurred because of the much-publicized failure of a large reinsurance brokerage firm during the mid-seventies. Many reinsurance brokers are also excess and surplus lines brokers and must be licensed to write those lines.

New York requires licensing of reinsurance brokers and makes them subject to examination by the superintendent of insurance. Regulation 98, adopted by the New York Superintendent of Insurance, establishes the regulatory pattern for that State. **New York Regulation 98** is shown in Exhibit 9-9.

New York's requirements do not apply to managers of reinsurance pools, syndicates, or associations.

Exhibit 9-9
New York Regulation 98

(1) Reinsurance intermediaries act in a fiduciary capacity for all funds received in their professional capacity and must not mingle them with other funds without the consent of the insurers and reinsurers they represent;
(2) Reinsurance intermediaries shall have written authorization from the insurers and reinsurers they represent, spelling out the extent and limitations of their authority;
(3) The written authority above must be made available to primary insurers or reinsurers with which the intermediary deals;
(4) No licensed intermediary shall procure reinsurance from an unlicensed reinsurer unless the reinsurer has appointed an agent for the service of process in New York;
(5) The intermediary must make full written disclosure of
   (a) any control over the broker by a reinsurer,
   (b) any control of a reinsurer by the intermediary,
   (c) any retrocessions of the subject business placed by the intermediary, and
   (d) commissions earned or to be earned on the business;
(6) Records of all transactions must be retained for at least ten years after the expiration of all reinsurance contracts.

Proposed Reinsurance Regulation

The present minimal regulation of reinsurance seems unlikely to continue. The NAIC has developed model reinsurance regulatory acts that have been submitted to the various state legislatures for possible enactment. One of the NAIC model acts deals with reinsurance ceded to nonadmitted reinsurers; the other is the NAIC Model Reinsurance Intermediary Act. The American Institute for Certified Public Accountants (AICPA) has promulgated guidelines for accountants to follow in auditing the reinsurance operations of either primary insurers or assuming reinsurers.[6] The Reinsurance Association of America (RAA) has also developed a model act. All of those documents are intended to solve essentially the same problems and take essentially the same approach to the solutions.

The principal problems addressed by the proposed regulations are as follows:

(1) Potential losses to primary insurers and their policyholders resulting from the insolvency of alien reinsurers

(2) Potential losses to primary insurers and their policyholders resulting from the insolvency or fraudulent activities of reinsurance intermediaries

(3) The difficulties for U.S. primary insurers in litigating disputed claims against alien reinsurers not licensed in the United States

(4) Potential losses to stockholders and policyholders of primary companies resulting from the fraudulent use of reinsurance by management

The regulatory acts use the leverage of reinsurance reserve credits to motivate primary insurers to require desirable provisions in their reinsurance contracts and to select reinsurers in sound financial condition.

They generally provide that reserve credit will not be allowed for reinsurance unless the reinsurer meets one or more of the following conditions:

(1) The reinsurer is licensed in the state concerned.

(2) The reinsurer is licensed in another state of the United States and meets solvency tests similar to those required by the state concerned.

(3) The reinsurer maintains a trust fund in the United States for the sole benefit of U.S. insureds, including primary insurers, of at least $20 million for insurers and of $100 million for associations of individual insurers (such as Lloyd's).

(4) The primary insurer holds assets of the reinsurer or an irrevocable letter of credit issued by a U.S. bank in an amount at least equal to the reserve credit.

In addition to the above, the reserve credits generally will not be allowed unless the reinsurance contract provides that:

(1) The reinsurer will submit to the jurisdiction of U.S. courts and be bound by the decision of such courts in any dispute under the contract.

(2) The state insurance commissioner is appointed the reinsurer's agent for the service of process.

(3) The liability of the reinsurer for loss under the contract shall not be reduced by the insolvency of the primary insurer.

The RAA model act includes provisions to control the use of bulk reinsurance, in which an insurer cedes all or substantially all of its business to a reinsurer. Bulk reinsurance has sometimes been used to deprive the stockholders of a stock company or the policyholders of a mutual company of all or part of their ownership rights in the company.

The model act provides that no bulk reinsurance contract can become effective without the prior written approval of the insurance commissioner. The commissioner can approve such a contract only if it is found (1) to be fair and equitable to the primary insurer and (2) not to reduce the protection provided to policyholders of the primary insurer. In addition, no director, officer, agent, or employee of either the primary insurer or the reinsurer can receive any fee, commission, or other valuable consideration for aiding or promoting the bulk transfer. For mutual primary insurers, additional provisions apply regarding approval by policyholder vote and payment in cash to policyholders for their equity in the business ceded.

Reinsurance and the Capacity Problem

One of the principal purposes of reinsurance, as discussed earlier in this chapter, is to provide capacity, both for large loss exposures and for premium volume. Without reinsurance facilities, meeting the insurance needs of the public would be very difficult for primary insurers. However, the success of reinsurers in providing the needed capacity varies from time to time, depending on several factors.

A major factor in capacity availability is price adequacy. Both primary insurance and reinsurance are subject to pricing cycles in which rates vary from grossly inadequate to excessive. Those cycles result from competition, inability to cope with inflation, and in the case of primary insurers, from excessive zeal on the part of state regulatory authorities in the control of rates. Of course, a reinsurer is less than eager to write business for which it has no reasonable expectation of profit.

Reinsurers can have poor loss experience for at least two reasons. One reason is inadequate rates. The other is that chance fluctuation in losses, especially from catastrophes, could cause poor loss experience in a single year even though rates are adequate for the long term. That is especially true, of course, of those reinsurers that write a substantial amount of catastrophe coverages. One or a few years of poor underwriting experience can restrict reinsurance capacity in two ways. First, existing reinsurers become less interested in writing new business and might even terminate some existing business, either because of poor profit expectations or because of shrinkage of surplus. Second, poor investment experience, especially sharp declines in the stock market, could have much the same effect because of the resulting drop in policyholders' surplus.

When capacity shortages in insurance and reinsurance have occurred, the insurance marketplace has sought new sources of capital. During the years when advisory organizations made rates and were successful in keeping primary insurance rates adequate by controlling competition, capacity shortages were less common. However, a return to that kind of rate control in the near future seems very unlikely.

Any move by reinsurance to fix rates at a prohibitively high level would be certain to run afoul of federal antitrust laws and probably would not succeed even in the absence of antitrust laws. Rates fixed at an unrealistically high level would merely attract new reinsurers willing to write business at lower rates. The ease of entry into the reinsurance business virtually precludes effective price fixing. In addition, primary insurers have resisted excessive reinsurance rates by increasing their retentions.

It seems likely that reinsurers shortages will continue to occur. Fortunately, they tend to be relatively brief and to cause fewer problems than might be expected from a casual reading of the speeches and magazine articles that usually accompany them.

Summary

The reinsurance program of a primary insurer consists of a number of reinsurance transactions. A primary insurer's reinsurance relationship may be with a single reinsurer, but, more likely, many reinsurers are involved. Several reinsurers may be involved in achieving a specific objective of the primary insurer. Such is the case when many reinsurers commit to one multi-line surplus share treaty.

The reinsurance program of a well-managed insurer plays a key role in the attainment of specific insurer goals. The usual goals served by reinsurance were described as reinsurance functions or purposes of reinsurance in the previous chapter. Those functions fulfill needs—needs created by the desire to achieve specific insurer objectives.

In designing a reinsurance program, insurers or their reinsurance brokers compare existing reinsurance arrangements with their ever-changing needs. To be effective, reinsurance programs must be flexible enough to meet known and anticipated needs. Designing a reinsurance program involves determining the reinsurance needs, gathering information to establish the retention and limits, setting retentions, and setting limits.

After the reinsurance program is in place, it must be administered. The level of administration varies by the type of reinsurance used. The cost of administering the reinsurance program is an additional consideration in selecting the components of a program.

Reinsurance is less regulated than primary insurance. The premise used by state regulators is that in the reinsurance transaction, both parties to the contract are knowledgeable concerning their rights and obligations. In reality, the traditional relationship of "utmost good faith" that permitted reinsurance to operate on a handshake has deteriorated because of unfulfilled promises. Insurance regulators have recognized that the insurance consumer could suffer if reinsurance contractual agreements are not met. In response, several proposals have been initiated to increase the level of regulatory supervision on reinsurers.

Glossary of Reinsurance Terms[7]

Broker—An intermediary who negotiates reinsurance contracts between the ceding company and the reinsurer(s). The broker generally represents the ceding company and receives a commission, almost always from the reinsurer(s), for placing the business and performing other necessary services.

Broker Market—The collective reference to those reinsurance companies which accept business mainly from reinsurance brokers. See Direct Writing Reinsurer.

Burning Cost—See Pure Loss Cost.

Combination Plan Reinsurance—A reinsurance agreement which combines the excess of loss and the quota share forms of coverage within one contract, with the reinsurance premium established as a fixed percentage of the ceding company's subject premium. After deducting the excess recovery on any one loss for one risk, the reinsurer indemnifies the ceding company based on a fixed quota share percentage. If a loss does not exceed the excess of loss retention level, only the quota share coverage applies.

Contingent Commission—An allowance made to the ceding company reinsurance contract or contracts.

Direct Writing Reinsurer—A reinsurance company which develops its business by using its own personnel and does not (ordinarily) accept business from a broker or intermediary.

Extra-Contractual Obligations (ECO) Clause—A clause in a reinsurance treaty that protects the ceding company against all or part of its liability arising from claim settlement activities and falling outside of strict policy provisions.

Gross Line—The total limit of liability accepted by an insurer on an individual risk (net line plus all reinsurance ceded).

Indexing—A procedure sometimes incorporated into an excess of loss reinsurance treaty to adjust the retention and limit according to the value of a specified public economic index (for example: wage, price, or cost-of-living).

Insolvency Clause—A contractual provision, generally required by statute or regulation as a prerequisite to receiving credit for reinsurance, under which the reinsurer agrees, in the event of the ceding insurer's insolvency, to pay its reinsurance obligations under the contract whether or not the insurer has paid its obligations.

Intermediary Clause—A contractual provision, generally required by statute or regulation as a prerequisite to receiving credit for reinsurance, in which the parties agree to effect all transactions through an intermediary and the credit risk of the intermediary, as distinct from other risks, is imposed on the reinsurer.

Letter of Credit (LOC)—Within the context of reinsurance, a banking instrument established on a "standby" basis to secure recoverables from non-admitted reinsurers to enable the ceding company to reduce the provision for unauthorized reinsurance in its statutory statement.

Offset (Setoff)—The reduction of the amount owed by one party to a second party by crediting the first party with amounts owed it by the second party. The existence and scope of offset rights may be determined by contract language as well as statutory, regulatory, and judicial law.

Pure Loss Cost (Also Burning Cost)—The ratio of the reinsurance losses incurred to the ceding company's subject premium.

Sliding Scale Commission—A commission adjustment on earned premiums whereby the actual commission varies inversely with the loss ratio, subject to a maximum and minimum.

Chapter Notes

1. Len Strazewski, "Intermediaries Historical Image Clashes with Modern Role," *Business Insurance*, October 10, 1983, p. 3.
2. Colleen Johnson, "Brokers Predict Revenue Rebound," *Business Insurance*, November 12, 1990, p. 3.
3. For a more thorough treatment of this subject, see Anthony M. Lanzone, "Analyzing Reinsurance Disputes," *National Underwriter*, Property & Casualty Edition, August 19, 1983, p. 19; and August 26, 1983, p. 15.
4. See Lanzone, "Analyzing Reinsurance Disputes," *National Underwriter*, Property & Casualty Edition, September 9, 1983, p. 27; and "Reinsurer Bound When Insurer Follows Policy," *Business Insurance*, September 26, 1983, p. 36.

5. "Supervision of U.K. Reinsurance Tightened Up," *International Insurance Monitor*, January/February 1983, p. 12.

6. Douglas McLeod, "New Guidelines to Spell Out Reinsurance Procedures," *Business Insurance*, October 8, 1983, p. 18; and William J. Kane, "Reinsurance Accounting: Whose Responsibility?" *National Underwriter*, Property & Casualty Edition, August 26, 1983, Part 2, p. 26.

7. The definitions in this glossary were adapted with permission from *Glossary of Reinsurance Terms* (Washington, DC: Reinsurance Association of America, 1992).

Chapter 10

Ratemaking Principles

Property-liability insurers require many actuarial services in order to function effectively. Among them are ratemaking, verification of loss reserves, collection and analysis of company data to evaluate the insurer's profitability, analysis of data from other sources to determine the insurer's competitive position, and preparation of statistical reports for management and regulatory authorities. This chapter, the first of two that explore these actuarial services, focuses on the principles of ratemaking.

Actuaries usually supervise ratemaking activities. An **actuary** is trained in applying mathematical techniques to insurer operations and must demonstrate competence by completing written examinations administered by actuarial professional organizations. For property-liability insurance, the principal actuarial professional organization in the United States is the Casualty Actuarial Society (CAS). The CAS has two levels of membership. A person becomes an Associate of the Casualty Actuarial Society (ACAS) by successfully completing seven examinations. Successful completion of three additional examinations qualifies the Associate to become a Fellow of the Casualty Actuarial Society (FCAS). Most members of the CAS are also members of the American Academy of Actuaries (AAA). The AAA performs certain educational, public relations, government relations, disciplinary, and other functions on behalf of various actuarial professional bodies in the United States and Canada. Members of the Academy may indicate membership by writing MAAA after their names.

Regulatory authorities generally require an actuary to be a member of the CAS or AAA, or otherwise demonstrate actuarial competence, before performing certain services for insurers, such as certifying the adequacy of loss and loss expense reserves.

Actuarial Services

Actuarial services can be obtained in several ways. Many insurers have one or more actuaries on staff to provide most of the actuarial services needed. Smaller insurers rely on actuarial consultants for such services. Insurers with actuaries on staff may occasionally retain actuarial consultants, either because their staff actuaries lack adequate expertise in a specific field or because they believe that an outside consultant will provide greater objectivity than a staff actuary. Persons or firms with which insurers are negotiating, such as regulatory authorities and reinsurers, sometimes require the insurer to provide an opinion by a consulting actuary to verify the accuracy and reasonableness of work done by staff actuaries.

Some actuarial services can also be obtained from advisory organizations. Advisory organizations usually perform the following actuarial functions:

1. Collection of ratemaking data
2. Analysis of the data and calculation of loss costs
3. Preparation of rate filings
4. Submission of rate filings to appropriate state regulatory authorities

They also maintain continuing contact with regulatory authorities to facilitate the approval of the rate filing if regulatory approval is required. If regulatory hearings or judicial proceedings are required relative to the rate filing, the advisory organization provides the actuarial and legal services necessary for such proceedings. A **rate filing** is a document containing rates along with the necessary data and statistical analysis to show that the rates comply with regulatory requirements. Advisory organizations also provide some services that are not actuarial in nature, such as drafting policy contracts.

Advisory organizations have moved away from the practice of calculating final rates and toward providing prospective loss cost information, to which each insurer must add its own expense information to determine its final rates.

The principal advisory organizations are (1) Insurance Services Office (ISO),

(2) American Association of Insurance Services (AAIS), (3) National Council on Compensation Insurance (NCCI), and (4) Surety Association of America. There are several additional, more specialized advisory organizations also exist.

ISO performs actuarial services related to most lines of property-liability insurance other than workers compensation insurance and surety and fidelity bonds. AAIS also provides services for several lines of insurance other than workers compensation and surety bonds. NCCI has jurisdiction over workers compensation insurance, and Surety Association of America specializes in fidelity and surety bonds.

Principles of Ratemaking

The remainder of this chapter is devoted to the principles of the ratemaking process.

Objectives of Ratemaking

The primary objective of ratemaking is to develop a rate structure that will enable the insurer to compete effectively for business while earning a reasonable profit on its operations. There are several subsidiary objectives, some imposed by corporate considerations and some by regulatory requirements.

Corporate Objectives

From the insurer's viewpoint, rates should (1) be stable, (2) be responsive, (3) promote loss control, (4) provide for contingencies, and (5) be easy to understand and apply. Because some of these objectives necessarily conflict with each other, compromises among them are necessary at several levels.

Stability of rates is highly desirable for several reasons. Implementing rate changes is an expensive process and should be kept to a practical minimum. Also, large and sudden changes in rates cause dissatisfaction among consumers and may lead to harsh regulatory actions and unfavorable legislation. The adoption of Proposition 103 in California in 1988 and similar rate regulatory legislation in several other states stemmed from public perception that insurance rates were not sufficiently stable.

Of course, rates that are too stable do not comply with the second objective that rates change promptly in response to external factors that affect losses.

Rates that are too stable may also conflict with the fourth objective that rates should provide for contingencies. This objective simply means that a reasonable allowance should be made in the rates to cover unexpected variations in losses and expenses.

Rating systems encourage the third objective—loss control—by providing lower rates for policyholders who undertake loss prevention measures. For example, policyholders who install burglar alarm systems are granted a reduction in their burglary insurance rates. Lower fire insurance rates are given to policyholders who install sprinkler systems. Also, higher rates may be applied to policyholders who engage in activities that tend to result in higher losses, such as persons who use their cars for business.

The final objective, simplicity, is a relative one. Rating systems should be simple enough to be understood by agents, brokers, underwriters, and policyholders. Of these groups, policyholders are the least likely to be sophisticated in insurance matters. The level of insurance expertise among policyholders varies from personal lines consumers, who may have little knowledge of factors affecting insurance pricing, to large corporations with well-staffed risk management departments that have considerable insurance expertise. The insurance product should have a pricing methodology that the person or firm buying it can understand.

Regulatory Objectives

The regulatory objectives are set forth in the statutes of the various states. These objectives are that rates (1) must be adequate, (2) must not be excessive, and (3) must not be unfairly discriminatory. These requirements are discussed in greater detail in a later section of this chapter.

The Ratemaking Process

Insurance ratemaking techniques are frequently described by complicated mathematical formulas. Consequently, many people consider the ratemaking process to be complex and esoteric. Others consider the process to be more akin to the ancient art of reading the future from tea leaves or animal entrails. This chapter attempts to strip away the mystery and present the principles of ratemaking in nonmathematical form. Several unfamiliar words and terms might be encountered in this chapter. They are explained in the text, and a glossary at the end of the chapter provides brief definitions for them. The next chapter will explore the ratemaking process in greater depth.

This chapter uses private passenger automobile insurance to illustrate the principles of insurance ratemaking. That line of insurance has been selected for illustrative purposes for several reasons. First, virtually everyone has at least some familiarity with private passenger automobile insurance, either professionally or as a consumer. Also, the same ratemaking principles that apply to auto insurance can be applied in varying degrees to other lines of property or liability insurance. Finally, auto insurance is the largest line of property-liability insurance written.

Ratemaking in a Stable World

In a stable world, where nothing ever changes, the insurance ratemaking process would be very simple. It could be carried out in three easy steps:

1. Calculate the amount needed to pay claims.
2. Calculate the amount needed to pay expenses.
3. Add (1) and (2) to find the rate to be charged.

An Example

To illustrate this simple process, assume that an actuary has been commissioned to calculate auto insurance rates for the Kingdom of Everstable, a country ruled by a benevolent despot. The king believes that his people will be very happy if nothing ever changes. Consequently, he has decreed the following:

1. There will always be exactly 100,000 cars in Everstable, and they will all be exactly alike and will never change.
2. All drivers in Everstable will be exactly equal in driving ability, temperament, and amount of driving.
3. All cars will be insured for exactly the same coverages and limits, and the limits and coverages will never change.
4. Driving conditions will be uniform throughout the kingdom and will never change.
5. Laws governing compensation for auto accidents will be uniform throughout the kingdom and will never change.
6. There will be no inflation in the kingdom, so prices will never change.

The insurance companies in Everstable find that they have paid out exactly $10 million in claims each year for the past ten years. All claims in Everstable are paid within an hour of the occurrence of the loss. Errors in estimating future loss payments are not a concern, since there are no loss reserves to estimate.

The insurers in Everstable have paid out $100 in claims each year for each car insured (calculated by dividing the $10 million in claims by the 100,000 cars). Since nothing ever changes in Everstable, the same amount will be paid next year. The first step in the ratemaking process is now completed, and $100 for each car insured will be needed to pay claims, not including any expenses.

The accountants for the insurers tell the actuary that they have incurred the following expenses each year for the past ten years:

Loss adjustment expenses	$1,000,000
Acquisition expenses	1,500,000
General administrative expenses	800,000
Premium taxes	200,000
Total expenses	$3,500,000

Dividing the expenses by 100,000 (the number of cars) yields a total of $35 in expenses for each car insured. So the total premium for each car will be $100 loss plus $35 expense, or $135.

Terminology

Actuaries have names for the two elements that are included in this gross rate of $135. The $100 needed to pay claims is known as the **pure premium.** Loss adjustment expenses are sometimes included in the pure premium, in which case Everstable's pure premium would have been $110. It is important to determine whether a quoted pure premium includes or excludes loss adjustment expenses.

The amount included in the premium for expenses is known as an **expense loading**. In the example shown above, the expense loading included loss adjustment expenses. As noted above, loss adjustment expenses are commonly included in the pure premium, in which case those expenses would not be included in the expense loading. The sum of the pure premium and the expense loading is called the **gross rate**.

The insurers of Everstable were as benevolent as the king. They did not include anything in their rates for profit. In the real world, an allowance known as **profit and contingencies** would be included in the expense loading. The amount included protects the insurer against the possibility that actual claims or expenses will exceed the estimated claims and expenses included in the rates, either because of errors in estimation or because conditions change. If not needed for excessive losses or expenses, the funds generated by the loading become profit for the insurer.

Ratemaking in the Real World

Unfortunately (at least for actuaries), the real world bears little resemblance to the imaginary Kingdom of Everstable. This section examines the major differences.

Loss Reserves

All claims are not paid immediately in the real world. In fact, for some liability lines, many years may elapse between the time a loss occurs and the time the resulting claims are paid. For example, many claims are in litigation now, in 1997, involving injuries allegedly sustained by workers using asbestos in shipyards during World War II, over fifty years ago. Although this is an extreme case, delays of ten to twelve years in the settlement of liability claims are not unusual.

Insurers are required by law (and by good business practices) to estimate the amounts that they will eventually pay on such claims. The estimated amounts to be paid in the future for claims that have already happened are shown as a liability on the insurer's balance sheet and are usually referred to as **loss reserves**. Unfortunately, all insurers are not equipped with perfect foresight, so these estimates are not always accurate. Any errors in estimating claims payment amounts are reflected in rates calculated on the basis of such estimates. If the claims estimates are too low, the resulting rates will be too low. If the claims estimates are too high, the resulting rates will be too high.

To illustrate this effect, assume that rates are to be calculated for an auto liability insurance line for which 25 percent of losses are paid in the same year the accident occurs, 50 percent are to be paid in the next year, and the remaining 25 percent are to be paid in the second year following the year in which the accident occurs. The rates are to be calculated on the basis of the losses that occurred in the most recent three-year period. Exhibit 10-1 shows the losses for each year in the three-year period, with year 1 being the oldest year and year 3 the most recent year. The paid losses in Column (1) are the amounts paid up to and including December 31 of year 3.

Exhibit 10-1
Paid Losses, Loss Reserves, and Incurred Losses for a Hypothetical Auto Liability Line Evaluated at 12/31/3

Year	(1) Losses Paid	(2) Loss Reserves	(3) Incurred Losses
1	$10,000,000	$ 0	$10,000,000
2	7,500,000	2,500,000	10,000,000
3	2,500,000	7,500,000	10,000,000
Totals	$20,000,000	$10,000,000	$30,000,000

The loss reserves shown in Column (2) are the insurer's estimates, as of December 31 of year 3, of the amounts that will be paid in the future for losses that happened during the period. All losses that happened in year 1 have been paid, so there is no reserve for that period. Column (3), which is the sum of Columns (1) and (2), is labeled *Incurred Losses;* this is a standard actuarial term.

The **incurred losses** for a given period of time are the sum of (1) all amounts already paid for losses that happened during that time period and (2) amounts that will be paid in the future for losses that occurred during that time period.

If the insurer for which losses are shown in Exhibit 10-1 insured 100,000 cars each year during the period, it would have provided 300,000 *car-years* of protection during the period. (A car-year represents the exposure of one car insured for one year.) If the 300,000 car-years are divided into the $30 million of incurred losses, based on past experience only, the insurer will need a pure premium of $100 per car (the amount needed to pay losses).

Now assume that the insurer's loss reserves proved to be inadequate. When all claims were settled, the incurred losses turned out to be $33 million instead of the estimated $30 million in Exhibit 10-1. In that case, the pure premium actually needed was $110; the insurer's rates would have been too low.

In theory, an insurer could avoid the problem of incorrectly estimating loss reserves by waiting for all claims to be paid before calculating rates. However, there are major problems with this approach. Several years may elapse before all claims are paid. Delaying the rate filing for several years to permit all claims to be settled allows a greater length of time for inflation, changes in traffic conditions, and other factors to affect incurred losses. Errors in estimating the effects of these factors may be greater than the errors in estimating loss reserves.

Exhibit 10-2 shows the payout pattern reported by one insurer for automobile liability insurance. In Exhibit 10-2, year 1 is the year the accidents happened, year 2 is the next year after the accidents happened, and so forth.

Exhibit 10-2
Payout Pattern: Automobile Liability Insurance Losses Incurred in Year 1

	(1)	(2)	(3)	(4)
		Losses Unpaid		Estimated Losses Incurred
Year	Losses Paid	Reported	IBNR	in Year 1
12/31/1	$ 5,051,145	$13,837,205	$9,592,239	$28,480,589
12/31/2	10,780,845	12,906,866	4,187,646	27,875,357
12/31/3	16,036,708	9,058,737	2,036,246	27,131,691
12/31/4	19,667,531	6,782,231	79,247	26,529,009
12/31/5	22,268,032	4,308,212	0	26,576,244
12/31/6	24,714,163	3,136,059	0	27,850,222
12/31/7	25,088,249	860,395	0	25,948,644

Column (1) of Exhibit 10-2 shows the actual amount paid by the company up to the end of the year indicated for claims arising from insured events that occurred during year 1. During year 1, the company paid out $5,051,145 on such claims. During year 2, the company paid out an additional $5,729,700 on such claims, bringing the total payments to $10,780,845. At the end of year 7, the company had paid a total of $25,088,249 for claims that arose in year 1.

Column (2) of Exhibit 10-2 shows the company's estimate at the end of each year of the amount it will eventually pay to settle claims that occurred in year 1 and have been reported to it but have not yet been paid. This figure drops each year as claims are settled and has become a relatively small $860,395 at the end of year 7.

The figures in Column (3) are the company's estimates of amounts that it will pay in the future to settle claims that happened in year 1 but have not yet been reported to it. These are known as **incurred but not reported (IBNR)** claims. The company assumed that all auto insurance claims incurred in year 1 had been reported to it by the end of year 5, so the IBNR figure is zero for years 5 and later.

The figures in Columns (2) and (3) are estimates of amounts to be paid at some future time. The figures in Column (2) are usually determined by claims department personnel as their estimate of the amounts to be paid on individual claims. The numbers in Column (3) are usually calculated by actuaries on the basis of historical data. The methods used to arrive at these estimates are discussed in Chapter 12. The amounts ultimately paid are seldom, if ever, exactly equal to the estimates, and the differences are sometimes substantial.

The company in Exhibit 10-2 estimated at the end of year 1 [see Column (4)] that it would eventually pay a total of $28,480,589 to settle all of the auto liability claims incurred by it in year 1. At the end of year 7, it had reduced that estimate to $25,948,644. With only $860,395 outstanding at the end of year 7, that estimate should be much more accurate than the original estimate at the end of year 1.

If the company in Exhibit 10-2 had used its estimated incurred losses at the end of year 1 for ratemaking purposes, the resulting rates would have been too high by approximately 10 percent. Such an error could cause it to become noncompetitive and lose market share. Of course, all insurers do not overestimate their loss payments. Some underestimate them, which could cause inadequate rates, underwriting losses, and possibly even insolvency.

Actuaries have developed methods for detecting and correcting consistent errors in the estimation of future loss payments. The method most commonly used is known as **loss development**, which will be discussed in some detail in

Chapter 11. It is based on historical data and assumes that the company is making the same errors in estimation now that it made in the past

Inflation

Errors in the estimation of loss reserves are not the only source of ratemaking error that actuaries must guard against. Unlike the mythical Kingdom of Everstable, the real world is subject to inflation and, sometimes, to deflation. Inflation, especially rapid inflation, presents a substantial actuarial problem. An inevitable lag occurs between the time losses are incurred and the time at which those losses are reflected in rates charged to consumers. The delay may be as long as three years, though some companies are able to keep it somewhat shorter.

The lag in reflecting loss experience in rates stems from several sources. The principal sources of delay are as follows:

1. Delay by policyholders in reporting losses to insurers
2. Time required to analyze the data and prepare a rate filing
3. Delays in obtaining approval of filed rates by state regulatory authorities
4. Time required to communicate the new rates to agents and brokers

In addition, rates are frequently in effect for one year. Thus, the last policy issued under a given set of rates would be issued one year after the effective date of the rate filing, and coverage under those rates would continue until the policy expires, possibly a year later. During periods of rapid inflation, these delays could result in substantially inadequate rates.

Exhibit 10-3 shows a reasonably typical schedule for the development, approval, and implementation of new auto insurance rates. Some insurers and some states might complete the process more quickly, and others might take longer.

Exhibit 10-3 assumes that the insurer is basing its new rates on its loss experience for a three-year period. This three-year period is usually called the **experience period**, and all pertinent statistics from that period are collected and analyzed in the ratemaking process. The data items used are usually (1) earned exposure units, (2) earned premiums, (3) incurred losses in dollars, and (4) the number of claims incurred. An **exposure unit** is a measure of the risk assumed under an insurance contract. The premium for a policy is calculated by multiplying the number of exposure units by the rate for each exposure unit. For private passenger auto insurance, the unit of exposure is one car-year, or one car insured for one year.

The experience period in Exhibit 10-3 begins on January 1 of year 1. Experience statistics are collected for the three-year period beginning on that date

Exhibit 10-3
Chronology of a Rate Filing

January 1, Year 1	Beginning of the experience period, first claim incurred.
December 31, Year 1	
July 1, Year 2	Midpoint of experience period.
December 31, Year 2	
December 31, Year 3	End of experience period.
March 31, Year 4	Begin data collection and analysis.
July 1, Year 4	File rates with regulatory authorities.
September 1, Year 4	Receive approval of rates.
January 1, Year 5	Begin using new rates.
December 31, Year 5	Stop using rates from this filing. Also, midpoint of period during which losses are incurred under this filing.
December 31, Year 6	Last claim incurred under this rate filing.

and ending on December 31 of year 3. The midpoint of the experience period is July 1 of year 2.

Exhibit 10-3 shows the analysis phase of the ratemaking process beginning only three months after the end of the experience period. Some insurers would prefer to wait longer to permit claims information to mature. As noted above, many claims incurred during the experience period would not have been reported to the insurer at that point.

Exhibit 10-3 assumes that the new rates will become effective on January 1 of year 5, one year after the end of the experience period. They will remain in effect until December 31 of year 5, two years after the end of the experience period. However, the policies issued on December 31 of year 5 will remain in force until December 31 of year 6. Consequently, the last claim under these rates will be incurred three years after the end of the experience period and six years after the occurrence of the first of the claims on which the rate calculation was based. Some insurers may shorten this process slightly by filing new rates every six months or issuing six-month policies. Others may follow an even longer cycle.

In Exhibit 10-3, the lag between the midpoint of the experience period and the midpoint of the period in which losses are incurred under the rates is 3.5 years. A delay of this length can result in substantial changes in loss severity and frequency resulting from inflation, changes in laws, traffic density, or other factors. Rates calculated without regard to these potential changes could prove to be grossly inadequate or grossly excessive, depending on the nature of the changes taking place.

Exhibit 10-4 shows that the cost factors underlying insurance claims have exceeded inflation rates. Inflation is measured by the consumer price index (CPI), which is calculated by the U.S. Bureau of Labor of Statistics. The CPI is a measure of the average change in prices over time for a fixed market basket of goods and services. Those goods and services include energy, food, shelter, apparel and personal maintenance items, and medical care. The cost factors underlying insurance claims include the cost of physicians' services and other medical services; hospital care and rehabilitation; lost time and wages; automobiles, including repair and parts; building materials; plate and safety glass; personal effects; lawyers' fees; and other legal and court costs. The top section of Exhibit 10-4 compares these underlying costs with the CPI. The bottom section of the exhibit compares the claim costs of selected lines of insurance with the CPI.

Exhibit 10-4
Claim Costs Relative to the Consumer Price Index

	1984	1994	% Increase
Consumer Price Index			
All items	103.9	148.2	42.6
Indexes of Costs Underlying Claims			
CPI, physicians' services	107.0	199.8	86.7
CPI, hospital room rates	109.0	239.2	119.4
Legal costs	103.9	182.5	75.6
CPI, auto body work	104.6	153.6	46.8
Indexes for Direct Claim Costs for Major Lines of Insurance			
Auto bodily injury	108.4	208.6	92.4
Auto property damage	104.4	162.3	55.5
Auto physical damage	102.5	142.3	38.8
Workers compensation	109.0	188.0	72.5
Other bodily injury	106.4	205.0	92.7
Other property damage	106.3	162.5	52.9
Homeowners	105.3	161.2	53.1
Commercial multiple peril	104.7	150.0	43.3

Adapted from William R. Van Ark, "Gap in Claim Cost Trends Continues to Narrow," *Best's Review*, Property/Casualty Edition, March 1996, pp. 22-23.

Other Time-Dependent Factors

Inflation affects the average cost of a claim. Other time-dependent factors affect the number of claims that occur. Among them are the following:

1. Changes in traffic density (the number of vehicles per mile of road)
2. Changes in law enforcement efforts
3. Changes in legal rules governing claims settlement

Some of these factors may be very difficult to identify and to reduce to mathematical expressions, but they nonetheless affect insurance claims. Ignoring them may result in inadequate or excessive rates.

The actuarial technique used to cope with these time-dependent factors is known as **trending**. Some of the factors that affect the size and frequency of claims cannot be identified or measured directly, but their aggregate effect on claims can be determined with reasonable accuracy by statistical means. Trending uses statistical techniques to measure these effects in the past and to project them into the future. Trending is usually done separately for the average amount of claim, called severity, and the average number of claims, called frequency. Trending is sometimes applied to pure premiums, which combine frequency and severity into a single number. Chapter 11 will discuss trending in more detail.

Risk Classification

In the Kingdom of Everstable, all drivers and all cars are exactly equal. In the real world, both cars and drivers vary widely, and their variations have very important implications for the cost of insurance. There is no satisfactory way to measure directly the propensity of a particular driver to have accidents, but certain groups of drivers are known to have more accidents than others. For rating purposes, drivers are grouped into classes according to criteria that provide at least a rough measure of the claims they are likely to generate. This process of categorization is usually referred to as **risk classification**. Among the rating criteria frequently used for private passenger auto insurance risk classification are the following:

1. Age of the driver
2. Sex and marital status of the driver
3. Nature of the vehicle
4. Use of vehicle
5. Driving record of the driver
6. Risk classification rating

Age

When immaturity is coupled with inexperience, age becomes a good predictor of accident frequency. Both insurance statistics and statistics gathered by state motor vehicle departments show that young drivers have more accidents than older drivers. Perhaps youthful operators are more reckless than older drivers or more inclined to take chances that result in accidents. As young drivers gain more driving experience and develop more mature judgment, their accident records improve.

Sex and Marital Status of the Driver

A driver's sex also seems to be a factor in accident experience, though it is less of a factor than age. Regulatory requirements prohibit the use of sex as a rating criterion in a few states. Marital status has been used in further subclassify youthful operators. The presumption is that young married operators are more settled than their unmarried counterparts. In Georgia, for example, the class factor used is 10 to 15 percent higher for unmarried youthful operators than it is for married youthful operators.

Nature of Vehicle

Unlike the fabled land of Everstable, all vehicles in the real world are not created equal. Cars differ as to (1) susceptibility to accidents, (2) damageability, and (3) protection provided to occupants. Several notable examples of accident susceptibility have become apparent in recent years. Some utility vehicles have been found to be unstable and likely to overturn when executing sharp turns, such as what might happen during emergency maneuvers to avoid collision accidents. High-powered sports cars, with rapid acceleration and high-speed capabilities, have also been found to have more accidents than more conservative vehicles, especially when operated by inexperienced drivers.

Cars also vary with regard to their resistance to damage when an accident occurs. This susceptibility to damage may result from weak bumpers, the complex shape of metal parts such as decorative fenders, or excessive use of materials that are difficult to repair, such as molded fiberglass-plastic.

Finally, cars differ in the protection they offer to passengers when an accident occurs. One car model became infamous because its gasoline tank frequently ruptured when it was struck from the rear, causing serious fires and many deaths to its occupants. Others have been found to provide less than satisfactory protection to passengers in collision accidents. Many studies have shown that small cars provide less passenger protection than larger cars.

Accident susceptibility is an important rating consideration for all lines of automobile insurance except possibly theft. Damageability is important primarily for collision coverage rates, while passenger protection is important primarily for no-fault and medical expense coverages. It would also be important for liability coverage because of possible injuries to passengers.

Auto insurance ratemaking practices differ among insurers. Some insurers may not take all of these factors into account in calculating their rates.

Use of Vehicle

The use to which a vehicle is put usually determines the mileage driven and is therefore an important determinant of losses. Consequently, it is an important factor in risk classification. Cars used for business purposes are likely to be driven more than those used only for personal use. Cars driven to and from work are likely to be driven more than those driven only for pleasure. There are exceptions to these general rules, but the rules are useful for risk classification despite the exceptions.

Although the use of the vehicle is an important classification criterion, mileage driven is sometimes used as a separate criterion. It may be specified in terms of total annual mileage driven or in terms of the one-way distance between the policyholder's home and place of employment.

Driving Record

Many auto insurers use the policyholder's driving record as an important risk classification criterion. Years of driving experience is sometimes used instead of age as a risk classification criterion. Past accidents and traffic violations are also used for rating purposes. Some statistical compilations indicate that a driver who has had one or more accidents in the past three years is significantly more likely to have another accident in the next year.

Risk Classification Rating

These and other risk classification criteria are used to categorize drivers into reasonably homogeneous groups so that all members of the class have substantially the same exposure to loss. A rate is then calculated for each class so that the members of each class pay a premium commensurate with the loss exposure of the class. Rates such as these applied to a class of individual insureds to reflect the loss exposures of the group are known as **class rates**. They are the most common kind of rates for private passenger auto insurance. Class rates are sometimes referred to as **manual rates** because they are usually published in rating manuals to make them readily available to agents, underwriters, and others who need frequent access.

For some other lines of property or liability insurance, a separate rate is determined for each policyholder. Such rates are sometimes called **individual rates** or **specific rates** to distinguish them from class rates. As a general rule, individual or specific rates are used in connection with lines of insurance for which (1) each policy produces enough premium to justify the added expense of developing specific rates and (2) the loss exposures are so varied that risk classification within the line is difficult or impossible. Class rates, on the other hand, are used in connection with lines of insurance for which the policyholders can be classified into groups with reasonably homogeneous loss exposures.

Merit rating is an intermediate step between class rates and individual or specific rates. Under most merit rating plans, the premium for a particular policyholder is first calculated by the use of class rates and then modified upward or downward to reflect one or more characteristics of the policyholder that affect the policyholder's loss exposures. The characteristics for which merit rating plans reduce or increase rates include past loss experience, loss control measures adopted by the policyholder, and other similar factors.

Territorial Rating

In Everstable, driving conditions and laws were uniform throughout the kingdom. Elsewhere, the area where the vehicle is driven may be a factor in determining insurance rates. Accident rates may vary from one place to another for many reasons. Among them are differences in traffic density, climate, road construction and maintenance, and law enforcement.

To provide an equitable distribution of insurance costs, states are divided into several rating territories, based primarily on loss experience. Urban areas usually have higher rates than rural areas for most auto insurance lines because the greater traffic density in urban areas results in more accidents. Also, the cost of medical treatment and car repairs is likely to be higher in urban areas.

The primary goal of both risk classification and territorial rating is an equitable allocation of insurance costs among the various groups that buy insurance. Failure to recognize these differences among groups of policyholders results in some insurance buyers' paying more than their fair share of insurance costs, while others pay less.

Credibility

As noted above, insured auto losses vary over time as a result of inflation, traffic density, law changes, and other identifiable, time-dependent changes in the insurance environment. They may also change because of pure chance. Trending is used to adjust past data to future conditions by reflecting projected changes in time-dependent environmental conditions. However, some reasonably stable, identifiable rate of change must exist for trending to work properly. If inflation has been causing losses to increase at 4 percent each year, that rate of increase can be projected into the future in the absence of any indication that it will change.

Chance variations, on the other hand, may cause losses to rise sharply in one year and fall sharply the next. Such random changes cannot be projected reliably into the future. Consequently, actuaries have developed a process for moderating the variations in rates that would otherwise result from purely chance variations in losses.

An essential element in this process is the **law of large numbers.** Stated in insurance terminology, the law of large numbers says that all other things being equal, the accuracy of loss forecasts improves as the number of exposure units in the database increases. In other words, the amount of confidence an auto insurance actuary has in the projected losses (and the resulting rates) increases as the number of insured vehicles increases. The confidence level is known to actuaries as **credibility**. Credibility factors vary from zero (no confidence at all) to one (full confidence).

Chapter 11 will discuss credibility in more detail. For the present, note that credibility factors are used to dampen variations in rates that result from purely chance variations in losses. One simple way of applying credibility is to multiply the projected rate change by the credibility factor. For example, if the credibility factor is .30 and the data indicate that a rate increase of 10 percent is needed, a rate increase of 3.0 percent (10 × .30) would be taken. The same approach would be used for rate reductions so that rates would be stabilized over time.

Additional Concepts

Two fundamental concepts of insurance ratemaking are written premiums and earned premiums. The **written premiums** for a period consist of all of the premiums for policies and endorsements recorded on the company's books during the period. The **earned premiums** for the period consist of the premiums used to pay for protection actually provided during the period. For example, assume that a company writes only one policy during the year, a one-year policy with an annual premium of $100 written on October 1. The written premium for the year would be $100, the entire premium for the policy. The earned premium for the year would be $25, since only three months of protection would be provided during the year. The remaining $75 of premium for the policy would be earned in the next year. The $75 not earned by December 31 would be shown on the company's year-end balance sheet as a liability called the **unearned premium reserve**.

Similar concepts apply to losses. Incurred losses for a period consist of all losses arising from insured events that happened during the period. **Paid losses** for a period consist of all losses for which checks or drafts were issued during the period. Some of the paid losses may also have been incurred during the period, while others may have been incurred in earlier periods. The loss reserve on a given date consists of all amounts the insurer expects to pay in the future for losses incurred in the past.

The concept of **earned exposure unit** is also important in ratemaking. An exposure unit is a measure of the loss exposure assumed by an insurer. For auto insurance, the most common exposure unit is a car-year. A car-year can consist of one car insured for one year, two cars insured for six months each, four cars insured for three months each, and so forth.

If ten auto policies, each covering one car for one year, are written on October 1, the written exposure units would be ten car-years. On the following December 31, the earned exposure units under the ten policies would be 2.5 car years, ten cars insured for 0.25 years each. Different lines of insurance use relevant exposure units. For example, workers compensation uses $100 of payroll, as do some general liability classes. Other lines of insurance use sales, square footage, or some other measure of exposure.

A loss ratio is calculated by dividing premiums into losses. Since there are two kinds of losses (paid and incurred) and two kinds of premiums (written and earned), four different loss ratios are possible. However, the one that is most useful for ratemaking purposes is the incurred-earned loss ratio, which is calculated by dividing earned premiums into incurred losses. The incurred-earned loss ratio is the most appropriate loss ratio for ratemaking purposes because it provides the closest match between losses and the premiums which that intended to cover them.

This point can be illustrated by examining an extreme case—professional liability insurance for physicians and surgeons. Historical data indicate that less than 2 percent of losses for that line, when measured by dollar amount, are paid in the same year in which the related malpractice events occurred. Or to state it differently, over 98 percent of the losses paid in any given year were incurred in some earlier year. On the other hand, about half of the premiums written in any given year will be used to pay for insurance actually provided in the following year. Consequently, a paid-written loss ratio for this line of insurance would be comparing losses that happened in the past to premiums for the future. The incurred-earned loss ratio, in contrast, would compare losses and premiums for the same period.

Ratemaking Methods

There are three approaches to ratemaking:

1. Judgment method
2. Loss ratio method
3. Pure premium method

Judgment Method

The **judgment method** is the oldest of the three and is still used for some lines of insurance. In this method, the underwriter selects a rate on the basis of his or her experience and judgment. Little or no statistical information is used in the process. The judgment method is still used for ocean marine insurance, some inland marine lines, and aviation insurance. In general, it must be used if sufficient statistical information cannot be found to apply the other methods.

Loss Ratio Method

The **loss ratio method** of ratemaking is a method for adjusting an existing rate either upward or downward to reflect changing conditions. In its simplest form, the loss ratio method involves comparing two loss ratios—the actual loss ratio and the expected loss ratio. The actual loss ratio is the incurred-earned loss ratio achieved by the insurer during the selected experience period. The expected loss ratio is the loss ratio that the insurer would need in order to achieve its profit objectives. It is found by subtracting the insurer's expense loading (including a profit allowance) from 100 percent. For example, an insurer with an expense loading (sometimes called an expense ratio) of 40 percent would have an expected (or permissible) loss ratio of 60 percent. The expected loss ratio and the expense loading always sum to 100 percent.

In its simplest form, the loss ratio method is represented by the following equation:

$$\text{Percentage rate change} = (A - E)/E$$

where A = actual loss ratio, and E = expected loss ratio. If the answer is negative, it indicates a percentage rate reduction. If positive, it indicates a rate increase. For example, if A = 54 percent, and E = 60 percent, the answer would be –0.10, indicating a rate reduction of 10 percent.

The loss ratio method cannot be used to calculate rates for a new line of insurance because there would not be an actual loss ratio for the calculation or an old rate to adjust. For a new line of insurance, either the judgment method or the pure premium method must be used.

Pure Premium Method

The **pure premium method** of ratemaking, in its simplest form, involves three steps: (1) calculating the pure premium, (2) calculating the expense loading, and (3) combining the pure premium and the expense loading into the gross rate.

The pure premium is the amount needed for each exposure unit for the payment of losses incurred. Loss adjustment expenses are frequently included in the pure premium, but they may be included in the expense loading instead. The pure premium is calculated by dividing the number of earned exposure units into the dollar amount of incurred losses. For example, if an insurer has 100,000 earned car-years and $4 million of incurred losses, including loss adjustment expenses, the pure premium would be $40 per car-year.

The expense loading, which usually includes a factor for profit and contingencies, is based on the insurer's past expenses. It includes an allowance for all of the insurer's expenses except investment expenses and possibly loss adjustment expenses. If loss adjustment expenses are included in the pure premium, they are excluded from the expense loading. Investment expenses are deducted from investment income and are not directly reflected in rate calculations.

Traditionally, the expense loading for property-liability insurance has been stated as a percentage of the gross rate. Consequently, it cannot be added directly to the pure premium. The two must be combined by a simple algebraic formula. The formula can be derived as follows:

$$G = P + (L \times G)$$

where G = gross premium, P = pure premium, and L = expense loading.

Subtracting (L × G) from both sides of the above equation yields:

$$G - (L \times G) = P$$

or

$$(1 - L)G = P$$

dividing both sides by (1 – L) yields:

$$G = \frac{P}{(1 - L)}$$

This final form of the equation indicates that the gross premium is calculated by dividing the pure premium by one minus the expense loading

A pure premium of $40 and an expense loading equal to 20 percent of gross premium yield a gross premium of $50. The calculation is as follows:

$$G = \frac{\$40}{1 - .20} = \frac{\$40}{.80} = \$50$$

Some insurers separated their expense loadings into two components: fixed expenses and variable expenses. Fixed expenses are stated as a dollar amount per exposure unit. Variable expenses are stated as a percentage of the gross rate. For example, the insurer in the above illustration might decide that its cost for issuing a policy and collecting the premium is $2.50 per car-year, which does not vary with the size of the premium, the rating class, or the rating territory. Its other underwriting expenses vary with the size of the premium, and the total of such expenses equals 15 percent of gross premium.

Based on these assumptions, its gross premium would be calculated by the formula:

$$G = \frac{P + F}{(1 - V)}$$

where F = dollar amount of fixed expenses, V = percentage of variable expenses, and the other symbols have the meanings previously assigned to them. Substituting the above numerical values yields the following gross rate:

$$G = \frac{\$40 + 2.50}{1 - .15} = \frac{\$42.50}{.85} = \$50$$

In this example, both the percentage loading and the loading separated into fixed and variable expenses resulted in the same gross rate. That usually is not the case. A percentage loading results in policyholders in higher-rated classes and higher-rated territories paying more of the insurer's expenses than policyholders in lower-rated classes and territories. If some of the insurer's expenses do not vary with premiums, policyholders in the higher-rated classes and territories will be paying more than their fair share of the cost of insurance. Adopting a fixed/variable expense loading may result in a more equitable allocation of expenses.

Investment Income in Ratemaking

A property-liability insurer operates two businesses. The insurance business writes policies, collects premiums, and pays losses. The investment business uses the funds generated by the insurance business to buy bonds, stocks, and other investment vehicles to earn an investment profit. Investment profits are derived from three sources: investment income, realized capital gains, and unrealized capital gains. **Investment income** consists of interest, dividends, rents, and similar regular income received from the invested assets held by the company. Investment income is the most stable source of income for most insurance companies.

Realized capital gains occur when an insurer sells an asset for more than its cost. If an asset is sold for less than its cost, a **realized capital loss** results.

An **unrealized capital gain** results when the market price of an asset exceeds its cost and the insurer continues to hold the asset. If the market price of an asset falls below its cost and the insurer continues to hold the asset, an **unrealized capital loss** results. An example of these sources of investment income is shown in Exhibit 10-5.

Exhibit 10-5
Investment Income

On January 1, Insurance Company bought 1,000 shares of Publicly Held Corporation stock for $100 per share for a total cost of $100,000. During the year that followed, Publicly Held paid Insurance Company $5,000 in dividends on the stock. On December 30, the Publicly Held stock was quoted on the stock exchange at $160 per share, for a total market value of $160,000. On December 31, Insurance Company sold the stock for $160,000. Insurance Company's investment income for the year would be $5,000, the amount of the dividends.

On December 30, it had an unrealized capital gain of $60,000, the difference between the cost and the market value of the stock. On December 31, when it sold the stock, Insurance Company converted its unrealized capital gain to a realized capital gain.

Traditionally, property-liability insurers did not consider their investment profits directly in the calculation of insurance rates, though they may have considered investment profits informally in determining the allowance for profits and contingencies in the rates.

Recently, it has become more common to consider investment profits explicitly in the rate calculation. Some states now require the explicit consideration of investment income. Fewer require the explicit consideration of capital gains, mostly realized capital gains. One method for reflecting investment profits in ratemaking is to estimate the amount of investment profits to be realized on the line of insurance and deduct that amount from the expense loading used in the rates. For example, if an insurer's expenses are expected to be 30 percent of the gross rate and its investment profit is expected to be 5 percent of earned premiums, it would include an expense loading of 25 percent in its rates.

The amount of investment profit earned on a line of insurance depends largely on the loss reserves and unearned premium reserves generated. Consequently, including investment profits in ratemaking is likely to affect liability insurance rates more than property insurance rates.

Rate Regulation

The ratemaking process is not entirely mathematical. Actuaries must also be cognizant of government regulation. All states regulate insurance rates to some degree, with some imposing more stringent regulations than others.

Statutory Standards

All of the states impose three standards by which rates are judged, but the methods of applying those standards vary among the states. The three standards require that a rate be (1) adequate, (2) not excessive, and (3) not unfairly discriminatory.

A rate is considered adequate if it is sufficient to cover the probable losses and expenses of the insured. Most insurers would prefer to have something left for profits as well, but the statutory standard usually does not require a profit.

A rate is usually considered not excessive if it does not generate an unreasonable profit for the insurer. There has been much debate in recent years about what constitutes an unreasonable profit.

A rate is considered not unfairly discriminatory if it equitably reflects the expected loss and expenses of the policyholder to whom it applies. Under this standard, to knowingly overcharge one policyholder and undercharge another would be unlawful.

Administration

Although all the states apply the same three standards for regulating insurance rates, there is a wide variation in the administration of the standards. The methods of administration used in the various states can be classified into the following five categories:

1. State-made rates
2. Mandatory bureau membership
3. Prior approval
4. File and use
5. No filing required

State-Made Rates

Massachusetts calculates the rates for compulsory automobile insurance coverages in that state. All insurers that write automobile insurance in that state must use the rates determined by the state. The only way they can compete on the basis of price is to pay dividends to policyholders. Texas follows a similar procedure for several lines of property-liability insurance.

Mandatory Bureau Membership

Several states have statutory rating bureaus for one or more lines of insurance. The statutory rating bureaus were created by state law but are owned and managed by insurance companies. They collect data from their member companies and calculate rates based on the data. All insurers that write the lines of insurance under the jurisdiction of the statutory rating bureaus are usually required by law to be members of the bureau and to use the bureau rates.

Prior Approval Laws

About half of the states have prior approval rate regulatory laws. Under a **prior approval law**, an insurer must file its rates with state regulatory authorities and receive formal approval of the rates from the regulatory authorities before the rates can be used. In some states, prior approval laws include so-called "deemer provisions," which provide that if the authorities fail either to approve or disapprove the rates within some specified period, such as forty-five days, the rates will be deemed to be approved.

File-and-Use Laws

Almost half of the states have **file-and-use laws**. Under these laws, an insurer must file its rates with the authorities before they are used, but it need not obtain approval before use. However, regulatory authorities can order the insurer to stop using the rates if they find that the rates fail to meet statutory requirements. A variation of this category is the **use-and-file law**, under which an insurer can begin using rates before they are filed but must file them within some specified period, such as fifteen days, after they are first used.

No-File Laws

The most liberal of the rate regulatory laws are the no-file laws. Under these laws, rates are not required to be filed with the state on a regular basis. However, regulatory authorities may require the insurer to provide data to support the rates if they have reason to believe that the rates do not comply with statutory requirements. Historically, California was the most notable of the no-file states. Proposition 103, adopted in 1988, converted California to a prior approval state beginning in 1991. The term "open competition law" is sometimes used to refer to no-file, file-and-use, and use-and-file laws, either individually or collectively.

There has been much discussion as to which category of rate regulation is most favorable to consumers and which is most favorable to insurers. To date, no credible evidence has been produced to show any great advantage of one type of regulation over the others for either consumers or insurers. However, the debate continues with unabated furor, and states frequently change from one regulatory form to another.

Summary

An actuary is a person trained to use mathematical techniques to solve problems related to insurer management. The two most prominent actuarial functions for property-liability insurers are ratemaking and verifying loss reserves. This chapter primarily introduced the principles of ratemaking.

Insurance ratemaking would be very simple if all insured persons and all loss exposures were identical and unchanging. The complexities of real-world ratemaking processes arise from having to cope with variations in policyholders and loss exposures and time-related changes in the insurance environment.

There are three methods of determining insurance rates. The judgment method relies heavily on the knowledge and experience of an actuary or an underwriter, with little or no use of statistics. The loss ratio method determines a new rate by modifying an old rate, using a comparison of actual and expected loss ratios. The pure premium method involves calculating a pure premium, the amount needed to pay losses, to which an expense loading is added.

The ratemaking process is further complicated by the regulatory requirements of the various states. Rate regulation in all states is based on the statutory requirements that rates must be adequate, not excessive, and not unfairly discriminatory. However, the methods used to administer these basic requirements vary from the relatively liberal no-file laws to relatively rigid state-made rates. It is not unusual for a state to change from one form of rate regulation to another.

Glossary

AAA—See American Academy of Actuaries.

ACAS—See Casualty Actuarial Society.

Actuary—A person trained in the use of mathematical techniques for the solution of problems related to insurance.

Advisory Organization—An organization owned and controlled by insurance companies and providing services to its members and subscribers. The services provided include actuarial services. Advisory organizations are sometimes called rating bureaus.

American Academy of Actuaries—A professional society for actuaries, including actuaries who specialize in pension plans, life insurance, health insurance, and property-liability insurance. Members of the Academy are entitled to use the initials MAAA after their names.

Car-Year—One car insured for one year. It is a common exposure unit used in connection with automobile insurance.

Casualty Actuarial Society (CAS)—The professional society of actuaries who specialize in property-liability insurance. It has two levels of membership. Associate of the Casualty Actuarial Society (ACAS) is the entry level of membership. Fellow of the Casualty Actuarial Society (FCAS) is the senior level of membership.

Class Rate—A rate that applies without modification to all members of a group (or class) of policyholders. See Risk Classification.

Credibility—The level of confidence that an actuary has in the available data as an indicator of future losses. A mathematical procedure for smoothing variations in rates resulting from purely random variations in losses.

Earned Exposure Units—The number of exposure units for which a full year of coverage has been provided. For example, three exposure units insured for four months each would equal one earned exposure unit.

Earned Premiums—The premium for coverage actually provided during a period. See also Written Premiums and Unearned Premium Reserve.

Expense Loading—The amount included in a rate to cover the insurer's expenses. It does not include investment expenses and may not include loss adjustment expenses. The expense loading may be stated as a dollar amount, a percentage of the gross rate, or a combination of the two.

Experience Period—The period of time for which loss, premium, and exposure unit data are gathered for ratemaking purposes.

Exposure Unit—A measure of the loss exposure assumed by an insurer. For example, a car-year in automobile insurance. See also Insurance Premium and Insurance Rate.

FCAS—See Casualty Actuarial Society.

Gross Rate—The sum of the pure premium and the expense loading.

Incurred But Not Reported (IBNR) Losses—Losses that have occurred but have not yet been reported to the insurer. Insurers are required to establish reserves for such losses.

Incurred Losses—The losses arising from insured events that occurred during a specified period of time.

Individual Rate—See Specific Rate.

Insurance Premium—The consideration paid by the policyholder under an insurance contract or policy. The premium is usually calculated by multiplying a rate by the number of exposure units insured.

Insurance Rate—The price per unit of insurance. See also Insurance Premium.

Investment Income—Interest, dividends, rents, and similar income an insurer receives from its investment assets.

Judgment Method—A method for determining insurance rates. It relies heavily on the experience and knowledge of an actuary or an underwriter, with little or no use of statistics. See also Loss Ratio Method and Pure Premium Method.

Loss Development—A mathematical technique used in ratemaking to recognize consistent patterns over time in the accuracy of reserves established for reported losses and to provide for incurred but not reported losses.

Loss Ratio Method—A method for calculating insurance rates based on a comparison of actual and expected loss ratios. See also Pure Premium Method.

Loss Reserve—A liability on the balance sheet of an insurance company reflecting the insurer's obligation to make payments in the future for losses that occurred in the past.

MAAA—See American Academy of Actuaries.

Manual Rate—A rate printed in a manual, sometimes used as a synonym for class rate.

Merit Rating—A process for modifying a class rate, either upward or downward, to reflect characteristics of a particular policyholder that are expected to result in that policyholder's having losses greater than or less than the average losses for other members of the policyholder's rating class.

Premium—See Insurance Premium.

Premiums Earned—See Earned Premiums.

Premiums Written—See Written Premiums.

Pure Premium—The amount included in a rate for the payment of losses. It may also include loss adjustment expenses.

Pure Premium Method—A method for calculating insurance rates. A pure premium is first calculated, and an expense loading is added to it.

Rate—See Insurance Rate.

Rate Filing—A document containing a schedule of rates and rating plans, along with data and statistical analysis to show that the rates comply with statutory requirements. Rate filings are prepared for submission to (filing with) regulatory authorities.

Rating Bureau—See Advisory Organization.

Realized Capital Gain—The excess of the proceeds from the sale of an asset over its purchase price. Usually applied to an insurer's investment assets. See also Unrealized Capital Gain.

Realized Capital Loss—The excess of the purchase price of an asset over the proceeds from selling it. Usually applied to an insurer's investment assets. See also Realized Capital Gain.

Risk Classification—The process of categorizing insureds according to characteristics that affect their expected losses. See also Class Rate.

Specific Rate—A rate calculated to apply to only one policyholder. The opposite of Class Rate.

Territorial Rating—The categorization of policyholders by geographic location to reflect geographic variations in loss exposures.

Trending—A statistical technique for analyzing environmental changes, such as inflation, that affect insurance losses and projecting such changes into the future.

Unearned Premium Reserve—Premiums that have been written but not yet earned. A liability shown on an insurer's balance sheet. See also Earned Premiums and Written Premiums.

Unrealized Capital Gain—The excess of the current market price of an asset over its purchase price, with the asset not being sold. See also Realized Capital Gain.

Unrealized Capital Loss—The excess of the purchase price of an asset over its current market value, the asset not having been sold. See also Unrealized Capital Gain.

Written Exposure Units—The number of exposure units insured under all policies and endorsements issued during a period.

Written Premiums—The premiums entered on an insurer's books during a period. It includes premiums for policies and endorsements issued during the period along with premium audits and retrospective rating adjustments. See also Earned Premiums and Unearned Premium Reserve.

Chapter 11

The Ratemaking Process

Chapter 10 introduced a number of basic concepts in ratemaking for property-liability insurance. This chapter integrates those basic concepts into a demonstration of the ratemaking process. Some additional, more advanced concepts are also introduced. As in Chapter 10, private passenger automobile insurance is used to illustrate the process.

Development of Ratemaking Data

Rates for most lines of insurance, including private passenger auto insurance, are determined separately for each state. This practice is reflected in the terminology used in this chapter. However, the ratemaking process is generally the same for the few lines of insurance for which rates are calculated nationally.

Exhibit 11-1 shows the major steps in the ratemaking process. The insurer's own staff might perform the steps, or an advisory organization might perform some or all of them.

Exhibit 11-1
Steps in the Ratemaking Process

- Collect statistics.
- Adjust statistics.
- Calculate statewide average rate.
- Calculate territorial relativities.
- Calculate classification relativities.
- Prepare rate filing.
- Submit rate filing to regulatory authorities.
- Follow up to obtain necessary regulatory action.

Collection of Statistics

With the possible exception of the judgment method of ratemaking, the first step in the ratemaking process is to collect the ratemaking statistics. The first step in collecting statistics is to determine the kinds of statistics to collect and the form in which they will be collected.

For the loss ratio method, the statistics needed are incurred losses, earned premiums, and the expense loading. For the pure premium method, earned exposure units also are needed. If rates are to vary by rating class and territory, the statistics, with the possible exception of the expense ratio data, must be collected separately for each class and territory.

Ideally, the same group of insured entities should generate the incurred losses, earned premiums, and earned exposure units. In practice, such precise matching is not always practical, so approximation techniques are used.

Policy-Year Method

The only method for gathering statistics that provides an exact matching of losses, premiums, and exposure units to a specific group of insured entities is the policy-year method, sometimes called the policy-year statistical period. A **policy year** consists of all of the policies issued in a given twelve-month period, frequently a calendar year. When the policy-year method is used to gather statistics, all premium transactions attributable to a specific policy are directly tied to that policy. These would include the original premium along with additional premiums or return premiums resulting from premium audits, retrospective rating plans, policy changes, and similar transactions. Exposure units are calculated in a similar manner. Incurred losses and allocated loss adjustment expenses are also tied back to the policies under which they are covered. With such data collected, the actuary need only add up the earned premiums, exposure units, and incurred losses attributed to the specific group of policies in order to obtain policy-year statistics.

There are two major disadvantages to the policy-year method. First, and perhaps most important, it involves longer delays in gathering statistics than do the other two methods discussed below. Also, it involves some additional expense, since policy-year statistics are used only for ratemaking purposes. The statistics used in the other two methods are gathered, in part, as a byproduct of the company's accounting operations.

Delays are inherent in the policy-year method. For example, assume that the policy year begins on the first day of the calendar year. Then, the last policy in the policy year would be issued on the last day of the calendar year and, assuming one-year policies, would expire on the last day of the following calendar year. Thus, a policy year spans two calendar years.

These delays can be overcome in part by estimating the ultimate values of data for which final values are not yet available. However, potential errors in estimating such values reduce the "apples-to-apples" advantage of the policy-year method.

Historically, the additional cost of compiling policy-year statistics was a major disadvantage of that method. With the advent of computers, however, the extra cost of compiling policy-year statistics has become much less significant.

Calendar-Year Method

The oldest and least accurate method of collecting statistics for ratemaking purposes is the **calendar-year method**, sometimes called the calendar-year statistical period. This method does have two advantages, however. The statistics are available quickly, and there is very little expense involved in compiling them. These advantages stem from the fact that the calendar-year statistics are derived from data that must be compiled for accounting purposes.

An insurer's accounting records do not show incurred losses, earned premiums, or exposure units. Earned premiums must be estimated from written premiums and unearned premium reserves. The formula usually used for that estimation is as follows:

Earned premiums = Unearned premiums at the beginning of the year
+ Written premiums for the year
– Unearned premiums at the end of the year

This formula provides a reasonably accurate, but not exact, estimate of the actual earned premiums. The earned premiums may not be precisely matched to a specific group of insured entities because of additional premiums or refunds resulting from premium audits or retrospective rating plans on earlier policies, but these problems should be relatively small for most insurers.

Incurred losses must also be estimated by formula under the calendar-year method. The formula for that estimation is as follows:

Incurred losses = Loss reserves at the end of the year
+ Loss paid during the year
– Loss reserves at the beginning of the year

That formula may sometimes result in serious errors in estimating the true incurred losses, especially for liability lines. When the formula is used, the estimated incurred losses for a given year may be distorted by changes in loss reserves for losses that occurred in earlier years.

A simplified illustration may clarify the problem. Assume that at the beginning of 1998, Insurance Company had only one open claim. The claim arose from an accident that happened in 1996, and Insurance Company showed a reserve of $100,000 for it at the beginning of 1998. At the end of 1998, the claim was still open, and Insurance Company decided to increase the reserve to $500,000.

During 1998, Insurance Company sustained two additional claims arising from two accidents that happened during 1998. One of these two claims was settled during 1998 for $200,000. The other was still open at the end of 1998, and a reserve of $300,000 was carried for it. Thus, Insurance Company's actual incurred losses in 1998 were $500,000 for these two claims, but the formula shown above would indicate estimated incurred losses of $900,000. The calculation is as follows:

Loss reserve at the beginning of the year	$100,000
Paid losses during the year	200,000
Loss reserve at the end of the year	800,000

Incurred losses = $800,000 + $200,000 – $100,000
= $900,000

It is unlikely that the estimating error would be so large proportionately for an actual insurer. However, errors can be very substantial in lines of insurance for which there is a long delay in the payment of claims. Errors are not likely to be large for lines such as inland marine and auto physical damage, for which losses are paid rather quickly. For those lines, calendar-year statistics may be sufficiently accurate for practical purposes.

Insurer accounting records usually do not contain exposure unit data. Consequently, calendar-year statistics usually do not include exposure unit data and cannot be used alone in the pure premium ratemaking method. Of course, exposure unit information can be collected separately from the usual accounting data if desired.

Accident-Year Method

The **accident-year method** of gathering statistics (or the calendar-accident year method) is a compromise between the policy-year method and the calendar-year method. It achieves much of the accuracy of the policy-year method while preserving most of the economy and speed of the calendar-year method.

Earned premiums for the accident-year method are calculated in the same way as for the calendar-year method. The only difference between the two methods is in the calculation of incurred losses.

In the accident-year method, incurred losses for a given period consist of all losses and claims arising from insured events that occur during the period. The claims may be either open or closed, but if they arose from an insured event that occurred during the period under consideration, they are included in incurred losses for that period.

Since incurred losses under this method consist only of claims arising from insured events that occur during the period, they are not affected by changes in reserves for events that occurred in earlier periods. Thus, the accident-year method avoids the largest source of error inherent in the calendar-year method.

However, neither earned premiums nor incurred losses are tied as directly to a specific group of policyholders under the accident-year method as they are under the policy-year method. The accident-year statistics are slightly more expensive to compile than calendar-year statistics, since accounting records do not distinguish between insured events that occurred during the period under consideration and those that occurred earlier.

Exhibit 11-2 illustrates several claims, indicating how each would be classified under the three methods of gathering statistics. All policies in Exhibit 11-2 are one-year policies. Each claim is assigned to only one year under both the policy-year and accident-year methods, though the year may not be the same for both methods.

The calendar-year method can result in parts of a single claim being included in several years, depending on the timing of loss reserve changes and the difference, if any, between the final reserve and the loss payment. These peculiar results under the calendar-year method make that method unsuitable

Exhibit 11-2
Illustrative Examples of Calendar-Year, Accident-Year, and Policy-Year Statistics—Hypothetical Data

(1) Claim Number	(2) Date of Occurrence	(3) Policy[1] Effective Date	(4) Date Claim Reported	(5) Original Loss Reserve	(6) Change in Reserve	(7) Date of Reserve Change	(8) Amount Paid to Close	(9) Date Paid	(10) Policy[2] Year	(11) Accident[3] Year	(12) Calendar[4] Year	(13) Calendar Year Reserve
1	7-1-96	1-1-96	2-1-97	$100,000	—	—	$100,000	6-3-98	1996	1996	1997	
2	11-1-97	12-15-96	1-1-98	200,000	—	—	200,000	9-1-99	1996	1997	1998	
3	10-3-96	2-4-96	12-20-96	100,000	+$200,000	3-1-98	300,000	4-6-99	1996	1996	1996	$100,000
											1998	200,000
4	9-13-96	2-2-96	3-14-97	50,000	+100,000	4-4-98	300,000	5-3-99	1996	1996	1997	50,000
											1998	100,000
											1999	150,000
5	12-1-97	12-15-96	1-10-98	100,000	–50,000	3-1-99	150,000	2-1-00	1996	1997	1998	100,000
											1999	–50,000
											2000	100,000

1. All policies are for one-year terms.
2. The year to which the loss would be charged under the policy-year method.
3. The year to which the claim would be charged under the accident-year method.
4. The year or years to which the claim would be charged under the calendar-year method.

for collecting ratemaking statistics for liability and workers compensation insurance, for which the delay in loss payment may be long and the loss reserves may be large relative to earned premiums. For those lines of insurance, either the policy-year or accident-year method should be used.

For some other lines of insurance, such as fire, inland marine, and auto physical damage, losses are paid quickly, and loss reserves tend to be small relative to earned premiums. For those lines, the calendar-year method may be satisfactory for ratemaking purposes, though still less accurate than the other two methods.

An insurer should decide which statistical method it will use early in its existence, preferably before it issues its first policy. The alternative is to adopt a statistical plan that is sufficiently flexible to permit the use of several statistical methods. Policy information is collected most conveniently when policies, endorsements, and invoices are issued. Claims statistics are collected when claims are reported, reserves are changed, checks or drafts are issued, or claims are closed. Each insurer must have a statistical plan to inform personnel about the statistics to be collected and the methods to be used for coding the data for computer compilation. Various advisory organizations provide such statistical plans, but some insurers may choose to develop or adopt statistical plans that collect more data than the advisory organizations require.

Adjustment of Statistics

The raw data, as initially collected, are not suitable for determining the adequacy of current rates or as a basis for calculating revised rates. The raw loss data reflect conditions from present and past periods, while the rates being developed will be used in the future. Also, the premiums in the raw data may have been written at several rate levels. Consequently, the actuary must adjust loss data and premium data to make a useful evaluation. In addition, the actuary must adjust the raw loss data to reflect systematic errors, if any, in the estimation of loss reserves. These adjustments are discussed below.

Loss Development Factors

Calculating the loss development factors is the first step in adjusting loss data. The purpose of loss development factors is to adjust the reported loss (paid losses plus unpaid loss reserves) data to correct for systematic errors in the estimation of reserves for unpaid losses.

Loss development factors are usually calculated through the use of a table of successive estimates of reported losses. Exhibit 11-3 shows such a table, using hypothetical data. Because of the shape of the table, it is sometimes called a **loss triangle**.

Exhibit 11-3
Reported Losses (000s omitted)

(1)	(2)	(3)	(4)	(5)	(6)
		Months of Development			
Accident Year	12	24	36	48	Final 60
1	10,000	11,000	12,000	11,500	11,000
2	9,000	10,500	11,000	10,750	
3	10,500	12,000	12,000		
4	9,750	11,000			
5	10,250				

Percentage Development
Months of Development

	12-24	24-36	36-48	49-60
1	1.100	1.091	0.958	0.957
2	1.167	1.048	0.977	
3	1.143	1.000		
4	1.128			
5	—			
Average	1.135	1.046	0.968	0.957

One-year loss development factor = 0.957
Two-year loss development factor = 0.968 × 0.957 = 0.926
Three-year loss development factor = 1.046 × 0.968 × 0.957 = 0.969
Four-year loss development factor = 1.135 × 1.046 × 0.968 × 0.957 = 1.100

Each line in the top table in Exhibit 11-3 shows successive estimates of reported losses for a different year. Year 1 is the oldest year in the table, and year 5 is the most recent year. Column (2) shows the company's estimate of its reported losses after twelve months of development. Assuming that the experience period is a calendar year, the losses would be considered to be twelve-months developed on December 31 of the year in which they occurred. Column (3) shows the company's revised estimate at twenty-four months of development. Column (6) shows the actual losses reported at sixty months of development. The incurred losses are assumed to be known accurately at that point. Only year 1 has matured to sixty months. The other years are too immature, with year 5 having developed only to twelve months.

The figures in the second table in Exhibit 11-3 are calculated from the data in the first table. They show the percentage change in reported losses from one period to the next. For example, for year 1, the reported losses increased 10 percent from twelve months of development to twenty-four months of development. An additional 9.1 percent increase occurred from twenty-four months to thirty-six months. After that, the estimate decreased each period.

The bottom line, labeled "Average" in the second table of Exhibit 11-3, shows the arithmetic average of the numbers above it in that table. That is, it shows the average change during the period for all years for which data are available. For this example, these averages will be used directly to calculate the loss development factors.

In practice, an actuary might make some modifications to the averages to reflect changing circumstances. For example, the claims department might have changed its reserving methods so that the past statistics are not a good indication of current reserve accuracy. Such adjustments are based largely on judgment.

The loss development factors to be used in this chapter are shown below the tables in Exhibit 11-3. The method used to calculate them is also shown.

Exhibit 11-4 shows the developed losses for the five-year period shown in Exhibit 11-3. No adjustment is made to the losses from year 1, which are assumed to be fully mature. The losses for year 2 are twelve months from maturity, so the one-year loss development factor is applied to them. Losses for year 5 are four years from maturity, so the four-year development factor is used to adjust them. The losses from the other two years are similarly adjusted.

Exhibit 11-4
Developed Losses

Year	(1) Reported Losses[1]	(2) Loss Development Factors[2]	(3) Developed Losses[3]
1	$11,000,000	1.000	$11,000,000
2	10,750,000	0.957	10,287,750
3	12,000,000	0.926	11,112,000
4	11,000,000	0.969	10,659,000
5	10,250,000	1.100	11,275,000
Totals	$55,000,000		$54,333,750

1. From Exhibit 11-3
2. From Exhibit 11-3
3. (3) = (1) × (2)

In this example, the developed losses are less than the reported losses both in total and for some individual years. However, that would not always be the case. Developed losses could be either more or less than reported losses, depending on the insurer's past record in estimating loss reserves. If loss reserves have been consistently underestimated in the past, developed losses will be higher than reported losses. If loss reserves have been consistently overestimated in the past, developed losses will be lower than reported losses.

The loss development factors calculated above were for the dollar amount of losses. Development factors can be derived in the same manner for the number of claims.

Exhibit 11-5 shows for each year the developed number of claims, the developed amount of losses, and the average amount per claim severity.

Exhibit 11-5
Developed Losses and Developed Claims

(1) Year	(2) Developed Losses	(3) Developed Number of Claims[1]	(4) Average Claim
1	$11,000,000	9,167	$1,200
2	10,287,750	7,913	1,300
3	11,112,000	7,880	1,410
4	10,659,000	6,995	1,524
5	11,275,000	6,860	1,644
Totals	$54,333,750	38,815	$1,400[2]

1. The developed number of claims in Column (3) would be derived through the use of loss triangles similar to those in Exhibit 11-3, using number of claims instead of loss amounts. The process is not illustrated in this chapter.
2. This is a weighted average of the amount of claims, using the number of claims as weights. Alternatively, it can be calculated by dividing the total number of claims (38,815) into the total amount of losses ($54,333,750).

Trending

Loss development is an attempt to correct for errors in reporting past losses and to estimate the ultimate settlement value of reported losses. An estimate of losses for a future period is needed for ratemaking purposes. The purpose of trending is to adjust the developed losses from the experience period to reflect conditions that are expected to exist in a future period. As currently practiced in the U.S. insurance industry, the adjustment is made by projecting past trends into the future.

An examination of Exhibit 11-5 shows that severity (the average amount of claims) was on an upward trend during the experience period. At first glance, it appears that claims frequency was on a downward trend, since the total number of claims decreased substantially during the period. However, as shown in Exhibit 11-6, the decrease in the number of claims resulted from a decline in earned exposure units over the period. The actual claims frequency, measured in claims per 100 earned car-years, actually rose slightly, from 2.00 to 2.11.

Exhibit 11-6
Calculation of Claims Frequency

(1) Year	(2) Developed Number of Claims	(3) Earned Car-Years	(4) Frequency[1]
1	9,167	458,350	2.00
2	7,913	386,000	2.05
3	7,880	380,676	2.07
4	6,995	333,095	2.10
5	6,860	325,118	2.11
Totals	38,815	1,883,239	2.06[2]

1. Claims per 100 earned car-years
   (4) = (2) ÷ [(3) ÷ 100]
2. Average frequency

A statistical technique known as least-squares regression is frequently used to project these trends into the future. Two methods of trending are in general use in the United States: linear trending and exponential trending.

Linear Trending

Linear trending assumes that the statistical series being trended will increase or decrease by a fixed amount each year. For example, frequency will increase by a fixed number of claims per unit, and severity (the average amount of claims) will increase by a fixed number of dollars each year.

Exponential Trending

Exponential trending assumes that the statistical series being projected will increase or decrease by a fixed percentage, rather than a fixed amount each year. Exponential trending will result in higher projected losses than linear trending in virtually all cases. Consequently, it will result in higher insurance rates in virtually all cases, all other things being equal. The differences can be substantial.

The choice between the two methods should be based on either theoretical grounds or observation of the trend indicated by the data to be projected. If the data series seems to be increasing or decreasing in a straight line, linear trending is recommended. If the rate of change appears to be accelerating, exponential trending may be appropriate.

Some theoretical basis exists for using exponential trending for claims severity. Inflation, which is an exponential process, is a major factor in increasing severity. However, there is generally little theoretical basis for using exponential trending for claims frequency. Its use for frequency should be supported by empirical data.

A detailed explanation of the mathematics of trending is beyond the scope of this chapter. Exhibit 11-7 shows the results of applying both linear and exponential trending to the frequency and severity figures from Exhibits 11-5 and 11-6. Both the frequency data and the severity data have been restated in Exhibit 11-7 to show twenty moving twelve-month periods, one ending each quarter, in lieu of the five annual periods shown in earlier tables. This is a common practice in trending calculations. The increased number of data points improves the reliability of the calculations. Also, the moving-average presentation of data helps to smooth chance variations in data, making the true trend more apparent.

Exponential trending produces both higher frequency and higher severity in comparison with linear trending. This is usually the case, but linear trending may produce higher results in some rare instances.

The data from Exhibit 11-7 can be used to adjust the developed aggregate loss data to the levels anticipated during year 7, the year when the new rates will be used. The midpoint of the experience period for which data were collected is 6/30/3, and the midpoint of the year in which the rates will be used is 6/30/7. Consequently, the developed loss data must be projected, on the average, four years (or sixteen quarters) in the trending process. Projected frequency and severity were calculated using least-squares regression. The details of these calculations are beyond the scope of this text.

The projected frequency figures in Exhibit 11-7 show that the frequency for any data point is found by multiplying the preceding frequency by 1.0031. The comparable multiplier for severity (average claim) is 1.0202. Since aggregate claims result from both frequency and severity, a combined trend factor can be

Exhibit 11-7
Trending Results: Frequency and Severity

12-Month Period	Actual Frequency	Actual Severity
3/31/1	1.98	$1,125
6/30/1	1.97	1,175
9/30/1	2.02	1,195
12/31/1	2.00	1,200
3/31/2	2.04	1,210
6/30/2	2.02	1,290
9/30/2	2.06	1,275
12/31/2	2.05	1,300
3/31/3	2.03	1,295
6/30/3	2.06	1,325
9/30/3	2.08	1,400
12/31/3	2.07	1,410
3/31/4	2.11	1,420
6/30/4	2.08	1,405
9/30/4	2.07	1,490
12/31/4	2.10	1,530
3/31/5	2.09	1,560
6/30/5	2.08	1,620
9/30/5	2.10	1,670
12/31/5	2.11	1,660

	Projected Frequency		Projected Severity	
	Linear	Exponential	Linear	Exponential
3/31/6	2.123	2.124	1668.95	1688.76
6/30/6	2.129	2.131	1696.68	1722.87
9/30/6	2.135	2.138	1724.41	1757.67
12/31/6	2.141	2.145	1752.15	1793.17
3/31/7	2.147	2.152	1779.88	1829.39
6/30/7	2.153	2.159	1807.61	1866.34
9/30/7	2.159	2.166	1835.34	1904.04
12/31/7	2.165	2.173	1863.07	1942.50

found by multiplying the two together. That combined factor is 1.023 (1.0031 × 1.0202), rounded to three decimal places. This indicates that aggregate losses increase by 2.3 percent each quarter, on the average. Consequently, the percentage increase for sixteen quarters would be found by raising 1.023 to the sixteenth power. That increase is 1.439 (1.023^{16}), rounded to three decimal points. If the developed aggregate losses of $54,333,750 from the bottom of Column (2) in Exhibit 11-5 are multiplied by 1.439, the product is the developed and trended losses at year 7 levels, or $78,186,266.

Dividing the earned car years (1,883,239) from Exhibit 11-6 into the developed and trended losses yields the estimated statewide average pure premium of $41.52 for year 7. An expense loading must be added to arrive at the gross rate.

The insurer for which these rates are being calculated has the following underwriting expenses, all stated as a percentage of the gross rate:

Commissions and brokerage	15.0%
Other acquisition	1.0
General administration	5.0
Taxes, licenses, and fees	2.0
Profit and contingencies	2.0
Total	25.0%

In this example, loss adjustment expenses are included with losses. The gross rate follows:

$$\text{Gross rate} = \frac{\text{Pure premium}}{1 - \text{Expense ratio}} = \frac{41.52}{1 - .25} = \frac{41.52}{.75} = \$55.36$$

This is the **statewide average rate**, which is used as the basis for calculating rates for various territories and rating classes. However, before proceeding to those calculations, the statewide average rate is again calculated, using the loss ratio method. Only one of the two methods would be used in an actual rate filing. Both are used here for instructional purposes.

In order to use the loss ratio method, premium data are required. Exhibit 11-8 shows such data, along with the raw reported loss data, loss ratios, and statewide average rates for each year. The statewide average rate for year 6, the year during which the rates are being calculated for year 7, has remained at $44.63, the same as for year 4 and year 5.

Although Exhibit 11-8 shows premiums, losses, and loss ratios for the experience period, those figures need to be adjusted before they are used in the formula for the loss ratio method. A new loss ratio will be calculated for use as the actual loss ratio in that formula. The losses used in that ratio will be the developed and trended losses as calculated above in the pure premium method, $78,186,266.

Exhibit 11-8
Data for Loss Ratio Method (000s omitted)

(1) Year	(2) Premiums Earned	(3) Reported Losses Incurred[1]	(4) Reported Loss Ratio	(5) Statewide Average Rate[2]
1	$14,286	$11,000	77%	$31.17
2	14,333	10,750	75	37.13
3	15,190	12,000	79	39.88
4	14,865	11,000	74	44.63
5	14,510	10,250	71	44.63
Totals	$73,184	$55,000	75%	$39.49

1. From Exhibit 11-4.
2. The statewide average rates were taken from prior rate filings.

The premiums in Exhibit 11-8 also cannot be used directly in the loss ratio method. The goal in ratemaking is to determine whether the present rates need to be changed, but the premiums in Exhibit 11-8 were based on several different rate levels used over time, not all on the current rate level. What is needed are premiums based on the *present* rate level, usually referred to in actuarial literature as "premiums on level" or "premiums on rate level." In this case, premiums on level are easy to calculate. The number of earned exposure units (1,883,239) and the current statewide average rate ($44.63) are known. Consequently, premiums on level can be determined by multiplying the two ($84,048,957). Therefore, the actual loss ratio is as follows:

$$\text{Actual loss ratio (A)} = \frac{78{,}186{,}266}{84{,}048{,}957} = .93 \text{ or } 93\%$$

Since the company has an expense ratio of 25 percent, its expected loss ratio is 75 percent. Given the loss ratio method formula from the preceding chapter, the rate modification factor is calculated as follows:

$$\text{Rate change} = \frac{A - E}{E} = \frac{.93 - .75}{.75} = \frac{.18}{.75} = .24 \text{ or } 24\%$$

Therefore, the new rate is $1.24 \times 44.63 =$ $55.34, which is virtually the same as the rate calculated by the pure premium. Actually, the two rates should be identical. The difference is due solely to rounding in the calculation.

It can be shown algebraically that the pure premium method and the loss ratio method are mathematically equivalent. However, the proof is beyond the scope of this chapter.

If earned exposure units were not available, as is frequently the case when the loss ratio method is used, the on-level adjustment of premiums would have been calculated by a different technique. Exhibit 11-9 and the paragraphs that follow illustrate that technique. Some simplifying assumptions have been made in this illustration to avoid undue complexity. These assumptions are (1) all rate filings are effective on January 1, and (2) all policies are one-year policies and are also effective on January 1. If these assumptions are not met, which is common, the technique would be somewhat more complex.

Exhibit 11-9
On-Level Premium Adjustment Using a Rate Level Index

(1) Year	(2) Reported Earned Premiums[1]	(3) Statewide Average Rate[2]	(4) Annual Rate Change[3]	(5) Rate Level Index	(6) Premiums on Level
1	$14,286,000	$31.17	—	1.431	$20,443,266
2	14,333,000	37.13	.191	1.202	17,228,266
3	15,190,000	39.88	.074	1.119	16,997,610
4	14,865,000	44.63	.119	1.000	14,865,000
5	14,510,000	44.63	.000	1.000	14,510,000
6	—	44.63	.000	1.000	—
Totals	$73,184.000				$84,044,142

1. From Exhibit 11-8.
2. No rate change occurred in year 5.
3. Statewide average rate year 2 ÷ Statewide average rate year 1, etc. – 1.

The purpose of this technique is to adjust reported earned premiums for all rate changes that occurred after the policies were written. The premiums for year 5 and year 6 did not require any adjustment, since there were no subsequent rate changes.

Column 4 of Exhibit 11-9 shows the annual rate changes, and Column 5 shows a rate change index computed from the annual rate changes. The rate change index for year 1 is calculated by $1.191 \times 1.074 \times 1.119 \times 1.000 \times 1.000 = 1.431$; for year 2, it is $1.074 \times 1.119 \times 1.000 \times 1.000 = 1.202$; and so forth. Multiplying the actual earned premium for each year by the index for that year yields the estimated earned premiums at the present rate level. In this case, this technique provides a result that is very close to the exact calculation using earned exposure units. This high level of accuracy results in part from the simplified assumptions used in this example.

Territorial Relativities

The next step in preparing a rate schedule is to determine territorial relativities. Insurers use several techniques for determining territorial relativities, including the much-used technique outlined here.

Exhibit 11-10 shows the basic data for this calculation. Three rating territories are in the state, and Exhibit 11-10 shows the data separately for each territory. Territorial relativities are calculated by comparing the estimated incurred loss ratio for each territory to the statewide average loss ratio. The earned premium figure used in the loss ratio is calculated on the basis of the statewide average rate currently in use, and not on the territorial rate now in use. In this instance, the premiums at statewide average rate level were calculated by multiplying the earned exposure units by the statewide average rate.

The initial territorial relativities are shown in Column (7) of Exhibit 11-10. Territory 3 is very small, with only 807 claims incurred during the experience period of Column (5). This is not a sufficient number of claims to give full confidence to the initial relativity. With that small number of claims, the loss experience could be expected to vary rather widely over time. To reduce chance variations in the relativity for territory 3, a credibility factor has been introduced into the calculation.

Exhibit 11-11 shows the table of credibility factors used for this purpose. There are many credibility tables, but the one shown here is frequently used for auto liability insurance. It is based on the Poisson distribution, a mathematical formula used extensively in actuarial calculations. The details of these calculations are beyond the scope of this chapter.

From Exhibit 11-11, the credibility factor for 807 claims is .80. Therefore, the modified relativity for territory 3 is calculated by the credibility-weighted formula, as follows:

$$\begin{aligned}\text{Credibility-weighted relativity} &= (Z \times A) + [(1 - Z) \times B] \\ &= (.80 \times .788) + (.20 \times 1.00) \\ &= .830\end{aligned}$$

where A = Initial relativity from Column (7) of Exhibit 11-10
Z = Credibility factor from Exhibit 11-11
B = Statewide average relativity

Exhibit 11-10
Calculation of Territorial Relativities

(1) Terr.	(2) Developed and Trended Losses	(3) Premiums[1] on Level at Statewide Average Rate	(4) Earned Exposure Units	(5) Developed Number of Claims	(6) Loss[2] Ratio	(7) Initial[3] Terr. Rel.	(8) Cred.[4] Factor	(9) Cred. Weighted Terr. Rel.	(10) Terr.[6] Average Rate
1	$43,283,841	$43,065,228	964,939	20,586	100.5%	1.086	1.00	1.086	$60.12
2	33,435,196	38,982,074	873,450	17,422	85.8	0.923	1.00	0.923	51.10
3	1,467,229	2,001,655	44,850	807	73.3	0.788	0.80	0.830[5]	45.95
State-wide	$78,186,266	$84,048,957	1,883,239	38,815	93.0%	1.000	1.00	1.000	$55.36[7]

1. The premiums in this column were calculated by multiplying the earned exposure units in Column (4) by the current statewide average rate of $44.63.
2. (6) = (2) ÷ (3)
3. $(7) = \dfrac{\text{Territory loss ratio from column (6)}}{\text{Statewide loss ratio from column (6)}}$
4. See Exhibit 11-11.
5. (.788 × .80) + (1.00 × .20). See text for explanation.
6. $55.36 × (9)
7. Calculated on page 130.

Exhibit 11-11
Credibility Factors

Credibility Percentage	Number of Claims Required
1.00	1,084 and over
0.90	878 – 1,083
0.80	694 – 877
0.70	531 – 693
0.60	390 – 530
0.50	271 – 389
0.40	173 – 270
0.30	98 – 172
0.20	43 – 97
0.10	11 – 42
0.00	0 – 10

Adapted with permission from Philipp K. Stern, "Ratemaking Procedures for Automobile Liability Insurance," *Proceedings of the Casualty Actuarial Society*, 52 (1965), p. 166.

This is not the only method for applying credibility factors, but it is a common one. In this example, the statewide data and the data for territories 1 and 2 are sufficient for full credibility. Consequently, no credibility calculation is required for them.

Class Relativities

Class relativities are calculated in the same manner as territorial relativities. In this example, there are three rating classes. Exhibit 11-12 shows the calculation of class relativities. The final relativities are shown in Column (7) of Exhibit 11-12. A rate table showing rates for each territory and class can now be calculated, as shown in Exhibit 11-13. This completes the ratemaking process for this example. The principles illustrated here are applicable to most lines of property-liability insurance, but some modifications in the process may be needed in some lines. Those will be discussed in later sections of this chapter.

Even for auto liability insurance, some variations are possible and may even be necessary in some cases. For example, consumer organizations and some regulators have objected to the expense loading technique used above. When the expense loading is stated as a percentage of the gross premium, as was done

Exhibit 11-12
Calculation of Class Relativities

(1) Rating Class	(2) Developed and Trended Losses	(3) Premiums[1] on Level at Statewide Average Rate	(4) Earned Exposure Units	(5) Developed Number of Claims	(6) Loss[2] Ratio	(7) Initial[3] Class Rel.	(8) Cred.[4] Factor	(9) Cred. Weighted Class Rel.	(10) Class[5] Average Rate
A	$27,811,791	$40,484,676	907,118	15,421	68.7%	.739	1.00	.739	$ 40.91
B	26,670,223	31,011,513	694,858	13,897	86.0	.925	1.00	.925	51.21
C	23,704,252	12,552,768	281,263	9,497	188.8	2.030	1.00	2.030	112.38
State-wide	$78,186,266	$84,048,957	1,883,239	38,815	93.0%	1.000	1.00	1.000	$ 55.36

1. The premiums in this column were calculated by multiplying the earned exposure units in Column (4) by the statewide average rate of $44.63 currently in use.
2. (6) = [(2) ÷ (3)] × 100
3. Class relativity = $\frac{\text{Class loss ratio from column (6)}}{\text{Statewide loss ratio from column (6)}}$
4. See text and Exhibit 11-11 for explanation.
5. ($55.36 × (9))

Exhibit 11-13
Final Rate Table Showing Rates by Territory and Class

(1)	(2)	(3)	(4)	(5)
		Rating Class		
Territory	All Classes[1] Combined	Class[2] A	Class[2] B	Class[2] C
1	$60.12	$44.43	$55.61	$122.04
2	51.10	37.76	47.27	103.73
3	45.95	33.96	42.50	93.28
All Territories Combined	$55.36	$40.91	$51.21	$112.38

1. From Exhibit 11-10, Column (10).
2. Calculated by multiplying the rate for all classes combined, Column (2), by the appropriate class relativity factor from Exhibit 11-12.

in the above example, persons with higher expected losses pay a larger amount of expenses as well.

Using the rates calculated in Exhibit 11-13, a person in territory 1, rating class C, would pay $30.51 (.25 × $122.04) for the company's underwriting expenses, while a person in territory 3, class A, would pay only $8.49. One way to reduce this difference is to state some of the expenses as a flat dollar amount, which does not vary with expected losses. Assume, for example, that the company used in the above illustration concluded that it needed a flat $3.33 per car-year for general administration and other acquisition costs and 19 percent of gross premium for commissions, taxes, profit, and contingencies.

In that case, the class and territorial relativities would be applied to the pure premium, producing a table of pure premiums like the one shown in Exhibit 11-14. The pure premiums for each territory and class are then loaded for expenses. This calculation is shown in Exhibit 11-15. The statewide average gross rate for all classes and territories combined is the same in Exhibit 11-15 as in Exhibit 11-13. The gross rates for the lowest-rated territories and classes have been increased slightly, while the rates for the highest-rated territories and classes have been reduced. In most states, the differences in gross rates between the lowest-rated territories and classes and the highest-rated ones would be much greater than in this example. Consequently, the changes in rates from using some fixed dollar expense loading might be somewhat greater than shown here.

Exhibit 11-14
Pure Premiums by Class and Territory

(1)	(2)	(3)	(4)	(5)
		Rating Class		
Territory	All Classes Combined	Class A	Class B	Class C
1	$45.09	$33.32	$41.71	$91.53
2	38.32	28.32	35.45	77.79
3	34.46	25.47	31.88	69.95
All Territories Combined	$41.52[1]	$30.68	$38.41	$84.29

1. From page 130.

Exhibit 11-15
Gross Rates by Class and Territory

(1)	(2)	(3)	(4)	(5)
		Rating Class[1]		
Territory	All Classes Combined	Class A	Class B	Class C
1	$59.78	$45.25	$55.60	$117.11
2	51.42	39.07	47.88	100.15
3	46.65	35.56	43.47	90.47
All Territories Combined	$55.37	$41.99	$51.53	$108.17

1. These gross rates were calculated from the pure premiums by territory and class from Exhibit 11-14 using the formula:

$$\text{Gross rate} = \frac{\text{Pure premium} + 3.33}{1 - .19}$$

Pure premiums for this formula are from Exhibit 11-14.

Another possible variation would be the selection of the experience period from which data were drawn. An experience period of five years was used above. A shorter period, ranging from one to three years, might be used. A longer period has the advantage of smoothing chance variations in losses and promoting rate stability. This advantage is offset, at least in part, because a long experience period tends to conceal important developing trends and, therefore, reduces the responsiveness of rates to environmental changes. Of course, the experience period should be sufficiently long so that the resulting data set is large enough to have substantial credibility.

Comparison of Ratemaking Methods

The foregoing example relied primarily on the pure premium method of ratemaking. The loss ratio method was introduced briefly, partly to demonstrate that the two methods produce the same rates when the same data are used in both. Despite their mathematical similarities, the pure premium method has some practical advantages over the loss ratio method. For example, using a mixed expense loading, part fixed dollar and part percentage, is difficult in the loss ratio method but simple in the pure premium method. Since mixed expense loadings are likely to be common in the future, the pure premium method may have a substantial advantage.

On the other hand, the pure premium method cannot be used unless meaningful exposure unit data are obtained. Therefore, the loss ratio method will likely continue in use for the foreseeable future for some property insurance lines, such as inland marine insurance, in which the insured exposures are so variable that they virtually preclude the collection of meaningful exposure unit data.

The judgment method of ratemaking, used alone, has limited application. It is used primarily in ocean marine, aviation, and some inland marine lines. However, judgment is an important part of the ratemaking process for all lines of insurance. For example, selecting an experience period is largely a matter of judgment, with statistical analysis playing only a minor role. The design of a credibility table, such as that in Exhibit 11-11, involves a substantial amount of statistical analysis but still depends heavily on the actuary's judgment.

Although trending is based on statistical procedures, primarily regression analysis, the choice between linear trending and exponential trending (and possibly other variations) is based largely on actuarial judgment. Loss development factors are also heavily influenced by judgment in most cases.

Ratemaking processes for some lines of insurance use all three ratemaking methods to one degree or another. In workers compensation ratemaking, for example, the loss ratio method is used to determine the statewide average rate increase or decrease, while the pure premium method is used to determine class relativities. Of course, judgment is used in several phases of the process, such as trending and developing credibility factors. Such combination methods, using two or all three of the basic techniques, might become even more common as the insurance environment continues to increase in complexity.

Other Lines of Insurance

The basic principles discussed up to this point and applied in the auto insurance example above apply to all lines of property-liability insurance. However, the details of application may vary widely from one line to another. These variations may result from characteristics of the loss exposures insured, regulatory requirements, political considerations, or other factors.

Experience Period

Although an experience period of one to three years is common for automobile insurance and other liability lines, a five-year experience period is used almost universally for fire insurance. The reason for that choice is simple: it is required by law in many states. However, the five years are usually not given equal weight. The most recent years in the experience period are given greater weight in order to promote rate responsiveness.

The experience period for extended coverage is even longer, frequently twenty years or more. The purpose of that long experience period is to avoid the large swings in insurance costs that would otherwise result when a major hurricane or a series of major tornadoes strike an area.

In summary, the factors to be considered in determining the appropriate experience period are (1) legal requirements, if any, (2) the variability of losses over time, and (3) the credibility of the resulting ratemaking data. Of course, items (2) and (3) are related to some degree.

Loss Development

The loss development technique illustrated in the foregoing auto insurance example is applicable to all lines of insurance. However, the desirability of loss development varies from one line to another. Loss development is essential for most lines of liability insurance because of the long delay in loss settlement and the resulting large accumulation of loss reserves. An error in estimating the loss reserves could result in a substantial error in rates, since the incurred losses used in ratemaking may include a substantial proportion of reserves for open claims.

On the other hand, losses for fire, inland marine, and auto physical damage insurance are settled much more quickly. Consequently, the loss reserves for those lines tend to be a relatively small part of incurred losses. Also, open claims for those lines can be estimated more accurately than liability losses. Consequently, loss development factors are frequently not used in the ratemaking process for those lines.

Trending

Trending practices also vary by line of insurance. For liability lines, trending claims frequency and claims severity (as measured by the average claim amount) is common. For fire insurance, the frequency is low and generally very stable, so trending is restricted to severity. However, the average claim is not used as a measure of severity because the average fire insurance claim is likely to be distorted by infrequent, very large claims. Consequently, a composite index, composed partly of a construction cost index and partly of the consumer price index, is used for trending.

In fire insurance, trending both losses and premiums is necessary. Losses are trended in part to reflect the effects of inflation on claims costs. However, inflation also increases the values of the properties insured, and people tend to increase the amount of insurance to reflect the increased values. This increases insurer premium income. If the amounts of insurance kept pace perfectly with inflation, there would be no need to trend losses for inflation. However, the increases in insured amounts tend to lag somewhat behind inflation. Consequently, insurers have adopted the practices of trending both losses and premiums and offsetting the growth in premiums against the growth in losses. Premiums are also trended in other lines of insurance for which the exposure units are affected by inflation. Examples include workers compensation and some general liability lines.

A somewhat unique trending problem exists in workers compensation insurance. Since the benefits for that line are established by statute, they can change rather suddenly, and sometimes unexpectedly, when the legislature is in session. A law amendment factor is calculated to adjust rates and losses to reflect changes in the statutory benefits.

The law amendment factor is calculated on the basis of a standardized workers compensation injury table and a standardized wage distribution table. The injury table shows the probability of workers incurring specified kinds of injuries, the probabilities of being disabled for specified periods of time, and the probabilities of incurring specified amounts of medical expenses. The standardized wage table shows the probabilities that injured workers' wages will fall within certain ranges.

By combining the two tables, it is possible to estimate with reasonable accuracy the effects of a statutory benefit change on the losses insurers will incur under their policies. Unlike other trending, rate increases resulting from statutory benefit changes may apply to outstanding policies as well as renewals.

For boiler and machinery insurance, some expenses are trended. The loss control expenses for that line exceed the amount paid to settle losses. Thus, trending is desirable for those expenses because they constitute such a large share of the rate.

Large Loss Limitations

In using loss data for ratemaking purposes, one must guard against unusual rate fluctuations resulting from occasional large losses, whether from large individual losses or from an accumulation of smaller losses from a single event, such as a hurricane. In liability insurance, this problem is controlled by using only basic limits losses in calculating incurred losses. Basic limits losses are losses capped at some predetermined dollar amount, such as $25,000.

A similar practice is followed in ratemaking for workers compensation insurance. No basic limits exist for that line, so individual claims are limited to a specified amount for ratemaking purposes. In addition to the limitation on an individual claim, another limitation applies to multiple claims arising from a single event. Both limitations vary over time and by state.

Loss limitations also apply in ratemaking for property insurance. When a very large single loss occurs in fire insurance, only a part of it is included in ratemaking calculations in the state in which it occurred. The balance is spread over the rates of all the states. The amount included within the state depends on the total fire insurance premium volume in the state, so it varies substantially by state.

Most losses from catastrophe events, such as hurricanes, are excluded from ratemaking data and replaced by a flat catastrophe charge in the rates. The amount of the catastrophe charge is determined by data collected over a long period of time to smooth the fluctuations that would otherwise result from such catastrophes.

Credibility

The concept of credibility is the same for all lines of insurance, but the applications of that concept vary widely by line. In automobile insurance, it is usual to assume that statewide experience is fully credible. That assumption may not be appropriate for some small insurers when basing their rates on their own data alone. Even some large territories and rating classes may be fully credible. For those territories and classes that are not fully credible, rates are calculated as a weighted average of the indicated rate for the territory or class and the statewide average rate for all classes and territories combined, using the credibility factor as the weight in the weighted average. This is the procedure followed in the auto insurance example in an earlier section of this chapter.

For fire insurance, even the statewide loss experience may not be fully credible. In that case, a three-part weighted average is used, combining the state experience for the rating class, regional experience of the rating class, and state experience of a major group encompassing several rating classes. Again, credibility factors are used as weights.

Pure premiums for workers compensation insurance are composed of three separate charges: a pure premium for medical costs, a pure premium for nonserious injuries, and a pure premium for serious injuries. A separate credibility table exists for each of these categories.

Rate Filings

The final product of the ratemaking process is a rate filing. A rate filing is a document prepared for and submitted to state regulatory authorities. The states vary as to the amount of information required in a filing and the form in which they require it to be prepared. In general, the filing must include at least the following:

1. A schedule of the proposed new rates
2. A statement about the percentage change, either an increase or a decrease, in the statewide average rate
3. If the same percentage change does not apply to the rates for all territories and rating classes, an explanation of the differences
4. Necessary statistics to support the proposed rate changes, including territorial and class relativities
5. If investment income is reflected directly in the rates, an illustration of the necessary calculations
6. Expense loading data
7. Sufficient explanatory material to enable state insurance regulatory personnel to understand and evaluate the filing

The rate filing may be transmitted to the authorities by mail or by hand delivery. Depending on state law, formal approval of the filing by regulatory authorities may not be required. In some states, approval must be obtained before the rates are used. In other states, formal approval is not required by law, but many insurers prefer to obtain approval before use to avoid the possibility of having to withdraw the rates later if the authorities decide that they do not meet statutory requirements.

An insurer should keep a log of all rate filings it submits to authorities. A log is especially necessary if formal approval of filings is required or desired. The log can be used to help keep track of filings so that a follow-up can be made if approval is not received in a timely manner. The log should show the date that the filing was submitted, the date of any follow-up by the company, the date any request for additional information or other contact is received from the authorities, and the date approval is received.

The actuarial department, either with or without assistance from the legal department, frequently conducts negotiations with the state insurance departments regarding rate filings. This seems like a logical approach, since actuaries are best qualified to answer any technical questions that the regulatory authorities may raise. However, some insurers prefer to delegate most of the contacts to the legal department, with actuaries being called in only as needed.

Advisory Prospective Loss Costs

In the past, many insurers, especially smaller ones, depended on advisory organizations, sometimes called rating bureaus, to calculate rates, prepare rate filings, submit the rate filings to state regulatory authorities, and obtain approval of the filings. However, advisory organizations have now discontinued the calculation of rates in most states and calculate and file prospective loss costs instead. Prospective loss costs are simply loss data that have been modified by necessary loss development, trending, and credibility processes, not including expenses.

The advisory organizations calculate the advisory loss costs, prepare the necessary filings, and submit them to the state insurance departments as required. Each insurer that is a member of or subscriber to the advisory organization can then use the advisory prospective loss costs by adding its own expense loading, based either on its own expense data or on industry data.

This process requires most insurers, especially smaller ones, to take an active role in preparing and filing rates. Consulting actuarial firms are willing to perform such services, but the expense of such services encourages many companies to take a do-it-yourself approach to the task.

Summary

The first step in the ratemaking process is the collection of data. The data to be collected include incurred losses, earned premiums, the number of claims incurred, and earned exposure units. Such data are best accumulated gradually as policies and endorsements are issued and as claims are reported and paid. Consequently, an insurer should decide very early in its existence what data will be collected and the form in which that data will be collected.

The policy-year method is the most accurate method for collecting ratemaking statistics. It is also the most expensive method and involves a longer delay than the other methods. A policy year consists of all policies issued during a year. The incurred losses consist of all of the losses covered under those policies. The earned premiums consist of all premiums under those policies, including additional premiums under endorsements, premium audits, and retrospective rating adjustments. Thus, the incurred losses are tied directly to the premiums that were intended to pay them.

The calendar-year method is the least accurate method of collecting ratemaking statistics. However, the statistics are available quickly and with little additional expense because they are taken from the company's accounting records. This method is inaccurate primarily because incurred losses must be estimated from paid losses and loss reserves. Such estimates may be grossly inaccurate because of changes in reserves for outstanding losses.

The accident-year method of collecting ratemaking statistics is a compromise between the other two methods. It preserves most of the accuracy advantages of the policy-year method while achieving most of the speed and economy of the calendar-year method. The incurred losses for the accident-year method consist of all claims arising from insured events that occurred during the year, whether closed or open. The earned premiums are the same as for the calendar-year method.

After statistics are collected, they must be adjusted before rates can be calculated. First, losses must be developed, a process intended to recognize consistent patterns in the accuracy of estimating loss reserves. Next, the trending process is applied to project the losses to the midpoint of the period in which the rates will be used. Earned premiums must also be adjusted to the current rate level.

When these adjustments have been made, the statewide average rate can be calculated, using either the loss ratio method or the pure premium method. Although the two methods can be shown to be mathematically equivalent, the pure premium method may enjoy some practical advantages. The pure premium method requires one additional step (the addition of an expense loading) in comparison with the loss ratio method.

Finally, territorial and class relativities must be determined so that rates for various classes and territories can be calculated. Credibility procedures may be applied at several stages of the ratemaking process to minimize the adverse effects of random fluctuations in losses.

The steps outlined above and the principles that underlie them are applicable to all lines of property-liability insurance, although the details of application may differ by line.

Most advisory organizations no longer calculate final rates for the insurers they serve. Rather, prospective loss costs are developed by the advisory organizations. Insurers then load these loss costs with a provision for their expenses and profit requirements.

Glossary

This glossary provides definitions for actuarial terms introduced in this chapter. Additional terms are defined in the glossaries at the end of Chapters 10 and 12.

Accident Year—A method of collecting ratemaking statistics. The incurred losses for an accident year consist of all losses related to claims arising from accidents that occur during the year. Earned premiums are estimated by formula from accounting records. See also Calendar Year and Policy Year.

Calendar Year—A method of collecting ratemaking data. Both the earned premiums and incurred losses are estimated by formula from accounting records. See text for detailed explanation.

Exponential Trending—A method of trending that assumes a fixed percentage increase or decrease for each period. See also Linear Trending.

Linear Trending—A method of trending that assumes a fixed amount of increase or decrease for each period, the amount being either in dollars or number of claims. See also Exponential Trending.

Loss Triangle—A triangular table of data used to calculate loss development factors.

Policy Year—A method of collecting ratemaking data. A policy year consists of all policies issued during a year. All losses, premiums, and exposure units are tied back to the policies to which they are related. See text for detailed explanation. See also Accident Year and Calendar Year.

Statistical Period—A term applied to various methods of collecting ratemaking data. See also Accident Year, Calendar Year, and Policy Year.

Chapter 12

Insurer Financial Management

Insurance companies are financial intermediaries. **Financial intermediation** occurs when surplus funds from individuals, businesses, or governments are made available to others. Commercial and savings banks, savings and loans, credit unions, pension funds, and investment companies (mutual funds) are other examples of financial intermediaries.

At the end of 1995, the total assets under the control of U.S. property-liability insurers totaled more than $265 billion. Annual receipts amounted to more than $259 billion. Policyholders' surplus was more than $230 billion.[1]

The magnitude of funds under the control of insurance companies and the public's dependence on the insurance product make the financial department an integral operation of an insurance company. This chapter focuses on financial management activities other than investment. These activities are primarily aimed at assisting insurer management in making better decisions. Many insurers rely on their actuarial staff to study these decisions because of the mathematics underlying them. The activities considered in this chapter are (1) loss reserve analysis and verification, (2) planning, (3) analysis of reinsurance requirements, and (4) the evaluation of insurers. Closely related to those topics is how insurers are viewed by others. The rating system used by A.M. Best Company and the tools used by regulators are fundamental to this understanding.

Loss Reserve Analysis and Verification

Loss reserves represent the largest liability on the insurer's balance sheet. Accurate loss reserving is crucial, particularly as the property-liability industry shifts from a predominately property insurance business to a predominately liability insurance business. Loss reserving consists primarily of establishing case reserves incurred but not reported, and analyzing and verifying already established reserves.

Case Reserves

The analysis of loss reserves begins with the case reserves. **Case reserves** are reserves established on each individual claim as it is reported. The claims department usually establishes these reserves, but the actuarial department may assist in some complex cases. Three methods, with variations of each, are used in establishing case reserves: (1) the average value method, (2) the judgment method, and (3) the tabular method. A fourth method, the loss ratio method, is also sometimes used. However, it is not properly classified as a case reserving method, since it deals with aggregate reserves rather than individual cases.

The case reserving method used is determined to a large degree by the nature of the line of insurance concerned. More than one method may be used for the same line of insurance in some cases. For example, some companies may use an average value reserve for liability claims when they are first reported. That reserve is then adjusted upward or downward, based on judgment or the tabular method, as more information becomes available.

For some lines of insurance, it may be desirable to divide the losses into homogeneous groups and analyze each group separately. Commercial multiple peril coverage is one example of such a line. The property losses under this line are settled much more quickly than the liability losses. Also, the final payment is likely to differ from the original reserve by a smaller amount for property losses than for liability losses. Consequently, the accuracy of the reserve analysis is likely to be improved if the property loss reserves and the liability loss reserves are analyzed separately.

Average Value Method

When the **average value method** is used, a predetermined dollar amount of reserve is established for each claim as it is reported. This average value may apply to all claims within a line of insurance, such as physical damage for private passenger automobile insurance, or it may vary by risk class within the line. For lines of insurance with relatively small variations in loss size and relatively short delays in loss settlement, such as automobile physical damage, the average value reserve may not be changed during the life of the claim. For example, every physical damage claim may be reserved at $750 until the claim is closed. For other lines, an average value reserve may be established when a claim is first reported, and then later adjusted, either upward or downward, as more complete information becomes available. For example, every automobile bodily injury claim may be reserved at an average value of $2,000 when reported, with that reserve to be replaced with an individually estimated reserve within ninety days.

The average values used in this reserving method are usually based on the insurer's past average claims developed and trended to reflect current conditions. If the insurer's past data are not adequate for that purpose, the average factors may be based on judgment, or industry data may be used.

Judgment Method

When the **judgment method** is used, a person in the claims department estimates the amount that will eventually be paid to settle the claim, and a reserve is set up in that amount. The reserve may be established solely on the judgment of the person involved, or management may establish some guidelines to assist in the process. Some insurers have recently used expert systems to assist in establishing case reserves. An expert system, in this application, is a computer program containing rules to assist in estimating loss and loss expense reserves. The details of a particular claim are entered into the computer, and the program applies the appropriate rules to estimate the amount of the claim and the amount of allocated loss expenses. An expert system provides greater consistency in reserving than a pure judgment-based system.

Tabular Method

The **tabular method** is based on the use of actuarial tables and an assumed interest rate to calculate the present value of a claim. This method may be used for claims that involve a series of fixed or determinable payments to the claimant over a prolonged period of time. For example, some disability insurance claims may require payment of a fixed sum over a period of many years, provided the claimant remains alive and disabled. That is, the payments will be terminated if the claimant dies or recovers from the disabling condition. Calculating the present value of the future payments requires assumptions about interest rates and the length of the disability. A mortality table may be used to estimate the probability of death and a morbidity table to estimate the probability of recovery. In some cases, such as widow or widower benefits under workers compensation, the claim may be terminated if the claimant remarries. A remarriage table, showing the probability of remarriage at various ages and periods of widowhood, is used to estimate the value of such claims.

To illustrate a tabular reserve calculation, assume that a thirty-year-old widow is receiving a widow's benefit of $300 per week for life, to be terminated on remarriage. The table of present values shows that the present value of her future benefit is 14.129 for each dollar of benefit, reflecting mortality, probability of remarriage, and interest. In this case, the tabular reserve would be as follows: ($300 per week) × (52 weeks) × 14.129 = $220,412.

The interest rate used should be one that the insurer can reasonably expect to earn during the expected life of the claim and should be based on the yield on low-risk investments, such as government bonds. It may be lower than the average yield currently earned on the insurer's investment portfolio.

The mortality, morbidity, and remarriage rates assumed in calculating tabular reserves will not be realized exactly in most individual cases. For example, most claimants will either live longer or die sooner than the mortality table shows. However, if an insurer has a large number of such claims, the average mortality, morbidity, and remarriage experience of all claims combined should approximate the tabular values rather closely.

Since the reserves have been discounted for interest, the average amount paid over the life of all claims combined should exceed the aggregate reserves. For any individual claim, the total amount paid may be more or less than the reserve, depending on how the mortality, morbidity, or remarriage experience of the person differs from the values shown in the tables.

Loss Ratio Method

The loss ratio method is discussed here to provide a complete exposition of reserving methods, but it is not a method of case reserving. Case reserving is concerned with establishing reserves for individual claims. The **loss ratio method** establishes aggregate reserves for all claims within a line of insurance or a class of risks. In its simplest form, the loss ratio method assumes that aggregate losses will equal the amount included in the premium to pay them. That is, the aggregate losses for a given year will equal the earned premiums for the year multiplied by the permissible loss ratio used in calculating the rates that underlie the earned premiums. A loss ratio other than the one used in calculating the rates might be used if the rates are believed to be excessive or inadequate.

The loss ratio method is usually used only if the other methods prove to be inadequate. For example, in medical malpractice insurance for physicians and surgeons, under occurrence policies, only a very small fraction (1 percent to 2 percent) of covered claims are reported to the insurer during the year in which they are incurred. Therefore, the loss ratio method is commonly used to establish aggregate reserves at the end of the first year (at twelve months of development), and other methods are used thereafter. A similar approach has been used by reinsurers because of the long delays experienced in reporting and settling claims in that segment of the insurance business.

The NAIC Annual Statement requires minimum reserves (sometimes called "statutory" reserves) calculated by the loss ratio method for workers compensation and liability insurance. The loss ratio used to calculate the minimum loss reserve for liability lines varies from 60 percent to 75 percent, depending on the past loss ratios of the insurer. For workers compensation insurance, the percentage ranges from 65 percent to 75 percent.

The **statutory minimum reserve** is found by multiplying the earned premiums for the year by the appropriate percentage and deducting losses and adjustment expenses already paid for the year. This statutory minimum reserve calculation only applies to the three most recent accident years.

IBNR Reserve

Insurers are required by law and good accounting practice to establish reserves for losses that have been incurred but not yet reported, the so-called **IBNR reserve**. Although the name of this reserve refers only to incurred but not reported losses, unreported losses account for only a part of the reserve in many cases. The balance of the reserve is for losses that have been reported but for which the case reserves that have been established are inadequate. A reserve for claims that have been closed and then reopened may also be included in the IBNR reserve. Of course, analysts usually cannot identify the specific claims for which inadequate case reserves have been established or the closed claims that will be reopened, nor can they determine the amount of inadequacy for specific claims.

In this chapter, the reserve for unreported claims is referred to as the *pure IBNR reserve*. The reserve for inadequate case reserves is called the *reserve for case reserve inadequacies*. The sum of the two will be called the *total IBNR reserve*.

Since the insurer does not know either the number or the amount of such unreported losses or case reserve deficiencies, the IBNR reserve must be based on estimates of some kind. There are two possible approaches to such estimates. One approach is to estimate the ultimate total amount of incurred losses for the period and subtract the paid losses and case reserves for reported losses. The remainder is the total IBNR reserve.

If the paid losses and case reserves are greater than the estimated ultimate losses, this calculation produces a negative total IBNR reserve. This result may indicate either excessive case reserves or an inadequate estimate of ultimate aggregate incurred losses. In any case, a negative total IBNR reserve likely indicates an error in the reserve calculation and calls for further analysis.

The second approach to IBNR estimation is to estimate the pure IBNR reserve independently, without reference to the case reserves. A separate calculation must then be made for the reserve for case reserve deficiencies in order to determine the total IBNR reserve. The report-year method discussed later may be used for this purpose. This approach requires that historic loss data files include both the occurrence date and the report date for each claim. With such data, it is possible to determine the proportion of incurred claims, both in number and amount, reported after some specified cutoff date (such as December 31) in past years. It is then assumed that the same proportion of claims for the year or years in question remains unreported. Of course, if there have been environmental changes that would be expected to lengthen or shorten the reporting period, appropriate adjustments must be made. For example, the enactment of a shorter statute of limitations might cause some claims to be reported more quickly than indicated by historic data.

Some actuaries use both methods when sufficient data are available. If the two methods produce total IBNR reserve estimates that are consistent, the level of confidence in the result is increased. If the results are inconsistent, further analysis is needed to determine why, and which, if either, is more likely to be correct.

In some lines of insurance, the total IBNR reserve may be a substantial part of an insurer's total liabilities. Consequently, insurers should take great care in estimating the IBNR reserve.

Loss Reserve Analysis and Verification Techniques

Insurers maintain two loss reserving systems. The case reserve system, discussed above, is concerned with individual losses and is primarily the responsibility of the claims department. Ideally, the case reserving system should provide a reserve for each claim that is equal to the amount that will be required to settle that claim. This ideal is seldom achieved and is probably impossible to achieve in most lines of insurance.

The second reserving system is the **actuarial reserving system** or the bulk reserving system. Its principal purpose is to determine the insurer's claims liabilities for accounting purposes. It is concerned with the insurer's total liability for all outstanding claims, and not with the amount of reserve for individual claims.

The previous section of this chapter discussed the case reserving system. This section deals with the bulk reserving system.

The purpose of loss reserve analysis and verification is to determine whether the loss and adjustment expense reserves established by a company are adequate to cover the losses and adjustment expenses that have been incurred but have not yet been paid. Such a study may be commissioned by management as a normal part of management control by the company's auditors to determine whether the company's financial statement accurately indicates the company's financial condition, or it may be undertaken to comply with regulatory requirements. The NAIC Annual Statement instructions now require most insurers to have their loss reserves certified by an actuary or other qualified person. The NAIC's definition of a "qualified actuary" is shown in Exhibit 12-1.

Exhibit 12-1
Qualifications Required To Certify Loss Reserves

"Qualified actuary" is a person who is either:

1. A member in good standing of the Casualty Actuarial Society, or
2. A member in good standing of the American Academy of Actuaries who has been approved as qualified for signing casualty loss reserve opinions by the Casualty Practice Council of the American Academy of Actuaries, or
3. A person who otherwise has competency in loss reserve evaluation as demonstrated to the satisfaction of the insurance regulatory official of the domiciliary state. In such case, at least 90 days prior to the filing of its annual statement, the insurer must request approval that the person be deemed qualified and that request must be approved or denied. The request must include the NAIC Biographical Form and a list of all loss reserve opinions and/or certifications issued in the last 3 years by this person.

Annual Statement Instructions—Property and Casualty, National Association of Insurance Commissioners, Kansas City, MO, 1996, p. 8.

Signing such opinions or certifications creates an exposure to potential professional liability claims. Consequently, such opinions or certifications ordinarily would not be provided without a careful analysis of the reserves.

One actuarial technique for analyzing and verifying loss reserves is very similar to the loss development process discussed in the preceding chapter. In the first step of the process, the actuary must become familiar with the techniques used by the claims department to establish case reserves and must determine whether there have been any changes in case reserving methods.

The loss reserve verification techniques in common use measure past patterns in estimating case reserves and project these past patterns into the future. Consequently, a change in reserving practices, if it affects the pattern of case reserves, will result in an error in the evaluation of those reserves, unless the change is detected and appropriate adjustments are made.

For example, a change in case reserving methods that resulted in an increase in case reserves could, if undetected, cause the analyst to assume that case reserves, having been inadequate in the past, are still inadequate. Actually, of course, the changed methods could result in reserves that are now adequate or even excessive.

Although this chapter emphasizes the mathematical methods for analyzing loss reserves, performing such an analysis is not an entirely mathematical process. The mathematical results must be evaluated very carefully using nonmathematical information and common sense.

Accident-Year Loss Analysis Technique

One technique for loss reserve analysis uses loss triangles like those illustrated in Chapter 11 in Exhibits 11-3, 11-4, and 11-5. The triangles in Chapter 11 are accident-year loss triangles. Each line of data represents one accident year, with the various columns showing how the accident-year losses developed over time.

The number of accident years included in a loss development triangle for ratemaking purposes depends on the number of years in the experience period used for ratemaking purposes. There should be one line for each year in the experience period. However, the number of lines in a triangle used for loss reserve evaluation is determined primarily by the length of the delay between the occurrence of a loss and the time it is paid. Ideally, there should be one line for each accident year for which one or more reported claims remain open or for which one or more unreported claims are expected to be reported.

As a practical matter, it may be necessary to combine very old years with very few claims outstanding into a single line in the triangle. For example, the triangle might include a separate line for each of the last ten accident years plus a single line for the combined data for the eleventh year and all years before then.

Exhibit 12-2 shows the initial accident-year loss triangle for loss reserve verification. Exhibit 12-2 shows the dollar amount of incurred losses as reported for each accident year at various stages of development: twelve months, twenty-four months, and so on. The losses are presumed to be fully developed at ninety-six months, and do not change thereafter. As noted above, Exhibit 12-2 differs from Exhibit 11-2 only in that it includes more accident years (ten plus a line for prior years instead of five years).

Exhibit 12-3 shows loss development multipliers calculated from the data in Exhibit 12-2. The multipliers for each accident year were calculated by dividing the amount of losses for one development period from Exhibit 12-2 by the amount of losses on the same line for the immediately prior development period. For example, the multiplier for development from twelve months to twenty-four months for 1992 was calculated by dividing the losses at twenty-four months of development ($66,968,794) by the losses reported at twelve months of development ($41,773,849). The resulting loss development multiplier is 1.603. The other multipliers were calculated in the same manner.

The figures on the line labeled "Mean" in Exhibit 12-3 are the arithmetic means of the multipliers above them. The figures on the line labeled "Selected" are the ones chosen by the analyst to calculate the loss development factors on the line below. In this instance, the analyst has chosen to use the mean values without modification. In an actual analysis, the selected values might vary from the means. For example, if the accident-year multipliers indicated an increasing trend, the analyst might use selected values higher than the means. If the data were liability loss data from a state that had just adopted a shorter statute of limitations, the analyst might use selected values higher than average for earlier years and lower than average values for later years, indicating an expectation of earlier reporting in the future.

The ultimate development factors are shown on the bottom line of Exhibit 12-3. The ultimate development factors for ninety-six months and later are not shown in Exhibit 12-3. However, all of them are 1.00, indicating that the losses are fully developed at ninety-six months, and no additional changes are expected after that time. The ultimate development factor for eighty-four months of development is simply the selected value from the line above. For each of the other periods shown, the ultimate development factor was calculated by multiplying the selected value for that period by the ultimate development factor for the following period.

Exhibit 12-2
Loss Triangle: Accident-Year Method
Hypothetical Data

Accident Year	Months of Development							
	12	24	36	48	60	72	84	96
1987 & Prior	$279,554,361	$487,695,483	$498,712,348	$501,462,834	$507,832,541	$512,664,798	$515,447,632	$516,112,436
1988	26,443,738	44,658,934	46,112,869	47,355,873	48,586,914	48,967,324	49,116,736	49,214,873
1989	29,163,357	48,995,673	51,444,538	57,579,832	53,461,854	53,892,346	54,213,128	54,304,736
1990	32,561,477	54,564,783	52,668,598	58,234,768	58,977,654	59,541,632	59,843,486	59,925,726
1991	36,112,748	59,879,765	62,861,528	64,146,732	64,981,374	65,476,497	65,879,324	
1992	41,773,849	66,968,794	70,981,932	73,859,431	74,779,541	75,417,614		
1993	50,174,593	83,947,351	87,979,482	89,875,483	91,463,572			
1994	57,673,841	93,258,873	98,998,237	101,443,218				
1995	63,688,419	105,548,765	110,774,315					
1996	67,448,941	112,234,985						
1997	73,814,284							

Exhibit 12-3
Loss Triangle: Accident-Year Method
Hypothetical Data

Accident Year	Months of Development						
	12-24	24-36	36-48	48-60	60-72	72-84	84-96
1987 & Prior	1.745	1.023	1.006	1.013	1.010	1.005	1.001
1988	1.689	1.033	1.027	1.026	1.008	1.003	1.002
1989	1.680	1.050	1.022	1.017	1.008	1.006	1.002
1990	1.676	1.057	1.010	1.013	1.010	1.005	1.001
1991	1.658	1.050	1.020	1.013	1.008	1.006	
1992	1.603	1.060	1.041	1.012	1.009		
1993	1.673	1.048	1.022	1.018			
1994	1.617	1.062	1.025				
1995	1.657	1.050					
1996	1.664						
Mean	1.666	1.048	1.021	1.016	1.009	1.005	1.002
Selected	1.666	1.048	1.021	1.016	1.009	1.005	1.002
Ultimate	1.840	1.105	1.054	1.032	1.016	1.007	1.002

Exhibit 12-4
Ultimate Loss Development Factors: Accident-Year Method
Hypothetical Data

Accident Year	Ultimate Loss Development Factors
1987 & Prior	1.000
1988	1.000
1989	1.000
1990	1.000
1991	1.002
1992	1.007
1993	1.016
1994	1.032
1995	1.054
1996	1.105
1997	1.840

Exhibit 12-4 shows the **ultimate development factor** for each twelve-month period from twelve months to ninety-six months and later. Exhibit 12-5 shows the ultimate projected losses for each year in Exhibit 12-2. These projected ultimate losses were calculated by multiplying the reported amount of losses for the latest period in Exhibit 12-2 by the appropriate ultimate loss development factor from Exhibit 12-4.

The projected ultimate losses in Exhibit 12-5 include both paid losses and reserves, including IBNR reserves. The total loss reserve, including total IBNR, can be calculated by deducting the total paid losses of $972,213,944 (not shown in the tables) from the total projected losses of $1,395,724,850, shown at the bottom of Exhibit 12-5.

The total IBNR reserve can be calculated by deducting the total reported losses of $1,310,585,083 from the total projected ultimate losses of $1,395,724,850. Exhibit 12-5 shows this calculation along with the total IBNR for each of the accident years.

The loss triangles in this chapter include all reported claims, both closed and open. Some actuaries also use closed loss triangles in the reserve analysis process. Closed loss triangles are constructed and interpreted in exactly the

Exhibit 12-5
Developed Losses: Accident-Year Method
Hypothetical Data

Accident Year	Reported Losses	Loss Development Factors	Projected Ultimate Losses	IBNR	IBNR As % of Total
1987 & Prior	$ 516,112,436	1.000	$ 516,112,436	$ 0	.000
1988	49,214,873	1.000	49,214,873	0	.000
1989	54,304,736	1.000	54,304,736	0	.000
1990	59,925,726	1.000	59,925,726	0	.000
1991	65,879,324	1.002	66,011,083	131,759	.200
1992	75,417,614	1.007	75,945,537	527,923	.695
1993	91,463,572	1.016	92,926,989	1,463,417	1.574
1994	101,443,218	1.032	104,689,401	3,246,183	3.101
1995	110,774,315	1.054	116,756,128	5,981,813	5.123
1996	112,234,985	1.105	124,019,658	11,784,673	9.502
1997	73,814,284	1.840	135,818,283	62,003,999	45.652
Totals	$1,310,585,083		$1,395,724,850	$85,139,767	6.100

same manner as reported loss triangles. The only difference is that only data for closed losses are used, whereas the reported loss triangles also include open losses. Using closed loss triangles has the advantage of eliminating the effects of errors in estimating case reserves. However, the delay between occurrence and closing losses can be substantially longer than the delay between occurrence and reporting. Consequently, the number of months needed until there is no further development in closed loss triangles would be larger than for reported loss triangles. This longer delay introduces a greater chance for changing circumstances to lead to errors in interpreting the results.

Triangles for the number of claims are constructed in the same manner as those for loss amounts. The projected ultimate number of claims can then be cross-checked against the projected ultimate amount of losses to be sure they are consistent. Careful actuaries make many such cross-checks when certifying loss reserves.

Report-Year Loss Analysis Technique

The loss triangles discussed up to this point have dealt with accident-year statistics. Loss data, either number of claims or dollar amount of losses, were grouped by accident year, the year in which the loss event occurred. This section discusses a technique in which the loss data are grouped by report year, the year in which the loss was first reported to the insurer. This technique can be used to calculate the reserve for case reserve deficiencies.

For some lines of property insurance, such as auto physical damage, a large majority of claims are reported in the same year in which the loss event occurred. For those lines, using the report-year technique for loss reserve analysis would add little information to the process.

However, for long-tailed liability lines, such as medical malpractice, the majority of claims may be reported to the insurer in years subsequent to the year in which the loss event occurred. Reporting such claims to the insurer ten years or more after the loss event occurred is not unusual. For such lines, claims included in *report-year* 1997, for example, would be quite different from those reported in *accident-year* 1997.

The report-year technique deals with a constant portfolio of claims. The dollar amount of claims within the portfolio may change as claims are settled or case reserves are amended, and claims may move from the open category to the closed category, but the total number of claims remains constant. Since only reported claims are considered, the exact number of claims in the portfolio is known on the last day of the report year and does not change thereafter.

This constancy of the portfolio is both a strength and a weakness of the technique. It is a strength of the technique because it permits the analyst to follow the development of a specific group of claims and to test the accuracy of early case reserving. This is not possible with accident-year data because new claims are added to the portfolio as they are reported to the insurer.

The constant portfolio of losses is a weakness of the report-year technique because it does not provide information needed to determine the amount of reserve required for losses that have been incurred but have not yet been reported to the insurer, the pure IBNR reserve. Note, however, that it does permit testing of a part of the total IBNR reserve: that part consisting of case reserve inadequacies for reported losses. Consequently, the report-year technique cannot be used as the sole technique for loss reserve testing. However, it can be used as an important tool to supplement the insight gained through the accident-year methods.

Adequacy of Case Reserves

The adequacy of case reserves is sometimes very difficult to determine, especially for a relatively new insurer writing long-tailed liability insurance. Small claims, especially those settled without payment, tend to be settled quickly. Since those are the claims for which excessive reserves are likely to be established, this pattern of settlement can give the appearance that all case reserves are excessive, especially for a company that has not been in business long enough to settle a representative number of larger, more complex cases.

In several cases, this phenomenon has misled the management of new companies into believing their reserves were adequate or even excessive when, in fact, they were grossly inadequate. The accident-year loss triangles, used alone, may not reveal this problem. Using the report-year technique may assist in avoiding the problem if sufficient data are available.

Report-Year Loss Analysis Example

Unlike accident-year loss triangles, which include loss data for several accident years, a report-year loss table includes data for only one report year.

Exhibit 12-6 shows a report-year loss table, using hypothetical data. Several such tables, one for each report year, would be needed for a typical loss reserve analysis.

Several things should be noted about Exhibit 12-6. First, the total number of claims never changes. At the end of the report year, all reported claims are known, so the number does not change thereafter. Claims move from the open column to the closed column when they are settled, even if they are settled without payment. Occasionally, a claim may move from the closed column back to the open column if it is reopened for some reason, but the total number of claims never changes. The total amount of losses does change. The change may be either upward or downward, depending on an insurer's reserving practices. The change is always upward in Exhibit 12-6, indicating that the insurer's case reserves were substantially inadequate initially. For many real companies, the change will be upward in some years and downward in others.

There is a tendency for both the average closed claim and the average open claim to increase as the claims mature. This results from the tendency for small claims to be settled first, with larger claims taking longer to settle. This increase in the average claims may not be as regular in real life as it is depicted in Exhibit 12-6, and a year-to-year decrease may occasionally occur. However, such a decrease calls for further checking to be sure that a data error has not occurred or to find the reason for the anomaly.

The report-year loss table in Exhibit 12-6 is for a *fully mature report year*, one for which all claims have been settled. Exhibit 12-7 shows a similar table for a year not yet fully mature.

A loss triangle very similar to those used in accident-year analysis can be compiled from a series of report-year tables. The first step in compiling such a triangle is to calculate loss development multipliers from the total loss amount columns of the tables. Exhibit 12-8 shows the calculation of such multipliers from Exhibits 12-6 and 12-7.

Exhibit 12-9 shows a loss triangle using the data from Exhibits 12-6 and 12-7, along with additional data from other report years. The bottom line shows the ultimate development factors, the factors that can be used to project immature loss data to full maturity. In this illustration, the various twelve-month development factors in the next-to-last line of the table have been taken as the arithmetic mean of the multipliers above them for the report years. In actual practice, an analyst might elect a value greater or lesser than the arithmetic mean. Such a selection might be made because the data indicate an increasing or decreasing trend in the multipliers, or because of changes in case reserving practices. There might also be other reasons for the analyst to conclude that the arithmetic mean was not the appropriate value to select in a given instance.

Exhibit 12-10 shows the ultimate development factors alone. The losses for report year 1993, which are sixty months developed in Exhibit 12-7, can be projected to ultimate value by multiplying by the ultimate development factor corresponding to sixty months, shown in Exhibit 12-10 ($68,933,369 \times 1.047 = 72,173,237$).

Exhibit 12-6
Report-Year Loss Table for 1990
Hypothetical Data

Report	Closed Claims			Open Claims			All Claims		
Year	Number	Amount	Average	Number	Amount	Average	Number	Amount	Average
1990	1,451	$ 5,117,677	$3,527	9,122	$ 49,597,598	$ 5,437	10,573	$54,715,275	$5,175
1991	4,794	18,562,368	3,872	5,779	41,111,644	7,114	10,573	59,674,012	5,644
1992	6,579	30,862,089	4,691	3,994	30,122,975	7,542	10,573	60,985,064	5,768
1993	7,841	40,059,669	5,109	2,732	20,967,687	7,675	10,573	61,027,356	5,772
1994	8,987	49,635,201	5,523	1,586	12,882,948	8,123	10,573	62,518,149	5,913
1995	9,898	57,814,218	5,841	675	6,057,275	8,974	10,573	63,871,493	6,041
1996	10,570	64,762,390	6,127	3	282,706	94,235	10,573	65,045,096	6,152
1997	10,573	65,097,961	6,157	0	0	0	10,573	65,097,961	6,157

Exhibit 12-7
Report-Year Loss Table for 1993
Hypothetical Data

Report	Closed Claims			Open Claims			All Claims		
Year	Number	Amount	Average	Number	Amount	Average	Number	Amount	Average
1993	1,687	$ 6,677,146	$3,958	9,330	$57,474,845	$6,160	11,017	$64,151,991	$5,823
1994	5,135	24,139,635	4,701	5,882	43,559,830	7,406	11,017	67,699,465	6,145
1995	6,738	34,559,202	5,129	4,279	34,164,844	7,984	11,017	68,724,046	6,238
1996	7,953	43,590,393	5,481	3,064	26,653,999	8,699	11,017	70,244,392	6,376
1997	9,188	52,849,376	5,752	1,829	16,083,993	8,794	11,017	68,933,369	6,257

Exhibit 12-8
Report-Year Method
Development Multipliers

Months of Development	Report Year 1990 Amount	1990 Multiplier	1993 Amount	1993 Multiplier
12	$54,715,275		$64,151,991	
24	59,674,012	1.091	67,699,465	1.055
36	60,985,064	1.022	68,724,046	1.015
48	61,027,356	1.001	70,244,392	1.022
60	62,518,149	1.024	68,933,369	.981
72	63,871,493	1.022		
84	65,045,096	1.018		
96	65,097,961	1.001		

The report-year triangle shows that the company in question has consistently established inadequate loss reserves during the period being analyzed. In the absence of an indication that reserving practices have changed, an analyst looking at these data would assume that current reserves are inadequate by approximately the same percentage.

The foregoing analysis is based solely on claims reported to the insurer in the report year in question. Those claims would include some that were incurred during the report year and some that were incurred in earlier years. The data do not include any claims reported after the end of the report year, regardless of when they were incurred. Consequently, the claims projected to ultimate by this method do not include any amount for claims incurred but not reported. This part of the loss reserve must be computed separately when the report-year method is used.

As noted earlier, the IBNR reserve reported in the NAIC Annual Statement includes two elements, although the elements normally are not separately identified. The first of these elements is claims incurred but not yet reported, the pure IBNR reserve. The second element is composed of the deficiency (or perhaps redundancy) in the case reserves for reported losses. The report-year method does not provide an estimate of the first of these elements of the IBNR reserve, but it does provide an estimate of the second element.

Report-year triangles can be constructed using the number of claims as well as the amount of losses. However, such triangles are not as useful in the report-

Exhibit 12-9
Loss Triangle
Report-Year Method

Report Year	Months of Development						
	12-24	24-36	36-48	48-60	60-72	72-84	84-96
1989 & Prior	1.065	1.031	1.023	1.022	1.034	1.016	1.003
1990	1.091	1.022	1.001	1.024	1.022	1.018	1.001
1991	1.084	1.019	1.025	1.023	1.026	1.017	
1992	1.071	1.021	1.018	1.019	1.027		
1993	1.055	1.015	1.022	.981			
1994	1.063	1.024	1.019				
1995	1.073	1.020					
1996	1.059						
Mean	1.070	1.022	1.018	1.014	1.027	1.017	1.002
Selected	1.070	1.022	1.018	1.014	1.027	1.017	1.002
Development Factors	1.182	1.105	1.081	1.062	1.047	1.019	1.002

Exhibit 12-10
Report-Year Method
Ultimate Development Factors

Months of Development	Ultimate Development Factor
12	1.182
24	1.105
36	1.081
48	1.062
60	1.047
72	1.019
84	1.002
96	1.000

year method as they are in the accident-year method because the total number of claims for a given report year does not change in subsequent development. A triangle could be used to compile a distribution of lag times between the reporting and settlement of claims. Such a table is an important element in discounting loss reserves. The discounting process is discussed below.

In conclusion, the report-year method, standing alone, is not an adequate method for loss reserve verification. It is, however, a useful tool when used in parallel with the accident-year technique. Because it deals with a fixed portfolio of claims, the report-year method is an excellent tool for measuring the past performance of the case-reserving process. One must rely on judgment to determine whether past performance indicates present performance.

Discounting the Loss Reserves

For workers compensation and liability lines, insurers accumulate large amounts of loss reserves. The funds that back these reserves are invested in income-producing assets, and the income they produce is a very important element in insurer profits.

Many people have suggested over the years that the loss reserves established by insurers should be reduced to reflect the future income to be received from these investments, a process known as **discounting the loss reserves**. This would be a substantial change from the industry's traditional practice of establishing reserves for NAIC Annual Statement purposes equal to the expected loss payments, without any reduction for future investment income.

The proposal for discounting loss reserves has been controversial. Most insurers and most state regulatory authorities have opposed discounting. They point out that the practice of establishing full-value or gross (undiscounted) loss reserves provides an extra margin of safety to protect the solvency of insurers and is, at least to that extent, in the best interest of insurance consumers. They also question the desirability of discounting an estimated quantity that is subject to such a large margin for error. They say that discounting gives an appearance of precision that is not justified by the facts.

Proponents of discounting say that establishing full-value loss reserves understates an insurer's net worth and profits and, consequently, its tax liability. Most states permit insurers to discount some workers compensation insurance loss reserves, primarily those for which case reserves are calculated by the tabular method discussed previously in this chapter. Those are primarily long-term disability income and dependents' income benefits.

Some states also permit discounting loss reserves for some very long-tailed liability lines such as medical malpractice. This practice was adopted to facilitate the entry of newly formed insurers, primarily doctor-owned companies, into the medical malpractice market during the severe shortage of malpractice insurance in the 1970s. One small insurer specializing in medical malpractice insurance found that discounting reduced its loss and loss adjustment expense reserves by over $40 million, or about 20 percent of the undiscounted reserve. Other insurers might experience either larger or smaller reductions, depending on the payout distribution and interest rate used.

With the exceptions noted above, the regulatory authorities in most states prohibit or strongly discourage the discounting of loss reserves. With the enactment of Section 846 of the Internal Revenue Code in 1986, discounting loss reserves became mandatory for federal income tax purposes.

Discounting loss reserves requires some assumptions regarding (1) the time lags between the time a loss occurs and the time it is paid, and (2) the interest rate that will be earned on the invested assets offsetting the loss reserves. The Internal Revenue Service publishes loss payout patterns for all lines of property-liability insurance, along with discount rates to be used for discounting loss and adjustment expense reserves for federal income tax purposes.

For other purposes, the distribution of payment lags should be based on the insurer's own data if such data have sufficient credibility. If the insurer's own data lack credibility, other industry data can be used. The interest rate used in the discounting calculation should be related to the average yield on the insurer's own investment portfolio. However, that average yield may be adjusted to reflect future interest rate expectations. Also, if the insurer's investment portfolio includes high-risk investments, a lower interest rate may be used to discount loss reserves.

Planning

An insurer's planning operations include persons from several sectors of the company, including personnel involved with investments, marketing, underwriting, human resources, and others.

Actuaries often participate because they have been trained to have broad knowledge of insurer operations and the planning process. Additionally, they are adept at the mathematical phases of the process, such as the construction of mathematical models.

Planning includes both short-term (tactical) planning and long-term (strategic) planning. Planning inevitably involves collecting and analyzing voluminous statistical data. A comprehensive planning program almost inevitably includes the use of computer models for testing various alternative actions available to the insurer. Such models use mathematical equations to represent various functions within the insurer's structure and operations. The models vary from small and simple to very complex. A small model might represent only a small part of a company, even a single line of insurance. A more complex model might depict all of the operations of a company or group of companies. A small, simple model might take only a few seconds to run under spreadsheet software on a desktop computer. A complex model might take many minutes to run on a mainframe computer.

Regardless of their size or complexity, the models serve the same basic purpose: to permit planners to test various scenarios for the future operations of the company or group of companies.

Some of the kinds of questions that might be answered by a computer model are as follows:

1. How is the profitability of various lines of insurance affected by an increase of one percentage point in the insurer's yield on invested assets?
2. What is the optimum mix of reinsurance for the insurer, considering its probable underwriting results, investment income, and policyholders' surplus?
3. What is the optimum mix of investments, considering investment income, taxes, regulatory requirements, and the insurer's needs for liquidity, stability, and solvency?

The answers to questions such as those are determined by many factors, and the interrelationships among the factors are very complex. Few individuals understand all of the factors and their interrelationships. However, an interdisciplinary team, working together, can build an appropriate computer model to assist in the analysis.

When analyzing very complex systems, an analyst is not likely to follow the same path of analysis each time. A computer model, on the other hand, always follows the same path of analysis. Whatever factors and relations were programmed into it will be analyzed in the same manner each time.

This can be either a strength or a weakness of computer models. If the model was designed properly, its consistency is an advantage. If the model was not designed properly, it may give consistently wrong answers.

There are two general categories of computer models: deterministic models and probabilistic models. Each type of model has an appropriate role in insurance company planning.

Deterministic Models

Deterministic models are characterized by consistent results. If a deterministic model is run many times with exactly the same values for all of the input factors, it will produce exactly the same output each time. This is, of course, not representative of the real world.

Despite this substantial abstraction from the real world, deterministic models are useful in planning. They permit planners to experiment with changing a single factor while holding all other factors constant, something that is seldom possible in the business world.

Probabilistic Models

Probabilistic models are sometimes called stochastic models. They may also be called Monte Carlo models, after the famous gambling casino in Monaco. This association with gambling stems from the fact that the output from such a model is not determined solely by the inputs but is also subject to some element of chance variation. The range of chance variation may be large in some models.

Two simplified examples that may help to clarify the difference between a deterministic model and a probabilistic model are shown in Exhibits 12-11 and 12-12.

Choosing the Best Model

Since the operating results of an insurance company are subject to chance variation, one might conclude that a probabilistic model would be the better

Exhibit 12-11
Deterministic Model Example

Assume that an insurer wants to estimate its loss ratio for auto liability insurance in a given state for a year five years in the future. It has an estimate that there will be five million cars registered in that state in the year concerned. Based on its past trend in market share, it believes it will insure 3 percent of registered vehicles at that time. Its current average auto liability premium for the state is $300, and it estimates that rates will increase 7.5 percent each year for the next five years. Consequently, it estimates its earned premiums for the year five years in the future as follows:

Number of registered cars		5,000,000
Company's market share	×	.03
Cars insured by company		150,000
Average premium: [$300 × $(1.075)^5$]	×	$431
Total earned premium		$64,650,000

The company estimates that 2.5 percent of its insured vehicles will be involved in an at-fault accident each year. The average cost of claims arising from one accident is now $6,000, and the company expects that amount to increase at the rate of 8 percent each year. Consequently, the incurred losses for the year five years in the future will be calculated as follows:

Number of cars insured		150,000
Percentage of cars in accidents	×	.025
Number of accidents		3,750
Cost per accident: [$6,000 × $(1.08)^5$]	×	$8,816
Total incurred losses		$33,060,000

The company's projected loss ratio would be calculated as follows:

Incurred losses / Earned premiums

33,060,000 / 64,650,000 = .511, or 51.1 percent

Note that there is no element of chance in this model. If the number of registered cars, the market share, average premium, accident rate, average claim, and the rates of increase remain constant, the model will always produce exactly the same answer, no matter how many times it is calculated. This is the characteristic that distinguishes a deterministic model from a probabilistic model.

Exhibit 12-12
Probabilistic Model Example

Assume that an insurer wants to estimate its hurricane losses under homeowners policies for the coming hurricane season. Past experience indicates that the number of hurricanes ranges from zero to five, with the following probabilities:

Number of Hurricanes	Probability	Mean
0	.20	0
1	.30	.30
2	.20	.40
3	.15	.45
4	.10	.40
5	.05	.25
		1.80

The arithmetic mean is 1.8 hurricanes per year.

The total amount of the company's losses from a single hurricane varies from $100,000 to $15,000,000, with an arithmetic mean of $1,500,000 following a specified probability distribution.

The first step in simulating the hurricane losses is to select the number of hurricanes. The computer program would be designed to select a number from zero to five so that the probability of selecting zero would be .20, the probability of selecting one would be .30, and so forth. This is accomplished by using random numbers generated by the computer. Next, the total amount of losses for each hurricane is selected, again through the use of random numbers. For example, the first three runs might produce the following results:

Run Number	Number of Hurricanes	Total Amount of Losses
1	0	0
2	4	$3,500,000
3	2	$6,435,000

This process would be repeated many times, perhaps 10,000 times, and the arithmetic mean of all of the runs would be used as the estimate of the total losses to be expected. It is possible that no two of the 10,000 runs would produce exactly the same answer because of the element of chance introduced into the model.

planning instrument for an insurer. Actually, a deterministic model is likely to be more useful for most planning tasks. Since the output from a probabilistic model varies by chance, it is difficult to draw any firm conclusions from the model without running it many times and comparing the results of the many runs. This can be an expensive process because it may involve substantial costs for both computer and employee time. In most cases, the additional expense of building and operating a probabilistic model is not justified by improved results.

One notable exception is the area of reinsurance planning. One major purpose of reinsurance is to protect the ceding insurer from excessive chance fluctuations in losses. The adequacy of a reinsurance program for that purpose can be tested adequately in advance only by using a probabilistic computer model. Investment operations may also be represented more realistically by probabilistic models. This is especially true for investments involving common stocks and real estate, for which market prices fluctuate widely and for which potential capital gains are a major consideration.

Analysis of Reinsurance Requirements

The goal of a primary insurer's reinsurance planning is to design a reinsurance program that provides the degree of stability needed by the primary insurer while keeping reinsurance costs to a practical minimum. Of course, compliance with state regulatory requirements is also a concern.

The degree of stability needed is determined by the necessity for preserving the insurer's solvency and ability to function effectively and the attitude of its owners and managers toward the stability of profits. The owners and managers of some insurers are willing to accept substantial fluctuations in profits from year to year, while others demand greater stability.

An insurer must make many decisions in planning its reinsurance program. Among those decisions are the following:

1. What kind or kinds of reinsurance should it buy?
2. What retentions and limits should it have on each reinsurance contract?
3. What is a reasonable price to pay for the reinsurance contracts it decides to purchase?

Among the factors that must be considered in answering these questions are the following:

1. The size of the insurer's capital and surplus
2. The sizes of the individual risks it insures and the limits of its coverage for them

3. The total premium volume of the insurer
4. The premium volume for each line
5. The territory in which it operates
6. The geographic concentration of risks insured
7. The liquidity of the insurer's investment portfolio

Unfortunately, these factors cannot be evaluated individually and independently because substantial interactions occur among them. The most satisfactory method for considering all of these factors simultaneously is through the use of computer modeling. A reinsurance planning model is rather complex. Constructing such a model requires a thorough understanding of insurance, reinsurance, and company finance as well as mathematical techniques. Since a major purpose of reinsurance is to reduce chance fluctuations, a probabilistic model is appropriate for testing various reinsurance programs to find the one most advantageous to the particular circumstances under which the insurer operates.

For quota share reinsurance alone, the model can be rather simple, since the division of premiums and losses between ceding company and reinsurer is based only on aggregate premiums and aggregate losses. If only quota share treaties are to be considered, a deterministic model may be adequate.

However, for excess of loss and surplus share treaties, individual losses must be simulated. Both the number of covered losses and the amount of each loss must vary in the model in a manner similar to the way they vary in the ceding company's actual insurance portfolio. For surplus share, each loss must also be associated with an amount of direct insurance in order to properly apply the ceding company's retention.

For catastrophe reinsurance, the frequency of catastrophes (such as hurricanes, tornadoes, and earthquakes) must be simulated along with the aggregate amount of losses from each catastrophe. Depending on the terms of the proposed reinsurance contracts, simulation of individual losses within each catastrophe may also be necessary.

The number and amount of losses from catastrophes depend in part on the number and size of risks the insurer covers in areas subject to catastrophes. Consequently, a model to test catastrophe reinsurance must reflect the geographic distribution of insured properties as well as the probability of a catastrophic event and the probable magnitude of the forces unleashed by the event.

Another more complex probabilistic model would simulate the results on the insurer's financial statements of various kinds of reinsurance under various loss scenarios.

Evaluation of Insurers

Insurers sometimes need to analyze another insurer financially. Such an evaluation may be made because of a proposed merger or acquisition, for tax purposes, or for other reasons. In the case of a merger or an acquisition, the evaluation may be conducted for either the acquirer or the acquiree. Due diligence requirements would mandate that an evaluation be performed by each side independently. Actuaries are frequently called on to perform that evaluation.

The Actuarial Standards Board listed the principal elements to be considered in an actuarial appraisal of an insurance company as follows:

> 5.2 *Estimated Value of Insurance Company*—Based on actuarial appraisal calculations, the value of an insurance company is normally expressed as the sum of the following three components as of the appraisal date:
>
> a. Adjusted Net Worth
>
> b. Appraisal Value of Business in Force
>
> c. Appraisal Value of Future Business Capacity
>
> 5.2.1 *Adjusted Net Worth*—This component consists of the following:
>
> - Statutory capital and surplus
> - Any statutory liabilities that, in essence, represent allocations of surplus (e.g., mandatory securities valuation reserves, statutory portions of casualty Schedule Preserves, etc.)
> - Any statutory non-admitted assets that have realizable value
> - Reduction for surplus items that represent obligations to others
>
> 5.2.2 *Value of Business in Force*—This component equals the present value of future earnings attributable to business in force on the appraisal date.
>
> 5.2.3 *The Value of Future Business Capacity*—This component is generally represented by the present value of future earnings attributable to business issued or acquired after the appraisal date and attributable to the existing structure of the enterprise. In certain cases, it could be based on the market value of the company's charters and licenses and similar components of goodwill. [2]

Of course, these broad categories include many items. Among the principal factors of an actuarial nature to be considered in evaluating an insurance company are the following:

1. Adequacy of loss reserves
2. Adequacy of the unearned premium reserve
3. Adequacy and competitiveness of rate structures

4. Adequacy of reinsurance arrangements
5. Adequacy of funding for employee benefit plans, especially health and pension plans

Item (5) above would most likely be evaluated by a person trained in life insurance and pension actuarial techniques. The methods used for that purpose are not explained here. The ratemaking techniques discussed in Chapters 10 and 11 would be used to test rate adequacy, along with an analysis of past loss ratios by line and territory.

Techniques discussed elsewhere in this chapter would be used to test the adequacy of loss reserves and reinsurance arrangements. A sample of claim files would also be examined to verify that case reserves were properly established. However, that task would probably be undertaken by claims personnel rather than actuaries. Testing loss reserves is also an important part of testing rate adequacy. Posting inadequate loss reserves results in an understatement of the loss ratio and, consequently, inadequate rates.

Rate testing for a contemplated merger or acquisition must consider not only the adequacy of rates but also their competitiveness. One proposed acquisition was dropped quickly after the acquiring insurer discovered that the company it proposed to acquire had priced itself out of the market. It had raised its rates well above its competitors. The result was high short-term profits but a rapidly declining market share and agency force. The acquiring company doubted that the damage could be successfully reversed.

Testing the unearned premium reserve is perhaps the least difficult part of the actuarial evaluation of an insurer. It involves checking to see that the records for policies in force have been maintained properly and that calculating the unearned premiums from the in-force file was performed correctly. Very little discretion is involved in calculating the unearned premium reserve, and significant misstatements of the reserve are rare. Because it is the second largest liability on an insurer's balance sheet, the reserve should be verified.

Best's Ratings

The A.M. Best Company (Best's) has been in business for almost a century and has published financial-strength ratings of both life and property-liability insurers during most of that time. Initially, its ratings were formulated only once each year, when insurers published financial statements. Recently, the ratings have been reviewed quarterly, although mergers, catastrophe losses, the insolvency of reinsurers, or other unusual events may necessitate additional reviews.

Best's property-liability insurance company ratings are published annually in two books, *Best's Insurance Reports—Property/Casualty Edition* and *Best's Key Rating Guide*. Both books are published in July. The discussion that follows is based on the Preface of the 1996 edition of *Best's Reports*.

Ratings that are changed during the year are reported in *Best's Rating Monitor*, a special section of the company's newsletter, *Best Week*. In addition, up-to-the-minute ratings can be obtained for a fee by calling *Bestline*, the company's telephone rating service. Changes in ratings for major insurers are often reported in the insurance trade press and sometimes in the popular press and on various computer on-line services. Best's prepares reports and ratings for almost all significant insurers. Small insurers that are exempted from filing the NAIC Annual Statement form, the primary source of rating information, are one exception.

Although the NAIC Annual Statement and quarterly statement forms are the principal sources of rating information, they may be supplemented by audit reports, SEC reports, reports of insurance department examinations, and internal company reports.

The A.M. Best Company publishes three types of ratings: a Best's Rating, a Financial Performance Rating (FPR), and a Financial Size Category rating. Each of these ratings is discussed in more detail below.

When a person within the insurance industry refers to a Best's Rating without further qualification, he or she is most likely referring to the financial strength rating, officially called a Best's Rating by the A.M. Best Company. The Best's Rating is generally considered to be the most important of the three ratings published for most insurers by the A.M. Best Company. The company states the objective of the rating process as follows:

> The objective of Best's rating system is to evaluate the factors affecting the overall performance of an insurance company in order to provide our opinion of the company's financial strength, operating performance, competitive market position and ability to meet its obligations to policyholders currently and in the near future. The procedure includes quantitative and qualitative evaluations of the company's financial condition and operating performance.[3]

In addition, Best's notes the following:

> Best's Ratings reflect our independent **opinion** of the financial strength and operating performance of an insurer relative to standards established by the A.M. Best Company. Best's Ratings are **not a warranty** of an insurer's current or future ability to meet its obligations to policyholders, nor are they a recommendation of a specific policy form, contract, rate or claim practice. (emphasis in original)[4]

Quantitative Tests

The quantitative phase of the rating procedure consists of over one hundred tests. The individual tests vary in importance from one insurer to another, depending on the characteristics of the insurer. However, the quantitative tests as a group are intended to measure the following characteristics of an insurer:

- Profitability
- Capital and leverage
- Liquidity
- Loss reserve adequacy

The tests are based on the insurer's reported data for at least the past five years. An insurer's test results are evaluated by comparing them to its peer group as established by the A.M. Best Company. The peer group standards are based on an analysis of the peer group's reported data for the past twenty years.

Profitability Tests

Profitability indicates management's ability to operate the company in such a way as to generate or attract sufficient capital to support its future operations and growth. The analysis of profitability encompasses underwriting profit or loss, investment profit or loss, and capital gains or losses. The insurer's profits and losses over the past five years are analyzed as to their magnitude and source. Profits are strongly affected by operational changes, so trends in premium volume and distribution, investment income, net income, and surplus are analyzed.

Capital and Leverage Tests

The company's ability to withstand losses from unfavorable management decisions, industry trends, and economic developments depends on its capital and leverage. An insurer's capital is measured by its surplus to policyholders. Its **leverage** is measured by its dependence on the use of money belonging to others to supplement its capital in financing its operations. Leverage can result from borrowing money from a bank or through a bond issue. The A.M. Best Company calls this **financial leverage**. Insurance companies do not use financial leverage much, but insurance holding companies do.

However, leverage from loss reserves, unearned premium reserves, or other funds generated by the insurance business is common and likely to be substantial, especially for an insurer that writes a great deal of liability insurance. A.M. Best Company calls this form of leverage **operational leverage**. Operational leverage increases as the insurer's written premiums increase.

Best's rating procedures identify and measure four kinds of operational leverage. The first of these is the leverage resulting from current premium writings. This form of leverage is measured by the ratio of net written premiums to the insurer's policyholders' surplus. Net written premiums are gross written premiums less reinsurance premiums ceded and less return premiums. Some analysts may calculate the premium-to-surplus ratio on the basis of the statutory surplus, as reported in the NAIC Annual Statement. The A.M. Best Company uses a modified surplus to policyholders, calculated by adjusting the statutory surplus to reflect the equity in the unearned premium reserve, inadequacy or redundancy in loss reserves, the difference between the reported value and the market value of assets, and other relevant factors. A premium-to-surplus ratio is considered unfavorable by Best's if it exceeds 2.0. In addition, a change in net written premiums greater than 10 percent is considered unfavorable.

The second form of operational leverage recognized by Best's rating procedures is the ratio of net liabilities to surplus. The net liabilities consist mostly of loss reserves and unearned premium reserves, which are adjusted to reflect relevant reinsurance transactions. A.M. Best Company considers this ratio unfavorable if it exceeds 2.0 for property insurers or 3.8 for liability insurers.

The third form of leverage analyzed is the insurer's dependence on reinsurers and exposure to credit losses, such as the possibility that it may not be able to collect amounts due from reinsurers. The analysis consists of two phases: (1) an assessment of the financial strength of the reinsurers, and (2) measurement of the relationship between (a) surplus and (b) the premiums and reserves ceded to reinsurers and the related amount due or to become due from reinsurers. If the ratio of the ceded values to surplus exceeds 1.3, it is considered unfavorable.

The fourth form of leverage recognized in Best's rating procedures is investment leverage, which measures the risk that the insurer's surplus will be adversely affected by declining market prices of the insurer's investment securities. It measures the reduction in surplus that would result from (a) a 20 percent decline in the market value of the insurer's common stock portfolio, and (b) the decline in the market value of the insurer's portfolio of bonds, preferred stocks, and mortgages that would result from an increase of two percentage points in market interest rates.

Liquidity Tests

The liquidity tests measure an insurer's ability to meet unusual claims obligations without selling long-term investments or fixed assets that may be sellable only at a substantial loss during unfavorable market conditions. The emphasis in the liquidity tests is on cash and short-term securities that can be converted to cash with little or no loss in all but the most severe market conditions. One test of liquidity is the **quick liquidity** test ratio, which evaluates quick assets against net liabilities. The quick assets used in the ratio are (1) cash, (2) short-term investments issued by companies not affiliated with the insurer, (3) bonds maturing within one year and issued by companies not affiliated with the insurer, (4) government bonds maturing within five years, and (5) 80 percent of common stocks issued by corporations not affiliated with the insurer. Securities issued by companies affiliated with the insurer are excluded from quick assets regardless of their term or nature because they may not be marketable quickly without a substantial loss. Net liabilities consist primarily of loss reserves plus ceded reinsurance balances payable. A.M. Best Company considers a ratio below 30 percent for property insurers or 20 percent for liability insurers to be unsatisfactory.

The **current liquidity test** is the ratio of (1) the sum of cash, unaffiliated invested assets, and encumbrances on other properties to (2) net liabilities and ceded reinsurance balances payable, expressed as a percentage. If this ratio is less than 100 percent, the insurer may have to depend on the sale of its affiliated assets to cover its liabilities. A ratio lower than 120 percent for property insurers or lower than 100 percent for liability insurers is considered unsatisfactory.

The **overall liquidity test** is the ratio of (1) total admitted assets to (2) total liabilities less conditional reserves. A ratio below 140 percent for property insurers or 110 percent for liability insurers is considered unsatisfactory.

The **operating cash flow test** measures the funds generated by insurance operations, not including stockholder dividends, capital infusions, unrealized capital gains or losses on investment assets, and some noninsurance transactions among affiliated companies. A negative result is unsatisfactory and probably indicates poor underwriting results, poor investment results, or both.

The final test in the liquidity series is the ratio of (1) noninvestment grade bonds to (2) policyholders' surplus. The NAIC assigns a quality rating to all bonds held by insurers. The ratings range from 1 to 6, with 1 being the highest quality and 6 being for bonds that are in or near default. Bonds rated 3, 4, 5, or 6 are considered to be below investment grade. A.M. Best Company considers a ratio greater than 10 percent to be unsatisfactory for this test.

Loss Reserve Tests

The A.M. Best Company uses several measures of insurer loss reserves. It uses a proprietary model (details not disclosed) to measure the adequacy or inadequacy of the reserves. The needed reserves, as calculated by the model, are discounted for anticipated investment income to derive an economic loss reserve position. If the insurer's reported reserves are less than the calculated economic reserve, a deficiency in reserves is presumed to exist. If the reported reserves are greater than the economic reserve, a redundancy is presumed to exist. Any deficiency or redundancy is incorporated in the BCAR model discussed below.

Best's rating procedures also include the ratio of reported loss reserves to policyholders' surplus. A ratio greater than 150 percent is considered above the acceptable range for property insurers. A ratio above 300 percent for long-tailed liability writers is considered unacceptable.

Another test is the ratio of loss development to policyholders' surplus. The development of loss reserves (increase or decrease from previously reported values) is shown in Schedule P of the NAIC Annual Statement. If the reported development is positive and exceeds 25 percent of policyholders' surplus, the ratio is considered unacceptable.

The ratio of loss reserve development to net premiums earned is also calculated. The development figure used for this test is the same as for the above test. This ratio, like the others, is calculated for the most recent five years. If a comparison over time shows that the ratio is falling, it may indicate that the company is not establishing adequate reserves. However, the ratios over time will be affected by rapid growth (or shrinkage) of earned premiums and possibly by changes in the mix of business, so the ratio must be interpreted with care.

The four leverage measures, along with liquidity and other tests discussed above, are combined in Best's proprietary model to calculate the insurer's capital adequacy ratio, which measures the adequacy of the insurer's capital relative to the risks it assumes in its operations. The capital adequacy ratio, in turn, is used to calculate Best's Capital Adequacy Relativity (BCAR), which measures the company's capital adequacy relative to the capital adequacy of its industry peers. In calculating BCAR, insurers are divided into thirteen broad categories reflecting the lines written, as follows:

1. Personal lines
2. Personal auto
3. Homeowners
4. Non-standard auto
5. Property
6. Commercial casualty
7. Commercial auto

8. Workers compensation
9. Medical malpractice
10. Excess and surplus
11. Fidelity and surety
12. Credit/Accident and health
13. Reinsurance

In addition to this categorization by line, the industry peers are divided into three or four categories by size. The BCAR for a company is calculated by dividing the company's capital adequacy ratio by the composite capital adequacy ratio of its industry peers.

The A.M. Best Company does not publish a detailed explanation of the calculation of the BCAR. Following is the explanation it provides:

> Beginning in 1995, A.M. Best began publishing Best's Capital Adequacy Relativity (BCAR) results for property/casualty insurers assigned letter ratings or Financial Performance Ratings. This test, which measures a company's relative capital strength compared to its industry peer composite, is an important factor in determining the appropriateness of its rating. Using our proprietary capital model, BCAR integrates many components historically viewed and measured separately within our leverage, liquidity and loss reserve quantitative analysis.
>
> While our BCAR model is structurally similar in some respects to the NAIC Risk-Based Capital Model, it significantly differs in several key areas. Fundamentally, the BCAR model has considerably higher capital thresholds for its various risk elements than the NAIC model. This is appropriate since BCAR is used for rating purposes, whereas the NAIC's model is used for solvency purposes. Generally, companies must meet Best's minimum relative capitalization requirements based on a number of factors, including their BCAR results, to qualify for a particular rating level.[5]

Qualitative Tests

In addition to the quantitative tests, several qualitative tests are used in evaluating the insurer's (1) spread of risk and exposure to catastrophes; (2) quality and appropriateness of its reinsurance arrangements; (3) quality and diversity of investments; (4) adequacy of loss reserves; (5) adequacy of surplus; (6) capital structure of the insurer and its affiliates; (7) management; and (8) market positions.

Spread of Risk

The analysis of spread of risk includes (1) the size of the insurer's premium volume, (2) geographic spread of business, (3) diversity of product lines written, and (4) the distribution systems used. The objective is to have a sufficiently diverse book of business so that the loss ratio will not be affected excessively by natural catastrophes, adverse economic developments, or other factors that might apply to a limited geographic area or a limited class of business. Insurers that operate in a limited geographic area may also be exposed to adverse underwriting experience resulting from regulatory actions.

Reinsurance Analysis

The reinsurance analysis includes a review of the appropriateness of the reinsurance contracts purchased and the financial strength of the reinsurers. The appropriateness of the reinsurance program depends on the insurer's underwriting practices, including the lines written, the size of risks written, territorial spread of risks, and catastrophe exposures, as well as its other financial resources. The reinsurance contracts are also reviewed to see whether they provide true risk transfer, or merely financial window dressing.

Quality and Diversity of Investments

The insurer's invested assets are carefully screened to determine whether they could be sold quickly in an emergency with minimal market loss. Particular attention is given to large individual investments constituting 10 percent or more of the insurer's policyholders' surplus and to large investments in subsidiaries or affiliates. Lack of diversification by industry or by geographic area is also cause for concern.

Loss Reserves

The analysis of loss reserves depends primarily on the quantitative tests discussed previously in this chapter. However, an estimate of the uncertainty in loss reserve estimates is also included. If the quantitative tests indicate that the estimated uncertainty is greater than any equity in the reserves as indicated by the quantitative tests, the insurer's rating may be adversely affected.

Surplus

An insurers' surplus is a proxy for its financial strength. Surplus serves as a cushion should unexpected events occur. The adequacy of any insurers' surplus must be evaluated relative to other factors specific to that insurer, such as its investment portfolio, reinsurance program, and underwriting book of business.

Capital Structure

The capital and surplus structure of the insurer and its holding company, if any, are analyzed to be sure that they are sound and able to meet their obligations. For example, if the holding company is heavily burdened by debt, the debt service costs may require large stockholder dividends from the insurer, thereby reducing its ability to accumulate surplus through retained earnings. In extreme cases, the dividend drain may hamper the insurer's efforts to provide efficient service to its policyholders.

Management

Although the experience, capabilities, and integrity of management cannot be measured with mathematical precision, they are crucial factors in assessing an insurer's future prospects. Those factors are analyzed partly on the basis of the insurer's past success if the present management has been in place for several years. Otherwise, the assessment is based on past experience of the managers in other positions and on the raters' opinions of the managers developed through extensive meetings with them.

Market Position

An insurer's market position depends on its ability to maintain or increase its market share. Market position, in turn, is based on factors such as (1) a low expense ratio; (2) superior service; (3) strong recognition by buyers and producers in the insurers's selected market; (4) access to plentiful and inexpensive capital; and (5) control over distribution channels.

Best's Financial Strength Ratings

Based on the analysis outlined above, the A.M. Best Company assigns a letter rating, called a Best's Rating, to most significant insurers licensed and operating within the United States. The rating may be based on the data from a single insurer and apply only to that insurer, or it may be based on the consolidated figures for several companies operating under common ownership and management and apply to all insurers within the group. There are fifteen letter ratings ranging downward from A++ to F. The rating of F is for insurers currently in liquidation.

Financial Performance Ratings

The A.M. Best Company assigns Financial Performance Ratings (FPR) to insurers that are too small to qualify for Best's Ratings or cannot provide data for five representative years as required for a Best's Rating. The process for determining an FPR is very similar to that discussed above for Best's Ratings but is based on three years of data instead of five years. The FPRs range from "FPR=9," the most favorable rating, to "FPR=1," which indicates that at the insurer's request, no FPR is published. Before 1994, the

Financial Performance Rating was known as the Financial Performance Index (FPI). Exhibit 12-13 shows all of the Best's Ratings and Financial Performance Ratings along with a brief explanation of their meanings. It also shows the number of individual insurance companies that qualified for each rating as of June 24, 1996.

No Rating Opinions

At the bottom of Exhibit 12-13 is a list of Best's "no rating opinion" designations. These designations are applied to insurers that have not been assigned a Best's Rating. Some of them may qualify for the FPR. The reason for not assigning a Best's Rating is explained in the full report on the insurer in *Best's Reports*.

Rating Modifiers

Best's Ratings may be accompanied by one or more modifiers, indicated by lowercase letters. These modifiers are as follows:

- g—indicates that the rating is based on consolidated information for the rated insurer and one or more affiliated insurers under common ownership or management
- p—indicates a pooled rating based on data from two or more insurers operating under common ownership or management and pooling all of their business, with all premiums, expenses, and losses prorated among member insurers
- r—indicates that the rated insurer reinsures substantially all of its direct business with a single reinsurer and has been assigned the rating of the reinsurer
- q—indicates a rating that has been qualified because the insurer's rating may be adversely affected by state legislation or losses from residual market programs
- u—indicates that the insurer's rating is under review because of recent events or changes in its operations, which may have either positive or negative rating implications
- x—indicates that the rating has been changed during the year
- c—contingent rating, indicates that there has been a slight decline in the insurer's financial performance but not enough change to warrant a reduction in rating (not used since 1992)
- w—watch list, indicates that the insurer is being closely monitored because of recent unfavorable developments (not used since 1993)

Exhibit 12-13
1996 Property/Casualty Rating Distribution Based on Individual Companies as of June 24, 1996

Best's Rating /FPR Level	Category Rating Opinions	Number	Percent
Secure Categories			
A++	Superior	141	6.8%
A+	Superior	301	14.5
FPR=9	Strong	0	0.0
	Subtotal	**442**	**21.3**
A	Excellent	547	26.3
A–	Excellent	475	22.8
FPR=8	Strong	1	0.0
FPR=7	Above Average	8	0.4
	Subtotal	**1,031**	**49.6**
B++	Very Good	161	7.8
B+	Very Good	143	6.9
FPR=6	Above Average	19	0.9
FPR=5	Average	51	2.5
	Subtotal	**374**	**18.0**
	Total Secure Ratings	**1,842**	**88.8%**
Vulnerable Categories			
B	Adequate	75	3.6%
B–	Adequate	33	1.6
FPR=4	Average	43	2.1
	Subtotal	**151**	**7.3**
C++	Fair	12	0.6
C+	Fair	11	0.5
FPR=3	Below Average	16	0.8
	Subtotal	**39**	**1.9**
C	Marginal	12	0.6
C–	Marginal	2	0.1
FPR=2	Below Average	5	0.2
	Subtotal	**19**	**0.9**
D	Very Vulnerable	5	0.2
E	Under State Supervision	14	0.7
F	In Liquidation	4	0.2
	Total Vulnerable Ratings	**232**	**11.2%**
	Total Rating Opinions	**2,079**	**100.0%**

Continued on next page.

Level	Category	Number	Percent
	No Rating Opinions		
NA-1	Limited Data Filing	771	69.3%
NA-2	Less Than Minimum Size/Operating Experience	126	11.3
NA-3	Rating Procedure Inapplicable	196	17.6
NA-4	Company Request	19	1.7
S	Rating Suspended	0	0.0
	Subtotal—No Rating Opinions	**1,112**	**100.0%**
	Total Rated Companies	**3,191**	

1996 Best's Insurance Reports—Property/Casualty, p. xiii.

Exhibit 12-14 shows the number of insurers to which the modifiers were assigned in 1996. The modifiers c and w do not appear in Exhibit 12-14 because they had been dropped before 1996. As noted in Exhibit 12-14, two modifiers were assigned to the ratings of fifty-four insurers. The remaining ratings were subject to only one modifier each.

Best's Financial Size Category

The Best's Financial Size Category indicates the size of the company as measured by its reported policyholders' surplus plus conditional reserves. There are fifteen financial size categories, indicated by Roman numerals. They range from Class I to Class XV, with Class I being the smallest insurers. Exhibit 12-15 shows the categories and the number of insurers assigned to each class in 1996. Exhibit 12-15 does not include insurers with a Best's Rating of E or F.

The Financial Size Category is not a measure of the insurer's financial performance or financial soundness. It is one measure of the insurer's capacity to assume large risks in either its insurance or its investment operations.

Risk-Based Capital

Risk-based capital (RBC) is a system, developed by the NAIC, to determine the minimum amount of capital needed by an insurer to support its operations given the insurer's risk characteristics. Before the implementation of RBC, state insurance codes made little or no allowance for risk differentials among insurers in the laws that specified minimum capital requirements. The NAIC RBC formula and the model law that authorizes it attempt to make the

Exhibit 12-14
Assignment of Rating Modifiers, 1996

Rating Modifier	Number of Companies
g – Group	332
p – Pooled	527
r – Reinsured	318
q – Qualified	4
u – Under review	71
Subtotal	**1,252**
Dual Assignments	**(54)**
Total Modified Ratings	**1,198**

1996 Best's Reports—Property/Casualty, p. xv.

minimum capital required for a company a function of the risks assumed by that company.

The RBC model law enables insurance regulators to take regulatory action when it is warranted. The NAIC RBC formula prescribes four levels of regulatory intervention that permit state regulators to take decisive action before an insurer becomes too financially weak to be rehabilitated. Before the NAIC developed an RBC formula, state regulators were required to petition the courts and prove that the insurer was in financial difficulty before intervention was allowed, subjecting the insurer to regulatory control. The NAIC RBC formula offers an objective test of the insurer's solvency and matches regulatory action to the level of solvency concern. For example, the first level of regulatory intervention is the Company Action Level. At this level, the insurer must submit a comprehensive financial plan that identifies the factors that caused the condition and proposes corrective action to solve the problem. At the fourth level of regulatory intervention, the Mandatory Control Level, the state regulators must seize control of the insurer. The four levels of regulatory intervention are shown in Exhibit 12-16. Thresholds between the levels are stated in terms of "Percentage of Authorized Control Level RBC." That percentage means that if the insurer's capital is less than 200 percent of the NAIC RBC minimum, the insurer comes under the first level of control.

The nondiscretionary operation of the RBC model has benefits for insurers, state regulators, and the insurance-buying public. Insurers perform the RBC calculation themselves, so they know whether they will come under regulatory scrutiny. Before RBC was implemented, insurers performed the calculation,

Exhibit 12-15
1996 Financial Size Category

Financial Size Category	Adjusted Policyholders' Surplus ($ Millions)	Number of Companies
Class I	0 to 1	522
Class II	1 to 2	223
Class III	2 to 5	391
Class IV	5 to 10	313
Class V	10 to 25	336
Class VI	25 to 50	249
Class VII	50 to 100	216
Class VIII	100 to 250	300
Class IX	250 to 500	149
Class X	500 to 750	86
Class XI	750 to 1,000	61
Class XII	1,000 to 1,250	77
Class XIII	1,250 to 1,500	15
Class XIV	1,500 to 2,000	64
Class XV	2,000 or greater	171
Total Companies		***3,173**

*Does not include 18 companies rated E and F.

1996 Best's Insurance Reports—Property/Casualty, p. xvi.

and many took early action to improve their total adjusted capital. **Total adjusted capital** is the result of an insurer's RBC calculation. State insurance departments that have been accredited by the NAIC do not have a choice about whether to implement the regulatory action specified; therefore, regulatory intervention is not arbitrary or motivated by political factors. State insurance regulators are given a clear mandate with RBC. Rehabilitation is no longer subject to delays caused by regulators' expectations that insurers' financial problems will solve themselves. The number of larger insurer failures in the 1980s increased public awareness that insurer solvency, the focus of insurance regulatory efforts, was not being achieved. RBC, part of a broader NAIC solvency policing agenda, is the insurance regulator's greatest weapon for ensuring solvency, which is fundamental to insurers' meeting obligations to policyholders and claimants.

Exhibit 12-16
Risk-Based Capital Levels

RBC Level	Percentage of Authorized Control Level RBC	Action Required
Company Action Level	200 percent	Insurer files comprehensive plan
Regulatory Action Level	150 percent	Regulator performs exam as necessary; insurer files comprehensive plan
Authorized Control Level	100 percent	Regulator may seize control
Mandatory Control Level	70 percent	Regulator required to place insurer under regulatory control

Brian K. Atchinson, "The NAIC's Risk-Based Capital System," *NAIC Research Quarterly*, vol. 2, no. 4, October 1996, p. 9. Risk-Based Capital (RBC) for Insurers Model Act, Official NAIC Model Insurance Laws, Regulations and Guidelines, National Association of Insurance Commissioners, vol. 2, 1995, pp. 312-4 through 312-9.

The NAIC has been adamant since initial discussions about the creation of an RBC formula that the RBC level should not be construed to equate with financial strength. Even insurers with 150 percent to 200 percent of total adjusted capital are subject to state regulatory scrutiny at the company action level. The NAIC was equally concerned that its RBC formula not be used for making competitive comparisons among insurers. The result of an insurer's NAIC RBC calculation is shown in its NAIC Annual Statement. The NAIC RBC results for all insurers should not be ranked or used in insurer advertising. Comparisons among insurer RBC results are meaningless and could mislead the public. RBC is a regulatory tool designed to promptly redirect regulatory attention to financially distressed insurers.

The following sections, though not a comprehensive discussion, highlight the components of the NAIC RBC formula. The NAIC booklet entitled *1996 NAIC Property and Casualty Risk-Based Capital Report Including Overview and Instructions for Companies* provides a more thorough description. Although the main components of the NAIC RBC formula are well established, many of the factors used in the formula are regularly evaluated for their appropriateness and may change periodically. The NAIC formula was designed so that it could evolve into a more effective regulatory tool. As a result, the discussion that follows addresses only the main components of the NAIC RBC formula, not the details that support it.

The NAIC RBC formula has four main components: (1) asset risk; (2) credit risk; (3) underwriting risk; and (4) off-balance-sheet risk. Each component of the formula weighs the risks assumed by an insurer, since those risks vary by insurer. For example, one insurer might invest solely in short-term government bonds, while another holds a large portfolio of common stocks. The components of the NAIC RBC formula attempt to evaluate these risks and consolidate them into a single index. Because it is unlikely that all of the risks measured by the formula would befall an insurer simultaneously, the NAIC RBC formula tempers the amalgamation of components using a statistical adjustment called covariance. The **covariance adjustment** reduces the sum of the risk categories in the NAIC RBC formula.

Asset Risk

Asset risk is the chance that an asset's value will be lower than expected. Virtually all assets involve some such risk, though some assets are riskier than others. Under the RBC formula, the riskier assets require more underlying capital than do less risky assets. The amount of capital required is determined by multiplying the NAIC Annual Statement value of the asset by a factor provided by the NAIC in the RBC booklet. Exhibit 12-17 shows some examples of the risk charges used. U.S. government bonds, for example, have a factor of 0.000. This indicates that they are considered risk-free; no underlying capital is needed to support them. On the other hand, bonds in default require $3 of supporting capital for each $10 of reported value of the bonds.

To determine the amount of risk-based capital required to support its asset risks, an insurer would multiply the NAIC Annual Statement value of each asset by the appropriate risk factor and sum the resulting products. Additional RBC charges are imposed if the insurer's investments are concentrated in securities issued by a small number of issuers, that is, if investments are not sufficiently diversified.

Credit Risk

Credit risk reflects the possibility that the insurer will not be able to collect money owed to it. One credit exposure is the chance that one or more of the insurer's reinsurers will not be able to pay amounts due under reinsurance contracts. Cessions to some reinsurers are not subject to the RBC charge. Such reinsurers include (1) state-mandated involuntary pools and federal insurance programs; (2) voluntary market mechanism pools that meet certain conditions

Exhibit 12-17
Sample of RBC Charges for Selected Asset Categories

Type of Investment	RBC Factor
U.S. government bonds	0.000
Highest-quality corporate bonds	0.003
Cash and short-term investments	0.003
High-quality corporate bonds	0.010 to 0.100
Bonds in default on principle or interest	0.300
Mortgages and collateral loans	0.050
Unaffiliated common stock	0.150
Real estate	0.100
Partnerships and joint ventures	0.200

Brian K. Atchinson, "The NAIC's Risk-Based Capital System," *NAIC Research Quarterly*, vol. 2, no. 4, October 1996, p. 7.

specified in the RBC booklet; and (3) the insurer's U.S.-based affiliates, subsidiaries, and parents.

Other credit exposures that require RBC are (1) federal income tax recoverable; (2) interest, dividends, and real estate income due and accrued; (3) receivables from affiliates, subsidiaries, and parents; (4) amounts receivable relating to uninsured accident and health plans; and (5) aggregate write-ins for assets other than invested assets. For each of the above categories, the value shown in the NAIC Annual Statement is multiplied by the appropriate RBC factor to find the required RBC component for credit risk. The factor for reinsurance receivable is 0.100, and the factor for interest, dividends, etc., is 0.010. The others in this category are all 0.050.

Underwriting Risk

Underwriting risk measures the volatility of the lines of insurance written by an insurer. For example, one insurer may specialize in physical damage insurance for private passenger automobiles, a line with virtually no exposure to large single losses and limited exposure to catastrophe losses. Another insurer may specialize in property insurance for large industrial risks, with an exposure to both large individual losses and catastrophe losses from earthquakes, tornadoes, and hurricanes.

The underwriting RBC varies by line of insurance. It is calculated by multiplying the written premiums and the loss and loss adjustment expense reserves for each line by their respective RBC factors. The RBC factors for each line can vary depending on the insurer's loss ratio (including loss adjustment expenses) and loss development experience for the line.

The experience adjustment to the RBC ratios is based on a comparison of the insurer's experience to the industry experience for the past nine years for most lines of insurance. Five years is used for special property, auto physical damage, and several other lines that do not have long loss development periods. This calculation reflects the underpricing of existing and future insurance products and the underestimation of loss reserves. Of all the components of an insurer's RBC, the formula places greatest emphasis on its underwriting risk.

Off-Balance-Sheet Risk

Off-balance-sheet risk recognizes those risks associated with contingent liabilities and excessive growth that do not appear on the insurer's balance sheet. If an insurer, for example, had significant investments in affiliates or had made financial guarantees on behalf of affiliates, the NAIC RBC formula would require additional capital to offset the risk present. Excessive growth is also penalized under the NAIC RBC formula. The excessive growth charge is based on a combination of the growth in gross premiums written for the most recent four years, the loss and loss adjustment expense reserves for the most recent year, and the net premiums written for the most recent year.

IRIS

The Insurance Regulatory Information System (IRIS) was developed by the NAIC in the 1970s, about two decades before the risk-based capital formula. It was originally known as the *Early Warning System*, a name that accurately indicates its original purpose. IRIS was developed to provide the regulatory authorities with an early warning that an insurer might be experiencing financial difficulty. An early warning might enable the regulators to rehabilitate the insurer or, if rehabilitation is not practical, to minimize the losses resulting from liquidation.

The Insurance Regulatory Information System consists of eleven tests. An insurer that fails more than three of the eleven tests is not presumed to be in danger of financial failure, but it is likely to be selected by the regulators for more detailed attention.

The eleven IRIS tests are listed below. The appearance of "(Best's)" after the test name indicates that the same test, possibly with some minor variations in calculation or interpretation, is used by the A.M. Best Company in formulating Best's Ratings. Detailed instructions for calculating the IRIS test ratios and more detailed explanations of their interpretation are given in the NAIC's publication *Using the NAIC Insurance Regulatory Information System*, published annually.

Premium-to-Surplus Ratio (Best's)

The first test in the IRIS system is the ratio of net written premiums to policyholders' surplus, stated as a percentage. A ratio of 300 percent or less is considered acceptable. If this ratio is near 300 percent, it may be reviewed jointly with the ratio of surplus aid to surplus, described below, which shows the financial assistance provided to the insurer through its reinsurers.

Change in Writings (Best's)

Ratio 2 shows the percentage change in the insurer's net written premiums during the most recent year. Experience has shown that excessive growth in premium volume is frequently associated with financial problems. An increase or a decrease of 33 percent or less is considered acceptable for this ratio.

Ratio of Surplus Aid to Surplus

Ratio 3 is the ratio of surplus aid to surplus. Surplus aid, as used here, is the increase in the insurer's surplus that results from its purchases of reinsurance. The surplus aid is derived from ceding commissions on reinsurance ceded to nonaffiliated reinsurers. If the ceding commissions on unearned ceded premiums exceed 25 percent of the ceding insurer's policyholders' surplus, the ratio is considered unsatisfactory.

Two-Year Overall Operating Ratio (Best's)

Ratio 4 is calculated as the insurer's two-year loss ratio plus its two-year expense ratio minus its two-year investment income ratio. The loss ratio is the ratio of incurred losses and adjustment expenses and policyholder dividends to net earned premiums. The expense ratio is the ratio of underwriting expenses (all expenses except investment expenses) to net written premiums. The investment income ratio is the ratio investment income to net earned premiums. A ratio of less than 100 percent is considered satisfactory.

Investment Yield (Best's)

Ratio 5 is the ratio of net investment income to the average cash and invested assets for the year, stated as a percentage. A yield greater than 5 percent is considered satisfactory. A lower ratio may indicate excessive investment in home office facilities or subsidiaries and affiliates.

Change in Surplus (Best's)

Ratio 6 is the percentage change in adjusted policyholders' surplus during the year. Adjusted policyholders' surplus is the statutory policyholders' surplus (shown in the NAIC Annual Statement) plus equity in the unearned premium reserve. The ratio is considered satisfactory if it is in the range between a decrease of 10 percent and an increase of 50 percent.

Large increases in policyholders' surplus may result from an increase in surplus aid from reinsurance, a manipulation of loss reserves development, or other undesirable accounting techniques. Of course, large increases can also result from favorable developments, such as the issuance and sale of additional capital stock by the insurer. However, the reasons for any large change must be known and understood.

Liabilities to Liquid Assets (Best's)

Ratio 7 is the ratio of total liabilities to liquid assets. Liquid assets are computed as follows:

> Installment premiums booked but not yet due + Cash, invested assets, and accrued investment income − Investments in affiliated companies − The value of owned real estate in excess of 5 percent of policyholders' surplus

The ratio is considered satisfactory if it is less than 105 percent.

Agents' Balances to Surplus

Ratio 8 is calculated by dividing agents' balances by policyholders' surplus, both as reported in the NAIC Annual Statement, with the result stated as a percentage. A ratio of less than 40 percent is considered satisfactory.

One-Year Reserve Development to Surplus (Best's)

Ratio 9 is the ratio of loss development during the past year to the insurer's policyholders' surplus at the beginning of the year (or the end of the prior year). The loss development is (1) the incurred losses for all years reported at the end of the year less incurred losses for the latest accident year minus (2) the incurred losses for all years reported at the end of the prior year. This figure is reported in Schedule P of the NAIC Annual Statement. The ratio is stated as a percentage, and a ratio of less than 25 percent is considered satisfactory.

A high ratio on this test may indicate that the insurer's loss reserves are inadequate and that its surplus has consequently been overstated. Ratios 10 and 11 also deal with the adequacy of loss reserves, indicating the importance attached to loss reserves as a factor in insurer insolvencies.

Two-Year Reserve Development to Surplus

Ratio 10 is calculated in the same manner as Ratio 9, except the loss reserves and surplus for the second prior year are used instead of those for the prior year. A ratio of less than 25 percent is also acceptable for Ratio 10.

Estimated Current Reserve Deficiency to Surplus

Ratio 11 is calculated by dividing the estimated current loss reserve deficiency by policyholders' surplus. The estimated reserve deficiency (or redundancy) is calculated by a rather complex formula based on the insurer's historical ratio of loss reserves to earned premiums. A work sheet for the calculation is included in the NAIC's publication *Using the NAIC Insurance Regulatory Information System*. This ratio is considered satisfactory if it is less than 25 percent.

IRIS and RBC are merely two of the many tools available to regulators to avoid insurer insolvencies or reduce the losses that result from unavoidable insolvencies. Other tools, such as investment regulation, on-site examinations, and financial reporting, are equally or more important. However, understanding and complying with IRIS and RBC are important for insurers for reasons other than avoiding regulatory problems. These indicators of financial strength are also watched by sophisticated insurance buyers and producers, who may apply an even higher standard than the regulatory authorities.

Summary

Insurance companies are financial intermediaries, and the assets controlled by U.S. insurers are considerable. The investment function of an insurer contributes significantly to its overall profitability. Although investment decisions are not discussed in this chapter, many other financially related management decisions are. Because of their analytical expertise, actuaries often participate in the decision-making process.

Establishing accurate loss reserves is crucial for an insurer. Loss reserves represent an insurer's largest balance sheet liability. Loss reserves established for liability lines of insurance are more volatile than those established for lines of property insurance. Although most property claims are quickly settled, liability claims might take years to resolve. Since liability loss reserves remain outstanding for several years, they are usually much larger than property loss reserves relative to earned premium. Interest in loss reserve analysis and verification have grown as the product mix of the U.S. insurance industry has transitioned from a predominately property insurance industry to a predominately liability insurance industry.

Success in marketing, underwriting, claims, and other insurer functional departments requires insurers to plan. Planning might be short- or long-term, and increasingly sophisticated models are used to project possible contingencies. Deterministic models are used when consistent results are expected. Probabilistic models are used when the results might be affected by some chance variation.

A key area of an insurer's financial well-being is the adequacy of its reinsurance program. Reinsurance provides an insurer with stability, yet that stability is obtained at a price. An analysis of an insurer's reinsurance program seeks to find the best balance between the stability afforded an insurer and the cost of reinsurance.

An insurer's promise to pay claims is no more valuable than its ability to do so. The A. M. Best Company established its ratings to simplify the complex task of evaluating insurer financial statements and to meet the needs of the unsophisticated public that needs that information. The A. M. Best ratings measure an insurer's financial strength in meeting policyholder obligations.

The primary purpose of insurance regulation is to monitor the solvency of insurers and safeguard the public from the effects of those insolvencies that do occur. The NAIC has developed several tools to assist in identifying financially weak insurers. The NAIC's Risk-Based Capital formula considers an insurer's asset risk, credit risk, underwriting risk, and off-balance-sheet risk and develops a minimum amount of capital each insurer should maintain. The Insurance Regulatory Information System (IRIS) consists of eleven financial ratios. Insurers that develop values outside an acceptable range on three of the ratios are subject to scrutiny by state regulators. Both NAIC tools serve the public interest by helping regulators address insurers with financial problems before they impinge on the insolvent insurer's claim-paying ability.

Glossary

Additional terms are defined in the glossaries at the end of Chapters 10 and 11.

Accident Year—A method for collecting and analyzing loss statistics. An accident year includes all losses for which the loss event occurred in a given twelve-month period. The period most often used is a calendar year. See also Report Year.

Actuarial Reserves—Aggregate loss reserves established for the total of all outstanding losses. The loss reserves shown on an insurer's balance sheet. See also Case Reserves.

Actuarial Standard Board—An organization established by the American Academy of Actuaries to formulate standards for the guidance of actuaries in the performance of their professional duties.

Bulk Reserves—See Actuarial Reserves.

Case Reserves—Loss reserves established for individual claims as they are reported to the insurer. See also Actuarial Reserves.

Computer Model—A computer program consisting primarily of mathematical equations that simulate the operation of a system, such as an insurance company or a part of an insurance company.

Deterministic Model—A mathematical model of a system, such as an insurance company, in which the outputs are determined solely by the inputs, without any element of chance variation. Used primarily for planning purposes. See also Probabilistic Model.

Discounted Reserve—A loss reserve that has been reduced to reflect future investment income produced by the assets backing the reserve. See also Full-Value Reserve.

Full-Value Reserve—A loss reserve estimated to be equal to the amount required to settle an insured loss, without reduction for future investment income. See also Discounted Reserve.

Gross Reserve—See Full-Value Reserve.

Monte Carlo Model—See Computer Model and Probabilistic Model.

Probabilistic Model—A mathematical model of a system, such as an insurance company, in which the outputs are determined partly by the inputs and partly by chance. See also Deterministic Model.

Pure IBNR Reserve—That part of the total IBNR reserve representing the reserves for losses that have been incurred but have not yet been reported to the insurer. See also Reserve for Case Reserve Deficiencies and Total IBNR Reserve.

Report Year—A method of collecting and analyzing loss statistics. A report year includes all losses first reported to an insurer during a given twelve-month period. The period most often used is a calendar year. See also Accident Year.

Reserve for Case Reserve Deficiencies—That part of the total IBNR reserve representing deficiencies in the insurer's case reserves for reported losses. See also Pure IBNR Reserve and Total IBNR Reserve.

Statutory Reserves—Minimum loss reserves required by the NAIC Annual Statement blank for liability insurance and workers compensation insurance. They are calculated by the loss ratio method.

Stochastic Model—See Computer Model and Probabilistic Model.

Tabular Loss Reserve—A case loss reserve calculated on the basis of one or more actuarial tables, such as a mortality, morbidity, or remarriage table.

Total IBNR Reserve—The sum of the pure IBNR reserve and the reserve for case reserve deficiencies.

Chapter Notes

1. A.M. Best Company, Inc., *Best's Aggregates & Averages*, 1996 Edition, pp. 2, 3, 196.
2. *Exposure Draft of the Actuarial Standard of Practice, Actuarial Appraisals of Insurance Companies, Segments of Insurance Companies, and/or Blocks of Insurance Contracts* (Actuarial Standards Board, April 1990), pp. 4, 5.
3. *1996 Best's Insurance Reports—Property/Casualty*, p. viii.
4. *1996 Best's Insurance Reports—Property/Casualty*, p. viii.
5. *1996 Best's Insurance Reports—Property/Casualty*, p. ix.

Chapter 13

Claims Adjusting

Individuals and businesses purchase insurance to protect themselves from the financial consequences of loss and to alleviate the worry associated with the possibility of loss. Once a loss occurs, the insurer is expected to fulfill its responsibility to the policyholder and satisfy the demand for payment. **Claims adjusting** is the insurance company function that handles demands for claim payments.

This chapter lays the foundations for the study of claims adjusting by exploring the objectives of claims adjusting and the environment in which it is performed. The chapter also provides an overview of the claims adjusting process, focusing on aspects common to most types of claims. Issues particular to specific types of insurance are discussed in Chapter 14—Property Claims Adjusting and Chapter 15—Liability Claims Adjusting.

The Claims Environment

The claims department exists to fulfill the insurer's promises to its policyholders. Since claims departments control over half of what insurers spend, their proper and efficient performance is important to an insurer's profitability. The loss payments, expenses, and other information generated by the claims department is essential to the marketing, underwriting, and pricing of insurance products. Claims personnel are among the most visible of insurer employees to policyholders and the public. Claims adjusters must work well with a variety of people. Managing, organizing, and delegating settlement authority within claims departments contribute to their success.

Objectives of the Claims Department

Managing an efficient claims operation requires that senior management recognize the importance of the claims function to both the insurance consumer and the insurer itself.

Complying With the Contractual Promise

The primary function of claims adjusting is to satisfy the obligations of the insurer to the policyholder as agreed to in the insurance policy. Following a loss, the adjustment process becomes the embodiment of the insurance policy, and in the course of this process, the promise of the insuring agreement to "pay," defend, or indemnify in the event of a covered loss is fulfilled.

That objective is achieved by providing fair, prompt, and equitable service to the policyholder, either directly when the loss involves a first-party claim made by the policyholder against the insurer or indirectly through the adjustment of a third-party loss to persons making a claim against the policyholder and to whom the policyholder may be liable. (Unfair claims practices laws have been enacted to ensure that policyholders and claimants are not being mistreated. An extensive discussion of the NAIC Unfair Trade Practices Model Act is presented later in this chapter.)

From the insurer's perspective, claims are expected, and adjusters must deal with them routinely. The occurrence of a loss and its consequences can be all-consuming. Adjusters must therefore deal with policyholders and claimants in extremely stressful circumstances. Insurance is marketed not only as a financial mechanism to restore policyholders to a pre-loss state but also as a way to ensure peace of mind. The manner in which an adjuster handles a claim can help soothe the policyholder who has suffered a devastating loss. This is perhaps most evident in a major disaster such as a storm or a serious accident in which multiple losses involve numerous people. Were it not for insurance, administered through the claims adjusting process, recovery would be slow, inefficient, and difficult.

Achieving the Insurer's Profit Objective

Most of the discussion involving insurer profit objectives focuses on the marketing and underwriting departments. Without their proper operation, insurers would have difficulty achieving success. It is shortsighted, however, not to recognize the operation of the claims function as central to the success of the insurance operation.

For example, overpaid claims will result in lower profits. Policyholders are entitled to a fair settlement of their demands and nothing more. By overcompensating a policyholder or claimant, the insurer is unnecessarily raising the cost of insurance for all of its policyholders.

Conversely, tight-fisted claims handling may result in angry policyholders, more litigated claims, or the wrath of insurance regulators. Policyholders and claimants are likely to accept the settlement offer of the insurer if they understand the insurer's position on the claim and believe they are being treated fairly. If a claims adjuster treats a policyholder or claimant unfairly, the insurer may find itself in a lawsuit. Claims that are mishandled and that eventually lead to litigation represent decreased goodwill and increased expenses for the insurer.

Insurers survive or fail to some extent on their reputation for providing the service promised. A reputation for resisting meritorious claims can invalidate the effectiveness of insurer advertisements or goodwill earned over years of operation.

Uses of Claims Information

The claims function provides valuable information that helps other departments guide the operational direction of the insurer. The three primary departments that receive management information from the claims department are the marketing, underwriting, and actuarial departments.

Marketing

The marketing department requires information relating to customer satisfaction, timeliness of settlements, and other factors that assist in marketing the insurance product. The marketing department recognizes that the other services performed by the insurer for the policyholder are quickly forgotten if the insurer fails to perform well after the occurrence of a loss.

Many insurers that market commercial policies have developed "niche" products that address the needs of specific types of policyholders. The intent of these insurers is to become the recognized expert in certain business classes, providing a product and service that cannot be easily equaled elsewhere. Niche marketers recognize that the claims adjusting process can be a possible source for new coverage ideas and product innovations that can be incorporated into future policy forms.

Producers must also have policyholder loss information to prepare renewal policies properly. Many commercial policies are subject to rating plans that affect the policy premium, based, in part, on the policyholder's loss experience. In personal lines, personal auto policies may be surcharged when property damage claims are paid during the policy year.

Claims personnel must inform producers of court rulings that affect the insurer's exposure or pricing, such as interpretations of policy exclusions or application of limits.

Underwriting

Individual underwriters are interested in claims information for the specific accounts they approved. A post-loss evaluation may reveal aspects of the risk that should have been detected when the application was first reviewed. Even if obvious clues were not overlooked initially, reviewing the claim file can uncover operations and activities that the underwriter would have investigated more thoroughly had they been apparent on the application. In some instances, material aspects of the insured exposures have changed since the policy was first underwritten. Discovering these changes could prompt discussion about immediate policy cancellation or nonrenewal of the account. Underwriters also recognize that losses occur on even the best accounts. The occurrence of a minor loss could therefore create the opportunity to take corrective action, through the service of the loss control department, that could prevent a subsequent major loss.

A number of similar claims may alert underwriting management to larger problems for a particular type or class of policyholder. These claims might be the result of new processes or technologies being used by the class of policyholders as a whole. For example, some roofing contractors may have tried to speed the process of replacing composite roofs by moving the tar smelter to the roof of the structure being repaired. This practice might have caused a number of fire losses. An adverse court ruling could also cause the loss experience of a class of business to deteriorate or could increase the number of claims presented.

Actuarial

Actuaries need accurate information not only on losses that have been paid but also on losses that have occurred and are reserved for payment. Such information helps actuaries establish reserves for IBNR losses and predict the development of open claims for which the reserves might change substantially over time before the claim is finally settled.

Claims Department Contacts

Other than the producing agent, the claims department is the branch of the insurer most visible to the public. It is therefore necessary for the claims department to interact effectively with outside contacts, such as the general public, plaintiffs' attorneys, defense attorneys, regulators, and claims organizations and associations.

General Public

Although many insurance companies have a public relations department affiliated with advertising, the insurer's public image is largely determined by the behavior of the claims department. When Consumer Union surveyed 34,000 readers of its publication *Consumer Reports*, those surveyed reported that "promptness in claims handling was the single most significant factor in deciding how much they liked a company's service." For the most part, these respondents had been paid promptly for claims, with 70 percent saying they got their check within fourteen days.[1] Delay in receiving payment for a claim is the primary claims-related complaint and causes many claimants or policyholders to seek attorney representation.

The nature of claims adjusting places the person adjusting a claim in a unique position to take advantage of unsophisticated policyholders and claimants. Adjusters must recognize that adjusting requires a high degree of integrity, which involves more than just honesty. The adjustment process requires keeping a promise made by the insurer, and the adjuster represents the insurer's sincerity to the policyholder.

Many states require adjusters to be bonded or to pass a written examination in order to become licensed, but this requirement is neither uniform nor universal. Exhibit 13-1 shows a list of states that require independent adjusters to be licensed. Fewer states require company-employed adjusters to be licensed.

Plaintiffs' Attorneys

In some areas of claims and in certain areas of the country, claimants are more likely to hire attorneys, often leading to costly litigation. Although attorney representation can result in a higher payment by the insurer, representation does not necessarily result in higher settlements to claimants, because they must pay expenses and attorney bills from the settlements. Attorney representation also does not guarantee a faster settlement.

Litigation of third-party claims has become one of the most visible and expensive problems facing liability insurers. Although litigation of first-party claims is also a costly problem, the immediate costs associated with the tort system have led many insurers to realize that litigation prevention must be an active part of the claims function.

Exhibit 13-1
Licensing of Independent Insurance Adjusters

States Requiring Adjuster Licenses

• Alaska	• Kentucky	• Oklahoma
• Arizona	• Maine	• Oregon
• Arkansas	• Michigan	• Rhode Island
• California	• Minnesota	• South Carolina
• Colorado	Mississippi	• Texas
• Connecticut	Montana	• Utah
• Delaware	• Nevada	• Vermont
• Florida	• New Hampshire	• Washington
• Georgia	New Mexico	• West Virginia
• Hawaii	• New York	• Wyoming
• Idaho	• North Carolina	• Puerto Rico (Terr.)

• States that require more than the payment of a license fee.

1996 Best's Directory of Recommended Insurance Attorneys and Adjusters.

Defense Attorneys

The duty to defend under liability policies is as important as, or more important than, the duty to indemnify. Many insurers spend as much money on outside defense attorneys as they do on claims department staff salaries and independent adjusting fees combined. Managing defense expenses is an essential component of managing the claims function.

Insurers typically hire an attorney from the jurisdiction where the claim is presented. Most attorneys limit their practice to one or two counties within a state, affording them a familiarity with the local legal system. Lawyers from a particular jurisdiction are more likely to identify with the community and potential juries. However, rising legal costs have made the use of in-house counsel for claims defense more attractive for many insurers, regardless of the advantages inherit in using local attorneys. Many insurers have created in-house law offices in the major metropolitan areas to defend claims.

Defense attorneys usually work on an hourly fee basis. Typical fees range from $75 per hour to $250 per hour, with $100 to $150 per hour being the most common. Because defense costs mount quickly at those rates, routine litigation can cost the insurer thousands of dollars.

The ideal situation for the insurer is to avoid litigation altogether through a prompt investigation and resolution. If a claim goes to suit, some aspect of the claims adjusting process may have failed to operate properly. Perhaps the claims department was understaffed, or the individual adjuster did not recognize a legitimate claim or offered an unrealistic settlement amount. Alternatively, the adjuster may not have explained the merits of the insurer's case well enough for the plaintiff to recognize a valid settlement offer. Of course, even if the insurer presents a valid case, the plaintiff could still be convinced that the claim is worth more and seek an attorney.

State Regulators

State insurance regulators monitor the insurer's activities in the claim settlement process. Regulators exercise controls through licensing adjusters, investigating consumer complaints, and performing market conduct investigations. Enforcement is usually handled through the Unfair Claims Settlement Practices Act or similar legislation.

Licensing

Not all jurisdictions currently license adjusters, and no standard procedure or uniform regulation exists for those that do. In some states, only independent adjusters who work for many insurance companies or public adjusters, who represent policyholders in first-party claims against insurers, are required to be licensed. In other states, staff adjusters must be licensed as well.

Most states or jurisdictions with licensing laws also require that the adjuster or his or her employer post a bond or show evidence of a fidelity bond. Many states with licensing laws also require the applicant to pass a written examination, which may be given on either a multiple-line basis or on specific lines of coverage. Some states also license vehicle damage or property appraisers, but others exempt such persons. A licensed attorney who is acting as an adjuster may be exempt from licensing requirements. Temporary permits or licenses are frequently granted to out-of-state adjusters brought in by insurers for major catastrophes, such as storms or other disasters.

Consumer Complaints

Claims departments must also pay attention to consumer complaints to state insurance regulatory departments. Most states have a specific time limit within which inquiries by the department must be answered or acted on. Failure to respond can result in expensive fines and even the loss of the adjuster's—or his or her employer's—license. Nevertheless, the relationship between state insurance departments and adjusters is usually positive.

Market Conduct Investigations

Insurance regulators periodically perform market conduct investigations either as part of their normal audit of insurance company activities or as a response to specific complaints. The typical market conduct audit concerns more than just claims practices; it includes a review of all departments that directly interact with policyholders and claimants.

Claims Organizations and Associations

Although claims personnel represent one of the largest segments of those employed by the property-liability insurance industry, there is no single national organization or association for people who work in claims. However, there are several organizations whose focus is important to claims personnel. The National Association of Independent Insurance Adjusters (NAIIA), of Chicago, is open to independent adjusters who meet certain standards. The NAIIA promulgates adjusting standards, maintains communications with insurance companies, encourages ethical practices, and conducts national, regional, and state meetings. The NAIIA publishes the *Blue Book of Adjusters*, which lists its members throughout the country and maintains educational resources available to any interested party.

The Property Loss Research Bureau (PLRB) and the Liability Insurance Research Bureau (LIRB) are divisions of the Alliance of American Insurers of Schaumburg, Illinois. These organizations are primarily dedicated to education and research. They exist to provide expert research and analysis of claims and legal issues important to member companies. They also conduct an annual education conference that is open to anyone in the insurance industry.

Property Claim Services of Rahway, New Jersey, a division of American Insurance Services Group, provides catastrophe management and educational services to the industry. Its educational services include various seminars, reference manuals, videos, and conferences.

The Loss Executives Association consists of claim experts in the property field. It conducts numerous seminars for its members. The Conference of Casualty Insurance Companies, of Indianapolis, provides arbitration and educational services to its members. Arbitration Forums Inc., of Tarrytown, New York, administers through its many local offices various intercompany arbitration agreements, such as the Nationwide Intercompany Agreement and the Fire and Allied Lines Subrogation Arbitration Agreement.

The National Insurance Crime Bureau (NICB), of Palos Hills, Illinois, was formed from the National Auto Theft Bureau (NATB) and the Insurance Crime Prevention Institute (ICPI). The NICB fights all forms of insurance fraud and crime, including automobile theft, medical fraud, and staged losses. It offers presentations on crime detection for claim representatives.

Local claim associations exist in most metropolitan areas. These groups are valuable sources of contacts within the local claims community and of information about local matters, such as defense law firms, public adjusters, plaintiff attorneys, and service providers. Most of the meetings held by these groups have both a social and an educational purpose. In fact, most meetings are organized around an educational presentation. Many state claim associations are likewise active and sponsor worthwhile educational programs.

Organization of the Claims Function

There is no ideal organizational structure for the claims function. What is best is generally what works. What works reflects the insurer's overall organization, its size, how it has grown, and its willingness to use outside providers of claim services.

Most claims departments can be distinguished by the degree of centralization and the division of labor along insurance product lines.

Centralized Versus Decentralized

Insurers can operate with either a centralized or a decentralized claims operation. Different insurers have been successful with each approach.

A centralized claims operation consists of one home office at which all claims are handled or a home office with very few regional offices. Centralized operations can be more efficient than decentralized operations regarding the cost of office rental, supervisory overhead, information systems support, and support staff. This approach works well when supervision is important or claims need not be inspected in person.

The advantages and disadvantages of decentralized operations are the reverse of those for centralized operations. Decentralization can be more costly and difficult to supervise, but it is preferable for claims that must be adjusted in person. Because many claims tasks, such as property inspections and witness interviews, cannot be done as well from a remote location, claims can never be centralized as effectively as underwriting or processing support functions.

The line of business, the volume of business, geographic location, and density of risks an insurer writes may determine how it will structure its claims operations, where it will locate its field offices, and whether it will use inside adjusting procedures or a large number of staff or independent field adjusters. An insurer that writes a large amount of workers compensation insurance, for instance, may locate a workers compensation claim office in an area where its policyholders have large numbers of employees, or it may contract with a local independent adjusting firm in that area to handle claims.

By Product or Line of Business

Some companies divide their workload by product or line of business—a property claims department handles first-party claims, a casualty claims department handles third-party claims, a marine department handles marine claims, and so forth. Other insurers divide the tasks by commercial and personal lines. Responsibility for those lines of business is usually subdivided into geographic regions. As mentioned above, some large personal lines insurers maintain a number of local claim offices, often several in a single metropolitan area. Some local offices may conduct only one activity, such as appraisal of automobile physical damage claims. These smaller claim offices report to the nearest regional service center. Many insurers also permit their producers to handle minor claims directly with their policyholders.

Management Structure and Settlement Authority

The claims department hierarchy and the flow of settlement authority within the department vary by insurer. Usually, the vice president of claims is a key member of the insurer's management team. Reporting directly to the vice president are one or more assistant vice presidents, who are responsible for individual coverage lines. Reporting to each of those may be one or more claims managers. The level of settlement authority required to settle or deny a claim usually follows the chain of command within the company. The settlement authority granted individual adjusters and examiners varies by experience, training, and education.

Beneath the senior level, claims adjusting personnel are organized by responsibility and authority into claims managers, examiners, supervisors, and adjusters. A diagram of an insurer's claims department structure is shown in Exhibit 13-2.

Claims Managers

In most claims organizations, the person below the top claims executive usually has the title of claims manager. Regardless of whether this individual works out of the home office of the insurer, a regional office, or a branch office, he or she is usually the senior person in the claims department involved with individual claim file decisions and loss management. The claims manager is often in charge of both claim files and the general administration and supervision of the claims department.

Examiners

Many insurers employ examiners at regional or home offices. Although the job description and actual title of an examiner may vary between companies, the examiner is primarily a claims analyst, assessing the coverage, liability, and

Exhibit 13-2
Insurer's Claims Department Structure

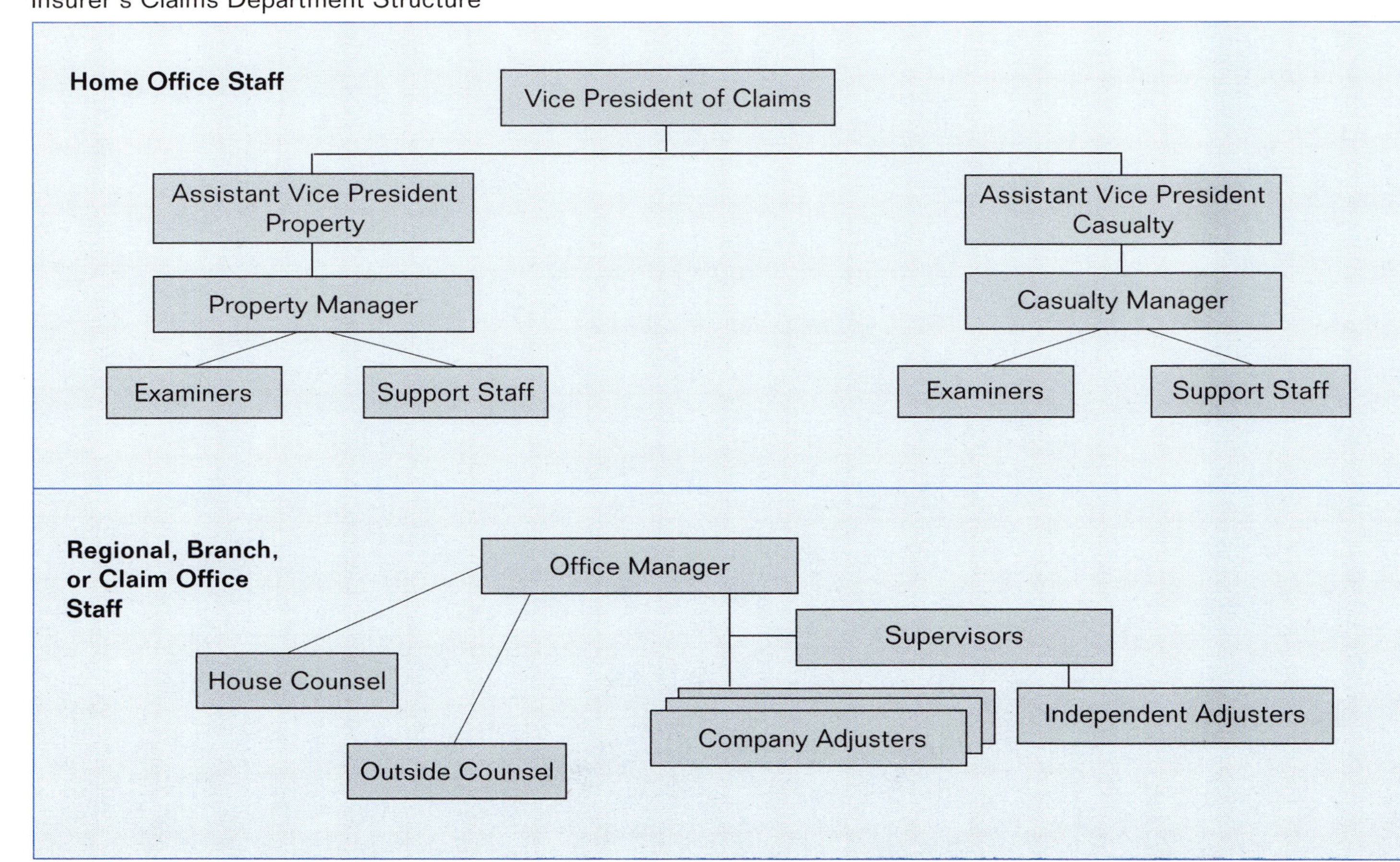

damage factors of any claim and extending settlement authority to adjusters or recommending a settlement amount or other authorization to a superior. The examiner may also be responsible for certain internal claims processes, such as preparing data input, reporting claims to a reinsurer, establishing a file reserve, or referring a claim file to counsel if a coverage or liability issue arises. Examiners are technical experts who do not usually supervise office staff.

Supervisors

Most claims managers structure their departments into various units or subsections, either by line of coverage or by geographic location. Each unit is under the direction of a supervisor. The claims supervisor is usually responsible for the daily activities of the unit. The supervisor may serve in two capacities, both as a supervisor of claims personnel and as a supervisor of the claim files, giving guidance to as many as ten or more adjusters, appraisers, and other representatives on the routine investigation, evaluation, and disposition of the files. The supervisor's authority is usually also extended to the activities of defense attorneys, independent adjusters, appraisers, and other outside service personnel with whom the insurer may contract.

The supervisor may have certain levels of settlement or denial authority and may also be responsible for the supervision of the file if it goes into litigation and is referred to outside counsel. Supervising the activities of the outside defense attorney may come from either the supervisor or the insurer's inside counsel, or in some cases from a staff adjuster. Many companies maintain a list of approved outside counsel in the localities where their losses are most likely to occur and often provide specific instructions and specify the authority granted to those attorneys.

Adjusters

The **adjuster** is responsible for investigating, evaluating, and negotiating the coverage, liability, and damages relating to each claim. Whether the adjuster's position is called "claims adjuster," "claim representative," or some other title, the adjuster is the insurer's direct contact with the policyholder, claimant, witness, or attorney; the liaison to the producer or broker; and the one, to a great extent, on whose shoulders rests the reputation of the insurer.

An adjuster may be an employee of the insurer, an employee of an insurer-owned adjustment bureau or subsidiary firm, or an independent adjuster retained either on a contract basis or on an individual assignment basis. Staff adjusters usually have some authority to act and issue checks on behalf of the insurer without prior clearance once coverage has been confirmed, whereas the authority of an independent adjuster may be limited.

Adjusters are usually employed either as "field" adjusters who operate outside of the claims office or as "inside" adjusters who adjust claims by phone and mail. Field adjusters spend much of their time visiting the scene of a loss, interviewing witnesses, investigating damages, and meeting with policyholders, claimants, attorneys, and other persons involved in the claim. They may inspect damaged property themselves or work closely with damage appraisers and may attend trials and hearings on the claims assigned to them.

Inside claims adjusting is appropriate for claims whose costs are known or when additional investigation would not be beneficial. Examples of claims handled by inside adjusters are personal auto comprehensive claims resolving policyholder losses such as stolen hubcaps, broken windshields, and towing or workers compensation claims involving only medical expenses. Inside adjusters may also be responsible for cases in litigation in which outside investigation is no longer necessary.

Independent Adjusters

Independent adjusting companies provide claims adjusting services to a variety of insurers and self-insureds. Independent adjusting firms derive revenue by charging insurers a fee for claim settlement services and may be owned by insurance brokers, insurance groups, or their own shareholders.

Two of the best-known national adjusting firms are GAB Business Services, Inc., and Crawford & Company. GAB Business Services was originally formed by several insurers to handle large property claims, but it is now independent of any insurer and handles all lines of claims. With its business divided almost equally between property and liability insurance loss handling, the firm also performs value appraisals and inspection surveys. Crawford & Company maintains about 700 offices domestically and internationally, offering loss adjustment services in liability, property, marine, environmental damage, flood, and aircraft insurance.

National adjusting firms serve not only insurance companies but also large self-insured corporations or government agencies. They may also offer related services, such as medical cost containment programs, health and vocational rehabilitation services, property and vehicle damage appraisals, loss data processing, and similar operations.

Many large insurer groups and brokerage firms own their own independent adjusting companies. These subsidiaries provide countercyclical revenue so that even during periods of heavy losses, fee income from adjusting services is available to partially offset losses. Whenever possible, the insurer-owner uses its own facilities. Additionally, most of these independent adjusters actively solicit nonrelated insurer accounts. Many independent adjusters operate in a specific geographic region. These adjusters cite their familiarity with the producers, policyholders, claimants, and legal environment as a reason to employ them when claims occur in their region.

Independent adjusters enable an insurer to have comprehensive coverage of a geographic area without the expense of leasing office space, hiring adjusters, and incurring other expenses associated with operating a claim office. Most companies use independent adjusters at some point in their claims program simply because claims can occur in places where the insurer does not have available staff. Many insurers keep full-time staff at minimal levels, so temporary employees or independent adjusters must be hired during periods of peak activity. In some instances, insurers hire independent adjusters to handle claims outside the normal expertise of the insurer's adjusters, such as pollution or asbestos claims. Access to specialized claims-handling expertise may be the deciding factor that wins the policyholder's account for the insurer.

In some "fronting" arrangements between businesses with a high self-insured retention (SIR) and the insurer, the insured may be instrumental in selecting the independent adjusting firm that will handle the claims on behalf of the insurer. Many of these adjusters operate autonomously, even maintaining trust accounts funded by the insured for payment of claims within the SIR and providing statistical data reports on the losses to the insurer and policyholders.

Insurance companies may also hire independent adjusters when they have been unable to hire skilled personnel on a permanent basis or to supplement staff during vacations. In the event of a catastrophic loss such as a hurricane or an earthquake, independent adjusting companies can supply claims adjusters to support the increase in claims.

An insurer that routinely employs an adjusting firm will usually provide instructions as to where to report and how much authority the adjuster will have to act on behalf of the insurer. Many insurers supply settlement checks to their approved independent adjusters and expect them to operate within the scope of their authority.

Producer Claim Services

Most independent-agency insurers permit their producers to handle minor claims within specific settlement authority or to make assignments to independent adjusters. Extending settlement authority to producers expedites claim service. Producers like the opportunity to be the insurer's representative when the coverage purchased is finally needed. They can remind their clients of the value of their services and can reevaluate the policyholder's coverage. Additionally, many larger commercial lines brokers and agents maintain claims personnel who assist policyholders with filing claims under policies serviced by the agent or broker.

Most of the large personal lines insurers have completely divorced their marketing and claims functions. Producers for these insurers may obtain the essential facts from the policyholder and forward the information to the regional service center for assignment to a local claim office. Some producers simply give the policyholder a telephone number of the insurer's claim service and a brief explanation of how the claim will be handled.

Public Adjusters

Many states permit the licensing of **public adjusters** who represent policyholders in property claims against insurers. These adjusters assist their clients in preparing the verification of loss, negotiating values with the insurer's adjuster, and preparing the settlement documents, such as the proof-of-loss forms. Public adjusters are generally paid a percentage, such as 10 percent, of the settlement the policyholder receives from the insurer, which gives them an incentive to seek the highest possible settlement for their clients.

Many individuals and small businesses, without the time to deal with all of the necessary documentation and negotiation required in a large fire or other property loss, find the services of the public adjuster convenient. When the insurance company is acting responsibly and in good faith, a public adjuster should not make a significant difference in the amount of the recovery. Any increase may be immediately offset by the public adjuster's fee. If policyholders do not believe that they are being treated fairly, they should initially consult their producer for help.

Other Claims Adjusting Personnel

Insurers rely on other experts to handle a specialized type or a particular aspect of a claim. Among these are specialist adjusters, cause and origin experts, material damage appraisers, reconstruction experts, private investigators, accountants, health and rehabilitation experts, medical cost containment consultants, professional engineers, and other support personnel.

Specialist Adjusters

Both independent and staff adjusters tend to specialize in certain areas of claims. Those who have completed certain educational requirements and have a certain amount of experience may be granted a special title, such as "general adjuster." An adjuster who handles only one line of coverage may use that specialty in his or her title, indicating that he or she is a "property adjuster" or a "marine adjuster."

One type of specialist adjuster is a catastrophe adjuster, who travels to the location of major disasters and remains there until all claims have been settled. These adjusters are trained to handle natural disasters (such as floods, hurricanes, tornadoes, hail losses, earthquakes, and volcanic eruptions), man-made disasters, or multiple liability losses.

Some insurers and independent adjusting firms maintain special pollution liability teams that are prepared to go anywhere a major loss has occurred. These teams mitigate damages as well as adjust claims. Their quick action may help improve the policyholders' perception of the insurance company and reduce the likelihood of class action suits.

Another type of specialty line adjuster is the marine surveyor, or "average" adjuster, who exclusively handles loss to freight, cargo, vessels (including everything from small watercraft and yachts to oceangoing ships), and, occasionally, aircraft. ("Average" is a marine insurance term for loss.)

Cause and Origin Experts

Cause and origin experts attempt to determine where and how a fire began. These experts are often consulted for fires that have a suspicious origin or when the possibility for subrogation exists.

Material Damage Appraisers

Many adjusters are also trained as property or vehicle damage appraisers or evaluators. Others who work directly for insurers or for independent adjusters specialize only in the appraisal of damages. The appraiser inspects the damage and, if it is reparable, writes an estimate of what it will cost to repair. The appraiser then obtains an agreed repair price with a repair facility, contractor, body shop, or other organization that has been selected by the policyholder or claimant to make the repairs.

If an item is irreparable or missing because of theft or other loss, the appraiser assists the adjuster in determining the value or replacement cost of the item and in disposing of salvage. Many insurers use wholesale replacement organizations that can obtain items commonly involved in losses at a lower price than can the policyholder. They also use automobile salvage "pools" to sell vehicles deemed to be a "total loss" to the highest bidder. Other companies assist adjusters in disposing of other salvage, such as merchandise from a commercial fire loss.

Reconstruction Experts

Some experts specialize in reconstructing the events of automobile accidents. They explain how an auto accident occurred and testify as to the rate of speed the vehicles were traveling, to the point of impact between the vehicles, and, in some cases, to what the various drivers were able to see before the accident.

Private Investigators

Many insurers also employ the services of detectives in the investigation of their claims for background and activity checks on claimants, surveillance of claimants who are allegedly injured, financial records checks, process serving, and other similar activities for which private investigators are licensed. Forensic engineers and highly trained arson investigators are also employed by insurers to investigate unusual or questionable losses. Many of these investigators operate as independent contractors. Most insurers also employ their own special investigations unit (SIU).

Accountants

Accountants may be required to examine the books of a policyholder in first-party claims for loss of use and claims for damaged inventory. Accountants may also be used in liability claims to verify the financial losses demanded by claimants.

Health and Rehabilitation Experts

Liability insurers rely on a variety of medical specialists to assist in claims and medical management. Medical consultants and rehabilitation nurses also help arrange independent medical examinations (IMEs) and obtain second opinions before agreeing to a treatment or surgical process suggested by the attending physician.

The workers compensation laws of many states now mandate a variety of vocational rehabilitation services, such as employment consultation and job retraining for disabled workers. Large workers compensation insurers may operate their own rehabilitation firm as a subsidiary of the insurer, and some independent adjusting firms have health and rehabilitation divisions that provide such services.

Medical Cost Containment Consultants

The insurer's health experts also review medical reports and audit bills from physicians and other medical providers. In a process called "utilization review," the nurse or medical technician examines the physician's report to ascertain the diagnosis and then determines whether the treatment being provided is reasonable and necessary to that diagnosis. Since most claims are for a specific injury or illness, the insurer does not want to pay for unreasonable charges or for services that may be unrelated to the claim.

Professional Engineers

Many slip and fall cases involve steps, stairways, or sidewalks. Product liability cases often allege improper design. Professional engineers can help the insurer determine whether any OSHA requirement or a building code was violated.

Support Personnel

In addition to the experts already described, claims departments may employ a variety of support personnel for technical and clerical functions. Larger personal lines insurers may employ auto damage appraisers who inspect damaged vehicles locally and reach either an agreed price for their repair or an assessment of their value if they are a total loss. The insurer may also have other staff technicians who can assist in certain aspects of loss, including special fraud investigators, coverage analysts, research librarians (especially for legal issues), and even laboratory and engineering assistants.

Clerical assistants may include transcribers, file room assistants, mail room clerks, data entry clerks, check typists, and others who help to make the claims department run smoothly.

Unbundled Claim Services

Larger commercial businesses commonly have both the necessary attributes and the desire to retain, rather than insure, losses. Although many of these businesses may have the financial resources and sophistication to manage claims without the services of an insurer, they may not have or want to maintain the necessary in-house talent to handle their own claims.

Many insurers "unbundle" their services, permitting these firms to purchase loss control, data processing, or claims adjusting services separately. Independent adjusters or third-party administrators also offer their services directly to businesses choosing to self-insure their loss exposures. For the insurers involved in these programs, the unbundling of insurer services offers an opportunity for the claims department to generate revenue for the insurer without the exposure to underwriting risk.

The Claims Adjusting Process[2]

There is no universal, uniform process for adjusting all claims. The steps that an insurer takes to settle a claim vary significantly by claim. Although settling similar types of claims requires taking similar steps, there are so many challenges in settling claims that insurers have developed extensive procedures for claims adjusters to follow.

The manner in which property and liability claims are handled differs significantly. This difference is reflected throughout the claims organization in terms of how personnel specialize, which internal forms are used, and which procedures are followed. Although the distinction between property and liability underwriting has been gradually eroding since the introduction of package policies, this distinction remains in most claims operations. Policyholder claims can usually be categorized as either property (first-party) or liability (third-party). Chapters 14 and 15 present the property and liability claims adjusting processes in detail. This section deals with some of the common elements of both processes.

Virtually all claims are legitimate demands on the insurer to fulfill its obligations. In evaluating a claim, the adjuster must consider whether the claim in question should be paid and whether any defenses to the claim exist. This approach appears to be a negative process, but it usually has a positive result and is similar to the screening process that underwriters use in reviewing applicants.

In deciding whether to pay a particular claim, an insurer must have a clear reason for its decision. Therefore, virtually all of an individual claims adjuster's efforts revolve around three distinct questions:

1. Is the loss covered by the policy in question?
2. Is the policyholder or insurer legally liable for the loss?
3. What are the damages?

An adjuster investigates, evaluates, and answers each of these questions in the course of handling a claim.

Coverage

The clearest example of mishandling a claim is payment of a claim not covered by the policy. However, such a blunder may be only the second worst coverage mistake a claims adjuster can make. Wrongful denial of coverage when it exists is unfair and abusive towards policyholders and can result in bad faith suits and enormous verdicts of extra-contractual damages. A proper coverage decision is fundamental to good claims handling.

Claims departments typically have experienced personnel who each work on claims resulting from only one, or very few, types of coverages. Claims adjusters must have detailed knowledge of the policies from which they work. Every individual line and clause from a policy may affect the outcome of a claim. Although experienced claims personnel have a well-developed sense of which situations are covered and which are not, good coverage analysis requires a methodical review of the specific policy on a given loss in light of the allegations and known facts.

Ultimately, coverage depends on (1) whether the loss or type of damage is within the insuring agreement, and (2) whether any exclusion or condition in the policy eliminates or restricts coverage.

Insuring Agreement

Insuring agreements are usually brief, as the following examples illustrate:

From the Personal Auto Policy, Part A:

> We will pay damages for "bodily injury" or "property damage" for which any "insured" becomes legally responsible because of an auto accident.

From the HO-3, Section I:

> We insure against risks of direct loss to property described in Coverages A and B only if that loss is a physical loss to property. . . .

From the Commercial General Liability policy, Coverage A:

> We will pay those sums that the insured becomes legally obligated to pay as damages because of "bodily injury" or "property damage" to which this insurance applies.

From the Building and Personal Property Coverage Form:

> We will pay for direct physical loss of or damage to Covered Property at the premises described in the Declarations caused by or resulting from any Covered Cause of Loss.

Despite their apparent simplicity, these insuring agreements contain numerous issues. Terms that are defined, such as "bodily injury," "property damage," and "insured," implicitly exclude from coverage anything that is not within the definition. For example, "property damage" is generally not considered to extend to fines, purely financial loss, or the diminution in value of property unrelated to physical damage. The "insured" in an auto policy does not include every person who might be driving an auto owned by the named insured (for example, a thief is not covered). The distinction between actual damage and loss of use is important in property coverages because different provisions may apply for each. Finally, insuring agreements typically incorporate other portions of the policy that must be fully understood before the insuring agreement itself can be understood.

Exclusions

Exclusions from coverage are too numerous to present here. Claims adjusters must carefully read and understand every exclusion contained in the policy applicable to a given loss. The evidentiary burden of proof of the application of an exclusion is the insurer's. The rationale for most exclusions usually falls into one of four categories, discussed below.

Coverage Provided Elsewhere

Policies generally exclude coverage that is provided elsewhere. For example, auto and workers compensation losses are excluded from general liability policies because they are the subjects of separate policies.

Coverage Not Needed by Most Policyholders

Some exclusions exist because most policyholders do not need the coverage and thus save premium expense by not having it. For example, insureds located in flat and stable terrain have no need for earthquake or volcanic eruption coverage. Those policyholders with out-of-the-ordinary exposures must cover them with endorsements or separate policies.

Occurrences Within Control of the Policyholder

Some exclusions are necessary because the policyholder should not have control over the occurrence of the loss. For example, general liability policies exclude claims arising out of intentional wrongdoing on the policyholder's part and (with some exceptions) out of the failure of the policyholder to perform his or her contractual obligations.

Uninsurability

Other exclusions relate to events that are uninsurable because of the difficulty in spreading the risk. For example, losses caused by war, flood, and nuclear accident would affect many policyholders at once. Thus, the insurance business does not cover such exposures under normal policies.

Conditions

The most important policy conditions with which a claims adjuster must deal are those concerning duties and procedures in the event of a loss. The exact wording of those duties and procedures varies by policy, but certain conditions are common to almost every policy. For example, the policyholder must promptly notify the insurer of any loss or suit and must cooperate in investigating, settling, and defending any claim. These and other duties of the policyholder are conditions precedent to the obligation of the insurer to pay the claim. However, the insurer, mindful of customer goodwill, cannot insist on a rigidly technical manner of performance, since the courts will not allow it.

Response to Coverage Issues

When a coverage issue arises, a claims adjuster must protect the interests of the insurer and resolve the issue quickly. If no coverage can be provided given the established facts, the claims adjuster must immediately inform the policyholder in writing, making reference to specific policy provisions.

If coverage is uncertain, the claims adjuster must continue to handle the claim under a **reservation-of-rights letter** or **nonwaiver agreement** while taking immediate action to resolve the coverage issue. Reservation-of-rights letters and nonwaiver agreements serve the same purpose. They allow the claims adjuster to continue to handle the claim without voiding the right of the insurer to later disclaim coverage. Otherwise, continued handling of the claim could be legally construed as a waiver of the rights of the insurer to deny coverage. The only difference between these instruments is that the reservation-of-rights letter is unilaterally issued by the insurer, and the nonwaiver agreement is signed and consented to by the policyholder.

Reservation-of-rights letters and nonwaiver agreements are not ends in themselves. They are means to allow the claims adjuster the time necessary to resolve the coverage issue. This resolution may require additional investigation or an opinion from an attorney experienced in insurance coverage matters.

Once a decision on coverage has been made, the policyholder should be advised immediately. Policyholders are naturally disgruntled whenever coverage for all or a part of a claim is denied. Policyholders in this position have frequently sued their insurer for both the denial of the claim and the way in which the denial was handled. Damages in such cases, including compensation for the policyholder's emotional distress and punitive damages, may be enormous. Consequently, most claims departments restrict authority to issue coverage denials to the claims manager, supervisory personnel, or home office.

An alternative to the unilateral resolution of a coverage issue is the filing of a declaratory judgment action. A **declaratory judgment** action is a lawsuit in which the court is asked to declare the rights between parties, rather than award monetary damages as in a typical lawsuit. Courts have acknowledged that the resolution of insurance policy coverage is a suitable issue for a declaratory judgment action. The drawbacks of this procedure are that it is expensive and that, in some jurisdictions, the declaratory judgment action may not move through the court system any faster than the underlying suit that is the subject of the claim. In that case, the declaratory judgement action may not be decided until the underlying action is decided.

Legal Liability

Legal liability is an important concept in third-party claims. The insuring agreements of the personal auto policy and the commercial general liability policy, quoted earlier, respectively refer to damages "for which any 'insured' becomes legally responsible" and "that the insured becomes legally obligated to pay." The phrases "legally responsible" and "legally obligated" are synonymous with the phrase "legally liable." **Legal liability**—the state of being legally liable for harm to another party—is thus a requisite of coverage under a liability insurance policy. The insurance company will not pay damages on behalf of the insured unless the insured is legally liable to pay such damages. Policyholders buy liability insurance to protect themselves against legal liability A complete knowledge of legal liability would require an exhaustive knowledge of the law, which would be difficult to achieve because of the many jurisdictions involved and the speed at which law changes. Nevertheless, the basics of legal liability are not difficult.

Sources of Liability

Other than criminal acts, which are almost invariably not covered by insurance, legal liability arises from three sources:

- Statutes
- Contracts
- Torts

Statutes

An individual or a business may be required to do something or refrain from doing something because a legislative body has enacted a law to that effect. For example, the obligation to pay taxes and file tax returns arises out of statute. Likewise, the obligation not to pollute the land, air, and water arises out of statute. Of great importance to insurance are traffic laws, which are primarily statutory. Many statutes are codifications of preexisting common law (judge or court-made law), but in such cases the statute preempts the common law. Breach of a statute is simultaneously a tort, in which such a breach is the proximate cause of damage to another.

Contracts

A legal liability to do something or to refrain from doing something can arise out of having made an agreement to that effect. The law enforces such agreements as long as the other party (or parties) incurs some reciprocal obligation and the agreement is not for some unlawful purpose. Contracts are common in both business and personal life. Generally, contractual obligations are not insurable. However, the exceptions to this general rule are common and important enough that claims adjusters need a good working knowledge of contract law. In particular, contracts are frequently used to transfer statutory and common law duties from one party to another. Only a few special types of contracts must be in writing. The remainder can be, and usually are, strictly oral.

Torts

This category of legal liability encompasses all noncontractual civil wrongs. Many criminal acts are also simultaneously torts, such as assault and battery or fraud. Claims adjusters must have a command of tort law, since most torts are covered by insurance and since their possibility is the very reason most policyholders have insurance policies. Torts are categorized by the behavior of the wrongdoer (called a tortfeasor). They may occur when the tortfeasor has acted intentionally or negligently or, in some circumstances, regardless of how the tortfeasor has acted.

Intentional torts include assault, battery, false imprisonment, false arrest, trespass, nuisance (a term that means interference with the use of land), fraud, libel, slander, conversion (a legal term for stealing), and others.

Although most insurance policies exclude coverage for intentional wrongdoing, a claims adjuster cannot expect to escape these types of claims. The "personal injury" coverage contained in some liability policies covers damages that are frequently the result of intentional conduct. In any event, the duty of the insurer to defend the policyholder exists if any part of a lawsuit is covered. Plaintiff attorneys include allegations of negligence, in addition to their allegations of intentional wrongdoing, in order to involve the insurer and its money in the case. Assault cases of this type are common. Furthermore, courts have interpreted intentional act exclusions narrowly by requiring that the policyholder intend the specific harm that results, not just the act that caused the harm. This interpretation has enabled policyholders to involve their insurer in cases by maintaining positions such as, "I intended to punch him, but I didn't expect him to fall backwards and hit his head."

Negligent behavior is the source of most torts and most insurance claims. The law of negligence is almost entirely common law, although some of it, such as traffic laws, has been codified. Negligence is the failure to act as a reasonable and prudent person would under the same circumstances. The "reasonable and prudent person" standard is not equivalent to what the average, or typical, person would do. The average person is often careless and thoughtless. The "reasonable and prudent person" standard is best understood as the behavior of someone who is always careful and prudent, a mythical person. The average person who is careless or thoughtless may be deserving of sympathy and understanding, but if that behavior causes damages to another, that behavior is negligent.

In some circumstances, tort liability may be found regardless of how carefully the tortfeasor behaved. These are the areas of absolute liability and strict liability. Absolute liability is only found in very narrow circumstances, such as blasting with dynamite. If the activity causes damage, liability exists, regardless of how much care was taken. The concept of strict liability applies in the area of liability for harm caused by products. A product manufacturer or seller is not absolutely liable whenever one of its products causes harm to someone. The manufacturer may have strict liability, however, if the product is somehow defective in a way that makes it unreasonably dangerous. Thus, liability depends on the nature of the product, not on the behavior of the manufacturer.

Investigation of Liability

Investigating liability is one of the claims adjuster's most important functions. It can also be one of the most challenging. Ideally, the claims adjuster should interview and obtain statements from all witnesses, inspect loss sites, review key documents, inspect products and advertising, and so forth. Witnesses include the parties directly involved and anyone else who knows anything about the case. Their statements should cover everything they know about the accident and the damages.

Claims adjusters take statements in one of two forms: handwritten or tape recorded. Handwritten statements have the advantage of forcing the claims adjuster to listen carefully in order to properly record what has been said. Tape recordings are more common today because of their convenience and accuracy. However, statements of either kind are rarely used in court. Most cases settle before they get that far. Furthermore, even among the cases that do not settle, witness statements taken out of court cannot be used unless the witness tells a different story on the witness stand. Despite their infrequent use in court, witness statements are considered the heart of any investigation. They are essential to determining liability, a prerequisite to any settlement. Their existence helps prevent witnesses from changing their story thereafter.

A problem for claims adjusters in liability investigations is inconsistency among the witnesses. This inconsistency does not usually result from deliberate lying, although that is a possibility. More often, the witnesses had different opportunities and abilities to observe, have a different quality of memory, or were emotionally upset by the events in question. The "truth" of most events is not available. Only the evidence of such truth, in the form of witness statements, is available.

Damages

No claim is complete without damages. Both first-party and third-party insurance policies provide for indemnification against damages. No subject is of greater interest to claimants. Claims adjusters spend a great portion of their time investigating and evaluating damages. Insurance policies generally extend their coverage to damages consisting of property damage, bodily injury, or both.

Property Damage

In first-party coverages, the term "property damage" means the direct physical destruction of or damage to property. The measure of damages for such destruction or damage is usually specified in the policy as either replacement cost or actual cash value. Replacement cost is the cost to replace what has been damaged. Actual cash value is usually replacement cost minus depreciation. Arguments about depreciation are common. Courts have held that any relevant factor may be considered in determining depreciation. This includes cost to replace, cost when purchased, expected life span, technological or style obsolescence, market value, identifiable physical wear and tear, and anything else.

As an alternative to paying money to settle a property claim, the insurer has the option to conduct repairs or procure a replacement itself. This option may be exercised with personal property losses and claims that seem suspicious.

Loss of use, which may be a result of property damage or destruction, is an element of damage but is not necessarily covered under first-party coverages. Generally, homeowners policies have some coverage for loss of use. Many commercial property policies must have such coverage added separately. In both cases, loss of use is usually not covered by property insurance unless it results from some type of damage or destruction to the property that is covered. In other words, loss of use is not covered when property simply ceases to function without having been damaged or destroyed. The measure of damages for loss of use is specified in the policy.

Property damages in liability claims also include damages for the direct physical damage to the property and for loss of its use. When property has been totally destroyed, claimants are not entitled to replacement cost unless the property truly had not depreciated at all. With property that is only partially damaged and can be repaired, the cost of repair is an accepted measure of damages. It is the least amount of money required to return the claimant to his or her original condition. Loss of use is measured by the cost of replacement services. However, all claimants in all liability claims are required to mitigate their damages. They cannot allow loss of use damages to accumulate beyond the value of damaged property or when destroyed property could be expeditiously replaced.

Bodily Injury Damages

Bodily injury damages may fall into at least nine categories: expenses for medical treatment, loss of earnings, pain and suffering, permanency, loss of consortium, future damages, punitive damages, survival and wrongful death, and extra-contractual damages. Punitive damages and extra-contractual damages can arise in property damage cases as well, but they are more often related to bodily injuries.

Expenses for Medical Treatment

These expenses include doctors' services, hospital expenses, nursing and rehabilitation treatment, medications, medical devices and equipment, and even transportation expense to receive medical care. All medical expense must be (1) related to the injury resulting from the accident (preexisting problems and unrelated problems that develop after an accident are not the responsibility of the liability insurer unless the injury exacerbates a preexisting condition), (2) for treatment that is necessary (excessive treatment that accomplishes nothing is not the responsibility of the liability insurer), and (3) reasonable in amount (insurers need not pay unreasonable and excessive charges). The statement of these parameters is easier than their enforcement. Medical care is usually controlled by the claimant and his or her doctor. Insurer arguments against the treatment prescribed are fruitless after the fact.

In many states, the medical expense must be paid by the defendant, even if it has been covered by some other source of insurance, such as health insurance. This is known as the **Collateral Source Rule**. The rationale of this rule is that defendants should not benefit from the prudence of injured parties in insuring themselves. This rule also extends to other collateral coverage, such as disability insurance for lost earnings. Recently, some states have modified or abolished the Collateral Source Rule, thus allowing a deduction from a plaintiff's recovery for expenses covered by other insurance.

Loss of Earnings

Any amount that a claimant would have earned during a period of disability is recoverable. Determining what the claimant would have earned is usually not difficult, especially if the claimant worked a regular job for salary or wages. Claimants who are businessowners sometimes present a problem. Their incomes may vary seasonally; they might have poor recordkeeping; and they might have typical personal expenses, such as an auto, paid by the business. In addition, everyone supplying information to the claims adjuster works for the claimant. If the magnitude of a loss of earnings claim is significant, the insurer might employ the services of an accountant to review the claimant's business.

The most difficult aspect of lost earnings claims is the determination of whether the claimant is disabled. Doctors should perform a detailed analysis of the physical demands of the claimant's job and compare those demands to the claimant's physical capabilities to properly reflect the extent of the claimant's disability. Abuse of disability is one of the most serious problems in claims. In first-party no-fault and uninsured motorist claims, the insurer can compel the injured person to undergo a medical examination. However, in third-party liability claims, disability cannot be controlled until litigation has begun, at which time the claimant can be compelled to undergo independent medical exams.

Pain and Suffering

Pain and suffering is an intangible factor in every injury case and usually the biggest element of damages. It includes inconvenience, anxiety, and other types of distress. The amount awarded in a suit, or agreed on in a settlement, depends on the amount of the medical expense, the length of the disability, the severity and nature of the injury, the locale where the case is tried, the respective skills of the attorneys in creating sympathy and favorable impressions, the sympathies created by the parties, and many other factors in a given case. The question faced by a claims adjuster in evaluating pain and suffering is "What would a jury award?" Proper evaluation requires a good deal of experience, but even experienced claims adjusters are well aware of how inaccurate they could be in a given case. Claimant attorneys are also under the same pressure, and this mutual pressure causes many settlements. In clear or fairly clear liability cases, settlements for pain and suffering are the largest element of damages and are usually for amounts that are several times the medical expense, loss of earnings, or both.

Permanency

In addition to chronic pain, claimants sometimes suffer scarring or some loss of bodily function that may not cause pain but has reduced the quality of life. Permanent injuries and scars are evaluated in the same manner as pain and suffering: unscientifically. However, permanent injuries that reduce earning capacity can be accurately determined.

Loss of Consortium

Loss of **consortium** is an element of damages that belongs to the spouse of the injured party. It consists of the three S's: sex, society, and services. "Sex" here refers to the loss of sexual relations because of the injury. "Society" means the loss of enjoyable companionship because of the injury. "Services" refers to the loss of useful services that the injured party formerly performed for the spouse. This element of damages is also difficult to evaluate. It is sometimes estimated as some smaller percentage of the underlying injury. Plaintiff attorneys do not usually emphasize this aspect of a case with a jury because of the common attitude that spouses take each other "for better or for worse." Nevertheless, this element of damages and a spouse who inspires sympathy can increase the settlement and verdict value of a case.

Future Damages

Any of the previous elements of damage that can be expected to continue into the future should be included in a settlement or jury verdict. With serious injuries, future damages, such as future lost earnings and future pain and suffering, may exceed the damages incurred. Because of inflation, future damages may be larger, in their face amount, than present damages. However, any future damages that can be specified in amount should be adjusted to their present value. This procedure (explained in any elementary finance text) recognizes that a dollar received in the future is worth less than a dollar received today.

Punitive Damages

Damages that can be established in known amounts, such as the medical expense and loss of earnings, are often called **special damages**, or the "specials." The other types of damages are **general damages**. Special damages and general damages together are called compensatory damages because they are designed to compensate the claimant for actual loss. Such compensation is generally all that a claimant can receive. However, in rare cases in which the defendant's conduct has been especially outrageous and wicked, the jury or court may award punitive damages. As the name suggests, these damages are levied against the defendant as punishment. Whether such damages are awarded and the amount awarded are unpredictable. They are requested by plaintiff attorneys far more often than they are awarded. In many states, such damages are uninsurable because of the law or policy language. However, other states do not prohibit insuring punitive damages, and some policies cover them.

Survival and Wrongful Death

This is both the name of the action and the name of the damages. Like "pain and suffering" and "assault and battery," these two actions are so frequently mentioned in the same breath that it is difficult to distinguish them. **Survival actions** are those legal causes of action that existed for the deceased before his or her death. In other words, had the deceased lived, these are actions that could have been pursued like any other. The claim for the medical expense, lost earnings, and pain and suffering up to the time of death are elements of a survival action and are evaluated in the normal manner. However, actions that precede a death lose some value upon death because the claimant cannot testify on his or her own behalf.

A wrongful death action is different. In concept, a **wrongful death action** belongs to the survivors of the deceased. It is designed to compensate them for the loss of the deceased and only arises upon death. Evaluation of wrongful death actions is complicated. Only certain people are entitled to recover under a wrongful death claim. If none of these people exist, the wrongful death action may be worth very little. Most deaths involve eligible beneficiaries, since most states allow spouses, parents, or children to recover, and most people have one or more such relatives. Even if eligible beneficiaries exist, their recovery may be limited to the benefits they would have received from the deceased. In the case of parents and adult children claiming for one another, the amount of the financial benefit from the deceased may be small. Recovery for loss of companionship is allowed in many states, but this element of damages is usually moderate, except in the case of spouses. Financial dependence allows for the largest recoveries. Minor children are presumed to be financially dependent on their parents, and spouses are presumed to depend financially on one another. Some states provide for a loss-to-the-estate measure of damages to the eligible beneficiaries. Under these formulations, the deceased's future cost of maintenance is subtracted from future earnings to arrive at a net contributions figure, or the deceased's likely estate at death is estimated. Under both loss-to-the-beneficiary or loss-to-the-estate measures of damages, the future damages should be discounted to their present value.

Extra-Contractual Damages

The terms of insurance policies describe the circumstances in which the insurer is to pay and the amounts. However, in certain circumstances, insurers may be liable to their policyholders for amounts not called for in the policy or in excess of the policy limits. This can occur when the insurer has behaved improperly toward its policyholder. **Extra-contractual damages** are usually awarded in these cases because of an excess verdict or because of the wrongful treatment of a policyholder, such as a violation of the Unfair Claims Settlement Practices Act.

Reporting

The adjuster's reports are vital to the claims function. Whether the report is from a staff or an independent field adjuster to a supervisor, or from a defense attorney to the adjuster or examiner, it serves as an important part of the evaluation process, updating information about each claim so that the proper action can be taken. Adjuster file notes serve as the basis of the more formal types of reports discussed below. Reports can be categorized as preliminary, investigative, status, and concluding. With widespread use of computers and networks, insurers and adjusters can now prepare and transmit many reports entirely by computer.

Preliminary Reports

The ACORD form is used by many producers to report the occurrence of a claim to a company. A copy of the ACORD Property Loss Notice is shown in Exhibit 13-3. Once the insurer has assigned the case to an adjuster, many insurers require a first report to be filed within a certain number of hours or days from the time the loss is reported. Such reports usually identify the names

Exhibit 13-3
ACORD Property Loss Notice

ACORD PROPERTY LOSS NOTICE

DATE (MM/DD/YY): 8/1/97

PRODUCER | PHONE (A/C, No, Ext):

PAUL PROCTOR
127 MAIN STREET
PLAINFIELD, OH

CODE: 39542 | SUB CODE:

AGENCY CUSTOMER ID:

MISCELLANEOUS INFO (Site & location code)

DATE OF LOSS AND TIME: 7/29/97 | X AM | PM

PREVIOUSLY REPORTED: YES | X NO

POLICY TYPE	COMPANY AND POLICY NUMBER		
PROP/HOME	CO: IIA INSURANCE COMPANY		EFF:
	POL: HO 1894370		EXP:
FLOOD	CO:		EFF:
	POL:		EXP:
WIND	CO:		EFF:
	POL:		EXP:

INSURED

NAME AND ADDRESS: LEONARD HILLMAN, 156 SIXTH AVENUE, PLAINFIELD, OH

SOC SEC #:

RESIDENCE PHONE (A/C, No): 215-555-8181

BUSINESS PHONE (A/C, No, Ext): 215-555-5000

CONTACT | CONTACT INSURED

NAME AND ADDRESS: JULIA HILLMAN

WHERE TO CONTACT: HOME

WHEN TO CONTACT: DAYTIME

RESIDENCE PHONE (A/C, No): SAME

BUSINESS PHONE (A/C, No, Ext):

LOSS

LOCATION OF LOSS:

POLICE OR FIRE DEPT TO WHICH REPORTED:

KIND OF LOSS: FIRE | LIGHTNING | FLOOD | OTHER (explain) | THEFT | X HAIL | X WIND

PROBABLE AMOUNT ENTIRE LOSS: $3,000

DESCRIPTION OF LOSS & DAMAGE (Use reverse side, if necessary)
WIND AND HAIL DAMAGED ROOF

POLICY INFORMATION

MORTGAGEE: PLAINFIELD FEDERAL SAVINGS AND LOAN ASSOCIATION

NO MORTGAGEE

HOMEOWNER POLICIES SECTION 1 ONLY (Complete for coverages A, B, C, D & additional coverages. For Homeowners Section II Liability Losses, use ACORD 3.)

A. DWELLING	B. OTHER STRUCT	C. PERSONAL PROP	D. LOSS OF USE	DEDUCTIBLES	DESCRIBE ADDITIONAL COVERAGES PROVIDED
$100,000	$10,000	$50,000	$20,000	$500	ON

COVERAGE A. EXCLUDES WIND

SUBJECT TO FORMS (Insert form numbers and edition dates, special deductibles)

FIRE, ALLIED LINES & MULTI-PERIL POLICIES (Complete only those items involved in loss)

ITEM	SUBJECT OF INS	AMOUNT	% COINS	DEDUCTIBLE	COVERAGE AND/OR DESCRIPTION OF PROPERTY INSURED
	BLDG / CNTS				
	BLDG / CNTS				
	BLDG / CNTS				

SUBJECT TO FORMS (Insert form numbers and edition dates, special deductibles): HO-290 REPLACEMENT COST COVERAGE

FLOOD POLICY: BUILDING: | DEDUCTIBLE: | CONTENTS: | DEDUCTIBLE: | ZONE | PRE FIRM | POST FIRM | DIFF IN ELEV | FORM TYPE | GENERAL DWELLING | CONDO

WIND POLICY: BUILDING | DEDUCTIBLE | CONTENTS | ZONE | FORM TYPE | GENERAL DWELLING | CONDO

REMARKS/OTHER INSURANCE (List companies, policy numbers, coverages & policy amounts)
ROOF LEAKING AFTER STORM. WATER DAMAGE TO CEILING IN ADDITION TO ROOF DAMAGE.

CAT # | FICO # | ADJUSTER ASSIGNED | ADJUSTER # | DATE ASSIGNED

REPORTED BY: LEONARD HILLMAN

REPORTED TO: ANN ADAMS

SIGNATURE OF PRODUCER OR INSURED: Ann Adams

ACORD 1 (1/96) NOTE: IMPORTANT STATE INFORMATION ON REVERSE SIDE and number of claimants and provide some initial evaluation of whether there are coverage issues that need to be explored, along with preliminary information on the liability factors involved. Above all, the report should guide the examiner in establishing the initial reserve for the claim.

Investigative Reports

The adjuster's next report is a detailed report on the claim investigation. Such a report is often called the "full formal," since it contains standard paragraph captions regarding coverage, liability, damages, and other factors involved in the loss. It also outlines the key information already obtained and the information that needs to be investigated. Each topic may be given a separate heading in the report.

Status Reports

After the preliminary investigation is completed, the insurer will require periodic reports on the status of the claim. These reports may be sent every thirty days or over longer intervals if the claim is slow in developing, as is the case with many injury losses. One important purpose of status reports is to facilitate the constant reevaluation of the reserves being maintained on the file. As factors involved in the claim change, the reserves may need to be increased or decreased. Example status reports are shown in Exhibits 13-4 and 13-5.

Concluding Reports

The adjuster's final report usually outlines the basis of settlement or other conclusion of the claim. It also contains the documents necessary to close the file, such as a copy of the settlement check, the release or proof-of-loss document, dismissal of any litigation, and final billings for any other services performed in the settlement, such as the defense attorney or independent adjuster's fees.

Reserving

Reserving the claim file is a crucial adjusting task. The reserve represents the amount of money that the insurer anticipates may be needed to pay for a particular claim. The reserve includes both the amounts owed to the policyholder or claimant(s) and, with some insurers, the moneys required to cover the expenses of the insurer. Estimating ultimate losses is a key adjusting skill that is acquired with experience and training. Failure to reserve properly, by either underestimating or overestimating the final cost of claims, can accumulate, causing distortions on the insurer's financial statements. Underreserving is one of the major causes of insurer insolvency and bankruptcy.

Exhibit 13-4
Six-Month Supervisor's Reserve Adequacy Review—Property

Supervisor Markham	Policy No. CPP 6106442100	Insured Westside Manufacturing	Loss Cause Fire	Suit ☐ Yes ☑ No

Claim Rep. Harrison	Amount of Coverage 500,000	Loss Date 4/5/X6	Date Rept'd 10/9/X6	Age (mos.) 6	LAE to date NA

ALL LOSSES	Y	N	N/A	A/N*
Scope—loss items defined in file content	☑	☐	☐	☐
Cause/Origin—clearly noted in file	☑	☐	☐	☐
Limiting Clauses Identified	☐	☐	☑	☐
Deductible Identified	☑	☐	☐	☐

BUILDING ONLY	Y	N	N/A	A/N*
ACV/RCV Calculated	☑	☐	☐	☐
Ownership Established	☑	☐	☐	☐
Coinsurance Noted	☑	☐	☐	☐
Mortgage Noted	☐	☐	☐	☐
R/C Holdback Applied	☑	☐	☐	☐
Statement Taken	☐	☐	☐	☐
CONTENTS				
Police Report Obtained	☑	☐	☐	☐
Property Verification of Items Involved	☑	☐	☐	☐

1. Are there any unresolved **COVERAGE** questions? ☐ Yes ☑ No
   a. If yes, are all property steps being taken to resolve them? ☐ Yes ☐ No
   b. Needed actions: (1)
      (2) Report underinsurance to underwriting
      (3) ______
2. **INVESTIGATION** completed? ☐ Yes ☐ No
   a. Specific investigation needed:
      (1) Check for other property liens
      (2) ______
      (3) ______
3. **DAMAGES/EXPOSURE**
   a. Is file properly documented to reflect the company's exposure? ☑ Yes ☐ No
   b. If no, does file contain a plan to document damages/exposure? ☐ Yes ☐ No
   c. If ALE/BI is involved, are steps begin taken to control expense? ☐ Yes ☐ No
4. **REPORTING**
   a. Are activity log notes clearly stated in file? ☑ Yes ☐ No
   b. Does the file contain a 90-Day Status Report? ☑ Yes ☐ No
   c. If defense attorney is involved, does the file contain an Initial Claim Analysis? ☐ Yes ☐ No
5. Does the file contain a **PLAN FOR RESOLUTION**? ☐ Yes ☐ No
   Steps or additional steps needed to resolve:
   1. Arrange for salvage to be sold
   2. ______
   3. ______
   4. ______
   5. ______
6. **RESERVE ANALYSIS**
   a. Have all reserve changes been posted in file? ☑ Yes ☐ No
   b. In view of your analysis of liability and damages, is the reserve adequate? ☑ Yes ☐ No

Reserve: $ 300,000 **REVISED RESERVE:** $ –

Signature: ______ **Date:** 10/9/X6

***A/N: Action Needed**

Exhibit 13-5
Six-Month Supervisor's Reserve Adequacy Review—Casualty

Policy #: WC 1238607 Claim Rep: Harrison
Date of Loss: ______ Super: Markham
Age (Months): 6 **SUIT?** ☐ Yes ☑ No
LAE to date: $ NA Policy Limits remaining: $ 200,000

1. Are there any unresolved **COVERAGE** questions? ☐ Yes ☑ No
   a. If yes, are all proper steps being taken to resolve them? ☐ Yes ☐ No
   b. Needed actions: (1) ______
      (2) ______
      (3) ______
2. **INVESTIGATION** completed? ☐ Yes ☐ No
   a. Specific investigation needed:
      (1) Index claimant-to review past claim
      (2) Consider peer review of chiropractic bills
      (3) ______
      (4) ______
   b. **LIABILITY** Analysis:
      undisputed
   c. Is legal advice needed to assist in evaluating liability? ☐ Yes ☐ No
3. **DAMAGES** and **INJURIES**
   a. Are medicals and specials in the file? ☑ Yes ☐ No
   b. If not, have we obtained the information by phone? ☐ Yes ☐ No
   c. Has the claimant returned to work? ☑ Yes ☐ No
   d. DIAGNOSIS: (1) Cervical strain
      (2) ______ (3) ______
   PROGNOSIS: full recovery
   SPECIALS: $ 3,750
4. **REPORTING**
   a. Does the file contain 90-day report(s)? ☐ Yes ☐ No
   b. Does the file contain an Initial Claim Analysis? ☐ Yes ☐ No ☐ N/A
   c. Does the file contain reports of depositions? ☐ Yes ☐ No ☐ N/A
5. Does the file contain a **PLAN FOR RESOLUTION**? ☐ Yes ☐ No
   Steps or additional steps needed to resolve:
   a. ______
   b. ______
   c. ______
   d. ______
6. **RESERVE ANALYSIS**
   a. Have all reserve changes been posted in file? ☑ Yes ☐ No
   b. In view of your analysis of liability and damages, is the reserve adequate? ☑ Yes ☐ No

   Reserve: $ ______ **REVISED RESERVE:** $______

Signature: ______ **Date:** ______

The amount insurers pay on claims is a key element in the calculation of future premium rates. Actuaries base future rates not only on the amount of money the claims department has paid on both open and closed files but also on the amount reserved on open files and reserved for incurred but not reported losses and reopened files. Accuracy in reserving eventually translates into premium rates that accurately reflect loss potential. Claims departments need to reserve claims consistently. Claims department management must communicate to the actuarial department any change in reserving practices so that any abnormalities that develop in loss reserve data can be recognized.

Improper reserving can (but should not) affect the outcome of individual claims. Reserving a file at an amount higher than its real value may create a tendency to overpay the claim or to settle too quickly without adequate negotiation. An underreserved claim, on the other hand, may cause the insurer to take too firm of a position, which may lead to litigation.

Allocated and Unallocated Expenses

In addition to the payment of the policyholder's loss, the insurer is responsible for the payment of the expenses associated with the claim. The NAIC Annual Statement requires that insurer claim expenses be apportioned between allocated and unallocated loss adjustment expenses. Claim costs that can be specifically identified with the settlement of a particular claim are **allocated loss adjustment expenses**. Specific charges that can be assigned to a claim include the fees paid (1) to an auto appraiser to inspect a vehicle damaged in an accident, (2) to a photographer to take photos of the scene, and (3) to a private investigator who does a background check on the claimant, as well as fees for the report(s) of a physician who examines an injured claimant and assesses the injury. In addition, all of the costs related to the defense of the policyholder if the claim goes into litigation—including the attorney's bill and the fees for court reporters, copy services, process servers, and the appeal bond—can be allocated to the individual file.

Some independent adjusters may bill in bulk for a number of settled claims on behalf of the insurer rather than identify individual claim files. These expenses, though no longer attributable to specific claim files, are directly attributable to the settlement of individual claims and are considered allocated loss adjustment expenses.

Expenses related to the overall operation of the claims function are called **unallocated loss adjustment expense**. These expenses include charges for the insurer's overhead expenses and adjustment expenses not included in the allocated adjustment expense category.

In some lines of insurance, certain aspects of medical coordination or vocational rehabilitation may also be allocated, but the use of rehabilitation and medical consultants for utilization review and other cost containment processes may be considered an unallocated expense.

The proper allocation of expenses between allocated and unallocated categories is significant because of state reporting requirements. Insurers frequently refer to these amounts to compare the efficiency of their claims operations with those of other insurers.

IBNR

Claims departments are involved in establishing case reserves. Case reserves are the ultimate loss expectations for each individual claim. There are also bulk (or aggregate) reserves, which are used to estimate losses that are assumed to have happened but have not yet been reported to the insurer. Insurers also use those reserves to reflect workers compensation claims that are reopened after having been settled and closed and to compensate for a general inadequacy in reported case reserves.

These IBNR losses are significant to the overall expectation of profitability of the insurer but only slightly relevant to an individual adjuster. The connection between the two is that case reserves are often used as a basis for the methodology employed to calculate IBNR.

The claims department usually assists in establishing bulk reserves. Many insurers use a committee made up of underwriting, actuarial, accounting, claims, and senior management personnel to review recommendations for bulk reserves. The mathematical procedures used in this process were discussed in Chapter 12. Although a significant part of this procedure is an actuarial function, claims department management can provide valuable information on the validity of the individual case reserves (on which the IBNR estimates are based), changes in the methodology used to determine case reserves, catastrophic or large losses that could skew results, and changes in the legal climate and benefit levels that might affect the ultimate cost of claims.

Case Reserves

No system of bulk reserving can be accurate unless the underlying reserves on individual files are reasonably accurate. That job often falls to the individual adjuster, supervisor, or claims examiner who is responsible for setting the initial reserve or to a special committee set up for the primary purpose of reserve evaluation.

The three standard methods of establishing case reserves, the judgment, average value, and tabular methods, were discussed in Chapter 12 and are reviewed below. The effectiveness of these methods depends on how they are used and on recognizing their inherent weaknesses.

Judgment

In the judgment method, the ability of the adjuster is crucial in determining the appropriateness of the reserve selected. Depending on the nature of the claim, the adjuster needs to know medical treatment costs, average repair or reconstruction time, local pricing factors, local plaintiff attorneys, treating physicians, local contractors, and other factors that will influence the final cost of the claim. This type of reserve-establishing ability is influenced by the adjuster's experience. The subjective nature of the judgment method makes evaluating the adequacy of case reserves difficult, except in the aggregate.

Average Value

The average value method is suitable for types of claims that occur with regular frequency, such as automobile physical damage claims. The claims department can readily establish a reserve amount that can be used for all claims of this nature, recognizing that the reserve amount will be high or low in specific claims but correct overall. Misinterpreting the average claim amount may cause problems. A low reserve may influence the insurer to ignore a potentially serious claim. Mishandled claims or claims that go to litigation usually settle for more than the average value.

For liability lines, the average value method is likely to produce inadequate loss reserves. This is especially true for those liability lines that usually do not settle readily, such as medical malpractice. In those situations, it is appropriate to use an average reserve when the claim is initially reported and to modify that average amount once the claim file can be reviewed in-depth.

Tabular

The tabular method is similar in concept to the average value method of reserving. Instead of using a selected average amount, the tabular method provides an "average" amount for all claims that have similar characteristics in terms of the age, health, and marital status of the claimant.

Reserving Work Sheets and Software

Insurers employ various reserve work sheets that force the claims adjuster to consider all the factors concerning the claim. For a workers compensation or bodily injury claim, the work sheet will take into account not only the known or anticipated medical costs but also the length and cost of disability, the degree of permanency of the injury, and other special damage items that influence the claim. Sophisticated computer programs are now available to help claims adjusters consider all relevant factors in setting reserves.

For liability claims, the adjuster must also take into account the general damage factors, such as pain and suffering, that a jury would consider in deciding on an award. Reserving work sheets also require careful evaluation of liability. Comparative negligence factors must be applied if any are applicable. If joint tortfeasors will contribute or if the potential for subrogation exists, those cost-reducing factors must also be considered.

Property claims can also be systematically evaluated to include not only the direct damages that can be quickly appraised but also the indirect damages, such as business interruption, extra expense, loss of use costs, potential recoveries for salvage and subrogation, and others, that will develop only after considerable time has passed.

Reserving Problems

Reserving becomes a problem when reserves are inadequate or redundant. During an investigation, it is expected that claims will be reevaluated and that reserves will be updated to reflect newly discovered facts.

Adjusters are often criticized for "stair-stepping" reserves, a practice that results when the claim is initially inadequately reserved and the reserves need to be continually updated. **Stair-stepping** (or "reserve creep") often occurs in workers compensation or other types of claims in which periodic payments are made. The adjuster, instead of adequately establishing a sufficient reserve based on the realistic value of the claim, sets only enough reserve to cover costs for the immediate future. Then, when payments meet or exceed the established reserve, the figure is increased for another round of payments. The problem with such a method is that the true value of the claim does not become evident to senior claims management until perhaps years after the initial reserve was set, meaning that cost control procedures that might have helped reduce the overall exposure were never considered. Further, stair-stepping methods may mislead the insurer into delaying a report to a reinsurer or, in a serious liability claim, notifying the policyholder of a potential excess loss situation.

Few initial reserves on claims that are open for more than a few weeks will remain accurate over the long run unless the loss is reserved for policy limits, which is the limit of what the insurer could pay barring any extra-contractual obligations. Most claim reserves must therefore be reevaluated as additional information about the loss is received. This may occur often enough that the file has the appearance of being stair-stepped, but the procedure is quite different, and the evaluation should more accurately represent both positive and negative factors of the loss.

Settlement

Even while the investigation of a claim is proceeding and the liability and reserves are being evaluated, the adjuster must establish personal relationships with a variety of people involved in the claim file in order to negotiate all of the factors that will be involved in the settlement.

Pre-Settlement Negotiation

Negotiation is a necessary step in the adjustment process at many levels. Aspects of coverage may need to be explored and agreed on by the policyholder and the insurer. Other insurers may be involved when a loss is covered by more than one policy or when more than one tortfeasor is responsible for the damages. All of the damages must be examined before any settlement can be reached. Disputes over the damages involved in a claim often require lengthy negotiations between not only the adjuster and the policyholder or claimant but also with repair facilities, public adjusters, and individuals or facilities providing care or treatment for the injured person.

Persons Involved in Claims Negotiations

The adjuster must become familiar with the producing agent, the policyholder, the third-party claimant or adverse party (if there is one), any witnesses, the specialists involved in repairs or damage restoration, the physicians, other experts who may be used, and the attorneys representing any parties involved in the claim. The success of the adjuster in settling any claim depends on his or her familiarity and ability to negotiate with the persons involved in the claim. Whether the claim is for a first-party loss or for damages caused by the policyholder, the relationship established by the adjuster will determine whether the claim is settled with great difficulty, perhaps involving litigation, or directly with the individuals involved.

In most metropolitan areas, many attorneys specialize in representing parties involved in insurance claims. Over a period of time, most adjusters establish either a relationship or a reputation with the local plaintiff bar, and vice versa. Most plaintiff's attorneys are sincerely interested in the welfare and best interests of their clients. Most adjusters are likewise interested in the best interests of all the parties concerned, primarily the policyholder, and those interests are best met when a claim can be quickly resolved by settlement rather than prolonged by litigation.

Negotiation of Settlements

Disposition of the claim is the final step in the adjusting process, whether the negotiation is carried on by the adjuster directly, through litigation, or by some other procedure such as appraisal or arbitration. Every claim must be resolved, and most means of resolution require some negotiation on the part of the adjuster, unless the claim simply involves payment of some fixed amount.

The key to settlements in which all the parties consider themselves to be winners is accurate information. Unless the adjuster has adequately investigated and evaluated all of the factors involved, the negotiating position will be weak and ineffectual and may result in litigation. When the adjuster wants to pay $5,000, but the claimant is demanding $50,000, some means of position justification must be used. Both parties, in light of the facts of the loss, may need to reevaluate their positions. Adjusting requires a large measure of personal control and salesmanship, a friendly disposition, and a degree of tolerance for frustration.

Information must often be shared. Some adjusters may believe that they should not discuss or share information that supports their position with a claimant or opposing attorney, but unless they do, negotiations may suffer. An opinion of value when intangibles, such as the value of pain or the loss of a loved one, are involved should not be artificially set by the adjuster. Flexibility might be necessary if the claim is to be settled.

Some insurers now routinely use some form of advanced payments on both first- and third-party claims. On major property losses, the insurer will often advance the policyholder moneys toward additional living expenses and even reconstruction costs and supplies before settlement of the claim. On liability claims involving both property damage and bodily injury, the insurer will settle the property portion of the claim (without waiting for the bodily injury settlement in accordance with the Unfair Claims Settlement Practices Model Act).

Denial of Claims

Denying the entire claim, or partial denial based on individual factors in a loss, can be difficult unless the adjuster has thoroughly researched the claim. Denial of claims, in order to be successful and not result in litigation, must be based on accurate information about coverage, liability, and damages. When a loss is not covered, the adjuster must be prepared to show the policyholder why the loss is not covered. Denial of coverage must be made as soon as practical after all facts are known.

Denying payment to a third party on the basis that the policyholder is not legally liable must likewise be handled in a way that does not leave the claimant angry and vengeful. The adjuster must be certain that there is no liability. If the denial is based on a contract, being able to identify the applicable provision can be helpful. If the denial is based on a coverage exclusion, the adjuster must involve the policyholder in order to protect the policyholders' interests against the liability exposure.

Settlement Documents

Once the adjuster has received settlement authority from senior claims department personnel and the parties have agreed on the value of a claim, the concluding documents will be executed. Property claims are sometimes settled with a sworn statement in a proof-of-loss form. This document is submitted by the policyholder as a sworn presentation of the claim and as an offer to settle, whereupon it can either be accepted or rejected by the insurer. In questionable first-party claims or those with disputed facts, the policyholder may be provided blank proof-of-loss forms to use in submitting a claim. If the claim is known to be fraudulent, the insurer may deny coverage based on the insured's act of submitting the "sworn" proof. Although some insurers treat the proof-of-loss form as a settlement document, others waive the formal filing of the form entirely, simply issuing a check for the agreed-upon amount.[3]

The final step in closing a third-party claim is obtaining a release from the claimant. A release is a legally binding document and provides that for the specific sums to be paid to the claimant, the claimant releases the policyholder from all claims arising out of the particular accident. There are a variety of release formats; the most commonly used is the **general release**. The general release is appropriate in almost all situations except when a specific type of release would be more appropriate. An example of a general release is shown in Exhibit 13-6.

Attorneys have drafted releases other than general releases to match certain situations, and, in many cases, the language of the releases varies to conform with individual state laws. These releases include joint tortfeasor release, covenant not to sue, high/low agreements, release for injury to a minor, parent's release and indemnity agreement, nominal or dollar releases, release draft, and telephone recorded releases.

Joint Tortfeasor Release

The **joint tortfeasor release** is used when a plaintiff is suing a number of different parties who are presumably responsible for the plaintiff's injuries. Under common law, the plaintiff cannot settle and release one tortfeasor without releasing all tortfeasors involved in the accident. Many states have adopted the Uniform Contribution Among Tortfeasors Act, which permits the plaintiff to release individual tortfeasors without releasing them all. The release shown

Exhibit 13-6
Release in Full of All Claims and Rights (General Release)

For and in consideration of the sum of ______________________
______________________________ ($ ____________________), receipt of which is acknowledged, I release and forever discharge ____________
____, their principals, agents, representatives and insurance carriers from any and all rights, claims, demands, and damages of any kind, known or unknown, existing or arising in the future, resulting from or related to personal injuries, death, or property damage, arising from an accident that occurred on or about the ______________ day of ___________, 19____, at or near_____________________________.

This release shall not destroy or otherwise affect the rights of persons on whose behalf this payment is made, or persons who may claim to be damaged by reason of the accident other than the undersigned or any other persons.

I understand that this is a compromise settlement of all my claims of every nature and kind whatsoever arising out of the accident referred to above, but is not an admission of liability. I understand that this is all the money or consideration I will receive from the above described parties as a result of this accident. I have read this release and understand it.

Signed this _______ day of ____________, 19____, at ___________ .

___________________ ___________________
WITNESS

___________________ ___________________
WITNESS

in Exhibit 13-7 protects the insured from a possible claim for contribution if the claimant is successful in an action against the remaining tortfeasors.

Covenant Not To Sue

A **covenant not to sue** is not a release but an agreement not to bring a suit. Like the joint tortfeasor release, this agreement is used in situations with multiple tortfeasors. In the event that the defendant does bring suit against the settling tortfeasor, the tortfeasor can sue for breach of contract and can recover the amount of legal costs for defense. As with the joint tortfeasor release, the use of this agreement varies by state based on the enactment of the Uniform Contribution Among Tortfeasors Act or similar legislation.

High/Low Agreements

High/low agreements are arrangements whereby the parties to the settlement agree to guaranteed minimum and maximum settlement amounts of claims in litigation or arbitration. A verdict below the minimum will result in the minimum limit being paid by the defendant. Likewise, a verdict above the maximum will be capped at the maximum. Any verdict between the two limits becomes the settlement amount. These agreements are made with the understanding that there will be no appeal.

This type of agreement is appropriate when the plaintiff's case is doubtful but, because of the seriousness of the injuries, could result in a significant judgment. The high/low agreement ensures that the plaintiff will recover something even if the case is lost. The insurer is able to limit its liability and avoid the threat of a bad faith claim for any excess verdict.

Release for Injury to a Minor

Because of a minor's legal status, a minor cannot give an effective release for his or her injuries. Although parents can release their claim for expenses and loss of services, they cannot legally release the claim of their minor child. In order to effectively release a minor's injury claim, therefore, the release must be obtained in accordance with the statutory provisions of the state in which settlement is made. In cases involving serious injuries, the claim should be closed only by means of a court-approved settlement through a guardian or by the procedure known as a "friendly suit." Ordinarily, the court will not approve the settlement unless it has reviewed a current medical report from the treating physician and is satisfied that the settlement fairly compensates the injured child. Since the procedure may vary by jurisdiction, adjusters need to be familiar with the accepted procedure in their jurisdiction.

Parent's Release and Indemnity Agreement

When a minor's injuries are slight and a full recovery is anticipated, many insurers forgo the time and expense of the court approval process and use a **Parent's Release and Indemnity Agreement**.

Although specific criteria may vary by insurer, this release should only be used in the following cases:

- The injury is healed and medical expenses are not great, or the medical report indicates that a minor was examined by a physician and released.
- No fractures were involved.
- No scarring is involved.
- There is no likelihood of future disability or impairment.

Exhibit 13-7
Release (Joint Tortfeasor Act)

We, the Undersigned, in consideration of ___($900.00) — Nine Hundred___ and 00/100___ dollars, the receipt of which is acknowledged, do hereby forever release and discharge ___(names of insureds responsible for the loss)___ herein after called the Payor, their heirs, executors, administrators, employers, employees, principals, agents, insurers, successors and assignees, from any and all liability, damages, actions and causes of action on account of personal injuries, death, loss of services or consortium, property damage and any and all other loss and damage of every kind and nature sustained by or hereafter resulting to the undersigned, his heirs, successors and assigns or any person or persons for whom the undersigned is acting as executor, administrator or guardian from an occurrence on or about the ___(loss date)___ day of ___(month)___, 19___ at ___(location of loss—address, street, highway, city, county, state)___.

It is further understood and agreed that all claims or damages recoverable by the undersigned against all other persons, firms, partnerships or corporation, jointly or severably liable to the undersigned in tort for injury to person or property as a result of said accidents are hereby reduced by ___(amount of settlement—$900)___.

The undersigned hereby warrant that I/we have not heretofore released any person, firm, partnership or corporation from any claims or liability for damages arising from said occurrence.

As inducement to the payment of the sum aforesaid the undersigned declare that we fully understand the terms of this settlement, and that we voluntarily accept said sum for the purpose of making full and final compromise, adjustment and settlement of all claims against the Payor, and that the payment of said sum for this release is not an admission of liability by the Payor, but that the Payor expressly denies liability.

This release is not intended to nor shall it be construed as releasing or discharging any other tortfeasor who may be liable for the injury and damage sustained in the above occurrence.

It is agreed that distribution of the above sum shall be made as follows ___(Entire amount to be paid to the undersigned.)___

___

In Witness Whereof, We hereunto set our hands and seals this ___day of ___, 19___. (today's date)

In presence of

Name ___(witness)___	___(claimant)___ (Seal)
Address ___	___(claimant's spouse)___ (Seal)
Name ___	___ (Seal)
Address___	___ (Seal)
Witnesses sign here	Claimants sign here

This release contains an indemnity agreement that states that if the minor later makes a recovery against the policyholder, the parents will indemnify (or reimburse) the policyholder for any payment made. The legal effect of this release is rarely tested, but in the situations in which this release is used, it probably does have the psychological effect of closing the issue.

Nominal or Dollar Releases

Some adjusters obtain a release from claimants who were involved in an accident but who sustained no injuries. A release without payment probably has no legal effect. When some liability exists, some adjusters settle for a nominal amount. Another approach to obtaining a claimant's release is to have the claimant make a "no injury" statement. In any case, the real value of these releases is to give the claimant some sense of finality and to preclude the claimant from seeking damages at a later time.

Release Draft

Where legal, many insurers use a specific statement of release on the reverse side of drafts. Such releases are most commonly associated with small to moderate property damage claims. The claimant's endorsement of the draft or check serves as a release of the claim. Adjusters must remember that many unfair claims practice laws restrict the use of **release drafts**. Adjusters should be familiar with any such restrictions in their states.

Telephone-Recorded Releases

Telephone-recorded releases are occasionally taken by adjusters in smaller claims in which the claimant is not represented by an attorney. The acceptability and use of telephone releases vary by company and, to some extent, by jurisdiction. Inside adjusters may find that releases are easier to obtain over the telephone, and a telephone release may occasionally be obtained instead of a telephone-recorded statement on smaller claims.

Litigation

Many insurers spend as much money on outside defense attorneys as they do for their entire claims department, yet defending policyholders is one of the key promises of liability insurance. It is essential to policyholders and the insurer that claims personnel handle litigation well. Because of the enormous expense of litigation and the delays existing in many court systems, claim representatives should explore alternatives to litigation. When litigation cannot be avoided, claim representatives must carefully select and direct defense counsel. They must actively participate in litigation strategy to ensure proper defense of the policyholder and careful control of litigation expenses.

Alternatives to Litigation

Adjusters use various procedures called **alternative dispute resolution (ADR)** as alternatives to litigation, including negotiation, mediation, arbitration, appraisals, mini-trials or summary jury trials, and pre-trial settlement conferences. The insurance industry and the courts encourage the use of these litigation alternatives. Approaches to alternative dispute resolution are discussed in Chapter 15.

Selection and Direction of Outside Attorneys

The selection of a defense attorney who will handle a lawsuit against an insured is an important decision. For a routine claim in which the amount of damages is specific (as in property damage) or where the action involves only subrogation collection, a new or unproven attorney who charges a minimum rate may be considered. But when the allegations against the policyholder are severe, liability is questionable, and the damages are so severe that a jury may award compensatory damages in excess of the policyholder's policy limits, the insurer must select an outstanding defense attorney.

The attorney's role is to be an advocate for the insured—regardless of how the attorney may personally view the policyholder's case or personal merits. The attorney must attack every aspect of the adverse party's claim, from the liability to the damages, seeking constantly to find something that will mitigate the claim against the policyholder and place the plaintiff in such a position that settlement may be a more attractive option than an unknown award from an unpredictable jury.

Decisions Relating to Defense

The first decision that must be made is whether to defend the lawsuit at all. If the lawsuit is the first notice of the claim and liability is probable, the adjuster handling the claim may request an extension from the plaintiff's attorney while some investigation is conducted and then try to settle the claim without incurring defense costs.

If the facts of the case are already known and the case is one of clear or probable liability, the adjuster should attempt to settle the case before incurring legal costs. The attorney may have filed the suit only to protect against a statute of limitations or to get the insurer's attention if settlement negotiations have failed to progress or have reached an impasse.

If, on the other hand, the claim may be owed but the plaintiff is seeking more in the settlement than the insurer feels is justified, the adjuster may decide to allow discovery to proceed to find whether the plaintiff has any proof that the damages are as severe as alleged.

When the previous investigation shows that the claim is not owed because of either a lack of liability or damages or the claim is owed by some other party, the insurer may elect to defend. The defense attorney might move to have the case dismissed on summary judgment (a pre-trial verdict in favor of the party requesting it) or might file a cross action or third-party action against the party believed to be the one responsible to the plaintiff. This is the sort of defense that can quickly become expensive as various motions before the court and the processes of discovery proceed.

Insurers often speak of "nuisance settlements" of a claim or lawsuit when there is either very little liability or no proof of damages. In order to save the cost of defending such a suit, the insurer may pay or contribute a minimal amount to a settlement to resolve the case. A valid argument might be made that nuisance payments produce more harm than good by encouraging unscrupulous claimants and attorneys to file more frivolous claims.

Selection of Experts

Whether or not a claim is in litigation, the adjuster may need a variety of experts to assist in the evaluation process. In complex claims involving traffic accidents, building or construction sites, products, mechanical processes, and other exposures that may require expert courtroom testimony, the adjuster must have available resources from which to draw the best witnesses. Someone with the most credentials, however, may not be the best technical expert if he or she cannot adequately use lay terms to explain to the jury what happened. The adjuster must select a specialist who is not only an expert in his or her field but who is also impartial and well-spoken.

Subrogation and Other Recoveries

Subrogation is the legal process through which an insurer assumes the right to pursue a legal action against a party who may be liable to the policyholder. Subrogation is one of the most effective post-loss control processes, not just in first-party claims but also in liability and other types of claims. Most subrogation occurs in workers compensation, property insurance, and automobile physical damage claims. The insurer may include the policyholder's deductible in a claim but otherwise may not pursue other loss suffered by the policyholder that is not covered by insurance.

A physical damage insurer will frequently seek to recover the collision damages that it has paid from the liability insurer of the driver who struck the insured auto. Insurers that have signed the Nationwide Inter-Company Arbitration Agreement sponsored by Arbitration Forums, Inc., may use arbitration via panels of local claims adjusters to resolve disputes between themselves over liability issues related to their subrogation. This agreement also permits insurers to pursue the amount of the deductible on behalf of the insured. The decision of the panel is binding and generally cannot be appealed. There are several other types of intercompany and special arbitration agreements to which insurers subscribe. Disputed uninsured motorists claims are often settled using arbitrators affiliated with the American Arbitration Association.

Measuring Claims Performance

The recovery of a community after a natural disaster is a testament to the success of claims activities. Yet insurers must have a more specific means of measuring the success of their claims departments and of individual adjusters.

There is no single convenient measure of the performance of an insurer's claims department. The claims-handling ability of an insurer should be measured in terms of two categories: financial measures and measures that evaluate claims-handling performance.

Financial Measures

The insurer's loss ratio is one of the most commonly used measures of evaluating the financial well-being of an insurance company. A rising loss ratio may indicate that the insurer is improperly performing the claims function. Rising losses could also mean that underwriting failed to select above-average risks or that the actuarial department failed to price the insurer's products correctly.

When the expense ratio of the insurer rises, the claims department, along with other departments, will face pressure to reduce expenses. Management often relies on superficial and shortsighted solutions to controlling claim expenses. Claims personnel can quickly reduce claims adjusting expenses by offering policyholders and claimants the settlement demanded rather than the settlement they deserve. A proper claim settlement requires incurring expenses. Inflated claim demands should be resisted, researched, negotiated, and, if necessary, litigated.

One way to reduce the cost of claims is to reduce the number of claims adjusting personnel. Reduced claim staffs or restrictions on the use of independent adjusters usually increase the workload of claims personnel. Increased workload without changes in job standards will likely result in adjusters' taking shortcuts in handling claims.

The long-term consequences of not following acceptable claims procedures is an increase in the total cost of claims. So, although there may be an immediate reduction in expenses because of these measures, claim costs are likely to rise as more claims go into litigation or are overpaid.

A better financial measure of claims performance is the accuracy with which claims are reserved. If the insurer must constantly transfer large sums on its financial balance sheet from surplus to reserves because of past underreserving, the claims department may be performing one of its primary jobs poorly.

Claims-Handling Performance

Claims-handling performance measures are internal standards by which claims departments and individual adjusters can be gauged. The criteria used to evaluate a claims department include the following:

- Turnover of claims
- Average cost of settlement
- Number and percentage of litigated files
- Litigation win/lose ratios
- Ratio of allocated to unallocated costs
- Average caseload per adjuster
- Turnover of staff

The performance of individual adjusters can be evaluated on the basis of the following factors:

- File turnover
- Ratio of litigated to settled files
- Average settlement costs compared to other adjusters with similar files

The adjuster's position, level of experience and education, and degree of supervision must be considered in the evaluation. An adjuster with a caseload that only grows, with few settled but many litigated files, is an adjuster in trouble. Overpaying claims is equally as troublesome, though it may reduce the caseload faster.

Unfair Claims Settlement Practices Legislation

The Unfair Claims Settlement Practices Model Act was developed by the National Association of Insurance Commissioners (NAIC) to establish standards for the proper handling of claims. Before its development, regulators relied on state unfair trade practices acts. These laws were often ineffective in protecting the public from insurer strategies to reduce or eliminate claims. Unconscionable insurer tactics included denying claims when there was obvious liability or slowing down the settlement process until policyholders and claimants finally gave up.

In creating the Unfair Claims Settlement Practices Model Act, the NAIC incorporated many of the provisions already included in New York statutes. The act was added as a new section to the existing Unfair Trade Practices Act. In 1990, the NAIC separated the provisions of the act to facilitate distinction between general unfair trade practices and the more specific unfair claim settlement practices. The insurer activities prohibited by the Unfair Claims Settlement Practices Act are listed in Exhibit 13-8.

Under the provisions of the model act, if the insurance commissioner has reasonable cause to believe that an insurer is conducting business in violation of the act, the commissioner can issue a statement of charges to the insurer and establish a hearing date. If it is determined after the hearing that the insurer has violated the act, the insurance commissioner will issue a cease and desist order and may impose a fine. The fine cannot be for more than $1,000 for each violation and no more than $100,000 altogether unless the violation was committed flagrantly and in conscious disregard of the act. In such cases, the penalty will not exceed $25,000 for each violation or $250,000 in the aggregate. The insurance commissioner may suspend or revoke the insurer's license if the insurer knew or reasonably should have known that the activity was in violation of the act. Additional penalties exist for violation of cease and desist orders.[4] *Some states may have adopted the model act but not the specific penalty provisions. Other states have altered the model act or deleted sections of it.*

The Unfair Property/Casualty Claims Settlement Practices Model Regulation is a companion to the Unfair Claims Settlement Practices Act. As with the model act, individual state legislatures must choose to adopt the model law or some version of it and enact it into law. In those states whose insurance commission has the power to devise insurance regulations to carry out the model act, the model regulation is available to serve as a basis for creating administrative guidelines. The regulation defines procedures and practices that constitute unfair claims practices in the following specific areas:

- File and record documentation
- Misrepresentation of policy provisions
- Failure to acknowledge pertinent communications
- Standards for prompt, fair, and equitable settlements applicable to all insurers
- Standards for prompt, fair, and equitable settlements applicable to automobile insurance
- Standards for prompt, fair, and equitable settlements applicable to automobile insurance
- Standards for prompt, fair, and equitable settlements applicable to fire and extended coverage-type policies with replacement cost coverage

Exhibit 13-8
Unfair Claims Settlement Practices

Committing or performing with such frequency as to indicate a general business practice any of the following:

A. Knowingly misrepresenting to claimants and insureds relevant facts or policy provisions relating to coverage at issue;

B. Failing to acknowledge with reasonable promptness pertinent communications with respect to claims arising under its policies;

C. Failing to adopt and implement reasonable standards for the prompt investigation and settlement of claims arising under its policies;

D. Not attempting in good faith to effectuate prompt, fair and equitable settlement of claims submitted in which liability has become reasonably clear;

E. Compelling insureds or beneficiaries to institute suits to recover amounts due under its policies by offering substantially less than the amounts ultimately recovered in suits brought by them;

F. Refusing to pay claims without conducting a reasonable investigation;

G. Failing to affirm or deny coverage of claims within a reasonable time after having completed its investigation related to such claim or claims;

H. Attempting to settle or settling claims for less than the amount that a reasonable person would believe the insured or beneficiary was entitled by reference to written or printed advertising material accompanying or made part of an application;

I. Attempting to settle or settling claims on the basis of an application that was materially altered without notice to, or knowledge or consent of, the insured;

J. Making claims payments to an insured or beneficiary without indicating the coverage under which each payment is being made;

K. Unreasonably delaying the investigation or payment of claims by requiring both a formal proof of loss form and subsequent verification that would result in duplication of information and verification appearing in the formal proof of loss form;

L. Failing in the case of claims denials or offers of compromise settlement to promptly provide a reasonable and accurate explanation of the basis for such actions;

M. Failing to provide forms necessary to present claims within fifteen (15) calendar days of a request with reasonable explanations regarding their use;

N. Failing to adopt and implement reasonable standards to assure that the repairs of a repairer owned by or required to be used by the insurer are performed in a workmanlike manner.

NAIC Model Laws, Regulations, and Guidelines, Tab: Unfair Trade Practices, 1991, p. 900-2-3.

Forty-five jurisdictions have adopted either the Unfair Claims Practices Model Act or similar legislation. Twenty-one states have adopted the Unfair Property/Casualty Claims Settlement Practices Model Regulation or similar regulations. In those states where the model regulations have not been adopted, the insurance regulators must decide on a case-by-case basis what is considered an "unfair" practice.

All state insurance codes contain various rules and regulations that govern the practice of claims adjusting. In addition, in many states, insurers, their adjusters, and independent adjusters are also subject to the state's consumer-oriented Deceptive Trade Practices Act. These laws often leave the issue of what constitutes an unfair trade practice to juries, which can award triple damages.

Various states can interpret their laws and regulations differently. One state may require an adjuster to advise an unrepresented claimant of the statute of limitations, but in another state without such a rule, volunteering information might be construed as the unauthorized practice of law. In another example, one state may require a vehicle damage appraiser to list one or more shops that will agree to repair a damaged vehicle for the appraised amount, but in another state, recommending any repair facility is a violation of law. Many of these rules deal with misrepresentation of policy terms, refusal to settle, or lack of response to inquiries.

Recognizing the need to internalize the provisions of the model act into the procedures of the claims department, insurers have rewritten its provisions and have added specific standards for company adjusters when the regulations have provided none. So even adjusters who may not be familiar with the act itself may be following company procedures that comply with the act. Enforcement of the Unfair Claims Settlement Practices Act is limited in most jurisdictions. In only a minority of states can individuals exert a right of action based on the act in first-party claims. Even fewer states permit a right of action in third-party claims. In the remainder of states, enforcement of the act is the full responsibility of the insurance department.

Summary

The insurer fulfills its contractual promise to the policyholder through the claim settlement process. Adjusters screen requests for payment to distinguish the valid from the invalid claims. Claims that fall within the bounds of coverage are assessed to determine their value and are then paid.

Most policyholders have little or no contact with their insurer other than when the initial policy is written or when the premium is due. When a claim does occur, the adjuster is responsible for the reputation of the insurance company. Fair and professional treatment of policyholders and claimants can do much to improve the image of the insurance industry, even on an individual, claim-by-claim basis.

Some insurers may think that any claim that goes to trial is a failure, even before the verdict is determined. When a claim does go to trial, the adjuster must manage the defense counsel and communicate to plaintiff's counsel the settlement philosophy of the insurer. Internally, adjusters must provide information to several departments, including the marketing, underwriting, and actuarial departments.

The structure of an insurer's claims organization is typically described in terms of its geographic or physical organization and its management/settlement authority. Claim offices are usually located close to policyholders so that service can be provided easily. Often, when claims occur outside the normal geographic scope of the insurer, independent adjusters are employed to service the policyholder. The management structure of a claims department is probably very similar to the management scheme of any other insurer functional area. A distinguishing feature in claims organization is that higher levels of settlement authority are assigned to individuals based on their responsible use of the claims authority already granted. Experience, knowledge, and the confidence of management are all factors considered in extending settlement authority.

In addition to handling claims outside the normal scope of operations, independent adjusters provide special expertise for complex or unusual claims. Many insurers employ independent adjusters as a normal part of their business rather than expanding their own staffs.

The claims adjusting process can be described in terms of investigation, evaluation, negotiation, and settlement of coverage, liability, and damage issues. The actual steps in this process may vary between property and liability claims. Specific claims-handling differences and the unique characteristics of individual lines of business are the subjects of Chapters 14 and 15.

Chapter Notes

1. "A Guide to Auto Insurance," *Consumer Reports*, October 1995, p. 642.
2. The following section is based on Bernard L. Webb, Howard N. Anderson, John A. Cookman, and Peter R. Kensicki, *Principles of Reinsurance*, vol. 1 (Malvern, PA: Insurance Institute of America, 1990), pp. 185-196.
3. Robert J. Prahl and Stephen M. Utrata, *Liability Claim Concepts and Practices* (Malvern, PA: Insurance Institute of America, 1985), pp. 385-403.
4. NAIC Model Laws, Regulations, and Guidelines, 1991, Tab: Unfair Trade Practices, p. 900.

Chapter 14

Property Claims Adjusting

Each of the final two chapters of this text addresses a specific type of claim: this chapter discusses claims for property losses (specifically claims for property damage under first-party insurance policies), and Chapter 15 discusses liability claims (primarily bodily injury claims under third-party insurance policies). This division is a natural one because claims adjusters are generally either property or liability specialists. Although claims for property damage can be asserted against third-party policies and injury claims can be covered by first-party policies, the majority of claims personnel do most of their work in either property-damage-first-party claims or in bodily-injury-third-party claims.

Property and liability claim specialists operate in different environments. Property claims adjusters are primarily concerned with the application of detailed insurance policy provisions to specific situations. Liability claims adjusters, on the other hand, are primarily concerned with how the legal system, which operates independently of insurance policy provisions, evaluates and compensates third-party claims. Property claims adjusters must indemnify losses that are supposedly objectively quantifiable, but liability claims adjusters must evaluate and settle claims that are largely subjective.

"Pain and suffering," for instance, is one of the major elements of damages in bodily injury liability claims.

The first part of this chapter addresses general issues that arise in all property claims. Who has an interest in, and who is insured with respect to, damaged property? What property is insured under a policy and for what locations and for what time period? For what causes of loss does the insurance provide coverage? What is the dollar amount of the loss? What procedures must the insured and the claims adjuster follow to conclude the claim? As noted above, the answers to those questions are derived from applying the insurance policy provisions to specific situations.

The second part of this chapter discusses specific issues pertinent to specific types of claims and how claims adjusters must deal with those issues. Although the settlement of all claims includes each of the issues described in the first part of this chapter, certain issues predominate in certain types of claims. For example, issues that are paramount in homeowners claims may be much less important in commercial crime claims, and vice versa.

General Issues in Property Claims Adjusting

The issues described herein pertain to every property claim and constitute a framework used by property claims adjusters to handle all kinds of property damage claims. The explicit language of insurance policies provides substantial direction and guidance to adjusters. For example, in order to determine who is insured, an adjuster can simply read the name on the policy. Although others may also be insured, the identification of the named insured is crucial. An adjuster can likewise resolve most of the issues described below by consulting the policy and applying the policy language to the given situation. The biggest exception to this approach is in determining the amount of loss. In contrast to the detail they provide concerning other matters, insurance policies are extremely general in how they state the value of insured property. Adjusters perform an in-depth analysis of property values on those policies that sustain a loss rather than all policies insured by the company. The critical time for property valuation is at the time of the loss, not at the time the policy was issued.

Who Has an Interest? Who Is Insured?

Insurance actually protects people, not property. So-called property insurance protects people or organizations from loss of the value of their interest in property. Accordingly, an interest in property is a prerequisite to asserting a claim under an insurance policy.

Good underwriting practice requires a prospective policyholder to have an interest in property before an insurance policy can be issued. The underwriting standard is reinforced by language in the policy that limits all claims payments to the extent of the insured's interest. One might wonder why claims adjusters concern themselves with this requirement. A review of all interests that may exist in damaged property is an excellent means of determining with whom the adjuster must deal in settling a claim. Since property insurance exists to protect people, the adjuster's first questions on every claim should be, "Who is affected? Who has a right to assert a claim?"

Interests in Property

In general, anyone who would be harmed financially by the destruction of property has an interest in that property. The simplest and most obvious example of an interest in property is a sole owner with a complete interest in the property. However, numerous other interests, less than complete and sole, may exist in a particular property, often simultaneously.

Ownership may not rest with a sole person—there are various legal forms by which more than one person can own property simultaneously. Under **joint ownership**, two or more owners each have a complete, indivisible interest in the property. If one joint owner dies, ownership need not be transferred, since the other owner already has a complete interest in the property. Joint ownership is often called "the poor person's will," since the property need never pass through the administration of the deceased's estate. Joint ownership between husband and wife is known as **tenancy by entireties**. **Ownership in common** involves two or more owners, each with an identifiable fractional interest in the property. This fractional interest is a financial interest and does not necessarily constitute any particular part of the physical property. Ownership in common is typical among partners.

A person or an organization can also have an interest in property that is not an ownership interest. Lessees of property have an interest in the use of the property for the life of the lease. Custodians of property, such as bailees, warehouse employees, and carriers, have an interest in the property to the extent of their fees and for their legal liability for the safe return of the property to its owner. Finally, security interests may exist in almost any property. The secured party is generally a creditor of the property owner. The existence of a security interest is usually not evident from an inspection of the property. The secured party usually does not have possession of the property, and the property is not marked physically to show the interest. Security interests are created by contractual agreement or by operation of law.

Policy Requirements for an Insurable Interest

Rather than listing the existence of an insurable interest as a precondition to coverage, insurance policies simply limit payment on any claim to the extent of the insured's interest. For example, the HO-3 policy states the following under Conditions 1:

> . . . we will not be liable in any one loss: a. to the insured for more than the amount of the insured's interest at the time of loss. . . .

Under Loss Conditions, paragraph 4.d., the business and personal property coverage form states:

> We will not pay you more than your financial interest in the Covered Property.

In addition, proof of loss forms usually require the insured to specify all interests in the property. Insurers typically provide these forms to insureds who have suffered losses and require that the forms be signed and sworn to by the insured. Some insurance policies explicitly require that all interests be specified on a proof of loss form. On other policies, the insurer may require the insured to file a signed, sworn statement listing all information required by the insurer. Invariably, the insurer will require complete information about interests in the property.

Since a proof of loss must be signed and sworn to, false information contained therein constitutes material misrepresentation that may void coverage. As noted later in this chapter, some insurers do not require a proof of loss on all, or even most, claims. However, any time the nature and extent of interests in the property are unclear, a proof of loss is invaluable to the insurer.

The limitation of claims payments to the extent of an insured's interest and the requirement that all interests existing in the property be specified are essential claims adjusting procedures. Were the insured able to collect more than its interest in the insured property, there would be a great incentive for deliberate destruction of the property by the insured. Even when a policy has been properly underwritten, an insured's interest can change (for example, through divorce, marriage, or additional mortgages), thus creating opportunities for false claims if the insured's recovery is not limited to its actual interest.

Identifying all interests in the property enables the adjuster to treat every party fairly, without compromising the insurer's rights, and may result in identifying other coverage. Whenever there are multiple interests in property, each party might have its own insurance protecting its own interest. Another party's property or liability insurance may reduce the payments required of the investigating insurer. Policies contain provisions to uphold the indemnification concept. The other insurance and subrogation clauses reduce recovery or limit unjust enrichment.

Possibilities for Other Coverage

The most common situations in which parties with different interests have separate coverages are landlord-tenant, bailor-bailee, and mortgagor-mortgagee arrangements.

Landlord-Tenant Arrangements

The lease determines the relationship between a landlord and a tenant. The lease should specify precisely what property is subject to the lease; what rights of use or access, if any, the tenant has to the landlord's other property; the rights in the leased property that the landlord retains; the rights of the tenant to make improvements to the leased property; and the rights of the landlord to any improvements to the leased property upon expiration of the lease. The lease should also specify whether the landlord and tenant waive rights of recovery against each other and whether the tenant is obligated to provide insurance for the landlord. An adjuster cannot determine the interests of either a landlord or a tenant in property without reviewing the lease.

Although the lease determines the respective rights regarding the leased property, it does not determine coverage under an insurance policy. The landlord or the tenant may be named as an insured under the other's policy, or there may be coverage for the property of others in the insured's possession. Neither the landlord nor the tenant has any rights under the insurance coverage of the other, however, unless the other's insurance policy so allows.

Thus, adjusters handling claims that potentially involve a landlord and a tenant must conduct a two-part analysis. First, what are the parties' respective interests in the property under the lease? Second, what rights does each party have under the insurance policy in question? In order to recover under an insurance policy, a party must have both the right to do so under the policy *and* an interest in some property that is covered by the policy.

Bailor-Bailee Arrangements

Bailor-bailee situations involve similar issues. The respective interests in the property are determined by contractual agreement or, in the absence of contractual terms, by the law. Rights under an insurance policy are determined solely by the terms of that policy. Because of their legal liabilities and because of industry custom, bailees such as warehouse employees, carriers, and repairers typically have some sort of coverage for the property of others while it is in their possession.

Adjusters handling claims for owners of property damaged in the hands of a bailee will usually look first to the bailee's insurer to handle the claim. Should the bailee's insurer fail to respond, or deny liability, the owner's insurer must handle the claim. Possible subrogation claims against the bailee may be waived or otherwise affected by the agreement between the owner and the bailee.

Mortgagor-Mortgagee Arrangements

The most common situation in which different interests are protected by common coverage is with owners and mortgagees. Mortgage agreements usually require the owner to name the mortgagee on the owner's insurance policy. Insurance policies grant rights to mortgagees that are separate and distinct from the owner's rights. Thus, adjusters may have to protect a mortgagee even when the coverage is void as to the owner.

In most claims, the mortgagee's interest is protected by having the property repaired with the claim settlement proceeds. The adjuster should include the mortgagee's name on any settlement draft. Failure to do so may render the insurer separately liable to the mortgagee. The adjuster should not become involved in disputes between the owner, mortgagee, and contractors over whether the property is reparable. Once the adjuster has agreed with the parties as to the amount of the loss and has named all parties on the settlement draft, the adjuster's task is complete.

Identification of Insureds

Adjusters must carefully distinguish among a variety of people with rights and duties under a policy. A policy may identify a "first named insured," "named insureds," spouse of a "named insured," "insureds," and people whose property may be covered under a policy.

Generally, only the "first named insured," "named insured," or spouse of the "named insured" is entitled to assert a claim. These specified individuals are likewise responsible for paying premiums and performing the insured's duties in the event of loss. In the event of the named insured's death, an adjuster can settle claims with the named insured's legal representative, either an executor or administrator of the estate. These legal representatives are included in most policies' definition of "insured." Loss payees are parties, such as auto finance companies, that do not have any rights greater than or independent of the policyholder, but the loss payee's name must be included on any claim settlement check.

The adjuster must deal with the proper party or parties. Failure to do so may obligate the insurer to pay the claim more than once if the proper party appears or may render ineffective any legal notices the insurer has given. An adjuster should be able to determine easily the proper party with whom to deal. The declarations of the policy will identify the named insureds. The policy language can be consulted to determine exactly who can assert claims and who must perform the insured's duties in the event of loss.

In any case in which the insurer can deny coverage to the first named insured or to the spouse of a named insured, the adjuster must carefully check the policy for the rights the other insureds may still have. If the policy language is unclear about such situations, the adjuster should consult legal counsel.

What Is Insured? Where Is It Insured?

Policy provisions regarding what property is covered and where it is covered are straightforward and usually do not cause disagreement between the insured and the adjuster.

Buildings

Being stationary, most buildings are easy to describe and identify. Most policies state the described buildings and structures at a given location. Although other policies provide blanket coverage, a schedule of locations is still necessary to identify which locations are intended to be insured.

Any inconsistency between the identification of an insured location on the declarations sheet and a purported insured location is probably caused by a clerical error that can be cleared up through research with the producer. The construction and occupancy of a building described on a declarations sheet are *not* conditions of the policy coverage unless the policy explicitly says so. Thus, if a claims adjuster finds that a house described as "brick" construction is actually wood frame construction, this discrepancy should be reported to the underwriter, but it will not void coverage, unless the policyholder engaged in misrepresentation. Intentional misrepresentation is a basis for voiding the policy from its inception.

Personal Property

Other than the coverages provided by inland marine policies, most personal property is covered under insurance policies that are written for a fixed location (and that may be primarily concerned with coverage for a building at that location). Such policies provide different coverage, depending on the circumstances. In general, the insured's personal property at the insured location is covered; the insured's personal property away from the insured location may or may not be covered, depending on the policy; and personal property not owned by the policyholder is covered only at the insured location and while in the insured's care, custody, and control, often subject to a tight limit of coverage.

Adjusters handling claims for personal property must be alert to two situations in which coverage may be sought even though it may not apply: (1) a claim for the insured's property that may have been damaged away from the insured location, and (2) a claim for damage to the property of another. In the first case, an adjuster may become suspicious if the property was damaged away from the insured premises because it is a certain type of property (for example, goods in the process of manufacture or goods that had been sold but not yet delivered). The cause of loss (for example, vehicle damage or theft without forcible entry) may also arouse suspicion. Additional documentation from, or investigation of, the insured is likely to confirm or disprove the suspicion. In the second case, the adjuster's job is easy if the insured acknowledges that the property in question belongs to another. The adjuster then need only check the policy to see what coverage pertains or whether other insurance covering the property is primary. The adjuster's job is harder if the insured tries to pass off the property of another as his or her own. The adjuster may suspect such a situation if the insured handles a great deal of other people's property without adequate coverage for this exposure. Careful research into the insured's records will usually reveal who owns the property. An adjuster may require assistance from an expert auditor for this task.

Fixtures are personal property that have become attached to and part of real property. In the event of a loss, the adjuster must be able to determine whether a given "fixture" is real or personal property. Real property is land and everything attached to it, such as buildings. Personal property is everything not considered real property. The distinction between real property and personal property is important to adjusters. The two types of property may be valued differently (actual cash value versus replacement cost), may have different limits of coverage (which may not be adequate for one type of property), and may have different coinsurance requirements. Adjusters can distinguish fixtures as real property by means of the following guidelines:

1. How permanently attached to the real property it is (for example, a furnace is a fixture, but a window air conditioner is not)
2. Whether the property is well adapted to the real property (for example, draperies that have been selected to match the interior decorating of a particular room)
3. The intent of the owner (for example, something may be bolted or screwed onto the real property yet be personal property because the owner so intends)

Certain policy provisions are helpful because they relieve the adjuster from classifying certain property. For example, the business and personal property coverage form allows fixtures to be classed as either "building" or "business personal property." The ISO Homeowners Special Form (HO-3) requires that carpets, awnings, appliances, and antennae be valued like personal property, regardless of whether they might actually be fixtures. In any doubtful case, an adjuster should categorize property in whatever way is most favorable to the insured. Specialized policies for electronic data processing equipment address all computer-related exposures, whether the computer hardware is personal property or a fixture, and extend to additional expenses, such as reconstructing data.

Property Not Covered

Adjusters quickly learn the types of property that are typically not covered, but they should always check the exact policy wording before denying any claim. Failure to provide a reasonable explanation for a claim denial with references to the insurance policy and the facts of the case is a violation of the Unfair Claims Settlement Practices Act.

Insureds who have a claim denied will usually accept a plausible and verifiable explanation from the adjuster. For example, the adjuster may simply have to explain that the property is the sort that is usually covered elsewhere (for example, motor vehicles) or through specialty lines of insurance (for example, valuable papers or livestock). Nevertheless, all claim denials should be in writing.

Additional Coverages

Following a loss, insureds will frequently consult with the adjuster about whether, and to what extent, they can incur certain expenses under the various additional coverages. It is considered good practice for adjusters to respond to requests from insureds for authorization of additional coverage expense. Unless the insured is asserting a suspicious claim, the common-sense approach is to reach agreement about an expense before it has been incurred, rather than to argue about it afterward. The adjuster's authorization of an expense under the additional coverages is regarded as contractually binding on the insurer, even if the expense in question should not have been covered.

Against What Causes of Loss Does the Insurance Protect?

Determining whether a loss was caused by a covered cause of loss is usually a simple matter for an adjuster. Causes of loss such as fire and windstorm, for example, cause very characteristic damage and are easy to verify. Adjusters may encounter problems verifying the cause of loss when certain perils or exclusions are involved. Water damage, collapse, theft, and vandalism, however, are troublesome perils to verify. The most troublesome exclusions are water damage (as an exclusion), wear and tear and other gradual causes of loss, ordinance or law causing increased cost to rebuild, faulty construction, and intentional acts on the part of the insured.

Direct and Indirect Physical Loss

Most property insurance policies provide coverage only in the event of direct physical loss. Thus, adjusters must recognize indirect or nonphysical types of losses that may be presented for coverage.

The most important type of indirect loss is loss of use of property. Coverage for loss of use is provided as part of the package of coverages in the typical homeowners policy. In contrast, some commercial property policies do not automatically provide loss of use coverage. Unless the insured purchases such coverage, loss of use of property is not compensated.

Even when there is coverage for loss of use, direct physical loss to property is essential to trigger such coverage and to measure its duration. For example, coverage for loss of business income applies only when the loss of business income is caused by a direct loss to covered property or when civil authorities close the business because of a hazardous situation nearby. Such coverage begins after a brief waiting period that follows when the covered property suffers direct loss and usually ends when the same property should be repaired or replaced.

Nonphysical losses include loss of value to property not caused by physical damage or destruction, such as obsolescence, loss of market, investment loss, and financial frauds. Loss of market is an important problem for claims adjusters. Insureds who operate seasonal businesses and who suffer losses at the busiest time of year frequently demand compensation for the diminished value of inventory that went unsold because of their loss. Assuming such inventory did not suffer physical loss, its diminished value is not compensable.

Water Damage

Property insurance policies that provide coverage for water damage generally limit such coverage to sudden and accidental overflow, breakage, or bursting of plumbing. In a given case, the exact wording of the coverage is crucial, since any type of water damage not within the defined cause of loss is not covered.

The most significant types of water damage that are usually not covered are gradual seepage and floods. Alone, these two types of water damage are easy to identify. Claims adjusters face difficulties, however, when these types of water damage are combined with covered losses. For example, a burst pipe may cause damage to property that has already suffered damage from gradual seepage.

Except under certain "all-risks" policies that may cover seepage, the adjuster must separate property damaged by seepage from other property and must determine how much of the damage to the former was caused by the seepage and the burst pipe, respectively.

Hurricanes frequently cause damage through a combination of wind, wind-driven water, and flooding. The typical property policy covers the damage caused by wind and wind-driven water (under specific circumstances), but not by flooding. The adjuster must separate damages by cause even if the owner purchased flood coverage through the National Flood Insurance Program (NFIP). Under the NFIP's Single Adjuster Program, one adjuster can handle both the wind and flood claims at a single loss site. This is an important procedure because adjusters are usually in short supply following a major catastrophe. As a result, all claims in the affected geographic area can be handled sooner.

Collapse

Collapse is actually a type of loss, rather than a cause of loss. In recent Insurance Services Office policy forms, collapse is treated as an additional coverage. The effect of treating collapse as an additional coverage is to limit the coverage for collapse to the specific wording of the additional coverage. Collapse is covered only when it is caused by the perils specified in the additional coverage. Adjusters must be careful when handling claims involving two specific causes of collapse: hidden problems and defective construction.

Decay and insect and vermin damage are covered causes of collapse only if they are *hidden*. Conspicuous decay or insect or vermin damage should be repaired by the insured before further loss occurs. In order to determine whether the insured should have known of the damage that caused the collapse, claims adjusters must reconstruct how a structure looked before its collapse.

Defective construction is a covered cause of collapse only if the collapse occurs during construction. Policyholders have presented numerous claims to insurers for loss caused by defective construction. The underwriters of most property insurance policies do not intend to have the policies serve in place of a surety contract that would protect the structure's owner from mistakes made by the builder.

Theft

Coverage for theft varies widely among property policies, from none to extensive. An adjuster handling a claim for loss caused by theft must be very careful to review thoroughly the relevant policy provisions.

Assuming that the policyholder has theft coverage for the type and location of property concerned, the adjuster's most difficult task is verifying the loss. Both the loss itself and its amount must be verified. Theft claims are the easiest for a dishonest insured to fabricate, since little or no evidence remains. Even in legitimate cases of theft, there is often no evidence that a thief acted, that the property involved ever existed, or of the values and quantities of property involved. The insured's statements as to the nature, quantity, and value of property allegedly stolen are admissible evidence in court. Thus, an adjuster cannot deny a claim simply because the insured fails to provide receipts.

Adjusters can (and should) require policyholders with theft claims to report such claims to the police. Most insurance policies require the policyholder to do so. Indeed, a policyholder's failure to do so will likely arouse the adjuster's suspicions. People who fabricate theft claims may be reluctant to involve the police because of the possibilities of criminal sanctions for false reporting. On legitimate claims, the police occasionally recover stolen property, thus mitigating the insurer's payment.

Disproving suspicious theft claims is difficult. Doing so usually requires statements from an unhappy spouse, a business partner, or an employee of the insured who turns against the insured. Otherwise, adjusters must judge theft claims by their reasonableness. Do the type and amount of property in question seem appropriate to the policyholder's standard of living? Does the policyholder claim unusual duplicates, such as two stereo systems or two sets of silver? Does the policyholder have documentation that is common, such as inventory records in a business or instruction manuals for consumer electronics? Ultimately, if the adjuster compels the policyholder to comply scrupulously with every duty following loss and the adjuster's suspicions remain unproven, the claim is likely to be paid.

Vandalism

Vandalism is the intentional or malicious destruction of property. Accidental or negligent destruction of property is not vandalism. Adjusters investigating unexplained damage to property cannot pay for such damage under the coverage for vandalism, unless there is evidence of intentional or malicious wrongdoing. For example, landlords might report a tenant's abuse of property as vandalism. Unless there is evidence of maliciousness beyond mere carelessness, such abuse would not be vandalism.

Vandalism is likely whenever damage appears to have been caused by the actions of a person, rather than forces of nature, and the circumstances do not appear accidental. Examples include windows broken by rocks, spray-painted graffiti, and other deliberate defacement.

Gradual Causes of Loss

Exclusions from coverage concerned with gradual losses, such as exclusions for wear and tear, rust, decay, deterioration, latent defect, and rot, are very important in claims handling. Losses from these excluded causes present the same problems as those caused by water seepage (described above).

Property that has suffered loss from any of these excluded causes may suffer a subsequent loss that is covered. In such a situation, the adjuster must separate property that suffered the gradual problem from that which did not. Damage to property that suffered gradual loss may be included in a claim for subsequent covered loss, but the claim for such property is limited to the extent its value has been further diminished by the covered cause of loss. The gradual cause of loss may have already diminished the property's value to nearly nothing.

Ordinance or Law

Local ordinances or laws may require the demolition of a damaged structure. The cost of demolition may be more than the cost to rebuild the structure. In addition, local ordinances or laws may require construction plans, methods, or materials that are different from, and more expensive than, what existed before the loss. In general, property policies do not cover these additional costs, unless a special endorsement has been added to the policy.

An adjuster handling a claim in which these costs are added should have contractors prepare estimates as though the building were to be rebuilt as it was, even though such rebuilding is not legal. Alternatively, realistic and practical estimates can be prepared, as long as the added costs not covered are identified and segregated.

Faulty Construction

As noted above with respect to collapse caused by faulty construction, property insurance policies are not designed to be surety contracts for construction work. Losses caused by faulty design, construction, or materials are generally excluded from coverage. The additional coverage for collapse, described above, actually "gives back" coverage for faulty construction in very limited circumstances, such as when the collapse occurs during construction, remodeling, or renovation. For example, if faulty construction was the cause of a fire, the adjuster must segregate damage caused by the poor workmanship from that caused by the fire and pursue subrogation.

Intentional Acts

The most obvious type of loss that should be, and invariably is, excluded from coverage is loss caused intentionally by the insured. For example, as noted above, theft claims can be easily staged by the policyholder.

Fires are the most common type of intentionally caused loss. Intentionally set fires are acts of arson, whether committed by the insured or not. Arson may also be committed for revenge, in the commission of a crime, or by vandals. In those cases, innocent property owners are entitled to insurance coverage. Nevertheless, in the insurance context, "arson" usually refers to a fire intentionally set by the insured. When arson by the insured is suspected, most insurers involve their special investigative units (SIUs) or outside legal counsel. The factors shown in Exhibit 14-1 are indicators of arson.

Exhibit 14-1
Indicators of Arson

General Indicators of Arson-for-Profit or Fire-Related Fraud

- Building or contents were up for sale at the time of the loss.
- Suspiciously coincidental absence of family pet at time of fire.
- Insured had a loss at the same site in the preceding year. The initial loss, though small, may have been a failed attempt to liquidate contents.
- Building or business was recently purchased.
- Commercial losses include old or non-saleable inventory or illegal chemicals or materials. Insured or insured's business is experiencing financial difficulties, e.g., bankruptcy, foreclosure.
- Fire site is claimed by multiple mortgagees or chattel mortgagees.

Indicators at the Fire Scene

- Building is in deteriorating condition and/or lacks proper maintenance.
- Fire scene investigation suggests that property/contents were heavily over-insured.
- Fire scene investigation reveals absence of remains of noncombustible items of scheduled property or items covered by floaters, e.g., coin or gun collections or jewelry.
- Fire scene investigation reveals absence of expensive items used to justify an increase over normal 50 percent contents coverage, e.g., antiques, piano, or expensive stereo/video equipment.
- Fire scene investigation reveals absence of items of sentimental value, e.g., family Bible, family photos, trophies.
- Fire scene investigation reveals absence or remains of items normally found in a home or business. The following is a sample listing of such items, most of which will be identifiable at fire scenes except in total burns. Kitchen: major appliances, minor appliances, normal food supply

in refrigerator and cabinets. Living room: television/stereo equipment, record/tape collections, organ or piano, furniture (springs will remain). Bedrooms: guns, jewelry, clothing, and toys. Basement/garage: tools, lawn mower, bicycles, sporting equipment, such as golf clubs (especially note whether putter is missing from otherwise complete set). Business/office: office equipment and furniture, normal inventory, business records (which are normally housed in metal filing cabinets and should survive most fires).

Indicators Associated With the Loss Incident

- Fire occurs at night, especially after 11 P.M.
- Commercial fire occurs on holiday, weekend, or when business is closed.
- Fire department reports fire cause is incendiary, suspicious, or unknown.
- Fire alarm or sprinkler system failed to work at the time of the loss.

Adapted with permission of the National Insurance Crime Bureau, Palos Hill, Illinois, 1992.

In order to prove arson, an adjuster must prove (1) an incendiary fire (one that has been set intentionally), (2) a motive on the insured's part, and (3) opportunity on the insured's part. An insurer should prove the cause of the fire with a cause-and-origin expert, who is usually a scientist or an engineer with special expertise in identifying the cause of fires.

The insured's motive is usually financial, and it may be shown by demonstrating that the insured is better off financially with the insurance proceeds and a vacant lot than with an intact building. This is done by examining the policyholder's books and records. Irrational motives, such as hatred of a spouse or business partner, may also be the cause of an arson.

Opportunity to set the fire may be proven by demonstrating that the insured was in the vicinity of the building soon before the fire started or by proving that the insured hired someone to commit the act.

Once the investigation concludes that arson by the insured was committed, the insurer need only deny the claim for breach of the policy conditions against misrepresentations and because losses caused by intentional acts are excluded. It is then up to the policyholder to sue the insurer for the claims payment. Sometimes, policyholders do not push the claim any further; this satisfies many insurance companies. Other insurance companies are more aggressive and will take every step possible to have the insured prosecuted by the criminal authorities, should the evidence be strong enough.

To prevail in a civil suit, the insurance company need only have the preponderance of the evidence in its favor. To prevail in a criminal action, the state must prove its case beyond a reasonable doubt. The criminal standard of proof is more difficult. Thus, even if the policyholder is acquitted of criminal arson or if the authorities have simply declined to prosecute, the arson defense may still be used successfully in a civil suit between the policyholder and the insurance company.

Amount of Loss

After determining that coverage is in order for the insured, the property, and the peril involved in a given loss, the adjuster must determine the amount of the loss. Although settlement of the amount paid may be the central event in claims work, insurance policies do not specify how adjusters should determine the amount. Policies usually value property at "replacement cost" or "actual cash value," without further guiding the adjuster as to how "replacement cost" can be determined or what "actual cash value" might mean (for example, does it differ from "cash value" or "value"?).

Replacement Cost

Replacement cost is the cost to replace property with identical property or with property of like kind and quality at the time of the loss. Replacement cost settlement provisions spare adjusters the difficulties of determining actual cash value and convincing the policyholder to agree with that value. Following the trauma of a loss, many policyholders are faced with actual cash value settlements that do not allow them to replace their lost property without substantial out-of-pocket expenditures.

Determining replacement cost is easier than determining actual cash value, yet several possibilities for disagreement with the policyholder exist. The adjuster and the insured must identify the property precisely. For personal property, the manufacturer's name, product description, and exact model or style numbers must be determined. For buildings, the exact measurements and descriptions and an exact specification of the type and quality of materials, including the manufacturer's name, are necessary.

Once the property is fully identified and described, the adjuster must determine the cost to replace it *at the time of loss*. The amount the insured originally paid for the property (generally less) is irrelevant. The cost at the time of loss should be the amount at which the policyholder can buy the property. It is improper for an adjuster to argue for a lesser amount based on a bulk purchase price unless that option is also available to the policyholder or based on prices that may be available in other parts of the country but are unavailable in the policyholder's locale.

If the exact type of property owned by the insured is no longer available, the adjuster can make settlement based on property of like kind and quality. Specific models and styles of goods are frequently discontinued. However, similar items are usually available, often from the same manufacturer. Settlement on the basis of such goods is rarely a problem with the policyholder, as long as the goods are of similar quality.

Adjusters obtain specific replacement cost information from catalogues, furniture retailers, and department stores. Retailers such as Sears, J. C. Penney's, Macy's, Wal-Mart, K-Mart, and local department store chains provide a good gauge of costs for most clothes and household items. However, for specific losses, adjusters should consult the retailer from which a policyholder bought his or her property. Business personal property is normally replaced through the insured's usual suppliers and, thus, may be available at "wholesale" prices. Many replacement service vendors specifically service the insurance industry and can provide insurance companies the best price on items such as cameras. Insurance companies have the option to replace property rather than pay money to settle claims.

Determining replacement cost for building damage requires construction estimates. Proper estimates are based on the following factors:

- *Specifications.* Specifications state precisely what must be done, including whether to repair or replace the property, the exact type of materials, and the quantity of materials in exact dimensions or count.
- *Materials.* The total quantity of materials is determined based on the specifications and priced according to prevailing material costs. The proper material cost is that which can be obtained for the sort of job required by the policyholder's loss. Bulk discounts cannot be considered unless such quantities are needed.
- *Labor.* The hours of labor required for a particular job depend on the amount and type of material to be installed and the working conditions. Skilled estimators can calculate labor amounts fairly accurately. In addition, there are published "standard" work rates that are generally regarded as fair. For example, such publications may indicate that a typical rate for hanging wallpaper is 200 square feet per hour. An estimate can be prepared using such a rate, regardless of whether the paperhanger who does the job happens to be faster or slower. Wage rates for common laborers can be used in estimating tear-out and demolition work, provided there is enough work to justify separate hiring. Otherwise, a skilled craftsman's rate must be used. For example, a plumber's wage rate may be appropriate for tearing out a wall to gain access to a burst pipe.

- *Overhead*. Overhead represents the contractor's fixed costs of doing business or fixed specific costs attributable to the job. Examples include office space, telephones, insurance, permits, and job site offices and toilets. Generally, overhead is calculated as a percentage of the cost of the job, usually 10 to 15 percent, depending on a contractor's circumstances. Costs that are specific to the job, such as permits, may simply be added in.
- *Profit*. Contractors are in business to earn profit. The amount computed for overhead is *not* profit. Overhead represents very real costs for the contractor. Once overhead costs have been added to the job, profit is calculated as a percentage of total costs, usually 10 percent.

Most adjusters simply ask or hire contractors to provide estimates. Policyholders, or public adjusters working for them, likewise engage contractors to provide estimates. Unless all contractors involved provide estimates with detailed specifications, material, and labor, resolving disparities is difficult. Round sum figures for an entire job are difficult for an adjuster to negotiate. Even when all parties have done detailed work, there is room for differences: Does property need to be replaced, repaired, or simply cleaned? Have measurements been rounded? What allowance is each contractor making for waste of materials or for difficult working conditions? What labor rate (dollars per hour) and rate of work does each contractor assume? Estimates may appear to be very precise but may include a great deal of judgment and assume a great deal of background information.

Computer software is available to help adjusters or contractors prepare estimates. The adjuster or contractor specifies the work to be done, the measurements, and the quantities, and the computer calculates the total material cost and the total hours and cost of labor and determines the total estimate. Computerized estimating programs are quick and provide neat output. The computer cannot, however, spot unusual circumstances. Computerized estimating programs are a useful tool for those who already understand estimating, but they cannot teach estimating to a novice.

Adjusters must be prepared to negotiate estimates in good faith and should be scrupulous in using only contractors who provide legitimate estimates and good workmanship. A policyholder who has suffered the loss of his or her home should not have to disprove fictitious estimates prepared by contractors with no intention of doing the work for the stated price.

Whenever losses are settled on a replacement cost basis, determining the insured's compliance with insurance to value requirements must likewise be done on a replacement cost basis. This can be tedious if the loss is small relative to the total value of insured property. The adjuster must estimate the value of a great deal of property not affected by the loss. Fortunately, there are shortcuts. With business personal property, the insured's accounting records will usually show what items were purchased by the business, when they were purchased, and for how much. The services of an accountant may be needed to extract this information from the accounting records. An estimation guide, which uses factors such as square footage and construction quality to determine how much it would cost to rebuild a building, offers a shortcut for determining a building's value.

Insurance policies generally do not permit replacement cost settlements until the property is actually repaired or replaced. Such policy provisions exist to prevent unjust enrichment of the insured and to discourage intentional losses. Nevertheless, the insured may need funds to pay a contractor or merchant before repair or replacement is complete. The adjuster will either (1) release to the insured an actual cash value settlement, with the balance paid upon complete repair or replacement, or (2) parcel out a replacement cost settlement as repair or replacement is gradually accomplished. Either of these approaches should be satisfactory to the policyholder.

Actual Cash Value

Actual cash value is often defined as replacement cost minus depreciation. Claims adjusters applying this formula must have a sophisticated understanding of depreciation. Although the formula is generally appropriate, claims adjusters must realize when it is not.

Depreciation represents loss of value. It is not limited to physical wear and tear, although physical wear and tear is obviously an important consideration in determining the depreciation of certain property, such as carpeting. When physical wear and tear is the chief cause of depreciation, adjusters usually apply straight-line depreciation, by which a fixed percentage of the property's value is deducted for every year of the property's useful life that the owner has enjoyed.

Aside from physical wear and tear, obsolescence is the main cause of depreciation. Obsolescence is caused by changes in technology and fashion and can have much more sudden and dramatic effects on the value of property than physical wear and tear. Clothing in last year's fashions, even if untouched by wear and tear, will have lost significant value. Property for which technology advances rapidly, such as electronics and computers, will also quickly lose value.

Age alone, absent wear and tear or obsolescence, should not cause too much depreciation. For example, the frame carpentry (wall studs, floor joists, and so forth) of a 100-year-old house may be in as good a condition as when it was installed. Although there may be some obsolescence in such frame carpentry, obsolescence can be difficult to identify in residential construction. Although the copper pipes used today are superior to lead pipes, found in older homes, frame carpentry techniques have changed little in 100 years. Furthermore, certain features of older construction are considered desirable.

Adjusters frequently rely on published guides to determine depreciation. Individual insurance companies have created such guides based on their experience. Trade groups have published guides for items such as clothing and household furnishings. However, adjusters should consider the characteristics of the specific property in question when evaluating actual cash value. In every loss in which there is to be an actual cash value settlement, the adjuster must determine depreciation for the specific property that has suffered loss.

In losses in which there is significant depreciation caused by obsolescence, guidebooks are likely to be obsolete sooner than the property in question. Guidebooks are primarily useful as a starting point for discussing depreciation caused by wear and tear. In many situations, the published rate of depreciation is perfectly appropriate. However, an adjuster who mindlessly applies guidebook depreciation to every loss will harm both policyholders and insurers. The reputation of the insurance company and the industry is harmed by such arbitrary and inflexible practices.

Other Definitions of Actual Cash Value

As long as depreciation is understood to represent loss of value of any type, the "replacement cost minus depreciation" definition of "actual cash value" is usually appropriate. However, it is not appropriate in all circumstances.

Application of the "replacement cost minus depreciation" definition requires an ascertainable figure for replacement cost. In some situations, no such figure exists. For example, antiques cannot be produced and sold new. Old buildings may feature construction methods that are simply not performed any longer. Finally, many adjusters mistakenly infer that the "replacement cost minus depreciation" definition only allows for deductions from the replacement cost. Certain property is known to appreciate in value, such as some collectibles.

As a result of adjusters' misapplying the definition of actual cash value, some courts have defined the term to mean fair market value. The fair market value of an item reflects both the "replacement cost minus depreciation" approach and the possibility that an item is irreplaceable. The market valuation of antiques and objects of art is generally regarded as fair. In addition, a well-functioning market will consider obsolescence and any other factor that affects value. A well-functioning market for a type of property is key to determining market valuation. Unfortunately, no substantial secondary market exists for many common items of property, such as used clothing, which most people regard as completely valueless. Adjusters should not apply market valuation unless there is a well-functioning secondary market.

Other courts have avoided definitions based strictly on a formula of actual cash value. These courts have required adjusters to consider all pertinent factors, including physical wear and tear, obsolescence, market value, and any other relevant factors. This approach is known as the **broad evidence rule.**

Deductibles

When a loss is otherwise fully covered, applying a deductible is a simple matter. The deductible amount is subtracted from the amount of the loss, and the insured is paid the remainder. However, applying deductibles to a loss that is not fully covered is more difficult.

When the application of a coinsurance penalty results in a reduction of the recoverable amount of loss, it is more favorable to the insured to have the deductible applied first, as shown in the following example of the settlement of a \$10,000 loss in which a policyholder maintained only \$60,000 of coverage when \$80,000 was required:

Deductible Applied First

\$10,000 loss – \$100 deductible = \$9,900

$$\frac{\$60{,}000}{\$80{,}000} \times \$9{,}900 = \$7{,}425$$

Coinsurance Applied First

$$\frac{\$60{,}000}{\$80{,}000} \times \$10{,}000 \text{ loss} = \$7{,}500$$

\$7,500 – \$100 deductible = \$7,400

Adjusters should use the first approach unless the policy explicitly states otherwise. The commercial building and personal property (BPP) form is an example of a policy that does state otherwise. The excerpt in Exhibit 14-2 shows that the BPP form requires the deductible to be applied after the coinsurance penalty.

A loss may also not be fully covered because of the application of a sublimit. The typical homeowners policy has numerous sublimits for specific types of property, such as cash, precious stones and jewelry, and firearms. Adjusters

Exhibit 14-2
Building and Personal Property Coverage Form Excerpt

1. Coinsurance

If a Coinsurance percentage is shown in the Declarations, the following condition applies.

a. We will not pay the full amount of any loss if the value of Covered Property at the time of loss times the Coinsurance percentage shown for it in the Declarations is greater than the Limit of Insurance for the property.

Instead, we will determine the most we will pay using the following steps:

(1) Multiply the value of Covered Property at the time of loss by the Coinsurance percentage;

(2) Divide the Limit of Insurance of the property by the figure determined in step (1);

(3) Multiply the total amount of loss, before the application of any deductible, by the figure determined in step (2); and

(4) Subtract the deductible from the figure determined in step (3).

We will pay the amount determined in step (4) or the limit of insurance, whichever is less. For the remainder, you will either have to rely on other insurance or absorb the loss yourself.

Example No. 1 (Underinsurance):

When:

The value of the property is	\$250,000
The Coinsurance percentage for it is	80%
The Limit of Insurance for it is	\$100,000
The Deductible is	\$250
The amount of loss is	\$40,000

Step (1): \$250,000 × 80% = \$200,000 (the minimum amount of insurance to meet your Coinsurance requirements)

Step (2): \$100,000 ÷ \$200,000 = .50

Step (3): \$ 40,000 × .50 = \$20,000

Step (4): \$ 20,000 – \$250 = \$19,750

We will pay no more than \$19,750. The remaining \$20,250 is not covered.

should first apply the deductible to any amount of the loss that is not covered because it exceeds a sublimit. For example, an insured with a \$100 sublimit for cash and a \$100 deductible who has lost \$500 cash would recover only \$100, and the deductible should not apply any further. The \$400 loss in excess of the sublimit is more than sufficient to absorb the deductible. Although insurance policies do not explicitly require this approach, it is regarded among adjusters as good and proper practice.

Stated Values and Agreed Amounts

Some property policies are written on a scheduled basis, such as personal articles floaters and endorsements to homeowners policies designed for scheduled property. Individual property items may be listed separately with a value assigned for each, or the property may be listed by class, such as cameras, furs, or jewelry. Some coverages provided on personal articles floaters are on a stated amount basis. The **stated amount** is typically determined by appraising the policyholder's property or by reviewing a sales receipt for the property in question. In the event of a loss, the insured is entitled to no more than the *least* amount of (1) the actual cash value of the property, (2) the cost to repair or replace, or (3) the applicable amount of insurance.

Many policyholders believe that they are entitled to the stated amount regardless of the valuation provision of the policy. In fact, the stated value is designed as a maximum amount the insurer will have to pay.

Fine arts and valuable papers are usually insured on an **agreed amount** basis. In the event of a loss, the insurer agrees to restore the property to its condition before the loss or pay the agreed amount. The distinction between these properties and those covered on a stated amount basis is that the more valuable property is typically impossible to replace. Insurers recognize that owners of this type of property want the company to "preadjust" for potential losses in the underwriting process.

In dealing with agreed value losses, adjusters can become overly suspicious of fraud since the policyholder can readily fake a theft or mysterious disappearance. Underwriters recognize the increased chance of moral and morale hazards and scrutinize those applicants accordingly. If fraud is, in fact, evident, procedures should be followed just as in any fraudulent claim.

Repair or Replace Option

Claims are generally settled with money. Occasionally, adjusters prefer to settle claims by actually repairing or replacing the property as the policy allows. Adjusters might prefer not to repair or replace property because doing so opens up a new area for potential disagreement with the insured. The policyholder might expect the insurer to guarantee the repairs or certify the quality of a replacement item.

Adjusters will choose the repair or replace option whenever it is significantly cheaper to do so. It may be cheaper to perform repairs or provide a replacement item when the insurer has discount purchasing arrangements through local contractors and retailers. Insurers frequently replace jewelry through wholesale channels. Repairing or replacing the property enables insurers to eliminate the financial incentive some insureds have to file claims.

Appraisal Clause

The appraisal clause found in every property insurance policy is used solely to settle disputes over the value of the property or the amount of loss. It is not used to determine coverage, to substitute for the proof of loss or the insured's examination under oath, or to preclude litigation between the parties.

Adjusters who work for years in property claims may never participate in an appraisal, but this does not mean that the clause is unimportant. The existence of the appraisal clause informally prompts the insured and the adjuster to do more formally what the appraisal procedure requires. The adjuster presents his or her position to the insured with estimates from contractors and other supporting documentation. The insured prepares similar information to present to the adjuster. The adjuster and the insured, or the contractors working for them, negotiate their differences and almost always reach an agreement. The possibility of an appraisal procedure in which an impartial umpire will settle the dispute gives both sides an incentive to negotiate in good faith.

Insured's Duties Following Loss

Every property insurance policy enumerates various duties the insured must perform following a loss. These duties are conditions of the policy. Thus, an insured is not entitled to payment for a loss unless these duties have been performed. The insured's performance of duties following a loss helps the adjuster complete the loss adjustment, verify the extent and the dollar amount of the loss, and protect against fraudulent or exaggerated claims. Adjusters may waive certain duties if the circumstances so warrant, but they are likely to hold the policyholder to strict performance whenever unusual circumstances surround the claim or the claim seems suspicious. Enforcing all the insurer's procedures, without violating the Unfair Claims Settlement Practices Act, protects the adjuster from a critical review in a subsequent claim audit. Additionally, making the policyholder follow legitimate claim settlement procedures may unnerve fraudulent claim makers or reveal misrepresentations by the policyholder.

Notice

Obviously, nothing can be done with a claim until the policyholder notifies the insurer of the loss. The policyholder need not provide notice in any special form or in any special wording. Typically, the policyholder will telephone his or her agent and say, "I've had a fire." The policyholder does not have to give written notice that says, "I've suffered losses to the building and personal property and will suffer loss of use caused by the fire and smoke perils."

Although policies do not require that the policyholder give notice in any particular form, they do require that the notice be "prompt." An adjuster cannot properly investigate and evaluate a loss after too much time has passed. The requirement of prompt notice does not often become an issue between insureds and insurers. Insureds are usually eager to report claims, and adjusters will generally not penalize delayed notice if a proper investigation is still possible. Courts generally require that the insurer suffer some prejudice to its rights before it can consider denying coverage. Nevertheless, lack of prompt notice (as well as breach of other policy conditions) is an issue, for example, when the insured repairs or replaces property before ever notifying the insurer of the loss.

In case of loss by theft, the insured is required to notify the police. In most states it is a felony to submit false reports to the police. Thus, the policyholder's duty to report thefts and other criminal violations discourages staged claims. The BPP requires the insured to notify the police if a law may have been broken, which includes the occurrence of a possible theft. The common-sense interpretation of the BPP limits this duty to violations of *criminal* law only.

Homeowners' policies provide coverage for lost or stolen credit cards. In case of such an event, the insured must notify the credit card or funds transfer card company. Thereafter, the insured is not liable for improper and unauthorized charges. Should the insured fail to notify the credit card company, the insurer is not liable for any charges incurred after a reasonable time in which notice could have been given. The insured's lack of timely notice to a credit card company is rarely an issue between an insured and the insurers because most credit card agreements limit the cardholder's liability for unauthorized use to some small amount, such as $50.

Protection of Property

The insured is required to protect the property from further loss by making emergency repairs and implementing emergency safeguards. Such measures are a reimbursable part of the loss (subject to policy limits) as long as they are "reasonable" and "necessary." The insured will usually seek pre-approval of such measures from the adjuster. Adjusters are happy to cooperate with these requests in order to preclude any misunderstanding. Nevertheless, the insured is obligated to take "reasonable" and "necessary" measures regardless of whether the adjuster's approval has been obtained. Failure to do so may void coverage for any additional loss that results.

Assistance With the Loss Adjustment Process

Insureds have several duties that help expedite and conclude the loss adjustment process. They must inventory all damaged property and, under certain policies, all undamaged property as well. Such an inventory must include quantities, values, and amounts of loss and may be required as part of, or independent of, the proof of loss. Without such an inventory, the adjuster would have difficulty organizing and analyzing the loss to personal property and would have to deal with continual additions to the claim for personal property.

The insured must show the damaged property to the adjuster. The purpose of this requirement is to preclude claims based on photographic or verbal evidence, thereby discouraging exaggerated or fraudulent claims.

The insured must also allow an inspection of the insured's books and other records. The adjuster might personally inspect the insured's books or might hire an accountant to do so. The evidence in a policyholder's books and records is often essential to verify the existence and value of property. For example, property is often destroyed in all-consuming fires or as a result of theft.

Some insurance policies generally require the policyholder to cooperate. For example, the BPP lists among the insured's duties in the event of loss the duty to "cooperate with us in the investigation or settlement of the claim." The absence of such a duty in other policies means that the insured has no general duty of cooperation, although the lack of such a duty does not usually create any problems for the adjuster. The specifically listed duties—and, in particular, the duties to submit a proof of loss—are sufficient for the adjuster to obtain whatever is necessary from the policyholder.

Proof of Loss

The proof of loss is a powerful adjustment tool, yet it is often not used, or is misused, by adjusters. A **proof of loss** is a written, signed, and sworn-to statement by the insured about the loss. Thus, it is the policyholder's official version of the loss. Since it is signed and sworn to, all statements contained therein are material and, if false, are grounds to void the coverage. The formality of the proof of loss impresses policyholders with the importance of the statements made therein.

In a proof of loss, the insured is typically required to provide the time, place, and cause of loss; the interests in the property; any other insurance on the property; and detailed estimates, inventories, bills, and other documentation that prove the loss. The proof of loss should contain all the information necessary for the adjuster to settle the claim, including an exact dollar figure for the loss.

Once a proof of loss has been submitted, the adjuster must respond promptly. Many states have laws specifying the number of days following receipt of a proof of loss in which an adjuster must either accept or reject the proof of loss or tell the policyholder specifically what is further required. An adjuster who rejects a proof of loss should do so in writing and state specific reasons why the proof is rejected. Such a rejection letter should explain to the policyholder that the claim cannot be settled without a proper proof and should invite the policyholder to submit a new proof if it is possible and still timely to remedy the original.

Many insurers routinely waive the proof of loss. On uncomplicated claims, doing so expedites the settlement and relieves the insured of a possibly tedious and intimidating exercise. When the adjuster eliminates technical policy conditions on simple, straightforward losses, the danger to insurers of routinely waiving proofs of loss is that the adjusters may not spot nonroutine cases soon enough to implement the proof of loss requirement and will thereby waive valuable rights.

Some adjusters do not require the insured to complete a proof of loss until the conclusion of the claim. At that point, the adjuster has presumably already agreed with the insured about the amount of settlement. Completion of the proof of loss form is likely to make little impression on the insured. To be most effective, the proof of loss should be required early in the adjustment process. A proof of loss that is completed after settlement is still a sworn statement of material fact and thus could be the basis of a fraud defense.

Examination Under Oath

An **examination under oath** is a statement in which the person giving the statement swears to tell the truth before an officer of the court. Insurers rarely require an examination under oath, but when they do, they usually suspect fraud by the policyholder.

The examination under oath is a policy condition that, if invoked by the insurer, must be fulfilled by the insured. The insurer may require an examination even though the claim is not in litigation. The insured may have counsel present, but such counsel has no right to interrupt, object, or ask questions. Although adjusters can conduct examinations under oath themselves, they are almost invariably conducted by an attorney working for the insurer and helping the insurer prepare its fraud case.

An examination under oath is usually conducted after the insured completes and submits a proof of loss. The proof of loss commits the insured to a certain story, and the examination under oath allows the insurer to clarify that story.

Public Adjusters

In certain states, the insurance department recognizes and licenses public adjusters. These adjusters work for policyholders and only rarely work for insurance companies. Public adjusters handle all of the insured's duties following loss (except that the insured must still sign and swear to the proof of loss and must appear for an examination under oath). The policyholder is free to engage a public adjuster just as the policyholder is free to engage an attorney. The adjuster is required to handle the claim with the policyholder's chosen agent.

Adjustment Procedures

Adjusters will usually guide the policyholder through his or her duties following loss. The procedures the adjuster follows are not the same in every case, but all concern (1) verifying the cause of the loss; (2) determining the amount of the loss; and (3) documenting both the cause and amount of the loss. Loss procedures vary according to the size and complexity of the loss.

Level of Investigation

Upon notice of a new claim, an adjuster must decide how to investigate. An adjuster can follow these three general procedures or some combination thereof:

1. The adjuster can accept the policyholder's word and settle the claim accordingly.
2. The adjuster can personally investigate the loss.
3. The adjuster can employ experts to investigate the loss or refer it to an SIU.

The smaller, simpler, and more straightforward a claim appears to be, the more likely an adjuster is to settle based on the policyholder's word. The larger, more complicated, and suspicious a claim appears to be, the more likely it is that an adjuster will hire experts or involve an SIU.

Experts may be consulted to determine the cause of a loss. Such experts include cause and origin scientists, accident reconstruction engineers, and private investigators. Other experts help determine the value of a loss. These experts include contractors, accountants, and appraisers. Expert services are expensive but are essential when litigation is foreseeable, either following a claim denial or pursuant to subrogation.

Avoiding Waiver and Estoppel

Waiver is the voluntary and intentional relinquishment of a right. It may be expressed explicitly or implied by conduct. **Estoppel** has a similar effect as waiver but results when one's words or behavior causes another to rely to their detriment on those words or behavior and serves to bar the first party from asserting any rights inconsistent with his or her words or behavior. An estoppel can result from a waiver but can also be based on thoughtless, unintentional action on which the other party relies.

An adjuster's words and actions can cause waiver and estoppel of the insurer's rights. Although insurance policies state that they may not be altered or amended without the insurer's written approval, courts invariably deem adjusters to be agents of insurers with the power (if not the authority) to waive contractual conditions. Thus, an adjuster's words and behavior can undo policy requirements. The most significant way by which adjusters do so is by continuing to adjust *after* a coverage problem is revealed. Such behavior may be deemed by a court as waiver, or the policyholder may rely on such behavior, leading to estoppel.

Adjusters avoid the problems of waiver and estoppel with nonwaiver agreements or with reservation of rights letters. Exhibits 14-3 and 14-4 show a general nonwaiver agreement and a notice of reservation of rights, respectively. In each of these documents, the insurer makes clear that nothing it does (through the adjuster) in handling the claim is intended as a waiver of any of the insurer's rights.

The general nonwaiver is used whenever a great deal about the loss is unknown and the adjuster wishes to investigate without compromising the insurer's rights. The notice of reservation of rights accomplishes the same tasks as the general nonwaiver and also brings to the attention of the policyholder any specific problems, such as property or perils that appear not covered, or failure of the policyholder to perform any duties following loss or to comply with other policy conditions. A reservation of rights is the same in content as a nonwaiver agreement. It is sent (usually by certified mail) to the policyholder in the form of a letter, usually because the policyholder would not sign a nonwaiver or as a convenience by inside adjusters. Assuming that proof of receipt by the policyholder can be shown, a reservation of rights letter is as effective as a nonwaiver.

Once either a nonwaiver or a reservation of rights has been issued, the adjuster must resolve promptly the coverage issue and inform the policyholder. Should

Exhibit 14-3
Nonwaiver Agreement

Policy of insurance number HO 302 7648 was issued to Len Watson by IIA Insurance Company to cover the period from 7-1-X6 to 7-1-X7. Coverage under this policy of insurance has been requested for occurrence which took place on 12-21-X6 at Malvern, PA. A dispute has arisen about whether or not there is insurance coverage under the policy to protect Len Watson for any liability which is a result of the reported occurrence. The reason for the question of coverage is whether water damage was caused by repeated seepage

Nevertheless, Len Watson requests that the IIA Insurance Company investigate, negotiate, settle, deny, or defend any claim or suit arising out of such accident or occurrence as it deems necessary. IIA Insurance Company agrees to proceed with such handling of this case only on condition that such action taken will not waive any right the Insurance Company may have to deny any obligation under the policy contract, or be considered an admission of any liability on the part of the company. It is further agreed that such action will not waive any rights of the insured.

There may be other reasons why coverage does not apply. We do not waive our right to deny coverage for any other valid reason which may arise.

Nothing in this agreement precludes Len Watson from retaining personal counsel for his or her own protection.

Either party to this agreement may at any time terminate the agreement upon notice in writing and proceed under his/her own unrestricted rights.

Signed this 4th day of May, 19X7.

Nancy Spellman
Witness

Len Watson
Insured

Additional Insured

Jackie Limongelli
Witness

IIA Insurance Company
Insurance Company

BY: Connor M. Harrison
For the Company

Exhibit 14-4
Notice of Reservation of Rights

5/8, 19 X7

TO:

RE: Insured: **Ruth Stewart**
Claimant:
Date of Loss:
Policy Number:

We have received notice of an occurrence which took place at **Malvern, PA** on **4-1-X7**. As a result of this occurrence coverage has been requested under policy number **BOP 5612112** which was issued to **Ruth Stewart's Country Kitchen** by **IIA Insurance**.
There is a question whether coverage under the policy applies to this occurrence.

The nature of the coverage question is as follows: **whether it was lightning that caused the air conditioning unit to fail**

IIA Insurance Company will continue to handle this claim even though a coverage question exists. However, no act of any company representative while investigating, negotiating settlement of the claim, or defending a lawsuit shall be construed as waiving any Company rights. The Company reserves the right, under the policy, to deny coverage to you or anyone claiming coverage under the policy.

There may be other reasons why coverage does not apply. We do not waive our right to deny coverage for any other valid reason which may arise.

You may wish to discuss this matter with your own personal attorney. In any event, we would be pleased to answer any questions you might have concerning our position as outlined in this letter.

Very truly yours,

IIA Insurance Company
Insurance Company

BY *Connor M. Harrison*
For the Company

the adjuster fail to rectify whatever problem existed and proceed to settle the claim, the claim payment will constitute a waiver, and the insurer will be estopped from ever again raising the problem.

Determining Cause of Loss

An adjuster who personally investigates the cause of a loss will inspect the property in question, take the policyholder's statement, or do both.

A personal inspection of the damaged property is a valuable adjusting practice. The adjuster sees exactly how the property was damaged and can identify the property for purposes of verifying coverage. The effects of perils such as fire, smoke, lightning, windstorm, hail, explosions, and vandalism are usually obvious, and a quick inspection can verify coverage.

The adjuster will take the policyholder's statement to answer any questions about the cause of loss and to gather other information. Such a statement is informal, compared to the proof of loss or examination under oath, but it will be recorded. In some states, taking the policyholder's statement may preclude a subsequent proof of loss or examination under oath. When the policyholder's statement can be taken, the adjuster will ask about the cause of loss, any other interests in or liens on the property, other insurance, steps taken to mitigate loss, the documentation of the extent of loss, and any subrogation possibilities.

Determining the Amount of Loss

An adjuster who personally determines the amount of a loss must take careful, detailed inventories of personal property that specify the exact quantities and types of property and must prepare his or her own estimates for losses to buildings.

Most adjusters leave the item-by-item preparation of a personal property inventory to the insured. The adjuster will then spot-check the physical property or double-check with the policyholder's books and records. The adjuster must check the physical property sufficiently to determine appropriate depreciation.

An adjuster who prepares his or her own estimates must have extensive knowledge of construction practices and of the numerous resources concerning material prices and labor allowances. Indeed, such adjusters usually have their own library of materials catalogs, manufacturers' price lists, and construction trade association guides. Using these reference sources, they can determine, for example, the material and labor costs for applying a coat of paint, building a wall of cinderblocks, or installing a network of fire-extinguishing sprinklers.

Adjusters who write their own estimates must also develop a methodology for taking thorough specifications at a loss site. For example, an adjuster may take all outside measurements first and then go inside to take room measurements and, finally, all mechanical and electrical specifications. Completed estimates are usually also organized by trade, such as demolition, frame carpentry, finish carpentry, drywall, painting and decorating, plumbing, and electrical.

Documentation and Reporting

The ultimate service performed by claims adjusters for insureds is payment with the settlement check. While the adjuster investigates and gathers the information necessary to determine the amount of the settlement check, he or she should simultaneously create a file that would enable any other person to understand and follow the claim and agree with the amount paid. Every piece of pertinent information should be in the file. Insurers need thorough claim files to justify payments, to conduct audits of claims procedures and claims-handling quality, and to transfer cases from one adjuster to another. State insurance regulators and reinsurers are also interested in complete and thorough claim files.

Although an adjuster handles a claim, he or she must submit various reports to the insurer. A preliminary report usually only acknowledges receipt of the assignment, reports initial activity, suggests likely reserves, and raises any coverage issues that are found. Status reports are submitted on a regular basis thereafter, such as every fifteen to thirty days.

Investigative reports are longer, more formal, narrative reports in which the adjuster reports on all aspects of the claim to date and the expected future activity. Topics contained in such a report include the initial assignment, a description of insured and other interests and liens, coverage, any coverage questions, facts of the loss, official and expert reports, the investigation with the insured and witnesses, the scope of the loss, inventory, suggested reserves, subrogation or salvage, and work to be done.

Final reports account for payments made and describe any ongoing subrogation or salvage efforts. Most insurers have preprinted forms or general written guidelines for these various types of reports.

Salvage and Subrogation

Adjusters usually only disburse money for insurers. However, in salvage and subrogation activities, the claims adjuster can minimize the insurer's losses.

Whenever an insurer pays the insured the full value of personal property that has suffered loss, the insurer is entitled to take ownership of the property and can subsequently resell it. Any amount realized in the sale reduces the true cost of the claim. Taking the salvage value of property that has been "totaled" is the insurer's option. The policyholder cannot require the insurer to pay full value for damaged property and then take over the salvage. On the other hand, should it appear that damaged property has some salvage value, insurers will usually not depend on the insured to realize that salvage value. Insureds are usually not familiar with salvage markets. It is also unfair for a claims adjuster to reduce the amount of a loss settlement because of the value of "expected" salvage that the insured could not be expected to sell. Instead, should there be promising salvage value, insurers will usually pay full value to the insured and will handle the salvage themselves.

Ordinarily, adjusters do not directly market salvage. They either sell or consign the property in question to professional salvage companies. The markets for salvaged goods are specialized, variable, and irregular. Even insurance companies that frequently see salvageable goods from their losses find that they cannot compete in salvage markets. Salvage companies typically sell goods on consignment for expenses incurred plus a percentage commission. Salvors can operate even when the insurance company has not taken title to the goods, as long as the insured agrees.

Salvors can provide more services to insurers than just selling damaged goods. Salvors are expert in protecting and inventorying property. In certain cases when insureds are themselves merchants of the goods in question, a salvor can advise the insurer on the percentage of value remaining in the goods. In those situations, the insurer will settle the claim for the value of the goods less their remaining salvage value. The insured will accept such a settlement whenever he or she is confident that his or her own efforts can realize more value from a "fire sale" than could the efforts of anyone else.

An insurer may have subrogation rights whenever some party other than the policyholder is responsible for causing the loss. Whenever an insurer pays the insured for a loss under an insurance policy, the insurer is substituted (subrogated) for the insured's rights against any responsible party. Thus, the insurer obtains the insured's rights. Handling a claim involving potential subrogation is no different for an adjuster than handling any other claim, except that the adjuster must be especially scrupulous in establishing and documenting the cause of loss and may put the responsible party on notice of the liability claim.

If the responsible party has liability insurance and the two insurers cannot agree on a settlement amount, a subrogation claim is likely to be handled through the nationwide arbitration system operated by Arbitration Forums Incorporated. A copy of the Property Subrogation Arbitration Agreement is reproduced in Exhibit 14-5. Although the jurisdiction of this agreement is limited to claims between signatory parties and amounts of $100,000 or less, this agreement keeps a vast number of cases out of the courts. The results insurers experience under this agreement are probably as fair as any court settlement and are far less expensive to obtain. Naturally, the claims adjusters for the two involved insurers are free to negotiate a settlement before arbitration.

Exhibit 14-5
Fire and Allied Lines Arbitration Agreement

PROPERTY SUBROGATION ARBITRATION AGREEMENT

WHEREAS, it is the object of companies which are now or may hereafter be signatories hereto to arbitrate disputes among themselves, the undersigned hereby accepts and binds itself to the following Articles of Agreement for the arbitration of property damage claims arising from fire and losses other than automobile:

ARTICLE FIRST:

Signatory companies are bound to forgo litigation and in place thereof submit to arbitration any questions or disputes which may arise from:

(a) any fire subrogation or property damage claim not in excess of $100,000;

(b) any extended coverage subrogation or self-insured extended coverage claim not in excess of $100,000;

(c) any additional extended coverage subrogation or self-insured additional extended coverage claim not in excess of $100,000;

(d) any inland marine subrogation to self-insured inland marine claim not in excess of $100,000;

(e) any first party property subrogation or self-insured claim not in excess of $100,000 that is not within the compulsory provisions of other industry inter-company arbitration agreements, except for subrogation or self-insured claims arising from accidents on waters subject to the International Rules of the Road, the United States Inland Rules of the Road, or the Great Lakes and Western Rivers Rules of the Road, provided the accident occurs on a body of water within the geographic limits of one state.

This Article shall not apply to:

(a) any claim for the enforcement of which a lawsuit was instituted prior to, and is pending at the time this Agreement is signed;

(b) any claim as to which a company asserts a defense of lack of coverage on grounds other than

(1) delayed notice

(2) no notice

(3) noncooperation;

Continued on next page.

(c) subrogation claims arising out of policies written under Retrospective Rating plans, Comprehensive Insurance Rating Plans, or War Risk Rating Plans unless prior written consent is obtained from the companies in interest.

ARTICLE SECOND:

Any controversy, including policy coverage and interpretations, between or among signatory parties involving any claim or other matter relating thereto and not included in Article First hereof or which involve amounts in excess of those stated therein may also be submitted to arbitration under this Agreement with the prior consent of the parties.

For matters within Article First, if the law on the issue is in doubt and has not been interpreted by the courts of the jurisdiction, a party to the controversy may petition AF's Board of Directors to authorize the disputing party to proceed through litigation rather than arbitration. The Board's validation will be influenced by the effect on the industry through litigation to clarify the law. The decision to waive the mandatory provisions of the Agreement and proceed through litigation will be at the sole discretion of the Board.

ARTICLE THIRD:

Arbitration Forums, Inc. representing signatory parties is authorized:

(a) to make appropriate rules and regulations for the presentation and determination of controversies under this Agreement;

(b) to select the places where arbitration facilities are to be available, and adopt a policy for the selection and appointment of arbitration panels;

(c) to prescribe territorial jurisdiction of arbitration panels;

(d) to make appropriate rules and regulations to apportion equitably among arbitrating companies the operating expenses of the arbitration program;

(e) to authorize and approve as signatories to this Agreement such insurance carriers, self-insurers or commercial insureds with large retentions as may be invited to participate in the arbitration program and also to compel the withdrawal of any signatory from the program for failure to conform with the Agreement or the rules and regulations issued thereunder.

ARTICLE FOURTH:

Arbitration panels, appointed by the AF from among full-time salaried representatives of signatory companies, shall function in the following manner:

(a) Arbitration panel members shall be selected on the basis of their experience and other qualifications. They shall serve without compensation.

(b) No panel member shall serve on a panel hearing a case in which his/her company is directly or indirectly interested, or in which he/she has an interest.

(c) The decision of the majority of an arbitration panel shall be final and binding upon the parties to the controversy without the right of rehearing or appeal.

ARTICLE FIFTH:

Any signatory company may withdraw from this Agreement by notice in writing to the Arbitration Forums, Inc. Such withdrawal will become effective sixty (60) days after receipt of such notice except as to cases then pending before arbitration panels. The effective date of withdrawal as to such pending cases shall be upon final settlement.

Whenever any amount is obtained through subrogation efforts, the attorney fees and other expenses of subrogation must be paid first. Next, the insured is reimbursed for any deductible or other amount of loss not covered. Finally, the insurer receives whatever is left.

Challenges Facing Specific Types of Property Claims

Specific types of property loss claims raise specific issues. That which is important in adjusting claims for residential structures may be unimportant when settling claims for common carriers, and vice versa.

The remainder of this chapter examines the challenges of adjusting losses to specific types of property. The general issues described in the preceding part of this chapter are not repeated, except when any such issue raises special concerns or is handled in special ways with regard to specific types of property.

Residential Dwellings

Probably no job in the property-liability insurance industry is more important or more rewarding than adjusting losses to people's homes. Protecting people from the financial and emotional devastation that can follow the destruction of a home is perhaps the insurance industry's most important task.

Adjusters handling losses to homes must balance their concern with alleviating the policyholder's needs with their obligation to enforce the insurance policy and protect the insurer's rights. Generally, there will be little conflict between these concerns, provided the loss is not suspicious and the adjuster continually communicates and cooperates with the policyholder.

Insured's Concerns

Fortunately, most insureds who suffer a loss to their homes have never experienced such a loss before. However, as a result, the emotional trauma of seeing their home damaged is compounded by uncertainty and anxiety about their insurance and the loss adjustment process. Many policyholders fear that an inadvertent lapse on their part might somehow void their coverage.

Following a serious loss to a home, an adjuster's priorities should be (1) ensuring the physical safety of the policyholder's family; (2) ensuring the safety and security of the damaged home from further damage; and (3) explaining the coverage and adjustment procedure to the policyholder. Should there be any doubts above coverage, the adjuster can issue a reservation of rights letter and immediately begin with these priorities.

Sometimes the policyholder will escape from a burning home with nothing but the clothes on his or her back, which may be pajamas. An adjuster who deals with the insured at such a time can provide reassurance that the coverage extends to living expenses and replacement of personal property. An advance on the settlement can be issued on the spot. Exhibit 14-6 shows an advance payment receipt that incorporates a nonwaiver agreement. If there is no doubt about coverage, the second paragraph of this receipt can be deleted.

The insurance policy requires the insured to protect the property from further loss, yet the policyholder is usually unsure as to what that means. The adjuster should advise the policyholder of what is necessary and should recognize that advice is equivalent to authorization of any attendant expense. Following a serious loss, the policyholder must usually turn off all utilities, drain all plumbing, secure or board up the windows and doors to keep out vandals and trespassers, and secure tarpaulins or plastic sheets over any openings in the roof or walls to keep out the elements. Policyholders can do this work themselves or can hire contractors to do it.

Once the insured's family and property are secure, the adjuster should thoroughly explain the coverage and the adjustment procedure and should answer any questions. Indeed, the adjuster should explain procedures and answer questions from the first moment of contact with the policyholder. For example, as noted above, the adjuster should immediately communicate the

Exhibit 14-6
Advance Payment Receipt

Advance Payment Receipt and Reservation of Rights

I, the undersigned, hereby acknowledge the receipt of Five thousand Dollars ($ 5,000) in partial payment of the claim for insurance benefits which I have asserted in connection with a policy of insurance issued by IIA Insurance Company (herein the Company) and bearing Policy Number HP 721 1025 . The claim I have made pertains to a fire loss which I reported as having occurred on or about the 13th day of May , 19 19X7 .

I understand and acknowledge that the Company is continuing to investigate, in good faith, the claim I have made, that my claim has neither been accepted nor denied, that the advance payment is not an admission of liability whatsoever on the part of the Company, and that the payment should not be considered payment under the policy.

I further understand that the Company is making this advance payment in good faith reliance upon the claim I have made, the representations I made to the Company in support of that claim, and my express request for an advance payment.

I further understand that the Company reserves its rights under the policy and will require full compliance with all the conditions of the policy including, but not limited to, my submission of a proper Sworn Statement in Proof of Loss, the submission of receipts, invoices, books and records, and that the Company may exercise its right to require me to take an examination under oath, if deemed necessary.

I further understand that if the policy or the claim is not valid and payment is not required by the Company, I will repay the advance to the company.

I further understand that if the policy and claim are deemed valid that the advance will be applied against any benefit due under the policy.

TO BE SIGNED BY ALL NAMED INSUREDS

Elliot Arnold
Named Insured

Coverage paid under C—Personal Property
(specify)

Deb Arnold
Spouse or Partner

State of Pennsylvania

County of Chester

Subscribed and sworn to before me this 15th day of May 19 X7 .

Notary Public for Brandon Insurance Agency

My Commission Expires: 1/1/X9

existence of coverage for living expense. The adjuster should reassure the insured that insurance policy conditions are not highly technical and should emphasize the importance of the insured's good faith compliance with those conditions. The adjuster should welcome any questions the policyholder might have about the policy conditions and should be prepared to answer them. The policyholder should know what he or she should do the next day, the next week, and the next month. As long as the adjuster is not suspicious about the loss, such direction is perfectly appropriate and is welcomed by the insured.

Additional Living Expense

In the time immediately following a loss, policyholders appreciate additional living expense coverage because it helps normalize their condition by paying for increased living expense following a loss.

The adjuster should try to explain the scope of additional living expense as clearly as possible. Misunderstandings about this element of loss can lead to anger and distrust that undermine all other aspects of the loss adjustment. Adjusters should emphasize to policyholders that they must get and keep receipts. Furthermore, although it is best to have receipts for everything, the policyholder must realize that he or she will be compensated only for *additional* living expense. Most policyholders can quickly grasp that normal living expenses are expenses for which they would be responsible even without the loss and are thus not compensable. The adjuster should explain that coverage is limited to the policyholder's normal standard of living. Adjusters should not require people to live or eat in places that are beneath their previous standard of living. Policyholders will usually follow the adjuster's advice as to what expenditures are appropriate and should be encouraged to check with the adjuster before making a doubtful expenditure.

The insured's residence must be uninhabitable (because of a covered loss) before additional living expense coverage is available. Fortunately, most losses are small. With large (total) losses, the inhabitability of a residence is obvious. With smaller losses, whether or not a home is inhabitable may be harder to judge. Adjusters can best approach this question by asking themselves whether they would expect their own family to live in a place damaged as badly as the insured's home. The stench of smoke may make a home uninhabitable, at least until it can be ventilated or fumigated. The loss of just a refrigerator or a stove probably does not make a home uninhabitable, but loss of the entire kitchen or an only bathroom probably would. Loss of a furnace (during a cold season) or loss of a hot water heater would likewise probably make a home uninhabitable.

Contractors

Damage to the policyholder's home is adjusted based on estimates. The insurance policy obligates the insured to prove and to present his or her damages. Contractors engaged by the insured should prepare detailed estimates that clearly show specifications, material costs, hours and costs of labor, and additional expenses such as overhead, permits, and demolition and debris removal. Estimates that show only grand total costs or trade-by-trade total costs are not suitable for loss settlements, because it is impossible to see how such estimates differ from other estimates and to negotiate those differences in a meaningful way.

Most adjusters prefer to negotiate differences in estimates directly with contractors, since they routinely handle construction issues. Estimates are likely to differ with respect to (1) specification of the work to be done; (2) quality of materials; or (3) hours of labor. Costs of materials and labor are generally well known, once the quality and hours have been specified.

Some insurance companies will recommend contractors to policyholders. Doing so is helpful to policyholders who may otherwise not know which contractors are honest, competent, and interested in insurance repair work. However, making such recommendations creates some real dangers for the insurance company. The adjuster's recommendation may be understood by the policyholder as a guarantee that the contractor's estimate will be accepted or that its work will be good. Furthermore, some insurance companies fear that allowing adjusters to make recommendations may lead to the adjusters' receiving kickbacks and gratuities from contractors.

Some contractors treat estimating for insurance repairs differently from other estimating. They may regard the work as harder or more complicated, since the work requires removing damaged sections and rebuilding. If all damaged property can be removed, estimating insurance repairs is identical to estimating new construction. Occasionally, access problems may justify more time and expense, or smoke, fire, and water damage may be hidden.

Restoration and Cleaning Services

Initially, many losses, and especially losses caused by smoke and water damage, look far worse than they are. Although many types of water damage are not covered, water damage resulting from fire-fighting activity is covered (under the fire cause of loss) and is often a significant problem. Both smoke and water can cause increasingly worse damage to property if they are allowed to sit. Furthermore, smoke and water will cause little or no damage to certain types of property if they are quickly removed. Professional cleaning and restoration services are available to do such work.

Although the adjuster may take an "arm's-length" approach to the policyholder's selection of a contractor, the adjuster must quickly get involved in hiring a professional cleaning and restoration service. Adjusters and insurance companies should have existing contacts with such services so that they can quickly be brought to the scene of a loss. The adjuster should agree on a price with the service providers and should concur with the policyholder to authorize them to begin work immediately. Quick work by such services can save a great deal of property, minimize additional living expense, and prove that cleaning alone is sufficient when it was first thought repainting would be necessary or that repainting alone is sufficient when it was thought replacement would be necessary.

Homeowners Personal Property

Claims for loss to homeowners personal property present adjusters with some of their most difficult professional challenges. Proof that the property ever existed or was lost is frequently scanty. Evaluation is difficult to do with any confidence or accuracy and may provoke strong emotions from the policyholder. Finally, the dollar amount of such claims is frequently small, so the adjuster must be constantly aware of the adjustment costs relative to the value of the damaged property.

Inventory

Damaged personal property is usually available for inspection by the adjuster, unless the loss is caused by fire or theft. Unfortunately, fire and theft are two of the most common perils affecting personal property. Even when personal property is burned beyond recognition or is stolen, the insured must prepare an inventory.

Most homeowners do not have written records of their personal property. Few people can even provide an accurate account of all the clothes they own. Often they cannot remember where or when various items were bought. Despite the often minimal evidence of personal property, adjusters cannot refuse to settle such claims. Most people own a collection of personal property that is consistent with their income and lifestyle. It would be unreasonable for an adjuster to deny a claim for a reasonable inventory of personal property just because the policyholder could not provide documentation. Large purchases can often be documented by bank statements or credit card bills. Personal photographs from relatives might show the policyholder's home and furnishings in the background. In most instances, the adjuster can jog the policyholder's memory by going through a checklist of types of property. Included in such a checklist might be major furniture in each room, clothes (by category) for each person in the household, drapes, rugs, towels and linens, kitchen appliances and utensils, food and liquor, pots and pans, dishes, televisions, radios, stereo equipment, tapes and compact discs, telephones, power tools and hand tools, gardening equipment, office supplies and books, home computers, toys, framed pictures and art objects, sports equipment, bicycles, firearms, and jewelry.

Depreciation

Homeowners generally cannot produce any better evidence of their property's depreciation than of its existence. Sometimes they can remember where major purchases were made, and those stores may have exact records.

In the absence of specific evidence of the age or condition of property, certain assumptions can be made. Clothes wear out and suffer fashion obsolescence at a predictable rate. Towels and linens likewise have predictable lives. Carpets become threadbare in a certain number of years. Kitchen appliances may be good for only a few years; kitchen utensils and pots and pans last longer. Major furniture can last a long time if it is not subject to abuse and is of classic styling. Policyholders and adjusters can usually agree on reasonable assumptions. Policyholders cannot maintain that virtually everything was new or was never subject to use. Adjusters cannot maintain that everything had depreciated to near worthlessness or that everything beyond a certain age was "100 percent" depreciated.

Depreciating items of property by groups, such as clothing, kitchen utensils, books, and children's toys, is undesirable, but may be necessary when the property cannot be inspected. Whenever the property is available for inspection, an item-by-item determination of depreciation should be possible. The National Flood Insurance Program forbids depreciation by group or category.

Sublimits

Applying special sublimits is usually straightforward. Sublimits do not seriously affect most policyholders. However, when a policyholder is seriously affected by policy sublimits, the adjuster has a difficult human relations/customer service problem.

Since the application of sublimits is unambiguous, the adjuster cannot misrepresent or overlook the situation. The adjuster should first apply the deductible to the entire loss amount. The adjuster can then use the uninsured portion of the loss to absorb the policyholder's deductible. The adjuster should explain the rationale of sublimits: some property is especially vulnerable to theft (for example, cash, jewelry, and firearms), and large limit coverage for such property would tremendously increase the exposure to loss and cost; other property is often covered by specialized policies (boats, valuable papers, and business property). Ultimately, the adjuster can only recommend that in the future the policyholder should increase coverage for special exposures.

Scheduled Property

When the policyholder has special coverage for individual items of property, the adjuster often has more loss settlement flexibility than with ordinary personal property.

Individual property usually gets scheduled coverage because it is valuable, and the policyholder wants the broader causes of loss or "all-risks" coverage typically associated with scheduled items. The scheduled coverage will usually identify the property very precisely. Thus, the adjuster can contact merchants and appraisers who specialize in such property to determine whether it can be repaired, whether it can be replaced through a secondary market, how much its value has decreased because of a loss, and whether the insurer can buy at discount. Jewelry, camera equipment, and firearms are precisely the types of property for which the insurer is likely to exercise its "repair or replace" option, because the insurer might be able to buy an exact replacement for less than the policyholder paid originally. The high value of these items also makes repair far more feasible than it is with lower-value property.

Thefts

After reporting a theft to the insurer, the adjuster should insist that the insured also report the theft to the police so that they might catch the perpetrator and recover the property. Unfortunately for the policyholder victimized by an actual theft, insurers have experienced many fraudulent attempts to collect because of alleged theft. Adjusters may take extra steps to ensure that theft occurred by taking separate statements from residents of the household and requiring independent verification of the existence of the stolen property.

Commercial Structures

Adjusting losses to commercial structures is usually limited to highly skilled and experienced adjusters because the value of commercial structures can easily reach millions of dollars. Additionally, experienced adjusters are needed to deal with complex issues such as alternative methods of property repair and the value of depreciated property. Rarely can an adjuster handle losses to commercial structures without expert assistance. The complexity of losses to commercial structures extends to investigating arson and to considering the loss of use.

Architects and Contractors

Adjusters with substantial experience and expertise in estimating residential losses are not necessarily able to estimate losses in commercial structures. The construction principles, methods, materials, and available contractors are different for commercial structures. The adjuster usually has to employ an architect to develop building specifications. The architect's fee is a legitimate element of the loss, whenever architectural services are necessary.

Architectural plans dating from the building's construction are often still available. Those plans can provide valuable information about a building's details if a serious loss has occurred. They can also serve as the basis of a precise reconstruction of the destroyed building. Even with such plans, the adjuster may have to hire another architect to identify changes in building codes or to design alternatives to obsolete construction features and techniques. An architect can develop precise cost estimates or can hire professional estimators to do so.

Local contractors may not be adequate for reconstructing certain commercial structures. Such contractors may not have sufficient expertise, equipment, or staff for large or complicated work. The insured or his or her architect may have to solicit bids from contractors throughout the region or throughout the country. The adjuster cannot necessarily settle the claim based on the lowest bid for the work. The low bidder may be lowest because the contractor's lack of experience has resulted in a miscalculation. The adjuster should only choose the lowest responsible and capable bidder. The architect can help the adjuster identify which bidders meet those criteria.

The adjuster must remember that the insurance company's duty is to settle with the policyholder, not to engage a contractor to perform the actual reconstruction. Soliciting bids from contractors is done to help the adjuster evaluate the loss. Only the insured should enter into contracts for the construction work.

Determining Actual Cash Value

The value of commercial structures is more variable than that of residences. In addition, commercial structures are more likely than residences to experience significant depreciation caused by factors other than wear and tear.

The principle of supply and demand determines the value of a commercial structure. A portion of a structure's value depends on the profit a business derives from its use, or demand. The remainder of the structure's value depends on the cost of rebuilding that structure or obtaining an alternative location, or supply. When demand is strong and supply is in shortage, the value of commercial structures rises significantly. Alternatively, when demand is weak and supplies are glutted, values decline.

The demand for commercial structures fluctuates with the overall economy and with business conditions in particular industries. The more specialized a building is, the more the demand for its use will parallel economic conditions in a particular industry. For example, the value of an auto assembly plant corresponds more to the demand for autos than to the value of other commercial structures.

The supply of commercial structures is characterized by frequent shortages and gluts. This phenomenon is caused by the amount of time required to build commercial structures. In times of shortage, buildings are planned that may not be completed until a glut of similar buildings exists.

An adjuster evaluating the actual cash value at the time of loss of a commercial structure must consider market conditions. The market may be such that the replacement cost of a structure has significantly appreciated since it was built. If so, the insured should be appropriately compensated. Alternatively, the value of a building may have plummeted, so significant depreciation should be applied to the claim.

Although commercial structures experience wear and tear, other factors may be the prime causes of depreciation. Commercial structures are more susceptible than residences to economic and technological obsolescence. For example, an old warehouse may still be useful but less desirable than a newer warehouse because its floor space is broken up by pillars, its lighting is inadequate, its access roads and parking lots are poor, its loading dock is not well designed, and its heating and ventilation are obsolete. Though still in use, the older, obsolete structure has far less value per square foot than a new structure. This difference is usually easy to document through commercial realtors. Realtors can quote the likely rental values of an old property and a new property. The difference in rental rates is a good gauge of depreciation.

The extent of depreciation a policyholder has taken in its financial records is irrelevant. Since financial depreciation reduces taxes, policyholders will take it as fast as the tax laws allow. Thus, most buildings will have less actual depreciation than the amount recorded in the policyholder's accounting records.

Problems With Mortgagee

The variability of the value of commercial structures, described above, creates more potential for problems with mortgagees than it does with residences. Commercial mortgage agreements usually make the mortgage amount completely due and payable upon the destruction of the structure on the property. During depressed markets for commercial properties, mortgagees may see an insurance claim as their most likely chance of being paid. The mortgagee may resist the owner's wish to rebuild the property and may want to be paid in full.

The adjuster cannot solve this problem, since it is between the owner and the mortgagee. The adjuster must put the names of both the owner and the mortgagee on the settlement draft and should keep both parties advised of the settlement. Beyond this, the adjuster has no obligation to either party.

Contamination and Pollution Cleanup

Serious losses at commercial structures, especially manufacture and storage sites, may result in contamination and pollution. Adjusters should be concerned about such losses for several reasons.

First, the adjuster's own health and safety may be at stake from exposure to the loss site. Firefighters may be obligated to notify the Environmental Protection Agency (EPA) or state environmental agencies whenever they know of contaminated loss sites. Whenever such agencies are involved, the adjuster should avoid the site until notified that entry is safe.

Second, the coverage for pollution cleanup is tightly limited in most policies. The adjuster must be familiar with these limitations and must communicate them to the insured. Nevertheless, pollution caused by a covered peril is often covered.

Third, the adjuster should have contacts with specialized technical services that can help the policyholder correct a contaminated site. The adjuster should not recommend such a service unless its cost will be covered or unless the insured provides clear acknowledgment (preferably in writing) that the insured is responsible for all costs. Although these technical services are expensive, they can often devise solutions that may be more practical, less expensive, and faster than the solutions of the EPA.

Arson Investigation

As in determining arson to a residence, the adjuster must prove three things to establish arson with a commercial structure: (1) incendiary fire, (2) motive, and (3) opportunity. As with suspected residential arsons, the incendiary fire can be proven by a cause and origin expert, and the insured's opportunity can be proven through an investigation of the insured and with SIUs. The only difference with commercial structures is that they experience a higher rate of incendiary fires not caused by arson. Commercial structures are frequently unoccupied at night and may be more tempting to vandals.

The main focus in cases of suspected arson to commercial structures is on the policyholder's motive. Such motive is almost always economic. Economic motive may exist even for a structure in regular use, provided the policyholder would be better off financially with the insurance settlement and vacant real estate. Usually in cases of suspected arson, the insured building is owned by a failing business in need of cash. Such circumstances can be established by having an accountant examine the policyholder's financial records. Indeed, considering the seriousness of the matter and the amount of money at stake, an adjuster should not consider asserting an arson defense without a solid accounting report that establishes motive.

Business Interruption

Adjusters regard business interruption claims as highly complex. Proper settlement of these cases requires detailed analysis of and considerable speculation about extensive financial records. Nevertheless, adjusters can organize and simplify their task by concentrating on just a few issues and reminding themselves that the ultimate effect of a business interruption settlement is to put the policyholder in essentially the same financial shape it would have been without the loss. The few important issues concern the best approach to loss determination, the determination of business income, and the determination of the period of restoration.

Loss Settlement Approach

Claims for business interruption can be settled prospectively or retrospectively. **Prospective settlements** are those made before the property has been repaired. **Retrospective settlements** are those made after the property has been repaired and the policyholder has resumed operations.

Prospective settlements are desirable whenever the insured intends not to repair the property at all or intends to make significant alterations. Prospective settlement is also available at the policyholder's request on any loss. The policyholder is not required to wait until the property is repaired and operations resume in order to conclude a settlement with the insurer. Provided the policyholder and the adjuster agree on all data relevant to the loss, settlement can be made immediately.

Nevertheless, retrospective settlements are probably more common. Once the property is repaired and the policyholder has resumed operations, the amount of time to make repairs and the expenses incurred during the interruption are known. Furthermore, during the interruption of business, the policyholder is likely to be so preoccupied with issues involved in reopening that the business interruption loss settlement becomes a secondary concern. Unfortunately, retrospective settlements hold more possibility for argument and disagreement over what the period of restoration *should* have been. The insurance only covers the time in which repairs *should* be made, not necessarily the amount of time actually consumed.

Determining Loss of Business Income

"Business income" is a quantity defined in the current ISO forms as essentially net profit (or loss) plus continuing normal operating expenses. This term is most easily understood when it is placed within the basic framework of business accounting.

A business determines its profit (or loss) by subtracting its costs from its revenue. Revenue consists mainly of sales. Costs consist of the cost to acquire the goods the business sells plus all other expenses. For retailers, the cost of goods is called "cost of goods sold" and represents the cost to the retailers of acquiring goods from their suppliers. For manufacturers, the cost of goods is their own cost of manufacturing the goods.

Excerpts from the Business Income Report/Work Sheet for a manufacturer are shown in Exhibit 14-7. This is a somewhat more elaborate version of the preceding paragraph. A business that completes this work sheet can determine its likely "business income." This amount can be understood as either sales minus cost of goods sold minus operating expenses that discontinue or as net profit (or loss) plus operating expenses that continue. These two amounts should be equivalent. Typically, both claims adjusters and policyholders find it easier to approach a loss settlement with the former definition: sales minus cost of goods and discontinued expenses.

The adjuster cannot directly use the Business Income Report/Work Sheet to settle a claim. This work sheet lists projected amounts, and the claim should be settled based on actual loss. This principle might seem to conflict with the prospective approach to settlement. In case of a prospective settlement, the adjuster and the insured must make new projections of what the insured loss of business income is likely to be for the expected period of restoration. Any actual experience that has developed since the policyholder completed the work sheet should be used to make the best projection of the actual loss of business income.

Determining the Period of Restoration

The "period of restoration" is the time starting seventy-two hours after the loss to the time when the repairs should be completed. This period is so defined to compel the insured to make repairs and resume operations with due diligence and to allow for settlement when the insured neither makes repairs nor resumes operations.

Exhibit 14-7
Business Income Report/Work Sheet

Business Income Report/Work Sheet
Financial Analysis
(000 omitted)

Income and Expenses	12 Month Period Ending 12/31/X4 Manufacturing	12 Month Period Ending 12/31/X4 Non-Manufacturing	Estimated for 12 Month Period Beginning 4/1/X5 Manufacturing	Estimated for 12 Month Period Beginning 4/1/X5 Non-Manufacturing
A. Gross Sales	$ 10,050	$ ______	$ 10,350	$ ______
B. Deduct:				
Finished Stock Inventory (at sales value) at Beginning	– 500	XXXXXX	– 550	XXXXXX
	9,550	XXXXXX	9,800	XXXXXX
C. Add:				
Finished Stock Inventory (at sales value) at End	+ 533	XXXXXX	+ 480	XXXXXX
D. Gross Sales Value of Production	$ 10,083	XXXXXX	$ 10,280	XXXXXX
E. Deduct:				
Prepaid Freight—Outgoing	– 0	– ______	– 0	– ______
Returns & Allowances	– 20	– ______	– 21	– ______
Discounts	– 30	– ______	– 32	– ______
Bad Debts	– 25	– ______	– 27	– ______
Collection Expenses	– 0	– ______	– 0	– ______
F. Net Sales		$ ______		$ ______
Net Sales Value of Production	$ 10,008		$ 10,200	
G. Add: Other Earnings from your business operations (not investment income or rents from other properties):				
Commissions or Rents	+ 0	+ ______	+ 0	+ ______
Cash Discounts Received	+ 0	+ ______	+ 0	+ ______
Other	+ 10	+ ______	+ 15	+ ______
H. Total Revenues	$ 10,018	$ ______	$ 10,215	$ ______

Page 2 of 5 **CP 15 15 06 95** □

	Income and Expenses	12 Month Period Ending 12/31/X4 Manufacturing	Non-Manufacturing	Estimated for 12 Month Period Beginning 4/1/X5 Manufacturing	Non-Manufacturing
	Total Revenues (Line **H.** from previous page)	$ 10,018	$ ____	$ 10,215	$ ____
I.	Deduct:				
	Cost of goods sold (see next page for instructions)	– 5,725	– ____	– 5,900	– ____
	Cost of services purchased from outsiders (not your employees) to resell, that do not continue under contract.	– 0	– ____	– 0	– ____
	Power, heat and refrigeration expenses that do not continue under contract (if **CP 15 11** is attached)	– N/A	XXXXXX	– N/A	XXXXXX
	All ordinary payroll expenses or the amount of payroll expense excluded (if **CP 15 10** is attached)	– N/A	– ____	– N/A	– ____
	Special deductions for mining properties (see next page for instructions)	– N/A	– ____	– N/A	– ____
J.1.	Business Income exposure for 12 months	$ 4,293	____	4,315	____
J.2.	Combined (firms engaged in manufacturing & non-manufacturing operations)....	$ ____		$ ____	
	The figures in **J.1.** or **J.2.** represent 100% of your actual and estimated Business Income exposure for 12 months.				
K.	Additional Expenses:				
	1. Extra Expenses—form **CP 00 30** only (expenses incurred to avoid or minimize & to continue operations)			$ ____	$ ____
	2. Extended Business Income and Extended Period of Indemnity—form **CP 00 30** or **CP 00 32** (loss of Business Income following resumption of operations, up to 30 days or the no. of days selected under Extended Period of Indemnity option)...........			+ ____	+ ____
	3. Combined (all amounts in **K.1.** and **K.2.**)			$ ____	

CP 15 15 06 95 **Page 3 of 5** ☐

Continued on next page.

	"Estimated" column
L. Total of J. and K.	$ ______

The figure in L. represents 100% of your estimated Business Income exposure for 12 months, and additional expenses. Using this figure as information, determine the approximate amount of insurance needed based on your evaluation of the number of months needed (may exceed 123 months) to replace your property, resume operations and restore the business to the condition that would have existed if no property damage had occurred.

Refer to the agent or Company for information on available Coinsurance levels and indemnity options. The Limit of Insurance you select will be shown in the Declarations of the policy.

Supplementary Information

	12 Month Period Ending 12/31/X4		Estimated for 12 Month Period Beginning 4/1/X5	
	Manufacturing	Non-Manufacturing	Manufacturing	Non-Manufacturing
Calculation of Cost of Goods Sold				
Inventory at beginning of year (including raw material and stock in process, but not finished stock, for manufacturing risks)	$ 1,050	$ ______	$ 1,110	$ ______
Add: The following purchase costs:				
Cost of raw stock (including transportation charges)	+ 5,715	XXXXXX	+ 5,820	XXXXXX
Cost of factory supplies consumed	+ 25	XXXXXX	+ 20	XXXXXX
Cost of merchandise sold including transportation charges (for manufacturing risks, means cost of merchandise sold but not manufactured by you)	+ 0	+ ______	+ 0	+ ______
Cost of other supplies consumed (including transportation charges)	+ 0	+ ______	+ 0	+ ______
Cost of goods available for sale	$ 6,790	$ ______	$ 6,950	$ ______
Deduct: Inventory at end of year (including raw material and stock in process, but not finished stock, for manufacturing risks)	– 1,065	– ______	– 1,050	– ______
Cost of Goods Sold (Enter this figure in item I. on previous page)	$ 5,725	$ ______	$ 5,900	$ ______

The time in which repairs should be made can be determined by consulting with the contractors hired to do the work. Adjusters must remember that any such estimate from a contractor, even if made with the utmost good faith and honesty, is uncertain. Contractors cannot control weather, interruptions in supplies, subcontractor behavior, or availability of subcontractors.

Thus, many adjusters and insureds prefer to settle business interruption claims only after the repairs have actually been completed. However, at that point, the adjuster and insured may disagree over whether the insured used due diligence to get the work done. In general, adjusters do not penalize policyholders for delays caused by factors beyond their control. It is also good policy for adjusters not to penalize the policyholder for any delays caused by a delay in the settlement of the property damage claim. Delays in settling the underlying claim may be caused by the policyholder, the adjuster, or both.

Extra Expense

Claims for extra expense can only be settled retrospectively. In order for extra expenses to be covered, they must be incurred to avoid or minimize the suspension of business. Thus, the policyholder could realize a windfall if the adjuster allowed extra expense based on projections. The adjuster cannot adequately monitor whether the insured incurred the expense legitimately or simply pocketed it.

Extra expense incurred to repair damaged property is covered *to the extent it reduces the business interruption claim*. Thus, as mentioned above, the adjuster can authorize expedited construction methods or relatively expensive contractors if the business interruption loss is thereby reduced.

Use of Accountants

Probably no type of claim requires as much use of professional accounting assistance as business interruption claims. Most adjusters have only a rudimentary knowledge of accounting, but they can follow a report from a professional accountant. Most adjusters are not competent to analyze the hundreds of entries that record individual transactions of an ongoing business. Adjusters cannot simply review historic data and determine the policyholder's "normal" operating expenses.

Some accounting firms specialize in claims work. These firms already understand the policy coverages and can explain them to the policyholder's accountant. Adjusters find that business interruption claims run smoothly when one of these accounting firms is hired to work with the policyholder's accountant.

Merchandise

Merchandise that the policyholder holds for sale is a special type of business personal property. Its valuation raises unique issues; it offers the best opportunities for salvage and use of salvor services; and claims for it must be settled in special ways.

Valuation of Merchandise

The replacement cost of merchandise is the cost to the policyholder of replacing that merchandise. The policyholder will usually have ongoing relations with its suppliers and can provide accurate information about their prices. If the policyholder regularly enjoys trade discounts and allowances from its suppliers, the effective cost to the policyholder will be less than what appears on supplier invoices. Replacement costs of finished goods in the hands of a manufacturer are the costs of manufacture.

Actual cash value standards can be difficult to apply to merchandise. In many cases, the goods have experienced no depreciation, and actual cash value is equivalent to replacement cost. Depreciation caused by ordinary wear and tear is not common, but many goods suffer "shop wear." They are picked over and handled by so many people that they are no longer presentable as first-quality goods.

Merchandise can also suffer significant depreciation caused by obsolescence. An adjuster can identify situations of obsolescence even when he or she is not familiar with the product. If, before the loss, the policyholder was offering the product to the public at a discounted price or had stopped offering it altogether, the product has likely suffered obsolescence. In fact, it is considered good accounting practice to reduce the inventory value of merchandise whenever its listed retail price is reduced. Such an accounting approach by the policyholder should be noted and cited by the adjuster as justification for settling claims at the reduced inventory figure. Fashion changes, technological changes, and seasonal selling patterns can all cause an inventory to become obsolete. Insurance is not designed to reimburse for such loss of value.

Salvage

Other than vehicles, merchandise is the only significant source of salvage for the insurance industry. As explained earlier in this chapter, adjusters and insurers rarely try to sell salvaged merchandise themselves; they employ professional salvage firms.

Salvage proceeds from the sale of damaged merchandise can be very significant. Some merchants refuse to deal in damaged goods, no matter how superficial the damage is. These merchants will refuse to consider a loss settlement based on a percentage of the goods' value, since in that merchant's markets the goods are "worthless." Adjusters find it easiest to settle with such merchants for 100 percent of the goods' value and to take the merchandise for salvage.

Professional salvage firms can act quickly to protect goods from further damage, can inventory and separate goods, and can give advice to claim representatives about the likely amount of residual value in damaged goods.

Reporting Form Losses

Inventories of merchandise are often insured under reporting form policies that require the policyholder to submit regular reports of value. Adjusters who handle claims for such merchandise must know what to do when the policyholder underreports its values or fails to report the values promptly. The following rules are based on ISO's value reporting form.

Following a loss to merchandise insured under a value reporting form, the adjuster must determine the value of the policyholder's inventory for the date of the last report. The adjuster is not concerned with the value of the inventory on the date of loss unless the inventory is totaled. Analysis of the inventory for a past date may require the assistance of an accountant. If the policyholder underreported the value of its inventory, it cannot recover the full amount of its loss. It recovers only a percentage of the loss equal to the percentage of inventory value it reported.

Should the policyholder fail to submit a report when due, the loss adjustment will be based on the last report submitted. The adjuster will not pay more than the amount last reported. This rule might penalize the policyholder. However, should the policyholder fail to submit even the first required report, the adjuster will not pay more than 75 percent of what would otherwise have been paid. Applying this latter rule always penalizes the policyholder.

Importance of Negotiation

As noted above with respect to salvage, adjusters will sometimes settle losses to merchandise based on a percentage of value. Under these settlements, the merchant keeps the merchandise and is reimbursed for its decreased value. The adjuster is not required to pay full value for the goods or to dispose of salvage. Adjusters should try to negotiate with policyholders towards such settlements, since they offer mutual benefit.

For example, suppose that following a loss to merchandise, the adjuster believed that salvage of the damaged goods would yield about 35 percent of their insured value. It would not be unusual for the policyholder in such a situation to believe it could sell the goods for a much higher percentage of value, perhaps 55 percent. This might be true because the policyholder is a merchant in the business and is already organized to sell such goods. On the one hand, the adjuster could total the goods and sell them as salvage for a net loss of 65 percent. Alternatively, the adjuster could try to negotiate settlement with the policyholder for some percentage less than 65 percent. The policyholder would be willing to take as little as 45 percent, because the policyholder believes it can still realize 55 percent by selling the goods itself. Any settlement figure between 45 percent and 65 percent is therefore fair *to both parties*.

This type of situation is common in losses to merchandise. Each party must assess the situation accurately to negotiate effectively. The adjuster can get advice from a salvor or can negotiate based on his or her personal experience with similar losses. Intelligent negotiating by the adjuster does not necessarily harm the policyholder. A policyholder, knowledgeable of the merchandise's value, can refuse unfavorable settlement proposals. If the adjuster is being unreasonable, the policyholder can invoke the appraisal clause or can challenge the adjuster to total the goods and try to realize the salvage value the adjuster claims still exists.

Transportation and Bailment Losses

Property is frequently in the possession of someone other than its owner. Losses to such property create complicated legal and insurance policy coverage issues. Adjusters may have to handle claims for either the owner or the party in possession of the property. An adjuster must carefully review the coverage, the law, and the contracts between the parties in these situations.

The most common circumstances in which property is in the possession of someone other than its owner are transportation and bailment situations. Carriers such as trucking companies, railroads, and air freight companies are in the business of transporting other people's property. Bailments include situations in which owners entrust their property to bailees such as cleaners, repairers, processors, consignees, and warehousers. These relationships are contractual, and the pertinent contracts can affect both legal liability and insurance coverage.

Insurance Coverages

An adjuster handling transportation and bailment claims must orient himself or herself to the insurance policy under which he or she is working. Insurance policies exist for both the owner and for the other party involved. Policies written for motor truck carriers, bailees, warehousemen, and so on, may provide certain coverage for other parties. Thus, adjusters may find themselves settling a claim for one party under a policy that names some other party as the insured. For example, an adjuster may settle losses under a dry cleaner's policy for the dry cleaner's customers, rather than for the named insured—the dry cleaner.

Owner's policies typically provide limited coverage for property away from the insured location. Thus, the owner of the property may have significant uninsured exposures. An owner with predictable off-premises exposures should obtain special coverage under floater policies or shipper policies. Unfortunately, an owner's coverage is often inadequate. An adjuster handling a claim for an owner should check for off-premises coverage. If such coverage is inadequate, the adjuster should quickly settle for the available coverage and should place the carrier's or bailee's insurer on notice of the claim. Owner's policies typically have "no benefit to bailee" clauses. These clauses make clear that the owner's coverage does not extend to the carrier or bailee and that the owner's insurer retains its right of subrogation. However, as discussed below, subrogation rights may be affected by agreement between the parties.

Policies for carriers and bailees typically protect the interests of both the owner and the carrier/bailee. An adjuster handling claims under a carrier/bailee policy must usually settle two claims arising out of the same property loss: the owner's and the carrier/bailee's. The carrier/bailee has an interest in the property to the extent of its earned fees. In addition, the carrier/bailee may be legally liable to the owner for return of the property (the extent of a carrier/bailee's legal liability is discussed below). An insurance policy of a carrier/bailee that extends to liability for the owner's property requires the adjuster working for the carrier/bailee's insurer to settle the owner's claim. Most policies of this sort allow the adjuster to deal directly with the owner and also allow the insurer to defend the carrier/bailee against the owner's claim, rather than to pay it. Some carrier/bailee policies protect the owner regardless of the carrier/bailee's legal liability. Such policies are purchased to maintain customer goodwill. Owners expect to be reimbursed for damage to their property, without hairsplitting over legal liability. This quasi-first-party coverage allows the adjuster to deal immediately with the owner before conducting an investigation of legal liability.

Legal Liability

Even in the absence of agreement between the parties, the law provides for the extent of legal liability of the carrier/bailee to the owner. Since the relationship between the owner and the carrier/bailee is contractual, the specific terms of the contract between the parties also affect legal liability between them.

In the absence of an agreement to the contrary, the law makes common carriers liable for damage to an owner's goods. The only exceptions to this liability are for acts of God, war, negligence of the shipper, exercise of public authority, and inherent vice of the goods. Carriers usually limit the dollar amount of their liability in their **bill of lading**, which is a receipt for the goods and a contract for transportation. A **released bill of lading** limits the carrier's liability to a specified dollar amount. Owners and shippers with greater exposures must pay higher rates for increased liability on the carrier's part. Adjusters handling losses in shipment *must* review the applicable bill of lading.

Other bailees are generally liable to the owner only for their negligence. Should a loss occur without any negligence on the bailee's part, the owner must bear the loss. Thus, owners with significant off-premises exposures must arrange special coverage. A bailee's coverage may not apply. As with a transportation contract, a bailment contract can modify the respective legal rights of the parties. A bailment contract might limit the dollar amount of a bailee's liability or make the bailee strictly liable. An adjuster handling an owner's claim against a bailee for legal liability must read and understand the contract between the parties. To the extent that the bailee's liability is limited, so too is any coverage for the owner that is based on liability. Furthermore, the subrogation rights of the owner's insurer may be limited. Most property insurance policies allow the insured to waive subrogation before a loss occurs. An adjuster who has paid a claim under an owner's insurance may find that the insured/owner has waived liability of the bailee beyond a certain dollar amount. Such a waiver likewise limits the insurer's subrogation rights.

Crime Losses

Property losses caused by crime present a significant challenge to adjusters. The property in question is usually gone from sight. Thus, the best evidence that the loss occurred and of what the property was worth is absent. Adjusters handling such cases can usually expect a higher level of doubt and uncertainty than is considered acceptable and comfortable in other property losses.

On crime losses, the adjuster's most important duties are to verify the exact cause of loss, verify the existence and value of the property, and investigate any fraud possibilities.

Verification of Exact Cause

Because crime insurance is expensive, policy forms covering crime losses are narrowly tailored. The policyholder should have just the form or forms needed for that insured's significant exposures. For example, under the ISO crime program, Coverage Form C provides very broad coverage (theft, disappearance, or destruction) to a very specific category of property (money and securities), but Coverage Form D provides protection to broad types of property (anything other than money or securities) for very limited causes of loss (robbery of a custodian and safe burglary only).

Once the adjuster has carefully determined the policyholder's coverage, the adjuster must determine the exact cause of the loss. The insurance policy forms provide definitions of the various crimes that control whether a particular loss is covered. For example, burglary is defined so that there must be signs of forcible entry or exit. This requirement may not exist under a particular state's definition of burglary in its criminal code. Nevertheless, for a policyholder to have a loss covered, the cause must satisfy the policy definition.

The adjuster must interview and obtain statements from every party with knowledge of the alleged crime. Although taking statements is not standard practice for ordinary property losses, it is for crime losses. A robbery victim should be able to furnish a complete account of the incident. The person who discovered a burglary should be interviewed in depth. The scene of a reported burglary must be inspected. The adjuster should require the policyholder to report the incident to the police and should obtain whatever report or investigation the police prepare. Unfortunately, police in many high-crime areas spend little time and effort tracking down burglars and may not conduct an investigation at all.

One of the most essential aspects of an adjuster's investigation into a crime loss is to conclude that the theft was not an inside job. "Theft" by the policyholder is not theft at all; it is fraud. Theft by employees is only covered by employee dishonesty (fidelity) policies. In the case of a reported burglary, the policy requirement of forcible entry or exit benefits the adjuster. In the absence of such evidence, the adjuster can deny the claim without necessarily accusing the insured or the insured's employees. In cases of employee theft, the policyholder is usually suspicious of employee involvement and may have good ideas about who is involved. Adjusters should not repeat unproven, slanderous accusations but should take statements from all suspects and then decide whether sufficient evidence exists to alert the police to likely suspects or to deny the claim.

Verification of the Property

It is difficult, but not impossible, for an adjuster to verify the existence and value of property that is gone.

Businesses should have inventory records that record the quantity and value of property in inventory. Although inventory records are not perfect, they are usually accurate within a few percentage points. Many crime policies preclude the use of inventory records to prove the occurrence of a crime because inventory "shrinkage" is a widespread phenomenon usually caused by unrecorded sales, discarding of damaged merchandise, and employee pilferage. However, inventory records can be used as part of the evidence concerning the quantity and value of property taken.

Should the adjuster be suspicious about the loss, he or she should check with the policyholder's suppliers. These suppliers should have complete records regarding the types, quantities, and values of goods shipped to the policyholder. The adjuster can also check with suppliers to determine whether the policyholder has submitted false inventory data to the adjuster claiming receipt and presence of goods that never existed.

Fraud Possibilities

Adjusters tend to be suspicious of all crime losses. Nevertheless, legitimate crime losses are the norm, so unless the adjuster can develop evidence to the contrary, insured crime losses must be settled.

The policyholder has a motive for fraud whenever its inventory is obsolete or not selling well. The adjuster should learn as much as possible about the policyholder's general business condition through credit reports, financial statements, and credit records. If those reports show deterioration in the policyholder's financial condition, the adjuster should further consider the possibility that the claim is fraudulent.

Employees are often the best sources of solid evidence of fraud on the policyholder's part. Employees may witness the removal of property that is subsequently reported stolen or may be aware of irregularities in the policyholder's bookkeeping. An adjuster investigating a suspicious loss may contact the employees at home, where they may feel more comfortable about discussing questionable business practices.

Catastrophes

Hurricanes, floods, tornadoes, earthquakes, and fires or explosions causing widespread damage affect entire communities at once. The insurance industry's role in helping communities recover from catastrophes represents the industry at its finest. Property adjusters are the specific individuals in the insurance industry who must respond to catastrophes. Such response includes preparation before loss and actions following loss.

Pre-Loss Planning

Claims departments would be overwhelmed by catastrophes if they did not plan for them ahead of time. They must respond to catastrophes by having a sufficient number of adjusters in potential disaster areas while maintaining acceptable service throughout the rest of the country.

Certain areas of the country, such as the Gulf and Atlantic coasts during hurricane season, are most likely to "host" disaster recovery teams. Claim offices in these areas should prepare kits that include forms, maps, telephone directories, temporary licenses, tape measures, clipboards, calculators, and anything else a visiting adjuster would need to operate on the road. Although state insurance regulators vary as to how strictly they enforce licensing requirements following a catastrophe, every adjuster who is likely to be called into an area should be licensed.

The insurance company's administrative departments must be prepared to rent office space; have telephones, copy machines, desks, and other equipment installed; and procure temporary living quarters and rented cars on short notice.

Local agents or the underwriting department must establish a system by which adjusters can confirm coverage simply and reliably.

Post-Loss Planning

Adjusters on "storm duty" must work long hours and be separated from their families and normal lives for long periods. In addition, the circumstances of catastrophes will cause the adjuster to modify normal claims adjusting procedures. Adjusters often pay claims with less documentation than usual. They may also reimburse the insured for the insured's own labor in cleaning up the property, a circumstance that is especially common following catastrophes. Claims that would normally require an in-person inspection may be handled by telephone.

Local agents should be familiar with the insurer's claims practices so that they can advise policyholders on how to begin recovery from a loss. The agents should advise the policyholders of what documentation they must maintain and what actions they should take immediately following a loss.

Contractor's services may be at a premium following a major catastrophe. However, contractors from around the country will flock to the disaster area to help mitigate the shortage. Policyholders should be advised to be very careful about to whom they release money. Unscrupulous persons may take advantage of people who are shocked, confused, and suddenly holding cash.

Summary

Several general issues pertain to every property claim and constitute a framework used by property claims adjusters to handle all kinds of property damage claims.

The first issue involves determining who has an interest in the property, interpreting policy requirements for an insurable interest, and identifying who is insured. Next, the adjuster must identify exactly what property is insured and at what location the coverage applies.

Although losses from fire and windstorm are fairly clear-cut, problems may arise from losses caused by water damage, collapse, theft, vandalism, wear and tear and other gradual causes, ordinance or law, faulty construction, and intentional acts on the part of the policyholder. Indirect losses are financial losses resulting from loss of income or extra expenses to remain in operation.

After determining that coverage is in order for the policyholder, the property, and the peril, the adjuster must address the amount of the loss. Policies usually value property at replacement cost or actual cash value without specifying how the adjuster is to determine those amounts. Determining replacement cost is usually easier than figuring actual cash value.

Every property insurance policy enumerates various duties the insured must perform following a loss. These duties include notifying the insurer of the loss, protecting the property from further loss, assisting the insurer with the loss adjustment process, providing proof of loss if required, and submitting to examination under oath if requested. Some policyholders hire public adjusters to handle the contractual duties imposed after a loss.

Loss adjustment procedures include verifying the cause of loss, determining the amount of loss, and documenting the cause and amount of loss. Salvage and subrogation activities offer the adjuster an opportunity to minimize the insurer's losses.

Claims for loss to homeowners' personal property present adjusters with some of their most rewarding yet difficult challenges. For example, adjusters helping homeowners after a devastating loss are able to help those traumatized by the loss of their home. Simultaneously, however, adjusters must control the adjusting process so that the insureds understand and follow adjustment procedures.

Losses to commercial structures can easily reach millions of dollars. In those cases, adjusters often confer with architects and contractors to determine the value of a commercial structure and the extent of the loss. Problems may arise with mortgagees. Serious losses at commercial structures may result in contamination and pollution. Suspected arson is also a concern.

Business interruption claims can be highly complex, and settlement often requires a detailed analysis of financial records by an accountant.

Merchandise that the policyholder holds for sale is a special type of business personal property. The valuation of merchandise for sale raises unique issues: it offers the best opportunities for salvage and the use of salvor services, and claims for it must be settled in special ways.

Transportation and bailment losses can create complicated legal and coverage issues. Adjusters may have to handle claims for either the owner or the party in possession of the property. A claims adjuster must carefully review the coverage, the law, and the contracts between the parties in these situations.

Property losses caused by crime are among the greatest challenges faced by adjusters. When handling crime losses, the adjuster's most important duties are to verify the exact cause of loss, verify the existence and value of the property, and investigate any fraud possibilities.

Catastrophes—hurricanes, floods, tornadoes, earthquakes, fires, or explosions—can cause widespread damage that affects entire communities. The adjuster's response to these losses should include preparation before the loss and actions following the loss.

Chapter 15

Liability Claims Adjusting

Liability claims work differs so significantly from property claims work that most insurance company claims operations are organized along property-liability lines. Within personal lines insurance companies, the liability side of claims work may consist primarily of auto claims. Within commercial insurance companies, the same personnel frequently handle auto liability and general liability claims, and auto physical damage and workers compensation claims may be organized into separate units within the claims department. (Although not traditional liability-based claims, auto physical damage and workers compensation are treated in this chapter.)

The specialization among claims personnel between property and liability claims exists because those claims differ from one another in several important respects. Once coverage is established, resolving liability claims depends more on the law of liability and damages than on the contractual terms of an insurance policy. The law of liability and damages exists apart from insurance policy terms. Liability insurance policies protect the policyholder against the financial consequences of liability law and the policyholder's own legal liability. Thus, liability claims adjusters spend most of their time and effort investigating and evaluating the legal aspects of liability and damages and relatively less time than property claims adjusters enforcing and performing insurance policy terms.

In liability claim situations, the policyholder is really not the person with the claim. The party with a liability claim *against* the insured is the real claimant. This party is referred to as the "third party," or "claimant." Thus, the insurer has no contract with, and the liability adjuster has no contractual obligations to, the claimant. Although most insurance companies consider it to be both ethical and in their own best interests to deal with claimants promptly and responsively, the adjuster has more leeway in dealing with a third-party claimant than with a policyholder. Most insurance department regulations and market conduct studies, for example, are more solicitous of the interests of first-party insureds than of third-party claimants. In addition, third-party claimants are more frequently represented by an attorney than are first-party insureds.

Liability claims include both property damage and bodily injury liability. Although liability claims for property damage exist, they represent a relatively minor percentage of the total dollars paid on all liability claims. The predominately injury-oriented nature of liability claims distinguishes their settlement from the settlement of property damage claims. The evaluation of injuries both by claimants and adjusters is more subjective and uncertain than property claims, and, thus, negotiation plays a greater role in settling injury claims than it does in settling liability claims.

This chapter begins by describing the issues that exist in all liability claims. Coverage for the claim in question must first be verified. The adjuster must investigate and evaluate both legal liability and damages. Finally, the adjuster must settle the claim, either through negotiation or through the courts. The second half of this chapter describes issues that are important in the settlement of specific types of claims, including auto liability and physical damages, premises, operations, products, workers compensation, professional liability, and environmental impairment liability.

General Issues in Liability Claims

In every liability claim, the adjuster must determine coverage, liability, and damages and must make settlement. The adjuster may have to investigate in order to determine coverage, liability, and damages; rarely are all three of these issues quickly and easily determined. Most of an adjuster's time is thus devoted to investigation and documentation. However, knowing how, when, and for what amount to settle provides the most difficult challenge to a liability adjuster's skill and judgment. This section describes how liability adjusters perform the core functions of determining coverage, liability, and damages and making settlements.

Coverage

The essential coverage clause of most liability insurance policies is a simple one. For example, Coverage A of the commercial general liability (CGL) policy states, "We will pay those sums that the insured becomes legally obligated to pay as damages because of 'bodily injury' or 'property damages' to which this insurance applies." Thus, any type of bodily injury or property damage for which the insured is allegedly liable is covered, unless it is specifically excluded. When determining coverage, adjusters are primarily concerned with the possible application of exclusions. Nevertheless, the essential coverage clause raises important issues. Under Coverage A of the CGL, the claim must be for "bodily injury" or "property damage." Under most auto liability coverages, the claim must also arise out of the use of certain autos by certain individuals. Thus, a claim that is not for "bodily injury" or "property damage" or that does not arise out of the use of certain autos is not within the essential coverage provisions.

This section describes how claims adjusters determine whether a claim is covered. Although it is not a comprehensive exposition of coverage, this section addresses the major issues faced by adjusters.

Claimants' Allegations

When a claim is first presented to an adjuster, the facts may be unknown or in dispute. Without knowing the facts, how can an adjuster determine coverage?

The claimant's allegations determine coverage, even if those allegations are disputed and even if they are eventually proven untrue. Liability policies protect the policyholder against legal claims and their cost to defend, regardless of whether the claims are valid or groundless. Protection against false, unproven, and unprovable claims is a crucial part of the protection provided by liability insurance policies. An adjuster evaluating coverage must first consider the claimant's allegations at face value. However, sometimes the claimant's allegations may not be covered, or coverage may be doubtful.

Coverage Problems

Adjusters face difficulty whenever coverage for a claimant's allegations is doubtful. This difficulty occurs when some aspects of a claim are covered and others are not or when coverage for the entire claim is questionable. Clear communication with the policyholder and prompt action on the part of the adjuster are essential to protect both the policyholder's and the insurer's interests. Whenever coverage is doubtful or not applicable to part of a claim, the adjuster must explain clearly, in writing, why this is so and what both the adjuster and the policyholder must do.

If part of a claim is clearly not covered, the adjuster must explain to the policyholder why not, with reference to specific policy provisions. The adjuster must explain that the insurer will continue handling the claim but that the policyholder may have to contribute to an eventual settlement or judgment. This being so, the adjuster should invite the policyholder to involve a private attorney in the claim. Often, in these situations, the policyholder neither involves private counsel nor contributes to a settlement. This is so because part of the claim *is* covered, and the insurer must continue to conduct the defense of the claim and must pay any settlement unless part of the settlement is clearly not covered. Since most liability claims are settled without a clear specification of the basis of liability or of the elements of damages, the insurer usually pays the entire settlement.

When coverage for the entire claim is doubtful, the adjuster must explain to the policyholder why, in writing, and must explain what the adjuster will do. The adjuster must usually conduct a further investigation. Pending this investigation, the adjuster will reserve the insurer's right to deny coverage should the facts so indicate. Upon issuing a letter advising the policyholder of a coverage problem and reserving the insurer's rights, the adjuster must promptly investigate and make a decision. If coverage is found to apply, the policyholder should be informed. If coverage is found not to apply, the policyholder should receive a prompt letter of denial.

Insurers can resolve coverage questions through declaratory judgment actions in court. As the name suggests, these lawsuits result in a court declaration of the rights between parties. Many jurisdictions allow the courts to declare rights between parties whenever a controversy appears to surface in the investigation of the claim. Unfortunately, there are practical drawbacks to declaratory judgment actions. They are likely to consume thousands or tens of thousands of dollars of legal expense; thus, they are not feasible for small and moderately sized claims. Furthermore, in many jurisdictions, declaratory judgment actions do not move through the courts any faster than other cases. A declaratory judgment that takes years may not serve its purpose. The insurer will have to pay to defend the policyholder throughout that time and may have had to settle the case in the meantime. Filing a declaratory action, if unsuccessful, will also complicate the defense of the underlying action.

Whenever coverage does not apply to a claim, the policyholder should receive a written explanation, and a copy should go to the producer. If a lawsuit has been filed, the policyholder must be told exactly how much time he or she has to file a response with the court. Additionally, an adjuster should direct the policyholder to seek personal counsel.

Bodily Injury and Property Damage

As noted above, liability insurance policies usually apply only to claims for bodily injury or property damage. The most likely exception to this rule is the personal injury coverage of the CGL, which extends to damages that are not limited to bodily injury and property damage. "Personal injury" is used by attorneys to refer to "bodily injury" claims as defined in insurance policies. In insurance, "personal injury" refers to specific policy coverage for defamation, false arrest, advertising injury, and malicious prosecution.

Generally, policyholders will only submit claims that are for bodily injury or property damage. However, not all policyholders have a clear idea of what is covered by their insurance and will submit any claim in the hope that it might be covered. Thus, adjusters occasionally see claims that are not for bodily injury or property damage.

Money damages are an appropriate remedy for both bodily injury and property damage and are normally included in the relief sought in a lawsuit. Lawsuits that seek only an injunction, and not money damages, are generally not for bodily injury or property damage. An adjuster must be careful not to deny coverage too hastily for a suit seeking injunctive relief. A number of such suits concern ongoing injuries and seek an injunction to stop further injury. This is especially true for claims of interference with use of property. Since loss of use of property is included within the definition of "property damage," a suit based on such an alleged injury may be covered.

Suits involving breach of contract resulting in financial harm only or suits alleging financial fraud are more clearly not covered, since they do not concern claims for "bodily injury" or "property damage." Likewise, regulatory fines or minor criminal fines do not constitute "property damage" and are not covered.

Claims for emotional injury alone, without physical injury, present more difficult coverage issues. Generally, if the court cases of the jurisdiction in question allow a tort claim based on emotional injury only, then an emotional injury will constitute a bodily injury for purposes of coverage. Increasingly, more jurisdictions accept emotional injury as bodily injury.

Intentional Acts

Consistent with the notion that insurance is designed to cover accidental events, liability insurance policies generally exclude coverage for the policyholder's intentional acts. This is an important exclusion for adjusters, since claimants often allege that the policyholder acted intentionally. Unfortunately, the application of this exclusion is difficult, because adjusters must uncover the answers to two questions: (1) whether the policyholder intended the result of his or her action or merely intended to commit the action without contemplating the injurious outcome, and (2) whether intentional acts can be excluded when the claimant also alleges negligence or strict liability on the policyholder's part. An additional issue can involve vicarious liability in which a principal, the policyholder, may be liable for the intentional acts of an agent or a servant.

Adjusters cannot rely on the intentional act exclusion unless they are familiar with the law in their jurisdiction regarding its meaning. For example, in some states, an assault might not be excluded as an intentional act unless the policyholder intended the harm that resulted. This standard makes the exclusion much harder to apply than in states that consider an assault intentional as long as the policyholder intended to commit the assault. When it must be shown that the policyholder intended the harm, it is usually unnecessary to show that the policyholder intended the precise harm that occurred. Furthermore, the intent to cause harm may be inferred from the commission of the assault. Unfortunately, an insurer cannot deny coverage in the hope that a court will infer intent.

The distinction between intending the act and intending the harm has been at the center of numerous suits by policyholders seeking coverage under their homeowners liability insurance for acts of sexual molestation. Many of these cases involve victims who are small children. The policyholders in these cases have alleged that they were insane or severely emotionally disturbed or that they did not believe they were causing harm. Some courts have accepted those arguments and awarded coverage. Other courts have rejected the policyholder's arguments and have ruled that the intent to harm exists, as a matter of law, regardless of what the policyholder says about his or her subjective state. As a result, most homeowners policies now have a specific exclusion for sexual molestation.

Application of the intentional act exclusion is difficult whenever the claimant also alleges negligence or strict liability on the policyholder's part. Based on the claimant's allegations, part of the claim is covered, and part is not. In such situations, the insurer must defend the policyholder. If the opportunity arises, the adjuster may also have to settle the claim completely. Upon settlement, no distinction is made between which parts of the settlement are for which allegations. The case is settled as a whole, and coverage issues cannot be resolved in a settlement. The same problem exists even when a case is litigated to a verdict. In a few states, courts require juries to identify damages awarded count by count. Otherwise, the verdict will be expressed as a single sum of money and will not resolve any coverage issues. Sometimes the insurer can prove through a lawsuit's discovery that the policyholder must have intended the behavior, and this may be the basis for denying coverage. However, an insurer acting this way is acting contrary to the policyholder's best interests and must do so through separate attorneys. The attorney hired by the insurer to defend the policyholder cannot simultaneously work for the insurer toward proving that the policyholder acted intentionally.

Contractual Obligations

In general, liability insurance does not exist to guarantee that policyholders will perform their contractual agreements. However, adjusters cannot deny coverage for all claims based on breach of contract. Contractual obligations are frequently involved in covered claims.

The consequences of a breach of contract may be covered even if the breach itself is not. For example, a contractor may be hired to erect a wall. Should the contractor do the work negligently and the wall collapse on a person, the cost of rebuilding the wall (the subject of the contract) would not be covered, but injuries to the person would be covered. Adjusters frequently see claims of this nature.

Certain contractual obligations may be directly insured by liability policies. For example, the CGL excepts from its contractual exclusion (therefore leaving coverage in place) liability assumed in a lease and the contractual assumption of liability for another's torts for bodily injury or property damage. Both of these contractual obligations play significant roles in claims work.

As with claims involving alleged intentional acts, claims of contractual breach may be joined with claims of negligence or strict liability. Such claims generally involve products or professional liability. The breach of contract aspect of these cases is usually incidental. Adjusters handling such cases often realize that they will not try to differentiate between the intentional act and the contractual breach so that they do not inform the policyholder that part of the claim should technically not be covered. Failure to so advise the policyholder is equivalent to granting coverage for the entire claim, which is probably what the adjuster intends.

Property Under the Policyholder's Control

Policyholders will often submit claims for property damage to another's property that was damaged while in the policyholder's care, custody, or control or while the policyholder was working on it. Such property damage is clearly excluded from coverage by the typical liability insurance policy.

Policyholders are usually not aware of what is or is not covered. They often do not read or understand their policy exclusions. Adjusters can identify care, custody, or control situations with a minimum of investigation. The adjuster can then usually direct the policyholder to the first-party coverage that deals with these situations.

Property damage to the policyholder's product itself, to the policyholder's work itself, or to property that the policyholder has sold or given away is likewise excluded from typical liability policies. However, consequential bodily injuries or damage to another's property is usually covered. Adjusters frequently encounter these situations and must carefully distinguish between damages that are covered and those that are not.

Legal Liability

Once coverage has been determined, the adjuster must determine legal liability and damages. This section describes the procedures an adjuster follows and explains the bases for legal liability.

Proper investigation is essential in determining legal liability. The ability to conduct a complete and proper investigation is one of the core skills of claims adjusting. The adjuster's investigation is guided by the essential facts that need to be established in order to determine legal liability. These facts are dictated by the legal principles applicable to the situation. Many legal principles are relevant to claims work, including tort liability, criminal liability, contractual liability, statutory liability, and vicarious liability. This section explains these principles as they apply to claims work and explains the defenses that may be asserted against liability claims.

Investigation

The initial report of a claim will usually state nothing more than, "Insured involved in auto accident at 10th and Washington," or "Claimant fell at insured's store." The adjuster must develop the additional facts.

The adjuster will organize the investigation according to what information needs to be known and what is most important. For example, regarding the loss reports cited above, the adjuster would want to know the potential claimants' names, addresses, and telephone numbers and whether any of them are injured. On learning this, the adjuster would want to know each claimant's version of the story. When a person's account of an accident is committed to a statement, he or she cannot easily change his or her story later.

It is as important for an adjuster to obtain a claimant's story as to obtain the insured's story. The policyholder is required to cooperate and will usually be eager to do so. The claimant may exaggerate, embellish, or falsify his or her story if not questioned promptly. In addition to preserving evidence, prompt contact reassures the claimant about the insurer's responsiveness and greatly reduces the chance that the claimant will hire an attorney.

Taking statements is standard practice with liability claims. A good statement will have a proper introduction of both the witness and the adjuster and will systematically cover all relevant factual issues in the case. An adjuster should even cover areas with which the witness is likely to be unfamiliar. Having a witness respond "I don't know" prevents that witness from later inventing evidence on the same point. As long as a witness is available to testify, a statement given out of court cannot be used as evidence, except for impeachment.

Most statements are recorded on audiotape. This is both convenient for the adjuster and preserves the witness's words. Tapes are easy and inexpensive to reproduce should the witness want a copy.

Adjusters also collect evidence in other forms, such as police reports, photographs and diagrams of accident scenes, and products or objects involved in claims. Information should be collected promptly to preserve the accident scene before changes occur. For example, skid marks wear away quickly. Such evidence is useful for checking the credibility of witness statements and as direct evidence of what happened. Police reports should never serve to substitute for the adjuster's own investigation, unless all parties agree as to the facts of the accident.

The most important aspect in any investigation is to obtain all of the relevant evidence. Once all of the evidence has been gathered, the adjuster must evaluate its credibility and decide what most likely happened. Adjusters should be constantly evaluating the credibility of evidence as it is received.

Adjusters quickly learn that in many cases, the "truth" is never known for sure. All that is available is evidence, and one set of evidence may contradict another. The best the adjuster can do is evaluate the relative credibility of the evidence. Although the credibility of evidence and "truth" may not be the same in every case, credibility of evidence decides the outcome of cases.

In order for witnesses to be completely credible, they must have had the opportunity to observe the facts in question, must remember those facts accurately, must have the ability to communicate what is in their memory, and must have no motive to distort. Most witnesses are deficient in at least one of those respects. They may have had a good chance to observe but may have a poor memory. They may have a good memory but are so inarticulate that the adjuster must lead them through their entire statement, thus introducing the possibility of distortion. An adjuster must also remember that a witness may be biased but honest, or may be articulate without having really seen what happened.

Tort Liability

A tort is a civil wrong not arising out of breach of contract. Some torts, such as assault, may also be crimes, and others, such as professional malpractice, may also be breach of contract. Generally, though, the law provides a remedy for torts because the wrongdoer (called a tortfeasor) has behaved in a manner that falls below acceptable legal standards and has caused damage to another.

Negligence is the usual basis of tort liability. Adjusters and attorneys use the term "negligence" to refer both to negligent behavior and to a cause of action in negligence. A claimant has a cause of action in negligence whenever all elements required for negligence exist. Those elements are a duty of care; a breach of that duty (these first two elements together are sometimes referred to as "negligence," meaning negligent behavior); proximate cause; and damages.

Whenever someone has failed to behave carefully and prudently, he or she has likely breached a duty of care. Negligent behavior is very common; few people are always careful and prudent. An adjuster investigating a situation of potentially negligent behavior will usually proceed by investigating what the policyholder could have done differently to prevent the accident. If the policyholder could have reasonably avoided the accident, the policyholder is probably negligent. Violations of certain laws, such as traffic laws, are deemed negligence per se. These laws are designed to fix the standard of behavior for all people subject to the law. Anyone who drives must observe the traffic laws, and failure to do so is negligence.

It is not enough for the injuries of a person to be "caused by" another for there to be compensation; there must be **proximate** (or legal) **cause**. This legal concept requires that there be an unbroken chain of events between the "cause" and the injurious "event." Although "proximate" means close, a proximate cause is not necessarily physically close or close in time to its outcome. The proximate cause requirement protects a wrongdoer from responsibility for remote, unforeseeable consequences. Proximate cause is most likely questioned when the injurious outcome is also caused by intervening negligence. The intervening negligence may eliminate proximate causation between the original negligence and the eventual outcome.

Damages are an essential part of an action in negligence. Unless negligent behavior causes damage to some other party, the wrongdoer escapes any legal consequences. Damages are virtually inevitable in liability claims, however; if no damage was done, then the claimant would not be complaining.

Tort liability may also be based on behavior other than negligence. **Intentional torts** include assault, battery, false arrest, false imprisonment, conversion (theft), defamation, trespass, and fraud. Although many of these torts are crimes and all involve intentional conduct, an adjuster cannot assume they are not covered. Indeed, personal injury coverage extends to many of these torts. Convicting the policyholder of a crime is generally conclusive evidence that a tort was committed.

Torts may also be based on **absolute** (or strict) **liability**, which is liability that exists regardless of whether the policyholder was negligent. The term strict liability is often used in regard to product liability claims. There is a lack of agreement in the insurance and legal fields as to the proper use of the terms "strict liability" and "absolute liability." Some use the terms interchangeably. Others try to distinguish between the two and the situations to which they apply. A major distinction used by some is that the term "absolute liability" implies that no defenses are available. Those who hold this view believe that there are some defenses to strict liability situations.

An adjuster investigating tort liability must know all of the elements of the tort(s) in question so that instances of tort liability can be recognized. Claimants are unlikely to say, "I have an action in negligence against your insured." Instead, they say, "I fell and was injured at your insured's store."

Crimes

Criminals are legally liable in civil courts to their victims. As noted above, criminal acts are generally intentional, but that does not automatically mean they are not covered by insurance.

Anyone, including a convicted criminal, who seeks insurance coverage for a victim's claim is required by the insurance policy to cooperate with the insurer. Adjusters frequently find that convicted criminals are not cooperative even though they have a duty to be so. Those accused of crimes are often unable to cooperate with the adjuster if doing so will jeopardize their Fifth Amendment rights.

A convicted criminal's lack of cooperation may have little practical significance. A conviction is conclusive evidence that the crime was committed. Therefore, the criminal's cooperation would not help defend the claim. An adjuster handling a claim filed against a convicted criminal must often concede liability, but not necessarily coverage.

In the case of an accused, the adjuster can usually wait until the criminal proceedings are concluded before demanding the insured's cooperation. Criminal court dockets generally move much faster than civil court dockets, so the insurer is generally not prejudiced by the adjuster's waiting.

Contractual Liability

A party who breaches a contract is legally liable to the other party to the contract. If such breach causes bodily injury or property damage, the breaching party's liability insurance may cover the claim. As noted earlier in this chapter, certain contractual obligations may be covered by liability insurance.

In cases of alleged breach of contract, the adjuster must thoroughly review the entire contract and understand all of its terms. The adjuster must investigate the policyholder's behavior to determine whether it constitutes a breach of the contract. Finally, the adjuster must investigate all potential contractual defenses. Did the claimant breach the contract first, thereby excusing further performance by the policyholder? Has a precondition for the policyholder's contractual obligations not occurred or not been met? Have the policyholder and the claimant substituted a newer contract for a previous one?

In cases of contractual hold-harmless agreements and assumptions of liability, the adjuster must carefully scrutinize the contractual language to determine whether it applies to the situation in question. Courts read such agreements very narrowly, and an adjuster should do so as well. For example, in many hold-harmless agreements, the policyholder agrees to hold another harmless for claims that arise out of the policyholder's conduct. Should the situation in question involve negligence on the part of others, especially the party seeking protection under the agreement, the agreement may not apply. Courts may also invalidate contracts that are against public policy, that attempt to transfer liability for a nondelegable duty, or that contain ambiguous language.

Statutory Liability

Except for workers compensation, insurance is generally not designed to cover a policyholder's statutory obligations. (Workers compensation laws create an obligation for employers even when negligence is not an issue.) Nevertheless, should violation of a statute cause bodily injury or property damage, the policyholder's liability coverage may apply to a resulting claim. For example, violating a traffic law and injuring someone would be covered by auto liability insurance.

Not all statutory violations that cause bodily injury or property damage are covered by liability insurance. For example, intentionally dumping pollutants would be excluded. The adjuster handling a case involving an alleged violation of statutes must determine exactly what the statute requires, exactly what the policyholder did, and whether any exclusion in the insurance policy is applicable.

Vicarious Liability

Adjusters must frequently investigate the possibility of vicarious liability, which is liability imposed on a party because of that party's relationship to a wrongdoer. For example, employers may be liable for the acts of their employees, and principals may be responsible for their agents. Most claims against commercial policyholders involve vicarious liability because corporations are simply legal entities that act through human employees.

For adjusters, the most important issue with respect to vicarious liability is the scope of employment or agency. An employer is only liable for the acts of its employees while they are acting within the scope of their employment. For example, if an employee goes home and assaults a neighbor, the employer is not liable. Unfortunately for adjusters, cases in which the "scope of employment" issue arises are not so clear-cut. For example, employees often make brief deviations from their employer's business to attend to personal matters. Whether such a deviation occurred and when it ended are difficult questions. An adjuster handling such a situation must thoroughly investigate. Another difficult situation for determining scope of employment is when an employee attempts to conduct the employer's business by prohibited means, such as driving at illegally high speeds from one appointment to another. Usually, the law deems these situations to be within the scope of employment. The adjuster handling such situations often faces difficulty because the employer may overstate the extent to which it made its rules and prohibitions known.

Defenses to Liability Claims

Adjusters are interested in possible defenses to any claim they handle. As they investigate liability, adjusters also investigate possible defenses. The most useful defenses are absence of negligence, comparative or contributory negligence, assumption of risk, and statute of limitations. Other available defenses, such as exculpatory notices and hold harmless agreements, are not discussed here because they are less commonly encountered.

Absence of Negligence

Strictly speaking, absence of negligence is not so much a defense as it is a failure to prove the claimant's case. Nevertheless, adjusters should consider absence of negligence as a possible defense. Many accidents occur through no fault of anyone. Claimants often assert claims based on the notion that the mere occurrence of the accident entitles them to compensation. For example, a claimant who twists an ankle while walking through undeveloped land may expect the owner to compensate him or her. Yet it is not due to the negligence of the owner that the surface of the undeveloped property is uneven. Nature does not provide smoothly paved walkways, and anyone walking through natural terrain cannot expect to find them. Another unfortunately common example is auto accidents involving child pedestrians who dart into traffic. In many of those situations, it would have been impossible for the driver to have seen or anticipated the child's behavior or to have stopped the car in time. Defending these cases requires very careful preparation, however, because any hint of negligence on the driver's part might render the driver liable. Children involved in these cases are frequently under seven years old and are thus legally incapable of negligence.

Comparative or Contributory Negligence

Comparative or contributory negligence exists whenever a claimant's own fault contributes to causing his or her injuries. This is very common. In the few states that recognize contributory negligence, any fault on the claimant's part completely bars the claimant from recovery. Under comparative negligence laws, the claimant's recovery is reduced in proportion to the claimant's share of fault. In other words, if a claimant's negligence is a 25 percent cause of the accident, the claimant's recovery is reduced by 25 percent. Under some comparative negligence laws, claimant fault in excess of 50 percent completely bars the claimant from recovery. However, in "pure" comparative negligence states, a claimant can be 99 percent at fault and still recover 1 percent of the damages.

Assumption of Risk

The assumption of risk defense applies whenever a claimant knows of a risk and voluntarily encounters that risk anyway. In order for the defense to be valid, the claimant's behavior must be both knowing and voluntary. Assumption of the risk is frequently confused with comparative negligence. Although assuming a risk may be negligent in many specific circumstances, it is not necessarily negligent. For example, participating in sports such as downhill skiing includes an unavoidable risk of injury, but it is not negligent to participate. Knowing that risk, many people choose to participate anyway.

Statute of Limitations

Each state has enacted time limitations on the right to bring suit. The amount of time varies by state and by the type of legal claim; time limits can range from two to fifteen years, depending on the circumstances. Failure to file a suit within the allotted time waives any obligation on the part of the tortfeasor so that an expired statute of limitations can serve as an absolute defense.

Damages

Adjusters must determine and document damages before a claim can be settled. Doing so usually requires less legwork but takes more time than the investigation of liability. A liability investigation often concludes within days, whereas determining damages can take weeks, months, or longer. Adjusters usually rely on outside experts for damage information, such as doctors on bodily injury cases; appraisers, contractors, or repairers on property damage cases; and accountants or economists for determining financial factors.

Damages in bodily injury liability cases are usually proven with medical reports and bills, hospital records, and employer information. The adjuster must assemble this documentation throughout the time in which the claimant continues to receive treatment. Thus, settling an injury claim often does not occur until treatment is concluded or until a clear prognosis and course of future treatment are known. Damages in property damage cases are proven with estimates for repair or with actual bills for repair and rental. Most of this section concerns damages in bodily injury cases because those cases account for the majority of claim dollars spent in liability cases. The latter part of this section describes property damage cases and how they differ from first-party property damage claims.

Elements of Damage in Injury Claims

Adjusters must understand every element of damages for which the law provides compensation in order to investigate and document the claims properly. The claimant has the burden of proving the damages. Nevertheless, the adjuster should take the initiative in investigating them in order to remain aware of the nature and value of the claim.

Medical expenses include all bills incurred for emergency care, visits to doctors, surgery, hospitalization, drugs, medical equipment, nursing care, and medical transportation. Both medical expenses already incurred and future medical expenses that are reasonably expected and provable are allowable elements of damages.

Lost earnings for whatever period of time the claimant was disabled can also be recovered. If loss of earnings is expected to extend into the future, it too can be compensated. Future lost earnings may be expected for either a limited time or indefinitely and may be partial or total. A partial loss of earnings is likely to exist when a claimant has lost some of his or her ability to earn but also retains some of that ability. Total loss of earnings exists when the claimant is unable to perform any work.

The damages for medical expenses and loss of earnings are called out-of-pocket expenses, or special damages. Special damages are recoverable even if they do not actually come out of the claimant's pocket. Many claimants have health insurance and disability insurance that cover these items. Nevertheless, special damages are recoverable despite these other sources of payment. The principle of the law is that a claimant should not be penalized, nor should a wrongdoer be rewarded, because of the claimant's prudence in having insurance coverage. This is called the collateral source rule, a rule that is phrased in the negative: any collateral source is *not* to be considered when settling third-party claims. Many accident and health insurers have policy provisions that allow them to recover their payments from a tort recovery from the accident.

In addition to special damages, claimants can recover general damages. General damages are compensation for intangibles such as pain and suffering, and scarring or disfigurement. Special and general damages together are called "compensatory damages" and are the damages for which claimants are usually compensated.

If a claimant is married, the claimant's spouse can assert his or her own claim for loss of consortium. Consortium is the companionship, household services, and sexual relations one spouse provides the other. Depending on the liability policy wording, a claim for loss of consortium may involve a separate per-person policy limit, a circumstance that can be important in cases of serious injury.

Should a claimant die, two other types of claims are possible. In a survival action, the claimant's estate is able to assert whatever claim the deceased claimant had during his or her life. In other words, a bodily injury claim that the claimant could have asserted during his or her life may be asserted by the claimant's estate. The estate will be compensated for the same damages, special and general damages, but they do not continue to increase past the date of death. A survival action may be asserted even if the death is completely unrelated to the bodily injury.

If the bodily injuries cause death, the deceased's survivors may assert a wrongful death claim. A wrongful death claim belongs to the survivors, not to the deceased. It may be prosecuted by the administrator(s) of the deceased's estate, but the beneficiaries are the survivors. Laws vary by state as to who is an eligible beneficiary and how damages are measured. In general, damages in a wrongful death claim should compensate the beneficiary for the support and benefits formerly received from the deceased.

Evaluation of Special Damages

A liable party is not required to compensate a claimant for special damages that *might* be incurred. Certain rules and limitations exist.

Medical expenses must be related to the injury, necessary to heal the injury, and reasonable in amount. Although unrelated medical expenses should not be compensable, adjusters often have them submitted for payment. Many people who become claimants have preexisting medical conditions for which they were already or should have been receiving treatment. Bills for these treatments are often included with bills for accident-related treatment.

Medical treatment must be necessary in order to be compensated. Second-guessing the treating physician is not easy, but with a solid case, an insurer can avoid payment for unnecessary work.

Finally, medical treatment must be reasonable in amount and cost. Although insurers do not have any statutory, regulatory, or contractual controls over doctors and hospitals, they are neither required to reimburse a course of treatment nor pay bills that they can show are excessive.

Because adjusters lack the experience and expertise necessary to evaluate the necessity and frequency of medical treatment, insurers have begun to employ utilization review services. These services represent a recognized specialty within the medical field. By assessing medical treatment and bills, they are able to advise when a course of treatment is unnecessary, unrelated to the specific injury, or redundant of other treatment.

Lost wages must be established by verifying the extent and period of disability and the earnings of the claimant. The extent and period of disability are medical issues that must be addressed by doctors with reference to the physical demands of the claimant's job. A physician who expresses an opinion about disability without knowing the demands of the claimant's job cannot be reliable, unless the claimant's condition would disable the claimant from any work at all. The adjuster must usually rely on a doctor's written report to evaluate a claimant's disability. Should the adjuster doubt the alleged disability, the claimant can be examined by a physician of the adjuster's choosing. An independent medical exam can always be obtained when a case is in suit. If not, the claimant might consent. Those who refuse to consent should raise the adjuster's suspicions.

Earnings are easily verified for a claimant who receives a salary or works regular hours for wages. The claimant's employer can verify earnings, or the claimant's tax returns can be used as evidence. Earnings of self-employed claimants and claimants who own their own businesses are more difficult to determine. Tax returns can be helpful, but business conditions for such claimants change yearly. The issue in every case is what the claimant would have earned during the period of disability, not what was earned just prior. It may be necessary to contact customers and clients of the claimant or to hire an accountant to review the claimant's books. A businessowner's lost time is especially difficult to evaluate because the business can often carry on temporarily without the owner.

Evaluation of General Damages

General damages are highly subjective, but they are the largest, and thus most important, element of damages in injury claims. Adjusters, claimant attorneys, and claimants often do not agree about how to evaluate general damages. Nevertheless, they regularly negotiate and settle claims involving general damages.

Both sides of an injury claim face the same pressure. If they cannot agree with the other side on an amount to settle the claim, a jury or judge will eventually evaluate the case. For a claimant, the jury's evaluation may be less than the insurer was offering before trial. For an adjuster, the jury's evaluation may be more than the claimant was willing to accept before trial. The possibility of a relatively bad outcome at trial, in addition to the expense, effort, and trouble of a trial, is a powerful incentive for both sides to negotiate.

Assuming liability is unquestioned, general damages are generally considered to be several times as great as special damages. Some adjusters only consider medical expense (often referred to as "medical specials") in determining a multiple for general damages and then add in the unmultiplied amount of lost earnings. Other adjusters multiply all specials.

The multiple-of-specials approach to general damages is often condemned as inappropriate in most cases. It has no logical basis nor any "official" recognition in case law. Nevertheless, both claimant attorneys and adjusters widely practice it.

The nature of the injury is a significant factor in determining general damages. Pain and suffering, disability, and disruption of daily routine are considered as relatively more or less severe for various injuries. For example, a broken tibia (the weight-bearing bone of the lower leg) is widely regarded as worse than a broken wrist, even of the dominant hand. Likewise, scars on the face are widely considered worse than scars on the abdomen.

In ordinary cases, loss of consortium is not usually evaluated separately. It may be regarded as worth some fraction of the value of the underlying injury. In more serious cases, the loss of consortium may be significant and worth a separate evaluation. It is difficult to defend a claim for consortium unless there is a separation or divorce pending.

Property Damage

In some respects, determining damages in property damage liability cases is easier than in first-party claims. The adjuster need not worry about deductibles, special sublimits, coinsurance, or damage being caused by both covered and noncovered causes.

The law allows a deduction for depreciation from replacement cost. Determining depreciation can be as complex as it is in first-party claims. The adjuster must consider physical wear and tear; obsolescence because of fashion, seasonal, and technological changes; market value; and any other relevant factors. However, as in first-party claims, depreciation may be negligible, and a replacement cost settlement may be appropriate in many cases.

One important difference between first-party claims and property damage liability claims is that the property owner's own negligence is irrelevant in first-party claims, but it can be a major factor in settling liability claims. In contributory negligence jurisdictions, the owner's fault in causing the loss is a complete bar to recovery. In comparative negligence jurisdictions, the owner's fault reduces the recovery by a proportionate percentage or may even completely bar recovery.

A property damage claimant is in a relatively weaker bargaining position with the adjuster than a bodily injury claimant because of the smaller or more definite value of property damage claims and the expense of litigating them. Some restrictions on adjusters exploit this situation. For example, adjusters do not wish to incur unnecessary legal expense. If liability and value are clear, most adjusters prefer to pay the claim and close their file rather than litigate. Claims managers strongly discourage having a property damage claim go into suit, and such a suit would be closely scrutinized to see whether the adjuster had neglected to make legitimate settlement efforts. Furthermore, the Unfair Claims Settlement Practices Act, a version of which is in effect in most states, requires adjusters to attempt settlement when liability is reasonably clear and forbids stalling on the settlement of one claim to influence the settlement of another. This latter rule is especially applicable to auto accident cases in which the property damage claim may be ready for settlement while the bodily injury case is still a long way from being complete.

Many property damage liability cases first appear as subrogation claims from other insurers. The adjuster for the liability insurer should respond to the claim like an adjuster would respond to a claimant. Should the adjusters for the respective insurers be unable to negotiate a settlement, the claim may be resolved by intercompany arbitration. As mentioned in Chapter 14, the Property Subrogation Arbitration Agreement covers most first-party subrogation claims. The Nationwide Inter-Company Arbitration Agreement covers subrogation of auto physical damage claims. The arbitrators in these cases decide issues of both liability and damages, and their decision is not appealable. The vast majority of insurers in the United States subscribe to these agreements.

Negotiation and Settlement

Everything an adjuster does on a claim should be directed towards settlement. The vast majority of liability claims are settled without going into suit. The vast majority of claims that go into suit are settled before trial. Settling liability claims is the most valuable service liability claims adjusters perform for policyholders, claimants, insurers, and society. The courts would be overwhelmed if even a small percentage of cases that are settled were tried. It is also in the best interests of the insurers for adjusters to settle liability claims. Insurers would pay more in legal fees and verdict amounts than they would pay in settlements if they were to try all the claims that they could settle.

An insurer's obligation to settle claims arises out of its duty to defend and indemnify its insured. Both the insurer and the claimant face pressure to settle without litigation or trial. The negotiation process may seem like a game to outsiders, but failure has its repercussions. Once negotiations are completed, claims can be settled in several ways.

Duty To Settle

Liability policies usually give insurers the right to settle claims, but they do not express a duty to settle because insurers may want to litigate a case to conclusion. The insurer must have the right to litigate in order to protect itself against frivolous, fraudulent, or unfounded claims. The threat that a claim may be litigated probably keeps many dubious claims from ever being asserted.

Adjusters tend to believe that settling claims is expedient and in the best interests of policyholders and claimants. However, a legal obligation to settle arises when the value of a liability claim approaches, or clearly exceeds, the insured's policy limit.

Policyholders buy liability insurance for peace of mind. Almost nothing disturbs that peace of mind as much as being party to a lawsuit and enduring a court trial. Even if they are ultimately successful, most people are unsettled by the experience of a trial. A settlement shields the insured from this experience. Indeed, a settlement protects the insured from even being sued. Policyholders generally want claims to be handled without troubling or involving them too much. Since settling is also in the best interest of the insurer, it seems to be the best option for all concerned.

When the value of a claim approaches or exceeds the insured's policy limit, making settlement becomes a legal obligation and is no longer just good judgment. The insurer, rather than the policyholder, controls the defense and settlement of a claim. If a verdict exceeds the insured's policy limit, however, the insured would have to pay the excess. This situation creates a potential conflict. Absent a duty to settle the claim and once the value of the claim approaches or exceeds the policy limit, the insurer has little to lose by trying the case to verdict. The insurer might be surprised by a low verdict. If not, the policyholder will end up paying everything over the policy limit.

To prevent insurers from exploiting this situation and gambling with the policyholder's fortunes, courts have required insurers to make reasonable efforts to settle within policy limits and to accept settlement offers within policy limits whenever the value of a claim exceeds the limits. An insurer that rejects a settlement offer within policy limits does so at its own risk. Although courts have not made insurers absolutely liable for excess verdicts following the rejection of a settlement, convincing a court that the excess verdict was unforeseeable after it has been rendered is difficult. If a court thinks an insurer unreasonably rejected settlement, it will probably hold the insurer responsible for the excess amount. This type of action against insurers is known as a **bad faith claim**.

Pressures To Negotiate

As mentioned, both sides to a claim are pressured to negotiate by the possibility of a worse outcome at trial. This pressure is probably more strongly felt by insurers than by claimants, except when claimants face a serious risk of a defense verdict.

Even claimants who face little chance of losing at trial overwhelmingly prefer to settle than to litigate. Indeed, the typical liability claimant probably underestimates his or her claim for settlement; claimants typically settle for less than they could reasonably expect after trial. This is probably true because claimants are far less able than insurers to risk an adverse result and because claimant attorneys make much more money for their time by settling cases than by trying them.

For most liability claimants, a claim may be a once-in-a-lifetime event. The claimant's injury may be a major trauma for that person. Claimants make an enormous emotional investment in their claims and can be devastated by an adverse result at trial. An adverse result need not even be a complete loss, but simply a verdict amount much less than anticipated. In contrast, each claim is just one more case for insurers, a piece of business to be disposed of as readily as possible. With such differing emotional investments, claimants and insurers will approach settlement differently. Claimants are generally much less willing to risk a bad result than are insurers.

Claimant attorneys and defense attorneys face similar professional pressures. It is almost always in their clients' best interests to settle. Yet in order to develop their professional skills and present a credible threat to the other side, they must gain trial experience. Trying cases, however, is enormously stressful. Juries are very unpredictable, clients can be very unforgiving, and professional reputations can be made or destroyed by a single case. In addition, during the course of a trial, the attorneys spend all day in court and then must return to their offices for a full day's work. It is no wonder that many attorneys seem eager to settle cases and that many so-called trial attorneys rarely try cases.

In addition to the possibility of a negative result, adjusters are very highly motivated to limit and control legal expense. Both claims department management and corporate management closely monitor legal expenses. Adjusters are reprimanded for allowing cases to go into suit unnecessarily and for failing to pursue settlement throughout the course of litigation.

Negotiation Strategies

In the settlement of a typical claim, negotiations begin with a demand by the claimant's attorney for a specific sum of money. The opening demand is usually a very high evaluation of the case. The adjuster will sometimes make the opening settlement offer to "adjust" the attorney's expectations. Usually, however, the adjuster responds to the attorney's demand with a settlement offer that is a lower evaluation of the case. The attorney and the adjuster discuss the merits of their case and the weaknesses of the other side's case and exchange further counterdemands and counteroffers. If they believe they can settle, they continue to negotiate until they agree on a specific settlement amount. With an unrepresented claimant, the adjuster is much more likely to make the first settlement offer. Claimants are often bewildered by or uncomfortable with the negotiation process. Typically, adjusters must establish trust and should try to make realistic initial offers with unrepresented claimants. Thereafter, if the claimant and the adjuster believe they can agree on a settlement, they continue to discuss the case until they reach settlement.

Neither adjusters nor attorneys consider willingness to negotiate a weakness. Both sides know that the vast majority of cases settle. Anyone who avoids or refuses negotiations looks inexperienced or disorganized. Good negotiators can take strong positions and encourage the other side to continue the process.

Proper preparation and intelligent evaluation of a claim are essential prerequisites to good negotiating. Proper preparation consists of the adjuster's investigation and documentation of liability and damages. The final step of proper preparation is the adjuster's review of the file to ensure that he or she can discuss all aspects of the case. Simultaneously, the adjuster must evaluate the claim intelligently. The adjuster should determine both a good first offer and a probable range of settlement. Every adjuster can settle cases without consultation only up to a specified dollar limit. Beyond that limit, the adjuster must obtain settlement authority from higher level personnel. Requests for settlement authority are usually presented in writing and summarize the facts, the liability picture, the injuries, and the special damages.

Adjusters wish to communicate several messages with their first offer and throughout the negotiation process. They wish to communicate an intelligent evaluation of the case; nothing discredits an adjuster faster than being obviously unaware of the value of a claim. They also wish to communicate their confidence in their position and their willingness to litigate the case. In this respect, both the adjuster and the insurer should have experience litigating cases. The adjuster must also be sure that a credible defense attorney is involved should the case already be in suit. Finally, it is important to communicate some flexibility in one's position. Undervaluing a case and inflexibility risk stalling the negotiations and incurring needless litigation expense. On the other hand, overly generous offers and concessions may make an opponent overly optimistic and inflexible.

Most adjusters and attorneys negotiate cooperatively and constructively. Such a negotiation style is safe and effective. Nevertheless, this is not the only style of negotiation. Some parties negotiate in a hostile, competitive, and belligerent manner, which can also be effective but is much riskier. Hostile, competitive negotiating works when it destroys the confidence of an opponent or extracts concessions from an opponent who wants to placate his or her adversary. The danger of hostile negotiating is that it can destroy the negotiation process. Since both sides benefit from negotiated settlements, most attorneys and adjusters prefer to avoid a hostile style.

Settlement Techniques

Most claims are settled with a general release, in which the claimant releases the insured of all liability for the accident in question and the insurer agrees to pay the claimant the agreed settlement amount. Other types of releases exist to handle particular situations, such as those concerning joint tortfeasors and minors. Those were discussed in Chapter 13 along with other settlement tools.

In cases of claims by married individuals, the claimant's spouse should also be a party to the release to dispose of his or her consortium claim. In cases in which suit has been filed, the settlement must include dismissal of the suit by the claimant. This can be done by the claimant's attorney, who files a simple notice in the court records that the case has been settled.

Claims are usually settled with a lump-sum payment. Sometimes, the settlement instead calls for payments at both the time of settlement and into the future. These are called **structured settlements**. Structured settlements are usually made on high-value claims, but there is no minimum-size claim below which they are inappropriate. Structured settlements are especially useful when the claimant is likely to experience regular damages into the future, such as loss of income, or when the claimant is likely to squander a large settlement. Experience shows that most claimants tend to squander large settlements.

Structured settlements are attractive to insurers because they enable them to offer more dollars in the total settlement at a lower present cost than with a lump-sum payment. This is true because insurers can fund their future obligations with annuities purchased from other insurers, usually life insurance companies. The present cost of an annuity is less than what the annuity will pay in the future.

Many insurers use **advance payments** to control claimants and to discourage them from hiring attorneys. Advance payments are made as the claimant incurs medical or other expense. They are paid without receiving a release in return, but the claimant must sign a receipt acknowledging payment and that the advance payments will count towards final settlement.

Some insurers practice **walk-away settlements**, in which the insurer pays the claimant a lump-sum settlement and takes no release. These settlements are most appropriate in smaller claims. The insurers that advocate this practice consider it excellent public relations, assertive claims handling, and encouragement to claimants not to consider bringing suit. In cases in which the claimant does sue, the insurer is entitled to credit for what it has paid.

Litigation

All liability claims adjusters should be familiar with litigation. Ultimately, courts will determine both liability and damages for any claim that is not settled. Claimants may have to go to court to obtain compensation. Insurers and adjusters must understand how courts operate and how courts balance the rights and interests of plaintiffs and defendants.

Defense of lawsuits is a significant aspect of the protection policyholders buy through liability insurance policies. Insurers have both the right and the duty to defend the policyholder. Adjusters must understand and properly handle this right and duty.

The conduct of lawsuits is governed by **civil procedure**, that part of the law that establishes rules for litigation in civil cases. Adjusters must understand civil procedure in order to contribute to case strategy and to control defense attorney conduct.

Since attorney fees are a major expense for liability insurers, adjusters implement a variety of controls designed to moderate legal expense. Thus, adjusters must simultaneously make sure the insured is properly defended, develop strategy, direct litigation, and manage legal expense. Properly handling litigation is one of the most challenging tasks within claims work and one of the most important of any insurance jobs.

Role of Courts in Resolving Claims

Although the majority of claims are settled before suit is filed and the majority of suits are settled before trial, the courts play an essential role in settling claims. Without the courts, there would be no incentive to negotiate. Policyholders could not be held legally liable without a determination from the courts. Insurers would not be needed to protect policyholders without the threat of legal liability.

Nevertheless, courts are not fast, inexpensive, or predictable. Claimants who might otherwise rely on courts to determine their rights against policyholders have an incentive to negotiate. Claimants who do rely on courts find that they wait many years, spend considerable sums on legal expense, and often end up with a result no better than they could have gotten in settlement.

The psychological effects of litigation tend to mount as time goes by, thus increasing incentives to settle. Leading up to trial, the pace of depositions and motions usually increases. These pretrial matters place great stress on the parties and their attorneys and give everyone involved a taste of what trial will be like. Following pretrial efforts, many parties conclude that they would prefer a settlement for a sure amount, with relief from the aggravation and stress of litigation, to the uncertain and difficultly obtained outcome a trial would provide.

The values that attorneys and adjusters place on cases derive from actual results of cases litigated to conclusion. Cases that are litigated to conclusion therefore have important effects on all other cases. Although only a small percentage of cases are decided by court verdicts, those verdicts influence the price of all cases.

Duty To Defend

In addition to paying amounts for which the insured is legally liable (up to policy limits), insurance companies are also obligated to defend their policyholders against suits. This protection is a very valuable aspect of liability insurance. In many cases, the insurance company's duty to defend is more important to the policyholder than the duty to indemnify. The insurance company may have to spend exorbitant amounts defending a case if the case cannot be settled.

Many cases take a long time and a great deal of effort to settle. Other cases cannot be settled at all and are concluded by a trial and verdict. In both of these types of cases, legal expense can be extraordinary. Thousands and then tens of thousands of dollars of legal expense can quickly accumulate on very ordinary cases, such as auto accidents and premises liability claims. Complex cases can result in legal expenses well into six figures.

Cases can be difficult to settle because of unreasonableness on the part of plaintiffs or defendants. Plaintiffs may make settlement demands that are so unreasonably high that the insurer for the defendant is not even tempted to settle. Likewise, insurers can make settlement offers that are far below what the plaintiff is likely to win in a trial or can simply fail to evaluate a case meaningfully. (Usually, once a case is in suit, the defense attorney hired by the insurer will realistically evaluate the case, even if the claims adjuster has failed to do so.) Another type of suit that is difficult to settle involves cases of multiple codefendants, all of whom insist they have no liability and refuse to offer anything. Complete mutual refusal by a group of codefendants to offer any settlement can ruin negotiations, even in cases involving clearly innocent and severely injured plaintiffs. The better practice, in such cases, is for the defendants to work in concert to settle the plaintiff's claim and then to arbitrate or to negotiate their respective shares of liability for the settlement. Unfortunately, this rational approach is often difficult to adopt because of the number of claims adjusters and attorneys involved.

The insurer's duty to defend is especially important in cases that are frivolous, fraudulent, or without merit. Absent the insurer's duty to defend, plaintiffs would be in a strong position to coerce settlements from defendants who lack the resources or the ability to resist lawsuits. In claims involving insurance coverage, plaintiffs face an opponent with tremendous resources and experience in defending lawsuits: the insurance company. When insurers defend frivolous suits to a verdict, they spend far more on defense than on indemnification of the claim. When insurers settle frivolous suits, they usually do so because settling saves an equal or a greater amount of legal expense.

The insurer's duty to defend is also its right. The insurer can select the defense attorney, and the insured is then obligated to cooperate with whichever attorney is chosen. As long as it is solely liable for the claim, the insurer can dictate defense strategy. The insurer can unilaterally decide to settle or to continue the defense of a claim. Although the defense attorney is professionally obligated to serve the insured's interests above all, the insurer pays the defense attorney and is thus able to dictate all defense decisions. As long as the insured is not financially exposed to the claim, the defense attorney will take direction from the insurer. Taking direction from the insurer in this situation does not compromise the insured's interest, as long as the defense attorney is not involved in matters in which the insured and insurer may be adverse, such as a coverage issue. Defense attorneys hired to defend the insured should never be used to advise the insurer on coverage in the same case.

The insurer's right and duty to defend lawsuits is complicated in cases in which coverage is doubtful or in which part of the case is clearly not covered. The general rule is that an insurer must provide defense to an *entire* claim whenever a plaintiff's allegations in *any part* of the claim are covered. Coverage applies according to the plaintiff's allegations, not according to the merits of the case. Otherwise, policyholders would be without coverage when they need it the most—when faced with unfounded claims. However, plaintiffs often assert claims that are clearly not covered (such as intentional wrongdoing) in the same lawsuit as claims that are covered (such as ordinary negligence) or assert claims that may not be covered at all (for example, a case in which it is doubtful whether the injury or damage occurred during the policy period). In these cases, the insurer must defend the entire lawsuit, but the policyholder has a right to involve an attorney of the policyholder's choosing at the policyholder's expense. When two attorneys are involved in the defense, the attorney selected by the insurer will have the right to control the case as long as the insurer's money is at stake. The insurance company's attorney will attempt to involve and get the approval of the policyholder's private counsel in all major decisions. Should the insurance company's attorney ever disagree with the policyholder's private attorney, the insurer is likely to be financially responsible for any consequences.

Civil Procedure

Court cases proceed according to rules of civil procedure. Although details may vary somewhat by state and county, the basic framework of civil procedure is the same throughout the United States. The principal stages of a lawsuit are pleadings, discovery, motions, trial, and appeal.

Pleadings

The **pleadings** are papers filed with the court clerk in which each side tells its story. A lawsuit is initiated with either a **summons**, a simple notice to the defendant that suit has been filed, or a **complaint**, a listing of allegations in which the plaintiff sets forth his or her case. Jurisdictions vary as to the extent of detail required in a complaint, but in all jurisdictions a complaint must notify the defendant of the nature of the case. Within a specified time, usually twenty or thirty days, the defendant must file an **answer** in which the defendant responds to each of the plaintiff's allegations and may raise affirmative defenses. The defendant may join additional defendants by filing a **cross-complaint** in the same manner that the plaintiff filed and served the initial complaint against other parties who may be ultimately responsible for the defendant's cause of action. Additional defendants must file an answer to the cross-complaint. The initial pleadings that join a party to a suit, whether a summons, complaint, or cross-complaint, are served on the party (usually personally) by a court officer called the "sheriff." Sheriff's deputies may likewise serve court papers. In the federal courts, this task is performed by U.S. marshals. Thereafter, court rules usually allow papers to be served by private parties or through the mail.

Discovery

Once all parties have filed their pleadings, the issues in a case are clear, and discovery can begin. **Discovery** is the formal process by which each party obtains the evidence and information known to the other parties. Discovery may be by written **interrogatories**, a series of questions the other party must answer in writing; by **deposition**, a session of oral questions and answers that are recorded by a court reporter; by **requests for documents**, whenever documentary evidence is at issue; or by **requests for admission**, written statements that the receiving party must either accept or dispute. Since depositions are the most expensive and time-consuming form of discovery, most attorneys prefer to first use the other forms of discovery to narrow the issues. Nevertheless, depositions are usually essential to the preparation of a case. Discovery may also include a right of inspection, whenever the physical makeup of an object or a place is important in a case, or a right of independent medical examination, whenever a party's health and physical condition are at issue. Once all discovery is complete, each side should thoroughly know the opposing side's case and what evidence the opposing side will use at trial.

Motions

Motions are not really a distinct phase of litigation, since they can occur at any point from the initiation of suit to the appeal. A **motion** is a formal request to the court for a decision or ruling. A motion can be narrow and specific, such as a request to the court to allow or disallow a specific item of discovery, or comprehensive, such as a request to the court to terminate the suit in favor of the moving party. An example of the latter is a **motion for summary judgment**, in which the moving party asks the court to decide the case in its favor, usually after only pleadings or discovery has been completed and before trial. A motion for summary judgment is essentially an argument that there are no real issues in the case and that, as a matter of law, the moving party is entitled to judgment.

Trial

Barring summary judgment or a settlement, a case goes to trial. At **trial**, each side presents its evidence and has the opportunity to cross-examine and counter the evidence of the other side. The trier of fact, either a judge or a jury, decides which party's case is more persuasive and renders a verdict accordingly. When a case is decided by jury, the judge explains to the jury the relevant law and explains what factual issues the jury must resolve.

Appeal

Following a verdict, the losing party can file an appeal. An **appeal** is a request to a higher court to overturn the trial decision. On appeal, the case is *not* heard again in its entirety. Only alleged errors of law, not issues of fact, may be argued on appeal. Examples of errors of law would be that inadmissible evidence was admitted or that the trial judge misstated the law to the jury. Occasionally, on appeal a party will ask the higher court to change the law or announce new law. Courts have the inherent power to change, add to, or interpret the law. Thus, the common law evolves. Common law is court-made law, as opposed to statutory law, which is enacted by legislatures. Since appeals can only succeed in cases of legal error, most trial verdicts are not appealed. The trial marks the end of most cases.

Control of Legal Expense

The defense of liability lawsuits is tremendously expensive. Consequently, insurers are extremely sensitive to legal expense and have adopted a number of strategies to control it. Adjusters are responsible for implementing and enforcing those strategies.

Most claims departments use only certain preapproved law firms to defend liability suits. Those law firms usually specialize in insurance defense work and are familiar with the types of cases insurance companies have and their needs. In exchange for a volume of business, such law firms will usually work at a somewhat lower hourly rate than other attorneys and law firms with comparable skills and experience.

Claims departments usually require monthly or quarterly bills on active cases. These bills must be broken down by tenth or quarter-hour segments and must show exactly which attorney did what work in the time billed. Adjusters or specialized legal auditing firms can check these detailed bills against the actual file and the attorney's original time sheets to verify all charges.

Many claims departments require law firms to submit budgets for each case or quote a fixed price for the entire case. Sometimes fixed prices can be established for predictable work, such as completing pleading (such as the complaint and answer in a lawsuit) or conducting a deposition. Many claims departments require adjusters to preapprove all depositions or motions. Adjusters must have a sophisticated understanding of trial evidence and strategy in order to exert such controls in a way that does not jeopardize the defense.

Ultimately, the best control of legal expense is complete avoidance of the legal process. Adjusters should settle cases that can be settled before they go into suit or before discovery and trial have caused enormous expenses to accumulate.

Alternative Dispute Resolution

For various reasons, potential litigants are often unable to resolve their disputes without the assistance of a third party. Traditionally, the courts were used in this role to resolve conflicts. The rising costs of allowing the courts to decide these cases and the enormous backlog of cases in the court system have caused potential litigants to search for alternative ways of resolving their disputes. **Alternative dispute resolution (ADR)** is an all-encompassing term used to refer to any number of methods for settling claims outside the traditional court system. The most common ADR forums are negotiation, mediation, arbitration, appraisals, mini-trials, and pre-trial settlement conferences. The courts have recently annexed some of these forums as a way of relieving the backlog of cases in the court system.

The most effective way of controlling litigation expenses is to resolve the dispute before litigation. Negotiation is the principal form of resolving claims outside litigation. **Negotiation** involves discussing all issues and arriving at a mutually satisfactory disposition of the case. Litigation is sometimes the sign of a poorly functioning negotiation process. Because of improper training or supervision, a claims representative might make inadequate offers to claimants. Claimant attorneys might also abuse the legal system by filing frivolous lawsuits in the hope of receiving a settlement because of the sheer "nuisance value" of the claim. Claim supervisors and managers should monitor the negotiation process to ensure that it is working properly. If the parties in dispute have acted in good faith, they should have fully explored the possibilities of resolution by direct negotiation before commencing a lawsuit.

When direct negotiations fail, disputants may turn to mediation. **Mediation** can be thought of as a negotiation conference with a referee, called a mediator. In mediation, the parties in dispute present their case to the mediator, whose role is to facilitate an amicable resolution. The mediator will listen to each side present its case, point out the weaknesses in the arguments or in the evidence presented, propose alternative solutions, and help improve the relationship between the participants. The mediator does not normally decide the case for the parties but instead assists the parties in reaching a mutually agreed settlement. The fact that both sides must agree with the ultimate outcome makes mediation an attractive choice for disputants. The downside to mediation is that disputes sometimes do not get resolved. The opposing parties must then, after investing time and money in mediation, consider some other ADR forum or litigation.

In **arbitration**, the participants present their cases to a disinterested third party (the arbitrator) who acts as a judge (and in many cases is an active or a retired judge) in weighing the facts presented and making a decision based on the evidence. The advantage to arbitration is that a decision is made. Whether the participants must accept this decision depends on the type of arbitration agreement the parties entered into. Binding arbitration requires the participants to accept the arbitrator's decision. In nonbinding arbitration, neither party is compelled to accept the decision of the arbitrator. However, the arbitrator's decision provides the "winner" with leverage in future negotiations. Arbitration Forums Inc. is one well-known national organization that is used by insurance companies to resolve intercompany disputes. Its most popular forum is the Nationwide Inter-Company Arbitration Agreement, which is used to resolve automobile subrogation claims.

Appraisals are a unique form of ADR. (They should not be confused with the damage estimates of an automobile or a property damage appraiser.) An appraisal, in this context, is a method of resolving disputes between insurance companies and their policyholders. The process of the appraisal and its scope are specifically described in the policy. Exhibit 15-1 shows the appraisal provision from the ISO HO-3 policy. The appraisal provision is designed to resolve disputes over the *amount owed* on a covered loss, but it is not used to determine whether coverage exists.

Exhibit 15-1
Appraisal Provision From ISO HO-3 Policy

Appraisal. If you and we fail to agree on the amount of loss, either may demand an appraisal of the loss. In this event, each party will choose a competent appraiser within 20 days after receiving a written request from the other. The two appraisers will choose an umpire. If they cannot agree upon an umpire within 15 days, you or we may request that the choice be made by a judge of a court of record in the state where the "residence premises" is located. The appraisers will separately set the amount of loss. If the appraisers submit a written report of an agreement to us, the amount agreed upon will be the amount of loss. If they fail to agree, they will submit their differences to the umpire. A decision agreed to by any two will set the amount of loss.

Each party will:

a. Pay its own appraiser; and

b. Bear the other expenses of the appraisal and umpire equally.

Copyright, Insurance Services Office, Inc., 1990.

Mini-trials or **summary jury trials** closely resemble the traditional legal system in that representatives (usually attorneys) present an abbreviated version of their case to a jury. The decision of the jury can be binding or nonbinding, depending on the agreement. The rules of evidence and procedure law will normally coincide with that of traditional courts. Critics argue that there is little cost savings achieved with this forum. The main advantage is that the litigants do not have to wait months or years to have their cases heard.

A **pre-trial settlement conference** is an ADR forum that almost all states now require. The conferences are sanctioned by the court and are normally conducted by the judge who is presiding over the case. In these cases, a lawsuit has already been filed. The purpose of the settlement conference is to force litigants to make one last effort to resolve the case in lieu of going to trial. The judge's role is similar to that of a mediator, but sometimes the judge will subtly express to the litigants his opinion of their positions.

Challenges Facing Specific Types of Liability Claims

The adjuster's general duties to investigate; to determine coverage, liability, and damages; and to settle are present in all liability claims. The challenges that exist in performing these duties vary by claim. General principles of liability and damages apply somewhat differently to different factual settings.

The remainder of this chapter describes the challenges that exist in various types of liability claims. This section first addresses auto bodily injury and auto physical damage, the two most common liability claims. It then discusses claims arising out of premises, operations, and products, the situations typically covered by general liability insurance. This section concludes by addressing the specialized areas of workers compensation claims, professional liability claims, and environmental and toxic tort claims.

Auto Bodily Injury

Auto accidents are the most common type of liability claim. Nevertheless, auto accidents can cause some of the worst injuries and most expensive claims. New adjusters begin in auto claims because there are, fortunately, a majority of relatively minor claims and because the liability principles are so well known.

Although auto claims are a traditional training ground for liability adjusters, auto claims can be complicated in regard to coverage; accident reconstruction; and coordination with no-fault, workers compensation, and uninsured motorists claims.

Coverage Problems

Analysis of coverage is simple only when the accident involves the named insured as the driver and a vehicle specifically listed on the policy. More complicated are situations in which the named insured, or some other insured, has coverage while driving a vehicle not listed on the policy or when someone other than the named insured is using a covered vehicle.

Usually, when an insured is driving the vehicle of another, that other vehicle's coverage covers any loss. However, the other vehicle's coverage sometimes does not apply or is inadequate. In the event of the insolvency of the vehicle's insurance company or the exclusion of coverage for any reason, the insurance company for the driver must be prepared to take over the claim. Adjusters who "inherit" cases under these circumstances often find the investigation and other control of the case completely absent.

Inadequate policy limits are more common than the inapplicability of the vehicle's coverage. The adjuster working for the driver's insurer may adopt different strategies, depending on the circumstances. If the underlying coverage is far less than the value of the case, the adjuster for the driver's insurer should become heavily involved in the case or should take over its handling. If the underlying coverage is adequate to pay the claim, the adjuster for the driver's insurer is likely to take a less active role.

Accident Reconstruction

The facts of most auto accidents are not difficult to ascertain. The points of impact on each vehicle indicate at what angle and from what direction the two vehicles came into contact. The extent of damage to the vehicles provides some indication of the speeds of the vehicles. The parties to an accident usually differ more over how blameworthy they think each party is than over what happened. Fortunately, for adjusters, there are clear right-of-way rules when two vehicles converge on the roads. Also, whenever the parties disagree about what happened, adjusters or accident reconstruction experts may be able to determine the facts.

Accident reconstruction experts are most helpful in determining the speed of a vehicle and what a driver should have been able to see at the time of an accident.

Vehicle speed is determined by examining skid marks and vehicle damage. Skid marks are reliable indicators of speed because once the brakes are locked, vehicles will stop according to their weight, the road grade, the road surface, and speed. All of these factors except speed are known or can be precisely measured following an accident. When, instead of coming to a complete halt, a vehicle collides with another vehicle, an accident reconstruction expert can determine that the vehicle was traveling no slower than a certain speed based on the skid marks. This information may be sufficient to disprove a party's statements or to establish liability. The point at which skid marks begin can establish when and where the driver first reacted to a danger, an essential piece of evidence when driver inattention is an issue.

Accident reconstruction experts can also determine what a driver should have been able to see just before impact. The exact time of day and weather conditions at the time of the accident can usually be established. The driver's lines of sight can be determined according to the type of vehicle and the height of the driver. The effects on visibility of curves or hills in the roadway are also considered. All of this information can be combined to determine whether a driver reacted promptly to a hazard or was slow and inattentive. That determination is essential in cases in which the driver alleges a sudden and unavoidable emergency or in which the claimant's comparative negligence is at issue. Comparative negligence is frequently an important issue in auto accident cases. In many cases, the policyholder may be primarily at fault, but the claimant is also substantially negligent for failing to respond to a hazard.

Coordination With No-Fault and Workers Compensation

An adjuster handling auto liability claims must frequently deal with other insurers that provide no-fault or workers compensation benefits to an injured claimant. The presence of another insurer can be either helpful or problematic to a liability claims adjuster.

Another insurer can provide the adjuster with detailed medical information. The adjuster can stay abreast of the claimant's injuries on a regular basis in order to be sure that the liability claim reserves for the case are adequate. The other insurer may provide medical information because it has a subrogation claim for the amount of the medical expense. In jurisdictions in which subrogation is possible, the other insurer is obligated to submit medical information to support its claim.

Difficulties may arise between the adjuster and the other insurer whenever subrogation rights do not exist or comparative negligence is an important issue. In the absence of subrogation rights, the other insurer should not turn over to the adjuster any medical information about the claimant without an authorization. Eventually, the claimant must reveal medical information to the adjuster, but the claimant is likely to want control over any such release. As a professional courtesy, another adjuster may be willing to comment on the adequacy of the liability claim reserves, but the other adjuster might be accused of invading the claimant's privacy should any real medical information be revealed.

Uninsured Motorists Claims

Policyholders purchase uninsured motorists (UM) coverage to protect themselves against motorists who fail to carry liability insurance. An awkward aspect of the coverage is that the policyholder must be treated in the same manner as a claimant; the uninsured motorist is often an unavailable and uncooperative party who must be treated like an "insured." Denying a claim under uninsured motorists coverage might have immediate legal ramifications for the insurer that would not be present if the claimant were a third-party.

Attorney representation in an uninsured motorists claim is almost inevitable in many parts of the country. Once policyholders realize the opposing driver is uninsured, they assume that legal representation is essential. Unfortunately, dealing with the policyholder as a claimant leaves the adjuster with no favorable witness. The uninsured party is usually unavailable or uncooperative. A person who drives without insurance or causes hit-and-run accidents is usually not a credible witness, even if he or she is available and cooperative. Thus, uninsured motorists cases are extremely difficult to defend with respect to liability or on the basis of comparative negligence.

The adjuster has limited powers to defend uninsured motorists claims. In the event of any disagreement over the settlement amount, the policyholder can compel an arbitration. The arbitration is less expensive and time-consuming than litigation in the courts. Furthermore, arbitrators selected for these proceedings are usually attorneys who are aware that the claim involves the policyholder versus the insurance company. Arbitrators tend to give the policyholder the benefit of every doubt. Unfortunately, most adjusters believe that fraud and exaggeration are at least as common in uninsured motorists claims as they are in third-party liability claims.

In many states, uninsured motorists coverage is required to be purchased in order to meet state financial responsibility laws. As is the case with any statutorily required coverage, the claim representative must be aware that some exclusions and other policy provisions might contradict the statutes. Courts have ruled that whenever policy language and state law conflict, state law controls. For example, in some states requiring uninsured motorists coverage for every vehicle, courts take the position that policyholders should be entitled to stack the limits of liability. Thus, if an insured has three cars with $100,000 uninsured motorists coverage on each, then the insured would be entitled to a total of $300,000 coverage despite the fact that this was not permitted by policy wording. Claim representatives must therefore be familiar with any state laws that might affect the coverage interpretation of the claims they are handling.

Underinsured Motorists Coverage

Uninsured motorists coverage rarely applies to claims in which the responsible motorist has some liability insurance coverage, even if that coverage is woefully inadequate. Because states' minimum liability limit requirements have not kept pace with rising medical costs, insurance companies have offered underinsured motorists (UIM) coverage to help counter that problem. The ISO Underinsured Motorists Coverage endorsement PP 03 11 defines an "Underinsured motor vehicle" as "a land motor vehicle or trailer of any type to which a bodily injury liability bond or policy applies at the time of the accident but its limit for bodily injury liability is less than the limit of liability for this coverage."

The following provides an example of an underinsured motorist:

- Allen, a policyholder for Company A, has a $100,000 UIM policy. He is involved in an accident with Bob, a policyholder for Company B.
- Bob, who is responsible for the accident, has a $25,000 bodily injury limit on his PAP.
- Bob's motor vehicle would be considered "underinsured" with respect to Allen's UIM policy.

Using the same scenario, the following explains how UIM coverage applies in most states:

- Allen suffers bodily injury with $200,000 in damages.
- Allen collects $25,000, the bodily injury limit, from Bob's policy.
- The ISO UIM endorsement limits coverage by the following provision, ". . .the limit of liability shall be reduced by all sums paid because of the 'bodily injury' by or on behalf of persons or organization who may be legally responsible. . . ." So, Allen is entitled to $75,000 from his own UIM coverage (Allen's $100,000 UIM limit *minus* Bob's $25,000 bodily injury limit).

The purpose of the UIM coverage is to guarantee the policyholder a specific limit of protection (in this example, $100,000). In this scenario, Allen would be left uncompensated for his damages over $100,000. For that reason, courts in some states have construed the policy wording differently in order to provide additional coverage above the liability limit collected from the responsible party's insurance policy. Courts that take this alternative view might find a total of $125,000 in compensation for Allen's injuries (Allen's $100,000 UIM limit *plus* Bob's $25,000 bodily injury limit).

Auto Physical Damage

Auto physical damage claims are not like liability injury claims, even when they are asserted by third parties. Many auto physical damage claims are, in any case, first-party claims. Claims departments usually have auto damage specialists handling auto damage claims. Determining damage in auto damage cases requires expert knowledge of auto body repair methods and costs.

Proper handling of auto damage cases is an essential part of good relations with both policyholders and third parties. Calculating constructive total losses correctly and obtaining agreed repair prices are key tasks in the proper adjustment of auto damage claims.

First-Party Claims

Proper handling of first-party auto damage claims is one of the most fundamental and important services insurers provide to their policyholders. Cars represent a significant investment without which the policyholder may have difficulty commuting to work or satisfying family needs.

Adjusters who handle first-party auto damage claims should contact the policyholder and arrange to inspect the vehicle promptly, explain the complete procedure, and remain in contact with the policyholder throughout the claims process should any problems develop. The adjuster should not require the policyholder to pursue a liability claim against another party who may be liable for the damage. Should the insurer successfully subrogate against a responsible party, the policyholder's deductible amount should be reimbursed promptly.

Policyholders are sometimes upset to learn that personal property lost when their car is stolen is not covered by their auto coverage. Adjusters should cite the language of the policyholder's auto and homeowners policies to explain the proper source of recovery. Policyholders are usually unhappy about absorbing two deductibles, especially when both coverages are through the same insurer.

Auto thefts represent a significant percentage of all claims that are suspicious. A claim denial can only be made upon proof that the policyholder had the motive and opportunity to stage the claim or upon proof that the policyholder still has the car. Adjusters who handle auto damage claims must guard against excessive suspiciousness. Real thefts of autos are more common than staged thefts.

Liability Claims

Adjusters handling third-party auto damage claims are much less prone to policy provisions and state insurance regulations dictating how they must act than when dealing with first-party claims. In addition, in liability claims, the adjuster can argue comparative negligence. Thus, although adjusters should handle first-party claims with a primary emphasis on customer service, they can adopt a more critical attitude on liability claims, should it be necessary.

Nevertheless, there are often good reasons to provide good service to liability claimants. If the claimant is injured, prompt, courteous service in handling the auto damage may prevent a bodily injury claim from being asserted. In cases in which the claimant is not injured, the law may require the adjuster to negotiate with the claimant. Although the law is not as solicitous of claimants as it is of insureds, adjusters cannot completely ignore the claimant when liability is clear. An adjuster is permitted to make good faith comparative negligence arguments but should be willing to negotiate with claimants.

Constructive Total Losses

Whenever the cost to repair a vehicle plus its remaining salvage value equals or exceeds the vehicle's pre-loss value, the vehicle is a **constructive total loss**. It is financially senseless to repair a constructive total loss, even if it is physically possible to make satisfactory repairs. By paying the pre-loss value of the vehicle and taking the salvage, the insurer pays less overall. For example, assume a car worth $3,500 before loss suffers $3,000 of damage and retains $1,000 of salvage value. Rather than pay $3,000 for repairs, the insurer should pay $3,500 for the title to the car and obtain $1,000 in the salvage market, for a net loss of $2,500. Insurers have frequent contact with salvage dealers and are in a better position to dispose of salvage efficiently than is the average person.

Neither policyholders nor claimants are required to "sell" their cars to insurers, as the preceding example implies. Should the insured want to keep the car, the adjuster is entitled to take account of the salvage value. For example, using the numbers above, the actual cash value of the vehicle before loss ($3,500) minus the ACV of the vehicle following loss ($1,000) equals the amount of the loss ($2,500).

Agreed Repair Prices

If a vehicle can be repaired, the adjuster should obtain an agreed repair price with the body shop selected by the policyholder (or claimant). This agreement demonstrates that the adjuster's evaluation of the loss is legitimate and prevents disputes between the insurer and the auto owner or between the owner and the body shop. Although the adjuster should try to reach an agreed price, the choice of a body shop should be left to the vehicle owner.

Premises Liability

Businesses that regularly have the public on their premises, such as retail stores, restaurants, banks, and hotels, probably experience more premises claims than any other type of claim. Premises liability claims are usually relatively minor fall-down cases but are nevertheless important to both the claimant and the policyholder. Good and responsive handling of such claims can reduce their cost to the insurer and can preserve public goodwill towards the policyholder.

Adjusters handling premises cases must establish good rapport with the claimant, both to establish the cause of the accident and to determine comparative negligence. Witnesses and employees of the policyholder can often help the adjuster in these efforts.

Determining Cause of Accident

Legal liability in premises cases is determined by negligence theories. The claimant asserts that the policyholder failed to maintain the premises in a reasonably safe condition. Under the law of negligence, the policyholder should be judged by how a reasonably prudent person would behave under the same circumstances.

The standard of care for property owners is traditionally qualified by the claimant's status on the premises. An owner owes only slight care towards a trespasser, primarily a duty not to intentionally injure. An intermediate level of care is owed to licensees, a group that includes social guests, letter carriers, and solicitors. A property owner owes a high duty of care towards business invitees, those who are on the premises at the invitation of the owner to do business with the owner. This group includes the customers of the various businesses that regularly have members of the public on their premises. Some jurisdictions have moved away from this classification scheme, requiring instead that reasonable care is the duty owed to all. Nevertheless, in substance, the law of these jurisdictions may differ little from the traditional classifications. What is "reasonable" in each situation largely depends on the claimant's status on the property.

Upon learning that a customer has had an accident on the premises, most policyholders are genuinely solicitous of the injured person, both out of human decency and a sense of self-protection. Most policyholders want to preserve their customers' goodwill and forestall possible legal actions against them. Injuries to pride and dignity are as common as bodily injuries, and policyholders find that injured customers respond well to genuine concern. Some policyholders in these circumstances will insist that the customer be seen by a doctor and will promise to pay whatever medical expense is incurred.

Policyholders that take this approach should have medical payments coverage. Medical payments coverage is usually obtained for exactly this situation: taking care of a customer without regard for liability. Policyholders that do not have medical payments coverage probably violate their liability insurance policy conditions by making promises of payment, yet such promises do not usually cause trouble with insurers. If it will settle the case, adjusters are usually willing to pay for minor medical expense, regardless of fault, under liability coverage.

Maintaining rapport with claimants in premises cases is very important. A dissatisfied claimant who seeks legal representation will usually cost much more to settle with. Thus, most adjusters handling premises claims do not push liability issues if a case can be settled for medical expenses only.

When premises cases cannot be quickly and easily settled, liability issues are important. In the case of business invitees, the policyholder owes a high duty of care. Thus, almost any factor in the environment of the insured premises contributing to the accident could indicate negligence on the policyholder's part. The floor may be uneven, slightly defective, or too slippery. The lighting may be insufficient or the environment too distracting. The policyholder may have failed to warn the public of a hazard or to barricade the hazard. The policyholder may have failed to conduct sufficient inspections of the premises to be aware of a new hazard. Sometimes (but rarely) claimants fall down on smooth, even, dry, clear, well-lit, and unobstructed surfaces. Usually, the claimant can blame something for the accident.

Adjusters investigating premises cases should solicit statements from the claimant and all witnesses who can testify about either the accident or the condition of the accident scene. If the scene is substantially the same as when the accident occurred, the adjuster should take photos. The adjuster should also determine the policyholder's cleaning, maintenance, and inspection practices and should get copies of any logs or records of such. Should the policyholder use an independent contractor for cleaning or maintenance work, the adjuster should determine the scope of that contractor's duties, obtain copies of the contracts, and determine what role in the accident the contractor may have played.

Determining Comparative Negligence

With respect to liability for their accident, claimants in premises cases are often in a difficult position. Unless their accident was caused by a hidden hazard, claimants must usually admit that (1) they have no idea what caused their accident; (2) they know the cause, but failed to observe and avoid it; or (3) they were aware of and observed the cause before the accident but encountered it anyway. With respect to liability, these three alternatives amount to (1) no negligence on the policyholder's part; (2) comparative negligence on the claimant's part; or (3) assumption of the risk by the claimant. A common example of the first situation is a fall down smooth, even, well-lit stairs. Most policyholders that have the public on their premises maintain their stairways very well, and a fall on the stairs is usually the claimant's fault. An example of the second situation is the claimant who falls on an obvious hazard, such as debris on the floor. The defense of claims of this sort is weaker whenever something in the environment, such as a sales display, was a conspicuous distraction or whenever the hazard should have been known to the policyholder and eliminated before the accident. An example of the third situation is the claimant who voluntarily walks across an obvious hazard, such as a torn-up or icy sidewalk. The defense of this third situation will be weakened if the claimant had no choice. The assumption of the risk defense cannot be applied unless the claimant acted voluntarily.

The adjuster handling a premises case should get the claimant's statement as soon as possible. Immediately following an accident, a claimant is usually eager to talk about it and will often give candid statements that may suggest one of the above three defenses.

Operations

With respect to the liability theories and defenses that apply, claims arising out of a policyholder's operations are similar to premises cases. The key difference is that operations claims usually focus on some unsafe act rather than an unsafe condition. In addition, the policyholder in operations claims is typically a contractor rather than an establishment open to the public.

Bases of Liability

A policyholder's operations are alleged to be responsible for an accident whenever the accident results from an unsafe or improper act by the policyholder or the policyholder's employees; whenever the policyholder fails to properly supervise another party for which it is responsible; or whenever the policyholder has contractually assumed liability.

Construction sites and construction operations are inherently dangerous. Unsafe acts and conditions are common in this environment. As a result, many contractors and construction companies face very high costs for workers compensation and general liability insurance. Such organizations often devote great effort to safety, to control costs, to avoid unfortunate injuries, and to comply with OSHA. As a result, following an accident, the adjuster will often find that determination of liability is an extremely sensitive issue. The policyholder's workers may not be forthcoming, honest, and complete in response to the adjuster's inquiries. The policyholder's supervisors may be defensive, brusque, or irrational.

When investigating claims arising out of operations, the adjuster should begin by establishing exactly how the claimant's accident occurred. Exactly where did the accident occur? What workers were in the vicinity? Who employs and supervises these workers? Exactly what were these workers doing at the moment of the accident? What equipment were they operating? What did each of them see? Even in the face of evasion and reluctance from the witnesses, an adjuster can usually establish what happened through a thorough and methodical investigation.

A contractor may be responsible for its own employees as well as the supervision of others. Under many construction contracts, a general contractor has duties to ensure workplace safety, and individual contractors may be responsible for their own subcontractors. The duty to supervise may be an explicit contractual obligation, a custom of the trade that is implied in the contract, or required under general tort principles. When faced with a case of potential improper supervision, an adjuster will usually take the position that the primarily responsible party is the employer of the workers who caused the accident or its insurer. Nevertheless, the adjuster should thoroughly investigate what supervisory steps the policyholder actually took. Did the policyholder communicate with its subcontractors about safety? Did the policyholder conduct inspections, give warnings, withhold payments, or otherwise enforce safe practices?

Contractual Assumptions of Liability

In addition to their direct responsibility for their workers and their duty to supervise others, contractor-insureds are often liable for the faults of another because they have assumed liability by contract. Liability assumed by contract is different from liability for failure to supervise. When a contractor assumes liability for another, it is responsible for that other party's liabilities. In contrast, liability for failure to supervise is based on the contractor's own failures, not the failures or liabilities of another.

The legal interpretation of contractual assumptions of liability can be complex. Generally, courts recognize contractual assumptions of liability as valid but interpret them narrowly. An adjuster examining an assumption of liability clause must determine whether it requires defense and indemnity or just indemnity. Does the assumption of liability extend to all liabilities of the indemnified party or just liabilities that arise out of the indemnifying party's behavior? Does the assumption of liability extend to the owner of the project site or to subcontractors of the indemnified party? If the adjuster has any doubts about interpreting the assumption of liability clause, he or she should seek the advice of supervisors, managers, or counsel.

Insurance coverage for contractual assumptions of liability varies. Thus, adjusters with cases of contractual liability must check their policy wording very carefully. Again, if coverage is unclear or in doubt, the adjuster should seek an opinion from superiors or staff advisers and should issue a reservation of rights letter to the policyholder until the matter is resolved.

When an adjuster handles a case of assumed liability, the adjuster must investigate with the indemnified party and its employees as though it were the insured. If the indemnified party has been sued, the adjuster may consider providing for its defense, even if the contract does not strictly require it. If the adjuster's insurer must indemnify the party in question, it may be sensible to provide for its defense as well. Whether or not to do so is a question of company policy that may also depend on the strength of the case and the willingness of the party in question to relinquish control of its defense.

Preservation of Accident Scene

In a claim involving operations, the adjuster should immediately try to preserve the accident scene through photos, diagrams, and detailed measurements. Construction sites change rapidly, and witnesses' memories can become confused and vague.

In addition to preserving the precise scene of an accident, photos can provide many important incidental details. Photos can show the exact stage of the project at the time of the accident, including the exact stage of each subcontractor's work. Photos can show which contractors were on the scene on the day of the accident. Photos can also show the presence or absence of safety measures and precautions. On large or well-organized projects, the owner, architect, or general contractor may have daily records of progress, including photos.

Product Liability

Any party that manufactures or sells a product that causes harm to another may be liable for that harm. Products liability claims may be based on traditional negligence theories, but also on other bases. An adjuster handling products claims must investigate all possible bases of liability and all defenses that apply to those bases.

Bases of Liability

Other than traditional negligence theories, product liability may be based on breach of warranty or strict liability in tort.

A **warranty** is any contractual promise about the product that accompanies the sale. The warranty that guarantees performance or durability is one type of warranty. An alleged breach of warranty may be based on an express warranty (described below) or on a warranty implied by law. Many written sales contracts explicitly disclaim any warranties, express or implied, unless set forth in the written contract.

An **express warranty** is any explicit statement about the product that accompanies the sale. For example, a statement that reads, "These hedge clippers can easily cut through branches up to a quarter-inch thick," could be the basis of liability if the hedge clippers failed to so perform and caused damage as a result. Express warranties may allow a claimant to assert a products claim that might not be sustainable on negligence or strict liability grounds. In the absence of an express warranty, the principal advantage to claimants of a warranty suit is that the statute of limitations is usually longer than for tort-based claims.

Strict liability in tort differs from negligence, yet the factual investigation for each theory is similar. Under strict liability theory, the nature of the product is the issue, not the behavior of the defendant. Specifically, the issue is whether the product is "defective" in a way that makes it "unreasonably dangerous," not whether the defendant was negligent. Yet asking whether a product is "defective" is very much like asking whether it should have been made differently by the defendant, and determining whether a product is "unreasonably dangerous" depends on how much less dangerous it might have been made.

Identification of Product and Manufacturer

The defense of product liability claims is significantly different for manufacturers than for those who merely sell the product. If a wholesaler or retailer resells a product in the same condition in which it left the manufacturer, the manufacturer is responsible for indemnifying the wholesaler or retailer from any product liability claim. An adjuster handling claims for a wholesaler or retailer can usually withdraw from the claim once the manufacturer's insurer is involved. Nevertheless, since the wholesaler or retailer is liable as far as the public is concerned, an adjuster for a wholesaler or retailer should be prepared to handle the claim should the manufacturer be out of business, not identifiable, insolvent, uninsured, or unwilling for any reason to handle the claim. Usually, however, manufacturers want to defend their products and their retailers for business reasons, over and above the law.

The product in question must be carefully identified in order to verify the manufacturer. Many retailers sell products with a store label that are manufactured elsewhere. Many products have component parts that come from sources other than the assembling manufacturer. Unless the manufacturer can be identified, the retailer will be responsible to the claimant. A retailer can usually verify whether it sold a particular type of product at a particular time. The retailer can usually also identify the source from which it bought its merchandise.

Use of Experts

Once a product is identified, the issue of liability depends on whether the product could have been made safer otherwise and still perform its intended function. Some products are inherently dangerous. For example, power tools cannot perform their intended function without simultaneously being capable of severe bodily damage.

Determining liability in products cases often involves redesigning the product after the occurrence of an accident. The feasibility of redesign can only be determined through expert testimony. Both the plaintiff and the defendant must hire an engineer or other expert who can provide an opinion. Resolving product liability claims is thus very expensive. Most manufacturers consider the expense worthwhile, since they might face potentially millions of claims from every user of the same products. Since the policyholder has often been in the business for years, it can be a good source of references for design engineers. However, adjusters must consider any financial stake such an engineer may have in his or her relations with the policyholder and whether the engineer is defending his or her own design.

Review of Warnings and Instructions

Often, in product liability claims, the product itself cannot realistically be redesigned, so the plaintiff argues that the warnings and instructions that accompanied the product were inadequate and that the product was thus defective.

When faced with such an allegation, the adjuster must review all literature accompanying the product. The adjuster should determine whether the warnings and instructions provided, if followed, would have prevented the claimant's accident. If not, the adjuster should try to determine what additional warning would have been necessary to prevent the claimant's accident. In all such cases, the adjuster should investigate whether the claimant ever read the instructions. If the claimant asserts that he or she did, the adjuster should ask the claimant to repeat whatever he or she remembers. Should it appear that the claimant never read the instructions, or forgot everything that he or she read, the claimant will have a difficult case to prove. Any alleged shortcomings in the manufacturer's instructions cannot be a cause of the claimant's accident if the claimant never read or cannot remember them.

Improper Use

Claimants are often injured while using products in ways that are not intended or foreseeable. For example, claimants may suffer injuries by using a lawn mower to trim hedges or by using prescription drugs for conditions other than those for which they were prescribed.

Adjusters who suspect an improper use should obtain a careful and thorough statement from the claimant. If the claimant is not available for a statement, the adjuster may be able to obtain an honest account of what happened from the claimant's emergency room records or from an initial report by the claimant to a state or federal consumer products regulatory agency.

Workers Compensation Claims

The workers compensation system is an exception to the liability system. Work-related injuries are compensated without regard to fault and usually without resorting to the courts. Although the compensability of work-related injuries is usually straightforward, adjusters handling workers compensation cases must investigate them diligently. In addition, the medical aspect of workers compensation cases may be extraordinarily complex and expensive.

Investigation of Compensation Cases

Workers compensation cases that only involve medical expenses, such as a single visit to the emergency room, are usually processed with no real investigation. The policyholder's word is accepted as proof that the accident happened on the job and that the injury is work-related.

Should an accident involve lost time from work, the adjuster is likely to conduct an investigation. Statements are obtained from the claimant, the employer, and any witnesses. The purpose of these statements is to establish that the injury is work-related, that the injury was not preexisting, what the likely period of disability will be, and whether relations between the employee and employer are such that the claimant might have staged the claim or might be inclined to exaggerate the disability. The adjuster must also obtain documentation of the employee's earnings so that the employee's disability compensation can be properly calculated.

The adjuster's investigation into the circumstances of the accident may be an important part of the employer's loss control program. Many policyholders are concerned about their workers compensation costs. In addition, these policyholders are interested in reducing workplace injuries for humanitarian reasons, to forestall any OSHA or state labor department investigation, and to maintain productivity in their business. Many insurers take an active role in loss control and depend on their adjusters' investigations for guidance as to where to devote their efforts.

Control of Medical Expenses

Workers compensation medical expenses are potentially unlimited. The law requires the employer (or its insurer) to pay all necessary and reasonable medical expenses related to the injury sustained on the job. Thus, workers compensation policies have no policy limits. A small percentage of workers compensation cases account for an enormous percentage of the medical expenses paid out by compensation insurers.

Compensation adjusters have limited tools with which to challenge medical expenses. The employee-patient is not required to co-pay any portion of the expenses, as is common with health insurance. Compensation insurers often do not have the bargaining power that health insurers have with medical providers. Furthermore, in many states, there are no fee schedules or other controls over medical bills. As a result, workers compensation medical costs have risen faster in the past decade than health costs in general.

Some compensation insurers have entered into agreements with **preferred provider organizations (PPOs)** by which the insurer receives a discount on the usual medical charges in exchange for a volume of referrals. This type of arrangement is only feasible in states that allow the employer or insurer to select the treating physician.

Most compensation insurers conduct **bill audits** to identify charges that are excessive, fabricated, or redundant. Specialized bill auditing firms can perform this service for compensation insurers. Bill audits usually result in more than enough savings to justify the expense of the audit.

Utilization review services, discussed previously, are also a valuable tool in determining whether medical treatment is necessary. However, before an insurer can deny reimbursement for a course of treatment, it must be certain that experts from the utilization review service are willing and able to testify on its behalf. Because workers compensation laws are designed to protect workers regardless of fault, insurers should not deny claims without clear grounds for doing so.

Claims for psychological injuries are very expensive. The causes of psychological problems are complex and may include a mixture of work-related and nonwork-related factors. Furthermore, the recovery from and cure of psychological conditions are often vague and unclear. Thus, claims for psychological conditions are expensive to investigate and difficult to terminate. Claims for allegedly work-related stress disability may involve a complex interaction of employer-employee difficulties, preexisting personality disorders, and current difficulties from outside the workplace. Adjusters are generally not competent to evaluate these cases. However, there are experts in the fields of psychology and psychiatry who specialize in defense evaluations of psychological conditions.

The most sophisticated form of medical cost control is **medical management**. Medical management is devoted to controlling medical expenses on the small percentage of cases that involve high medical costs. Those cases usually involve permanent injuries that require tens of thousands of dollars of medical expenses annually for the remainder of the claimant's life. Medical management ensures that the claimant receives care in appropriate facilities with appropriate specialists. Rehabilitation facilities may specialize in certain injuries, such as brain trauma, quadriplegia, burns, or blindness. Medical management may enable an injured claimant to live independently rather than be institutionalized. By specializing in the care of serious permanent injuries, medical management specialists can both ensure optimum treatment for claimants and control costs for insurers.

Control of Disability

Controlling disability expenses is probably the foremost issue for compensation adjusters. Cases in which the claimant loses no time from work and cases in which the claimant returns to work promptly are relatively simple and straightforward. Cases in which disability extends over a long or an excessive period are the biggest problem and expense for compensation insurers.

Compensation insurers generally do not have the legal power simply to cease making payments on cases in which they believe the disability should have ended. Once a case has been initially accepted as compensable, the insurer can only end disability payments by agreement with the claimant or by order of the compensation commission. If the claimant is not agreeable, cases before the compensation commission can take months to resolve. Compensation commissions generally decide in favor of the claimant and will probably resolve doubtful cases against the insurer. Should the commission find in favor of the insurer and allow disability payments to cease, the claimant is not required to reimburse past payments. Thus, in jurisdictions where compensation cases take months to resolve, the claimant is assured of compensation for those months, no matter what the outcome.

Some claimants in difficult disability cases are antagonistic towards the employer or hate their work. The adjuster can do little about those circumstances. However, such circumstances usually become obvious during the adjuster's investigation and act as "red flags" to the adjuster that the case in question could be difficult.

Adjusters can control disability by insisting that the treating physician explain why the claimant cannot perform the demands of his or her job. Many treating physicians will certify disability without any real understanding of the physical demands of the claimant's work. For almost any physical impairment, there are jobs, or aspects of jobs, that can be performed by someone with that impairment. Thus, physicians cannot simply assume disability because of the existence of certain impairments.

Adjusters can also work with the employer to modify the employee's job by removing the most physically demanding parts of it. Claimants who return to limited-duty work are usually on the road to recovery. Adjusters handling disability claims can encourage claimants to think in terms of returning to work by constantly asking them what aspects of their work they are still incapable of performing. Adjusters can then suggest job modifications to the employer.

Professional Liability

Liability claims for professional malpractice are generally handled by specialized insurance companies and adjusters. These cases require a specialized determination of liability and a complex determination of damages. Because of the importance of these cases to the professional reputation of the policyholder, the policyholder is usually involved in his or her own defense, and these cases are likely to be litigated to verdict rather than settled.

Professional liability claims can be asserted against people who provide professional services, such as physicians, engineers, architects, attorneys, accountants, or insurance agents. Most of the law of malpractice has developed from claims against physicians, not because they are more careless than other professionals, but because they work with people's health in an environment in which a bad outcome is always possible.

Determining Standard of Care

Physicians cannot guarantee a complete cure for every patient. Attorneys cannot win every case. Accountants cannot guarantee the financial health of a business or an investment. Professionals are not necessarily at fault for bad outcomes.

Professionals are required to exercise the standard of care accepted in their profession. In other words, professionals should perform their services in the manner of a competent, careful member of their profession. Malpractice cases are usually proven by expert testimony to the effect that the defendant should have behaved otherwise or should have made a different decision, given the facts and circumstances known when the professional services were rendered. An adjuster investigating a malpractice case should constantly ask what could have and should have been done differently at every point.

There are laws in certain jurisdictions to the effect that physicians are to be judged by the standards of their community. This means that a physician practicing in a rural community should be judged by a lower standard of care than a (presumably) more sophisticated big city physician. In probably the majority of jurisdictions, the once significant differences in care between rural and urban communities have diminished. Physicians are part of a nationwide profession with professional journals and modern communications readily available. On the other hand, no physician is held to the standard of the leading expert in the field. If appropriate care of a patient would require leading edge expertise, the average physician should not be judged as negligent for failing to provide such expertise.

Many physicians are found at fault for failing to obtain a patient's informed consent. Physicians are required to explain their care to their patients; they should explain the treatment options and risks associated with each. Should a physician fail to explain the risks inherent in a course of treatment, the physician may be liable to the patient, even if the adverse outcome is an unavoidable risk. Physicians must exercise judgment in how much they tell patients, since exhaustive explanations would befuddle most patients. Nevertheless, a physician who fails to fully inform a patient of the risks of treatment runs the risk of being responsible for any negative outcome. Obtaining informed consent is a difficult area to defend, since many physicians do not document their discussions with their patients, or do so in very brief fashion. After a negative outcome, patients will often claim not to have understood the risks they faced, and the physician cannot prove otherwise.

Determining Damages

Damages in medical malpractice are similar to those of other bodily injury cases, except that the physician is not liable for the underlying condition that was the cause of treatment initially. Determining damages requires expert testimony as to how much the patient's condition would have improved or progressed with proper treatment. Often these issues can only be determined as matters of probability.

In cases of alleged attorney malpractice, the underlying legal matter from which the malpractice claim arose must be relitigated or reconsidered in the professional liability claim. The damages in the malpractice case depend on how much better the result obtained in the underlying matter should have been.

Determining damages in other types of malpractice cases is similar. Expert testimony must be used to establish what the claimant's condition would have been had proper professional services been rendered.

Defense of Malpractice Cases

In general, malpractice cases are litigated by only the most sophisticated plaintiff and defense attorneys. The insured professional is also likely to be heavily involved in the defense of the case.

As malpractice suits became more common, the insurers that handled them resisted easy settlement. In many of those cases, the insured professional had to consent in writing to any settlement. Absent such consent, the verdict had to be litigated. As the strength of the opposition became obvious, only the most talented plaintiff attorneys would accept these cases. To match the skills of the plaintiff bar, insurers increasingly relied on specialized defense attorneys. It is currently very rare for a general practice attorney to handle a malpractice case.

Many professional malpractice policies require the policyholder's consent to settlement. The insured professional is more personally concerned about the outcome of professional malpractice claims than about the outcome of other claims, since the professional's reputation is at stake. Some policies require the professional who rejects a proposed settlement to be responsible for any verdict in excess of the proposed settlement.

An adjuster involved in a professional malpractice case must investigate the possibility of defenses. In medical malpractice cases, for example, the patient could be responsible for failing to divulge all relevant information to the physician, for failing to follow the prescribed course of treatment, or for failing to report complications.

Environmental and Toxic Tort

Liability claims for environmental impairment and cleanup and for injuries caused by toxins are a growing area of claims work. Like professional malpractice, these areas are handled by specialists. The typical adjuster never handles such cases. Insurance companies that face significant exposures in these areas have usually established special units to handle them, have referred them to outside attorneys, or have consulted adjusting firms with the skills and experience needed.

All aspects of these cases are complicated. Determining coverage, liability, and damages may require the assistance of outside experts. The complexity of these cases has often resulted in multiple levels of litigation: litigation between the plaintiff and various defendants, between the various defendants and their insurers, and among the insurers. Some environmental and toxic tort cases also include bankruptcies of one or more of the parties, thus involving another court and adding complexity to each case.

Determination of Coverage

The specifics of the coverage issues involved in these cases are beyond the scope of this course. However, adjusters handling these cases must understand that coverage problems revolve around both a determination of the correct policy period and certain substantive coverage issues. The adjuster must understand company policy for handling those issues. Some insurers handle coverage issues with inside staff, and others always use outside legal counsel.

When different policy periods are at issue, coverage may be determined by when the harmful exposure occurred, by when the damage or injuries first occurred, or by when the damage and injuries were first discovered. Some jurisdictions require coverage to apply whenever any of these criteria exist. Thus, numerous different insurers are usually involved in the same claim, often with different policy limits or terms.

Aside from difficulties with policy periods, these cases also involve substantive coverage issues, such as the application of intentional act or pollution exclusions or the meaning of the phrase "property damage." Given the amount of money at stake in these claims, insurers that face a significant number of them usually litigate the meaning of their policy provisions through the courts. Courts, however, have generally resolved any coverage ambiguity against the insurer.

Determination of Liability

Liability for release of pollutants or other toxins depends on state and federal laws. Common law may have a role in determining liability, but the specially enacted environmental statutes are more significant. The specifics of those laws are beyond the scope of this course.

Adjusters with questions about environmental or toxic tort liability are usually required to consult with outside law firms that specialize in these issues. The typical insurance defense law firm does not have any expertise in environmental matters.

The law firm that consults about liability or that defends the policyholder should be different from the attorney or law firm that the insurer consults regarding coverage issues. When coverage questions exist, it is a conflict of interest for a law firm or an attorney to serve both the insurer and the policyholder simultaneously.

Determination of Damages

Because of environmental statutes, and especially the federal Superfund law, few commercial firms are willing to perform environmental cleanups. As a result, the services of these firms are expensive. More firms provide environmental consulting. Those organizations can provide expert opinions on the scope and cost of a cleanup effort, whether there are valid alternatives to the cleanup procedure required by the government, and whether a particular policyholder's chemical waste can be identified and segregated in a general dump site. These consulting firms are also expensive, even though they do not perform the cleanup.

In toxic tort cases, the plaintiff usually has a difficult burden of proof unless the cause-and-effect relationship between the toxin and the injury has been well established in scientific literature. Generally, in these cases, the plaintiff alleges exposure to a toxin caused by the defendant that results in a physical malady, such as cancer. Pioneering plaintiff attorneys do not mind losing a long string of these cases if they can eventually win one. Once a jury has decided in favor of a plaintiff, all subsequent cases have a certain settlement value. Courts have begun to recognize that this roulette-like approach to what is supposedly a scientific issue is inappropriate. Courts have therefore disallowed purported expert testimony on behalf of plaintiffs unless it would be acceptable in scientific literature.

Summary

Liability claims adjusters are primarily concerned with the laws of liability and damages, which exist apart from the insurance policy. Once coverage has been verified in a liability case, the insurance policy plays a much smaller role than in the settlement of property loss claims.

The basic law of negligence is applicable to most cases that liability adjusters handle, but adjusters must be alert to other possible legal theories, such as strict liability for products and specific statutory liability for certain auto accidents.

Damages in injury cases include medical specials, loss of earnings, and general damages. Determining and evaluating general damages are essential skills for liability claims adjusters, since general damages are the main element of the claimant's case. Because general damages are subjective, there is great room for negotiations in liability claims. Most successful liability claims adjusters are excellent negotiators who enjoy the challenge of negotiation.

Should negotiations not prove successful, liability claims adjusters must know how to steer cases through the court system. This requires knowledge of court procedures and the ability to deal with and manage attorneys.

Specific types of liability claims present their own unique challenges. Experienced liability claims adjusters are familiar with the difficulties that can arise in the various types of cases.

Index

A

Absence of negligence, 329-330
Absolute liability, 327
Accident, cause of, determining, 355-356
Accident reconstruction, 349-350
Accident scene, preservation of, 359
Accident-year loss analysis technique, 154-160
Accident-year method, 121-123
Accountants, 215
  use of, 305
Actual cash value, 271-272
  definitions of, other, 272-273
  determining, 297-298
Actuarial department, claims information and, 202
Actuarial reserving system, 153
Actuarial services, 88-89
Actuary, 87
Adjusters, 210-211
  independent, 211-212
  public, 213, 280
  specialist, 213-214
Adjusting, claims, 199
Adjusting companies, independent, 211
Adjusting process, claims, 216-250
Adjustment procedures, 280-289
Adjustment of statistics, 123-133
Administration, reinsurance, 66-71
Administration of rate regulation, 109-111
ADR (alternative dispute resolution), 244, 346-348
Advance payments, 340
Age, risk classification and, 100
Agents' balances to surplus, 194
Aggregate excess treaty, 24-25, 74
Agreed amount, 275
Agreed repair prices, 354
Agreement, insuring, 218
  nonwaiver, 220
  Parent's Release and Indemnity, 241-243
Agreements, high/low, 241
Allocated and unallocated expenses, 233-234
Alternative dispute resolution (ADR), 244, 346-348
Alternatives to litigation, 244
Amount of loss, 268-276
  determining, 284-285
Analysis, reinsurance, 182
Analysis of reinsurance requirements, 172-173
Answer, 343
Appeal, 345
Appraisal clause, 276
Appraisals, 347
Appraisers, material damage, 214
Arbitration, 346
Architects and contractors, 297
Arson investigation, 299-300
Asset risk, 190
Associations, claims organizations and, 206-207
Assumption of risk, 330
Attorneys, defense, 204-205
  outside, selection and direction of, 244
  plaintiffs', 203

Audits, bill, 363
Auto bodily injury, 348-352
Auto physical damage, 353-354
Average value method, 149, 235

B

Bad faith claim, 337
Bailment losses, transportation and, 308-310
Bailor-bailee arrangements, 257-258
Bases of liability, 357-358, 359-360
Best's financial performance ratings, 183-184
Best's financial size category, 186
Best's financial strength ratings, 183
Best's ratings, 175-186
Bill audits, 363
Bill of lading, 310
  released, 310
Bodily injury damages, 224-228
Bodily injury and property damage, 321
Bordereau, 17
Broker, reinsurance, 63
Buildings, property claims adjusting and, 259
Bureau membership, mandatory, 110
Burning-cost method, 73
Burning-cost rate, 73
Business income, loss of, determining, 301
Business interruption, 300-305

C

Calendar-year method, 119-121
Capacity problem, reinsurance and, 82-83
Capital, risk-based, 186-192
  total adjusted, 188
Capital gain, realized, 107
  unrealized, 108
Capital and leverage tests, 177-178
Capital loss, realized, 107
  unrealized, 108
Capital structure, 182-183
Case reserves, 148-151, 234-235
  adequacy of, 161
Catastrophe excess, 21
Catastrophe protection, 7
Catastrophe treaties, 74
Catastrophes, 312-313
Catastrophic loss, exposures subject to, 48-49
Cause of accident, determining, 355-356
Cause of loss, determining, 284
Cause and origin experts, 214
Causes of loss, gradual, 265
  protected by insurance, 261-268
Ceding commission, 6
Centralized versus decentralized claims function, 207
Certificate of reinsurance, 27
Challenges facing liability claims, 348-369
Challenges facing property claims, 289-313
Change in surplus, 194
Change in writings, 193
Civil procedure, 340, 343-345
Claim, bad faith, 337
Claim investigation, level of, 280-281
Claim services, producer, 212-213
  unbundled, 216
Claim settlement, 70-71
Claimants' allegations, 319
Claims, denial of, 238-239
  first-party, 353
  injury, elements of damage in, 331-332
  liability, 353-354
    challenges facing, 348-369
    defenses to, 329-330
    issues in, 318-348
  property, challenges facing, 289-313
  resolving, role of courts in, 341
  uninsured motorists, 351-352
  workers compensation, 362-365
Claims adjusting, 199
  property, issues in, 254-289
Claims adjusting personnel, miscellaneous, 213-216
Claims adjusting process, 216-250

Claims department, objectives of, 200-201
Claims department contacts, 202-207
Claims environment, 199-216
Claims function, organization of, 207-208
Claims-handling performance, 247
Claims information, uses of, 201-202
Claims managers, 208
Claims negotiations, persons involved in, 237
Claims organizations and associations, 206-207
Claims performance, measuring, 246-250
Clash cover, 21
Class of business, territory or, withdrawal from, 8
Class rates, 101
Class relativities, 135-139
Classification, risk, 99-102
Clause, insolvency, 78
  intermediary, 78
Cleaning services, restoration and, 293-294
Collapse, 263
Collateral Source Rule, 225
Collection of statistics, 118
Commercial structures, 296-300
Commission, ceding, 6
Commissions, reinsurance, 65
Comparative or contributory negligence, 330
Comparative negligence, determining, 356-357
Comparison of ratemaking methods, 139
Compensation cases, investigation of, 362-363
Competition, effect of, on reinsurance pricing, 75
Complaint, 343
Concluding reports, 230
Conditions, policy, 219
Construction, faulty, 265
Constructive total losses, 354
Consultants, medical cost containment, 215
Consumer complaints, 205
Contacts, claims department, 202-207
Contamination and pollution cleanup, 299
Contract, loss portfolio transfer, 32
Contractors, 293
  architects and, 297
Contracts, 221
  financial reinsurance, 30
  time and distance, 31
Contractual assumptions of liability, 358-359
Contractual liability, 328
Contractual obligations, 323
Contractual promise, complying with, 200
Contributory negligence, comparative or, 330
Corporate objectives, ratemaking and, 89-90
Cost, replacement, 268-271
Cost of reinsurance, 59-60
Courts, role of, in resolving claims, 341
Covenant not to sue, 240
Coverage, 217-220, 319-324
  determination of, 368
  miscellaneous, possibilities for, 257-258
  underinsured motorists, 352
Coverage issues, response to, 219-220
Coverage not needed by policyholders, 219
Coverage problems, 319-321, 349
Coverage provided elsewhere, 219
Coverages, additional, 261
  insurance, 308-309
Credibility, 102-103, 142-143
  defined, 103
Credit risk, 190-191
Crime losses, 310-312
Crimes, 327
Cross-complaint, 343
Current liquidity test, 179
Cut-through endorsement, 9

D

Damage, auto physical, 353-354
  elements of, in injury claims, 331-332
  property, 224, 334-335
    bodily injury and, 321

water, 262-263
Damages, 223-228, 330-335
bodily injury, 224-228
determining, 366-367, 369
extra-contractual, 228
future, 226-227
general, 227
evaluation of, 333-334
punitive, 227
special, 227
evaluation of, 332-333
Decisions relating to defense, 244-245
Declaratory judgment, 220
Deductibles, 273-275
Defense attorneys, 204-205
Defense of malpractice cases, 367
Defenses to liability claims, 329-330
Denial of claims, 238-239
Deposition, 344
Depreciation, 271, 295
Deterministic models, 169
Development of ratemaking data, 117-139
Direct and indirect physical loss, 262
Disability, control of, 364-365
Discounting the loss reserves, 166-168
Discovery, 344
Documentation and reporting, 285
Documents, settlement, 239-243
Driver, sex and marital status of, 100
Driving record, 101
Duty to defend, 341-343
Duty to settle, 336-337
Dwellings, residential, 289-294

E

Earned exposure unit, 104
Earned premiums, 103
Earnings, loss of, 225-226
Elements of damage in injury claims, 331-332
Endorsement, cut-through, 9
Engineers, professional, 216
Environmental and toxic tort, 367-369
Estimated current reserve deficiency to surplus, 195
Estoppel, 281
waiver and, avoiding, 281-284
Evaluation of insurers, 174-175
Examination under oath, 279-280
Examiners, 208-210
Excess of loss facultative reinsurance, 28-30
Excess of loss or nonproportional treaties, 18-25
Excess of loss reinsurance, 11
Exclusions, 218-219
Expense, extra, 305
living, additional, 292
Expense loading, 92
Expenses, allocated and unallocated, 233-234
medical, control of, 363-364
Expenses for medical treatment, 225
Experience period, 96, 140
Experts, cause and origin, 214
health and rehabilitation, 215
reconstruction, 214-215
selection of, 245
use of, 361
Exponential trending, 127-133
Exposure unit, 96
Exposures subject to catastrophic loss, 48-49
Express warranty, 360
Extra-contractual damages, 228
Extra expense, 305

F

Facultative obligatory treaty, 10
Facultative reinsurance, 10, 25-30
excess of loss, 28-30
functions of, 30
pro rata, 28
Facultative treaty, 10
File-and-use laws, 110
Filings, rate, 143-144
Financial intermediation, 147

Financial leverage, 177
Financial measures, 246-247
Financial performance ratings, 183-184
Financial reinsurance, 7, 30-32
Financial reinsurance contracts, 30
Financial resources, available, 50
Financial size category, Best's, 186
Financing (surplus relief), 4-7
First-party claims, 353
Fraud possibilities, 312
Future damages, 226-227

G

General damages, 227
  evaluation of, 333-334
Glossary of reinsurance terms, 37-42, 84-85
Gradual causes of loss, 265
Gross rate, 92
Growth plans, 50-51

H

Health and rehabilitation experts, 215
High/low agreements, 241
Homeowners personal property, 294-296

I

IBNR (incurred but not reported), 95, 234
IBNR reserve, 151-152
Identification of insureds, 258-259
Income, investment, 107
Incurred but not reported (IBNR), 95, 234
Incurred losses, 94
Independent adjusters, 211-212
Independent adjusting companies, 211
Indirect physical loss, direct and, 262
Individual rates, 102
Inflation, 96-98
  effect of, on reinsurance pricing, 75-76
Information, claims, uses of, 201-202
Information needed, reinsurance negotiations and, 60-63
Injury, auto body, 348-352
  bodily, property damage and, 321
Injury claims, elements of damage in, 331-332
Insolvency clause, 78
Instructions, warnings and, review of, 361
Insurable interest, policy requirements for, 256-257
Insurance, lines of, miscellaneous, 140-143
Insurance coverages, 308-309
Insurance Regulatory Information System (IRIS), 192-195
Insurance written, kinds of, 47-48
  volume of, 49
Insured's concerns, 290-292
Insured's duties following loss, 276-280
Insureds, identification of, 258-259
Insurer, primary, 1
Insurer's profit objective, achieving, 200-201
Insurers, evaluation of, 174-175
Insuring agreement, 218
Intentional acts, 265-268, 321-323
Intentional torts, 327
Interests in property, 255
Intermediary clause, 78
Interrogatories, 344
Interruption, business, 300-305
Inventory, 294-295
Investigation, arson, 299-300
  claim, level of, 280-281
  compensation cases and, 362-363
  legal liability and, 324-326
  liability, 223
  market conduct, 205-206
Investigative reports, 230
Investigators, private, 215
Investment income, 107
  in ratemaking, 107-108
Investment portfolio, stability and liquidity of, 50
Investment risk, 30

Investment yield, 193-194
Investments, quality and diversity of, 182
IRIS (Insurance Regulatory Information System), 192-195

J

Joint ownership, 255
Joint tortfeasor release, 239-240
Judgment, declaratory, 220
Judgment method, 105, 149, 235

L

Landlord-tenant arrangements, 257
Large-line capacity, 4
Law, ordinance or, 265
Law of large numbers, 103
Laws, file-and-use, 110
  no-file, 110-111
  prior approval, 110
  use-and-file, 110
Legal expense, control of, 345
Legal liability, 220-223, 309-310, 324-330
  defined, 221
Leverage, 177
  financial, 177
  operational, 177
Leverage tests, capital and, 177-178
Liabilities to liquid assets, 194
Liability, absolute, 327
  bases of, 357-358, 359-360
  contractual, 328
  contractual assumptions of, 358-359
  determination of, 368
  investigation of, 223
  legal, 220-223, 309-310, 324-330
    defined, 221
  premises, 355-357
  product, 359-362
  professional, 365-367
  sources of, 221-223
  statutory, 328
  strict, 360
  tort, 326-327
  vicarious, 328-329
Liability claims, 353-354
  challenges facing, 348-369
  defenses to, 329-330
  issues in, 318-348
Licensing, 205
Linear trending, 127
Lines of insurance, miscellaneous, 140-143
Liquidity, quick, 179
Liquidity of investment portfolio, stability and, 50
Liquidity test, current, 179
  overall, 179
Litigation, 243-245, 340-348
  alternatives to, 244
Living expense, additional, 292
Loss, amount of, 268-276
    determining, 284-285
  cause of, determining, 284
  causes of, gradual, 265
    protected by insurance, 261-268
  insured's duties following, 276-280
  physical, direct and indirect, 262
Loss adjustment process, assistance with, 278
Loss analysis technique, accident-year, 154-160
  report-year, 160-166
    example of, 161-166
Loss of business income, determining, 301
Loss of consortium, 226
Loss development factors, 123-126
Loss development, 95, 140
Loss of earnings, 225-226
Loss experience, stabilization of, 2-3
Loss experience in reinsurance, 71
Loss limitations, large, 142
Loss portfolio transfer contract, 32
Loss portfolio transfers, 32
Loss ratio method, 105, 150-151
Loss reserve analysis and verification, 148-168
  techniques for, 152-168

Loss reserve tests, 179-181
Loss reserves, 92-96, 182
 defined, 93
 discounting the, 166-168
Loss settlement approach, 300-301
Loss triangle, 123
Losses, constructive total, 354
 crime, 310-312
 incurred, 94
 paid, 104
 reporting form, 307
 transportation and bailment, 308-310

M

Malpractice cases, defense of, 367
Management, 183
Management structure and settlement authority, 208-216
Managers, claims, 208
Manual rates, 101
Manufacturer, product and, identification of, 360-361
Market conduct investigations, 205-206
Market position, 183
Marketing, claims information and, 201-202
Material damage appraisers, 214
Mediation, 346
Medical cost containment consultants, 215
Medical expenses, control of, 363-364
Medical management, 364
Medical treatment, expenses for, 225
Merchandise, 306-308
 valuation of, 306
Merit rating, 102
Mini-trials, 347
Model, choosing best, 169-172
Models, deterministic, 169
 probabilistic, 169
Mortgagee, problems with, 298-299
Mortgagor-mortgagee arrangements, 258
Motion, 344
Motion for summary judgment, 344
Multi-line mutual insurer, small, example of, 51-52
Multi-line stock insurer, large, example of, 52-53

N

Negligence, absence of, 329-330
 comparative, determining, 356-357
 comparative or contributory, 330
Negotiation, defined, 346
 importance of, 307-308
 pre-settlement, 237
 pressures surrounding, 337-338
Negotiation and settlement, 237-238, 335-340
Negotiation strategies, 338-339
Negotiations, claims, persons involved in, 237
 reinsurance, 60-65
New York Regulation 98, 79
No rating opinions, 184
No-fault and workers compensation, auto bodily injury and, 350-351
No-file laws, 110-111
Nominal or dollar releases, 243
Nonproportional treaties, excess of loss or, 18-25
Nonwaiver agreement, 220
Notice, 276-277

O

Objectives of claims department, 200-201
Objectives of ratemaking, 89-90
Occurrences within control of policyholders, 219
Off-balance-sheet risk, 192
One-year reserve development to surplus, 194-195
Operating cash flow test, 179
Operational leverage, 177
Operations, 357-359
Ordinance or law, 265
Overall liquidity test, 179

Ownership, joint, 255
Ownership in common, 255

P

Paid losses, 104
Pain and suffering, 226
Parent's Release and Indemnity Agreement, 241
Payments, advance, 340
Per occurrence excess of loss, 21-24
Per policy excess treaty, 18-20, 73-74
Per risk excess treaty, 18-20, 73-74
Period of restoration, determining, 301, 305
Permanency, 226
Personal lines insurer, large, example of, 51
Personal property, 259-261
  homeowners, 294-296
Personnel, support, 216
Persons involved in claims negotiations, 237
Physical loss, direct and indirect, 262
Plaintiffs' attorneys, 203
Planning, 168-172
  post-loss, 313
  pre-loss, 312-313
Plans, growth, 50-51
Pleadings, 343-344
Policy conditions, 219
Policy requirements for insurable interest, 256-257
Policy year, 118
Policy-year method, 118-119
Policyholder's control, property under, 323-324
Policyholders, coverage not needed by, 219
  occurrences within control of, 219
Policyholders and reinsurance, 8-10
Pollution cleanup, contamination and, 299
Pool, reinsurance, 32
Pools, reinsurance through, 32-33
Portfolio reinsurance, 8
Post-loss planning, 313
PPOs (preferred provider organizations), 363
Pre-loss planning, 312-313
Pre-settlement negotiation, 237
Pre-trial settlement conference, 348
Preferred provider organizations (PPOs), 363
Preliminary reports, 228-230
Premises liability, 355-357
Premium, pure, 92
Premium-to-surplus ratio, 193
Premiums, earned, 103
  written, 103
Preservation of accident scene, 359
Prices, repair, agreed, 354
Pricing, reinsurance, 71-76
Primary insurer, 1
  reinsurance planning for, 46-60
  role of, 66-69
Principles of ratemaking, 89-109
Prior approval laws, 110
Private investigators, 215
Pro rata facultative reinsurance, 28
Pro rata or proportional treaties, 13-17
Pro rata reinsurance, 11
Pro rata treaties, 71-73
Probabilistic models, 169
Producer claim services, 212-213
Product, improper use of, 362
Product liability, 359-362
Product or line of business, claims function divided by, 208
Product and manufacturer, identification of, 360-361
Professional engineers, 216
Professional liability, 365-367
Profit and contingencies, 92
Profit objective, insurer's, achieving, 200-201
Profitability tests, 177
Proof of loss, 278-279
Property, interests in, 255
  personal, 259-261
    homeowners, 294-296
  protection of, 277-278
  scheduled, 296
  verification of, crime losses and, 311-312

Property claims, challenges facing, 289-313
Property claims adjusting, general issues in, 254-289
Property damage, 224, 334-335
  bodily injury and, 321
Property not covered, 261
Property under policyholder's control, 323-324
Proportional treaties, pro rata or, 13-17
Prospective settlements, 300
Protection of property, 277-278
Proximate cause, 326
Public adjusters, 213, 280
Punitive damages, 227
Pure premium, 92
Pure premium method, 106

Q

Qualitative tests, 181-183
Quantitative tests, 177-181
Quick liquidity, 179
Quota share treaty, 13-15

R

Rate, burning-cost, 73
  gross, 92
  statewide average, 130
Rate filing, 88
Rate filings, 143-144
Rate regulation, 109-111
Ratemaking, investment income in, 107-108
  objectives of, 89-90
  principles of, 89-109
Ratemaking data, development of, 117-139
Ratemaking methods, 105-107
  comparison of, 139
Ratemaking process, 90-99
Ratemaking in real world, 92-99
Ratemaking in stable world, 91-92
  example of, 91-92
  terminology and, 92
Rates, class, 101
  individual, 102
  manual, 101
  specific, 102
  state-made, 109-110
Rating, merit, 102
  risk classification, 101-102
  territorial, 102
Rating modifiers, 184-186
Ratings, Best's, 175-186
    financial performance, 183-184
    financial strength, 183
Ratio, premium-to-surplus, 193
  two-year overall operating, 193
Ratio of surplus aid to surplus, 193
RBC (risk-based capital), 186-192
Realized capital gain, 107
Realized capital loss, 107
Reciprocal reinsurance, 35
Reciprocity, 35-36
Reconstruction experts, 214-215
Recoveries, miscellaneous, subrogation and, 245-246
Regulation, rate, 109-111
  reinsurance, 77-82
    proposed, 80-82
  reinsurance broker, 79
  reinsurer, present, 78
Regulators, state, 205-206
Regulatory objectives, ratemaking and, 90
Reinsurance, 1
  cost of, 59-60
  excess of loss, 11
  facultative, 10, 25-30
    excess of loss, 28-30
    functions of, 30
    pro rata, 28
  financial, 7, 30-32
  functions of, 2-8
  loss experience in, 71
  policyholders and, 8-10
  portfolio, 8
  pro rata, 11
  reciprocal, 35
  regulation of, 77-82

surplus-aid, 7
treaty, 10, 11-25
types of, 10-30
Reinsurance administration, 66-71
Reinsurance analysis, 182
Reinsurance broker, defined, 63
regulation of, 79
use of, 63-65
Reinsurance and capacity problem, 82-83
Reinsurance commissions, 65
Reinsurance limits, setting, 58-59
Reinsurance market, 33-36
Reinsurance needs, factors determining, 47-53
Reinsurance negotiations, 60-65
Reinsurance planning for primary insurer, 46-60
Reinsurance pool, 32
Reinsurance through pools, 32-33
Reinsurance pricing, 71-76
Reinsurance regulation, proposed, 80-82
Reinsurance requirements, analysis of, 172-173
Reinsurance terms, glossary of, 37-42, 84-85
Reinsurer, 1
role of, 69-70
Reinsurer regulation, present, 78-79
Reinsurers, multiplicity of, 34
Relativities, class, 135-139
territorial, 133-135
Release draft, 243
Release for injury to a minor, 241
Released bill of lading, 310
Releases, joint tortfeasor, 239-240
nominal or dollar, 243
telephone-recorded, 243
Repair prices, agreed, 354
Repair or replace option, 275-276
Replacement cost, 268-271
Report-year loss analysis technique, 160-166
example of, 161-166
Reporting, 228-230
documentation and, 285
Reporting form losses, 307
Reports, concluding, 230
investigative, 230
preliminary, 228-230
status, 230
Requests for admission, 344
Requests for documents, 344
Reservation-of-rights letter, 220
Reserves, case, 234-235
Reserving, 230-236
Reserving problems, 236
Reserving work sheets and software, 235-236
Residential dwellings, 289-294
Response to coverage issues, 219-220
Restoration and cleaning services, 293-294
Retention, 2
Retentions, setting, 53-58
Retrocedent, 2
Retrocessionaire, 2
Retrocessions, 2
Retrospective settlements, 300
Risk, asset, 190
credit, 190-191
investment, 30
off-balance-sheet, 192
spread of, 181-182
timing, 30
underwriting, 191-192
Risk-based capital (RBC), 186-192
Risk classification, 99-102
Risk classification rating, 101-102
Role of primary insurer, 66-69
Role of reinsurer, 69-70

S

Salvage, 306-307
Salvage and subrogation, 285-289
Scheduled property, 296
Selection and direction of outside attorneys, 244
Selection of experts, 245
Settlement, 237-239
claim, 70-71
negotiation and, 237-238, 335-340

Settlement authority, management structure and, 208-216
Settlement documents, 239-243
Settlement techniques, 339-340
Settlements, prospective, 300
  retrospective, 300
  structured, 339
  walk-away, 340
Software, work sheets and, reserving, 235-236
Sources of liability, 221-223
Special damages, 227
  evaluation of, 332-333
Specialist adjusters, 213-214
Specific rates, 102
Spread of risk, 181-182
Stability and liquidity of investment portfolio, 50
Stair-stepping, 236
Standard of care, determining, 365-366
State-made rates, 109-110
State regulators, 205-206
Stated amount, 275
Statewide average rate, 130
Statistics, adjustment of, 123-133
  collection of, 118
Status reports, 230
Statute of limitations, 330
Statutes, 221
Statutory liability, 328
Statutory minimum reserve, 151
Statutory standards, 109
Strict liability, 360
Structured settlements, 339
Structures, commercial, 296-300
Sublimits, 295-296
Subrogation, salvage and, 285-289
Subrogation and miscellaneous recoveries, 245-246
Summary jury trials, 347
Summons, 343
Supervisors, 210
Support personnel, 216
Surplus, 182
Surplus-aid reinsurance, 7
Surplus relief, 7
Surplus share treaties, 15-17
Survival actions, 227
Survival and wrongful death, 227-228

T

Tabular method, 149-150, 235
Telephone-recorded releases, 243
Tenancy by entireties, 255
Territorial rating, 102
Territorial relativities, 133-135
Territory or class of business, withdrawal from, 8
Tests, capital and leverage, 177-178
  liquidity, 178-179
  loss reserve, 179-181
  profitability, 177
  qualitative, 181-183
  quantitative, 177-181
Theft, 263-264, 296
Time-dependent factors, miscellaneous, 99
Time and distance contracts, 31
Timing risk, 30
Tort, environmental and toxic, 367-369
Tort liability, 326-327
Torts, 222-223
  intentional, 327
Total adjusted capital, 188
Toxic tort, environmental and, 367-369
Transportation and bailment losses, 308-310
Treaties, catastrophe, 74
  excess of loss or nonproportional, 18-25
  pro rata, 71-73
    or proportional, 13-17
  surplus share, 15-17
Treaty, aggregate excess, 24-25, 74
  facultative, 10
  facultative obligatory, 10
  per policy excess, 18-20, 73-74
  per risk excess, 18-20, 73-74
  quota share, 13-15
Treaty reinsurance, 10, 11-25

Trending, 99, 126-133, 141
exponential, 127-133
linear, 127
Trial, 344
Two-year overall operating ratio, 193
Two-year reserve development to surplus, 195
Types of reinsurance, 10-30

U

Ultimate development factor, 158
Unallocated expenses, allocated and, 233-234
Unbundled claim services, 216
Underinsured motorists coverage, 352
Underwriting, claims information and, 202
Underwriting assistance, 7-8
Underwriting risk, 191-192
Unearned premium reserve, 103
Unfair Claims Settlement Practices legislation, 247-250
Uninsurability, 219
Uninsured motorists claims, 351-352
Unrealized capital gain, 108
Unrealized capital loss, 108
Use-and-file laws, 110
Use of vehicle, 101
Uses of claims information, 201-202

V

Valuation of merchandise, 306
Vandalism, 264
Vehicle, nature of, 100-101
use of, 101
Verification of cause, crime losses and, 310-311
Verification of property, crime losses and, 311-312
Vicarious liability, 328-329

W

Waiver, 281
Waiver and estoppel, avoiding, 281-284
Walk-away settlements, 340
Warnings and instructions, review of, 361
Warranty, 360
express, 360
Water damage, 262-263
Work sheets and software, reserving, 235-236
Workers compensation, no-fault and, auto bodily injury and, 350-351
Workers compensation claims, 362-365
Working covers, 18
Written premiums, 103
Wrongful death action, 227